D0726084

JUMBO'S HIDE, ELVIS'S RIDE, AND THE TOOTH OF BUDDHA

More

Marvelous

Tales of

Historical

Artifacts

Jumbo's Hide,

Elvis's Ride,

AND THE

TOOTH OF
BUDDHA

HARVEY RACHLIN

Henry Holt and Company   New York

Henry Holt and Company, LLC
Publishers since 1866
115 West 18th Street
New York, New York 10011

Henry Holt® is a registered trademark of
Henry Holt and Company, LLC.

Published in Canada by Fitzhenry & Whiteside Ltd.,
195 Allstate Parkway, Markham, Ontario L3R 4T8.

Library of Congress Cataloging-in-Publication Data
Rachlin, Harvey.
Jumbo's hide, Elvis's ride, and the tooth of Buddha:
more marvelous tales of historical artifacts /
by Harvey Rachlin.—1st ed.
p. cm.
Includes bibliographical references (p.) and index.
ISBN 0-8050-5683-1
1. History—Miscellanea. 2. Antiquities. I. Title.
D10.R334 2000   99-39456
909—dc21   CIP

Henry Holt books are available for special
promotions and premiums. For details contact:
Director, Special Markets.

First Edition 2000

DESIGNED BY KELLY S. TOO

Printed in the United States of America
10 9 8 7 6 5 4 3 2 1

CONTENTS

Introduction

From our lifetime of reading and learning, we may wonder what great artifacts of history have survived the ages. The annals of human experience are filled with objects that figured prominently or obliquely in manifold triumphs and calamities, and we may imagine a vast catalog of these objects spread around the earth, reposing in locations anywhere from obscure mountain hideaways to great metropolitan museums, testifying to natural disasters, wars, feats of heroism, tragedies, explorations, crimes, inventions, artistic creations, religious ceremonies, affairs of state, weddings, celebrations, and uncounted other events of record. We may be curious about whether objects ranging from the biblical Noah's Ark and Ark of the Covenant to later items such as the three caravels in which Christopher Columbus and his men sailed to the New World in 1492 and James Hargreaves's original spinning jenny still exist, and if so, where they are today.

My own insatiable desire to seek out these treasures—and the stories behind them—led me to write my first book on the subject, *Lucy's Bones, Sacred Stones, and Einstein's Brain*. I continue in this volume with a new collection of stories based on actual objects that exist today, which I hope will intrigue and inspire you, as they have me, to contemplate their role in shaping civilization and what they ultimately tell us about ourselves.

It is not difficult to wax romantic about artifacts. They are the props of history, portals to the past that afford the beholder a glimpse back in time. They offer edifying excursions that reveal as much as the eye—and imagination—is willing to see. Not only do they evoke insight into a particular era or event, but they carry the imprint of the individuals associated with them.

For many, artifacts associated with legendary figures of the past offer the greatest thrill. If you see or touch an object that was beheld by Newton, Washington, Lincoln, or Darwin, for example, you have formed a common bond with that icon of human history. Observe the Rosetta Stone at the British Museum, and you and Napoleon, centuries apart, have both examined the same object, and perhaps experienced the same awe.

It is terrifically interesting to research existing artifacts and discover their underlying history, which is not always apparent at first. It is like reaching into the drawers of history and rummaging through them. Sifting through a plethora of historical riches, I have pulled out a number of items that fascinated me, and which I thought readers would likewise find absorbing.

Why do we have such an avid interest in history? Clearly, history enables us to learn from the mistakes of our ancestors so we are not condemned to repeat them, and understanding the themes that animated past eras illuminates the present. But perhaps there is something more.

History is important, I believe, for identity and perspective. Not having knowledge of our roots would be like going through life with amnesia; history provides us with the emotional context of where we came from and how we came to be who we are. History also gives us the intellectual perspective to guide our own journey through life. It lets us know where we're going in relation to where our predecessors have been. Without that identity and perspective, we are aimless wanderers.

Not only is the future carved out of the past, but *we ourselves* are the direct result of history. Each of us is a product of the deeds, machinations, habits, policies, discoveries, humanitarian efforts, religious commitments, and much more, of all past peoples from peasants and slaves to nobles and kings, all trying to establish themselves securely in their worlds.

In our human ancestral chain, if but one link, just one person, had been different—no matter how far back—we might never have been born! Now, that is truly amazing, considering the countless factors that drew our ancestors together to meet and mate exactly as they did to produce the genetic sequence that led eventually to ourselves. You—every one of us—came into this world against truly incalculable odds: not just those of one individual sperm among 300 million winning the competition for a single egg in your unique conception, but of billions upon trillions of events and actions and decisions of the past that in precise concert resulted in the remarkable occasion of your birth. In one sense, your being here to read these words is vanishingly, stupefyingly unlikely. Paradoxically, in another and far deeper sense, it is inevitable.

I hope this book will be a voyage of discovery for the reader. Some of the artifacts may be familiar, but there is always more to learn about them, always the opportunity to move beyond the familiar and be surprised by history. Perhaps some readers may be inspired to undertake their own quests after objects of special interest. But one shouldn't be disappointed to find that some objects that played a major role in an important event of history do not survive. Alas, Columbus's 1492 fleet—the *Niña, Pinta,* and *Santa María*—and James Hargreaves's original spinning jenny no longer exist; and despite some claims to the contrary, to the best of scholars' knowledge, neither do Noah's Ark or the Ark of the Covenant.

So feast your mind on the tales of the trials and victories of humankind that yielded the artifacts we may see, touch, and savor for their rich historical value today. From the Magna Carta to the Emancipation Proclamation, from John Harrison's fourth marine timekeeper to ENIAC, from a horse's hoof to a tablecloth fragment, a pigtail to a smoking stand, they are all part of the stuff of history—the stuff of which you yourself are made.

JUMBO'S HIDE,
ELVIS'S RIDE,
AND THE
TOOTH OF BUDDHA

The Tooth of the Buddha

DATE: circa 483 B.C.E.

WHAT IT IS: A tooth venerated by Buddhists, said to have come from Gautama Buddha, the founder of Buddhism; according to tradition, the relic has demonstrated supernatural powers.

WHAT IT LOOKS LIKE: The tooth is white and brownish and is encased in seven gold and silver caskets. Larger than an ordinary tooth, it is about the size of the first digit of a pinky, or about one inch.

Seven days after life ceased to exist in the Buddha, flames engulfed his body, reducing it to a pile of seedlike ashes—save for seven body parts that miraculously retained their entire original form: the forehead bone, two collarbones, and four front teeth. The Buddha, it was said, had used his psychic powers to bequeath these relics to his followers because he wanted them to understand the impermanent nature of life.* After devoting his adult life to giving humanity the dharma, his teachings on how to lead a righteous and correct life, it was for him a way to guide his followers after his physical death.

The Buddha's bodily relics, tradition holds, went to different destinations over time. One, the sacred tooth, performed miracles as it was passed down from king to king, and has over the ages been revered by Buddhists as a holy object.

Buddhism is a religion based not on worship of a deity but on wisdom of the self, and it is rich and complex in its history, traditions, and teachings on such issues as natural law, worldly matters, human problems,

---

*Buddha taught that all conditioned things are transient (*annica*), sorrowful (*dukkha*), and soulless (*anatta*), or impersonal. By leaving his ashes and parts of his body as relics, the Buddha wanted to teach people the impermanent nature of things as they are; by respecting the relics, it is believed, devotees can achieve merit.

mindfulness, actions (*karma*), discipline, ethics, psychology, metaphysics, truths, and re-becoming, or existence after death. It was founded by Siddhartha Gautama, who, after six years of searching as an ascetic for an end to suffering, discovered a philosophy that delivers adherents from evil and guides them to perfect wisdom and pure living. Gautama became known as the Buddha, or Enlightened One.

Siddhartha Gautama was born to a royal family in Lumbini Park at Kapilavatthu on the Indian border of present-day Nepal around 563 B.C.E. A sage told his father, King Suddhodana, that if the prince were exposed to the sufferings of the common people, he would not succeed his father as king but would rather embrace a life of asceticism and devote himself assiduously to teaching religion. Fearing the prediction, the king secluded his son and tried to keep him ignorant of the misfortunes and woes of others.

But after Prince Siddhartha married as a young man, trips to the local village exposed him to suffering, old age, sickness, and death. On another trip he met a religious man who inspired him to seek a solution to people's problems. A compassionate person, Siddhartha pondered how he could bring happiness to humankind. His ruminations were fruitless, and he decided to devote his life to this goal. Renouncing his royal station, he became a hermit.

Siddhartha sought out all the major religious teachers in India—there were sixty-two prominent religions in the country then—and asked what solution they had to the problems of suffering and unhappiness. These teachers imparted their wisdom to Siddhartha, who saw two kinds of extremism in their views. One was to mortify the self—that is, to lead a humble life by giving up comforts and avoiding everything that gave pleasure. The other was to revel in gratification of the senses.

Siddhartha didn't believe a person had to go to either of these extremes to find happiness, so he searched for a solution somewhere in between self-mortification and hedonism. Eventually he had the profound insight that the reason for unhappiness is craving or desire, and that fulfilling desires causes even greater unhappiness because the satisfaction never lasts. If people could extinguish or eradicate their cravings, Gautama Buddha realized, there would be no unhappiness. To this end he formulated the four Noble Truths: life is suffering; the cause of suffering is desire; the remedy for suffering is the extinction of desire; the way to extinguish desire is to follow the Noble Eightfold Path: right understanding, right purpose, right speech, right conduct, right livelihood, right effort, right mindfulness, and right concentration.

Gautama Buddha's dharma, or philosophical teaching, was designed to

During the Portuguese invasion of Sri Lanka in the early sixteenth century, King Vimala-dharmasurya I offered his palace in Kandy to safeguard the Buddha's tooth. The sacred tooth, which had been taken from a Buddhist temple in the town of Ratnapura and hidden in various places so it wouldn't be seized or destroyed by the invaders, has ever since remained in the Temple of the Sacred Tooth Relic.

help people find happiness. It preached that people should not do evil deeds but good deeds, practice morality and discipline, and develop knowledge, or wisdom. To control one's mind, or keep it clean from unwholesome thoughts, was vital. Buddha said there were three kinds of unwholesomeness: craving, which includes greed or desire of any kind; anger or resentment; and delusion, or not having an understanding of how things really are.

Gautama urged Buddhists to follow five precepts: not to kill any living thing; not to steal; not to commit adultery or engage in any kind of sexual misconduct; not to lie, slander, utter obscenities, or engage in frivolous talk; and not to take any kind of intoxicants. The Buddha taught that people should rather practice loving kindness, compassion, sympathetic joy, and equanimity. Buddhists must always try to maintain these four states of mind, which is to say that they must always be mindful, or aware, of their thoughts, words, and activities.

The Buddha passed away in his eightieth year, about 483 B.C.E.* Ten months before his death, he traveled from city to city in India, stopping only at night to help people or to preach to them. At the end of his journey he settled in the northern Indian city of Kusinara (later called Kushinagar). A blacksmith prepared a meal for the Buddha in his house, and after eating it, the Buddha told the blacksmith that in the evening he was going to die. After the meal the Buddha was struck by a stomach pain, and he left for the

*According to Buddhism, the Buddha passed away to nirvana in 543 B.C.E., eighty years after he was born in 623 B.C.E. The reason the year dates differ from the Gregorian calendar is that ancient calculations, according to the traditional Eastern practice, were based on lunar months, whereas Western calculations are based on solar months.

place where he would die—the Sala garden of King Mallas. In this garden he asked the attendant monk to give him water, then urged all the monks to go meditate and not to be disheartened by his death. The Buddha opened his eyes and attained the four mental ecstasies, or absorptions (*jhanas*), then passed away and attained nirvana.

Many people attended the Buddha's cremation a week later in King Mallas's Sala garden in Kusinara. According to tradition, the remains of the Buddha were unusual. The ashes were like lentil seeds, and seven bones and teeth remained unchanged, according to the Buddha's determination. Eight powerful princes, all related to the Buddha, came to the cremation, each deeply desiring the Buddha's ashes. They quarreled among themselves vociferously about who was closer to the Buddha and therefore rightfully entitled to the ashes, and it seemed the clashes would soon become physical.

A Brahmin named Drona who had been a teacher to all the princes heard about the dispute and interceded, saying that arguing would lead only to bitter quarreling and bloodshed, and that the Lord Buddha would disapprove of it. Drona told the princes that he would distribute the ashes to them, and that as a teacher he would be impartial. With a measuring bowl he divided the seedlike ashes in an equitable manner among the eight princes, who then built shrines for the ashes in their own kingdoms for people to venerate.

The tooth of the Buddha, known as the Sacred Tooth Relic, is enshrined in a valuable golden casket. The threshhold and door frame of the casket chamber are covered with silver and gold. The sacred relic is located inside the seventh casket.

The Buddha's forehead bone, two collarbones, and four front teeth were more sacred than the ashes and dispersed to different locations. The three bones were taken by *arahants,* the foremost disciples of Buddha, and eventually were enshrined in separate monuments. The forehead bone went to a shrine called Seruvila Cetiya in the Trincomalee district in northeastern Sri Lanka. Of the two collarbones, the right one was put in the Thuparama shrine in Anuradhapura, the ancient capital of Sri Lanka; and the other was sent to the shrine of Selacetiya Mihintale, near Anuradhapura in north-central Sri Lanka.

Of the four teeth, one, according to tradition, was hidden by the Brahmin Drona in a lock of his hair under his turban, and was in turn taken by Sakra, the king of devas (divine beings), to heaven, where it was enshrined. Another tooth was taken to Nágaloka, described in Buddhist literature as a heavenly place that is under the ground. A third tooth was given to a Sri Lankan king and later enshrined at Somávati Cetiya, near Polonnaruva.

The fourth tooth was taken by a saintly monk, Arahant Khema. It has a long earthly heritage, traveling to many different shrines over time, and has been continually venerated by Buddhists.

Many stories of miracles are associated with this relic. For instance, there was once a non-Buddhist king who doubted the power of the relic and pummeled it on an iron anvil with a sledgehammer in an attempt to crush it. The tooth did not crush but instead embedded itself inside the anvil, where it could not be touched. The king then announced he would grant a reward to anybody who could take it out. Many people came from all over to try to extract the Buddha's tooth relic from the anvil, but no one was successful. Then one day a grandson of the wealthy Buddhist Anatha Pindika, who had lived at the time of the Buddha, came and knelt before the anvil. Reverently, he said, "Lord, please come out and show your miraculous power to the people who do not believe in the Buddha." And indeed the tooth came out from the anvil and soared to the sky, where it emitted a colorful rainbow. The grandson of the Buddhist follower then placed a lotus in the palm of his hand and asked the relic to come down from the sky. The tooth sailed down and rested on the lotus, which the man held above his head as he walked to the temple. This event was witnessed by thousands of people who cheered and shouted enthusiastically. The king also witnessed the miracle, and, surrendering to the power of the relic, bowed down to it. In a different time another king did not believe in the miracles of the Buddha's relic and threw it into a muddy body of water. Suddenly, out of the water rose a lotus upon which the tooth, completely dry, rested. The king henceforth became a believer in the tooth of the Buddha. The relic has many miraculous stories like these associated with it.

The tooth was passed down from king to king without much threat to its existence until the fourth century C.E. During the reign of King Guhasiva, a Buddhist who possessed the relic, a non-Buddhist king named Citrayana attempted to conquer Guhasiva's kingdom in India.* Guhasiva entered into

---

*At this time Hindus opposed Buddhism because the Buddha's teachings were contrary to the practices of the Brahmins, the Hindu priestly caste. The Hindus wanted Buddhism out of their land, which is why Buddhism began to separate from the country where it originated. What elements of Buddhism the Hindus did not eradicate, the Muslims later finished off, and after the fourteenth century Buddhism was almost completely stripped

battle with Citrayana but realized his forces could not defeat the stronger king. Fearing that Citrayana would seize the sacred tooth relic, Guhasiva summoned his only child, Princess Hemamala, and her husband, Prince Danta, and instructed them to deliver the tooth to the king of Sri Lanka.

Disguised as a Brahmin and his wife, the prince and princess slipped out of the city of Dantapura (later called Orissa) with the tooth relic hidden inside a lock of Hemamala's hair. Then, according to tradition, they entered a thick forest where a tribe of spiritlike beings called Nagas lived. The Nagas, who could appear like people but were not human, caused a fierce storm that alarmed the prince and princess. When they tried to take shelter, they were surrounded by Naga warriors, who searched the princess and found the relic. But to the delight of the prince and princess, the tooth performed a series of miracles. First, it stopped the thrashing storm. Then it jumped to the sky and began to shine brightly. The Nagas fell to their knees in awe, and the prince and princess slipped away unnoticed. The tooth then returned to the hand of Princess Hemamala, who was a devoted Buddhist.

The next obstacle for the prince and princess was to get across the shallow ocean that separated India from Sri Lanka. They set out on their voyage on a large boat, but a severe storm came up that threatened to overturn the vessel. Danta and Hemamala knelt down before the relic and reverently asked for help in completing their voyage. The tooth again rose to the sky and illuminated it with bright colors, whereupon the storm cleared and the travelers on the boat below cheered heartily. Then the relic returned to its carrier.

Prince Danta and Princess Hemamala arrived safely in Sri Lanka, and to avoid being recognized they traveled through the jungle to reach Anuradhapura, the capital, in the north-central part of the country. At the palace they presented a letter of introduction from the princess's father, which offered the sacred relic to King Meghavarnabhaya of Sri Lanka (who ruled from 301 to 328 C.E.), in the hope that he would protect it from the enemies of Buddhism. The king, greatly pleased with the gift, obliged, calling for a festival and procession to celebrate the tooth. The relic brought joy to the people of the Sinhala kingdom; Meghavarnabhaya placed it above his throne, where it began to shine, so the king built a special temple in the city to enshrine it.

Every king since Meghavarnabhaya who possessed the sacred tooth con-

---

from India. In the 1920s a Sri Lankan teacher named Anagarika Dharmapala went to India and reestablished Buddhism there. The British government assisted in this effort by restoring ancient Buddhist shrines in places where they had been as early as the third century B.C.E.

A mural from Kelaniya Raja Maha Vihara, a Buddist temple in Sri Lanka, depicting the arrival in the country from India, in the fourth century, of Princess Hemamala, daughter of King Guhasiva, and her husband, Prince Danta Kumara, with the sacred tooth relic. The prince and princess are disguised as a Brahmin ascetic couple and the relic is hidden in a lock of the princess's hair.

sidered himself the inheritor of the realm of the country until 1815, when Ceylon* became a British crown colony. In the early 1800s, the British occupied and controlled parts of Ceylon, and tried to take over the country, but met resistance, especially from the capital city of Kandy. In 1815, Robert Brownrigg, the governor, entered into a conspiracy with some of the king's ministers, and his soldiers captured the king, who had been hiding in a remote jungle village. On March 2, an agreement was signed by the British with rebellious ministers in which the ruling power of Ceylon was turned over to the British. (In a famous incident, a brave Buddhist monk named Wariyapola Sumangala took down the British flag that had been hoisted before the pact and stomped on it as a gesture of defiance.)

In the nineteenth century the British were bound by a treaty Brownrigg had made to protect the Ceylonese people's practice of Buddhism, which included maintaining and safeguarding the relic. Later, the British requested to be released from the treaty and appointed a custodian for the tooth.

The relic is encased in seven caskets, one inside the other, which were made especially for it by the sixteenth-century Sri Lankan king Vimaladharmasurya, the last king to give the tooth a home in his palace. During the Portuguese invasion of his country, he did not have time to build a shrine for the relic, so he gave his palace in the city of Mahanuvara (later called Kandy) to house the tooth, and he moved to a small building nearby.

* The name of the country was originally Sinhala Dvipa, according to ancient Pali (Buddhist-language) commentaries. The Indian Ocean island was later known by such names as Lanka, Sri Lanka, and beginning around the sixteenth century, Ceylon, when the country was occupied by the Portuguese, who had difficulty pronouncing the name "Sri Lanka." The country continued to be called Ceylon under later Dutch and British occupation, and through a series of peaceful political reforms was granted independence in 1948. In the 1970s the country became the Democratic Socialist Republic of Sri Lanka.

According to Buddhism, the magic of the relic is an extension of the supernatural powers of the Buddha. Buddha was said to have many such powers, including levitation, mind reading, clairaudience, and clairvoyance, but he used them only sparingly, to prove himself to skeptics or when they were urgently needed. For example, in only three instances did he use his "twin miracles" power, in which he would ascend to the sky and water and fire would pour forth simultaneously from his body: in the fourth week after he attained enlightenment, to remove doubt from the minds of divine beings;* when some older, haughty relatives refused to kneel before him; and when some religious leaders called Niganthas tried to discredit him. Once the Buddha used his psychic powers to catch a criminal who was running away. As the criminal ran, he perceived the ground rising steeply to the incline of a mountain, while the Buddha walked casually in pursuit of him on the flat land. When the criminal, known as Angulimala, tired out, Buddha caught him, and through his teachings tamed him. Angulimala, who had previously killed more than 1,000 people, became a well-respected disciple of the Buddha.† On other occasions, if someone needed the help of the Buddha, he would disappear from his temple and appear in front of the person in need.

Today, the sacred tooth continues to be venerated by Buddhists as well as some non-Buddhists for the wholesome thoughts and feelings of holiness it

*According to Buddhist teachings, invisible divine beings, or deities, live in the land and sky. Humans are powerless in their merits to see divine beings, who have gone beyond human meritorious power, and the happiness enjoyed by divine beings in heaven cannot be seen by humans because by birth they are powerless to do so. In Buddhism, all actions have reactions; bad actions have bad reactions, and good actions have good reactions. One's actions result in karma, and depending on one's karma, one will be reborn in a bad station or good station. A person who performs bad deeds such as stealing or killing will be reborn in hell, or in woeful states. There are four hells, according to Buddhism: the one visible woeful state is the animal world, and the three invisible states are the hungry-ghost world, burning hell, and the world of deformed spirits. Inhabitants in these worlds suffer according to their past deeds.

† Angulimala was the brilliant disciple of a Brahmin. His jealous fellow disciples conspired to get him into trouble by telling the Brahmin that Angulimala was having an affair with the Brahmin's wife. The Brahmin became enraged, demanding that Angulimala present him with a gift of 1,000 fingers, otherwise he would not teach him anymore. Angulimala was so desperately eager for spiritual knowledge that he took up the master's challenge and killed by sword more than 1,000 people, but animals carried away most of the body parts, and he was left with only 999 fingers. He was determined to acquire the one remaining finger he needed, but people ran away when they saw him, so he decided to kill his mother, who he knew would never run from him. At that point Buddha used his magical powers to stop the maddened student, who would be reborn in hell for killing his mother. Appearing to Angulimala in the chase scene described, Buddha preached to him and taught him how to obtain enlightenment, inducing Angulimala to give up his sword and follow the Buddha's teachings. Angulimala became an *arahant*, or saint.

gives them, as well as for its miraculous powers. In times of drought, for instance, the tooth may be taken out of its caskets, and followers will place their faith in the relic to produce rain. Others have claimed healing miracles, such as improved eyesight.

The relic remains locked in its seven caskets, one inside the other. The four outer caskets have locks, and four people have the keys to unlock them—two chief high priests, the custodian of the tooth relic, and a government representative; they must all be together to open the caskets.

The tooth relic is taken from its caskets for public exhibitions every four or five years, and on special occasions such as royal visits or government exhibitions. The four key holders are summoned to open the caskets, whereupon the sacred tooth is customarily placed on a decorated stage in its temple for public viewing a few hours each day but may not be touched. By means of a golden wire, the relic sits on top of a golden lotus. When the relic is not exhibited, people pay respect to it by standing or kneeling before it with their hands together, fingers extended, or by placing flowers in front of it. There is never any praying to or worshiping of the tooth by Buddhists.

Every year in Kandy, Sri Lanka, usually in July or August, a weeklong celebration is held to venerate the relic. For seven days festive processions are held (all in the evenings, except for the last day, when one is held in the morning), during which the smallest of the seven caskets (not containing the relic) is carried by a decorated elephant.

This is the foremost pageant in the country, a tradition that began in the fourth century with King Meghavarnabhaya and has continued to the present; the customs and practices of the procession have changed very little over time. Scores of gaily dressed drummers, trumpeters, dancers, elephants, lamp-holders, flag-bearers, representatives of the local deities, dignitaries, and monks march through the streets as throngs of people from all around the world, including the mostly Buddhist nations of Burma, Thailand, Singapore, and Nepal, enjoy the pageantry and celebrate the tooth relic. The perahera, or procession, moves through Dalada Vidiya, the central street in the city, and continues to the tooth relic's home, which is located in front of an artificial lake in the city. The celebration ends on the morning of the eighth day, when the last procession is held.

For Buddhists, the impermanent nature of life that the Enlightened One was determined to demonstrate to them is exemplified by the sacred fifth-century B.C.E. tooth of the Buddha.

LOCATION: Temple of the Sacred Tooth Relic (Dalada Maligawa), Kandy, Sri Lanka.

The Gold Larnax of King Philip II

DATE: 336 B.C.E.

WHAT IT IS: A funerary chest containing the burnt bones of King Philip II of Macedonia that was placed in a tomb more than two thousand years ago and not discovered until the twentieth century.

WHAT IT LOOKS LIKE: The larnax is made of pure gold sheets folded and hammered into the shape of a box with four legs sculpted in the shape of a lion's paws. It is ornately decorated with reliefs of intertwining plants, rosettes, and lotuses in two horizontal rows on its outer sides and, on its hinged lid, a Macedonian star with sixteen rays radiating from a circular center, which encloses a large gold rosette with a smaller blue enamel rosette inside it. The larnax measures approximately 16 inches by 13½ inches and weighs 17 pounds, 3.6 ounces.

Aigai (ancient Vergina), 336 B.C.E.

A special celebration is to take place in the city, the capital of the kingdom of Macedonia, an eastern Mediterranean state of southern Europe settled about seventeen hundred years earlier by the Thracians. Macedonia, the most powerful political entity in the region, is ruled by Philip II, who ascended the throne in 359 B.C.E. and judiciously continued his predecessors' strategy of conquering independent city-states and uniting them under his leadership. Philip, a son of King Amyntas III, is at the peak of his power now, and has his eyes set on expanding his empire by conquering the formidable Asian kingdom of Persia.

Before daylight a large crowd gathers at the city's amphitheater to watch the athletic games that are part of the wedding celebration of the daughter of King Philip II. Fanfare and revelry, not to mention, in these precarious times, an element of unease, fill the large outdoor arena where the Macedonian king will soon be joining the festivities in a royal procession. The wedding is a conciliatory gesture arranged by Philip after an altercation erupted at his own wedding the previous year to a high-born woman named Cleopatra. His new bride's uncle had the indiscretion to deride another of Philip's wives, Olympias, and in a drunken rage the king turned on his and Olympias's son, Alexander. Olympias, shrewd, quick-tempered, and impetuous, fled with Alexander to her native Epirus, and to keep peace in his subjugated northern kingdom, Philip offered his and Olympias's daughter to Olympias's brother, the king of Epirus.

This was a turbulent time in Greece to be sure, but it was also a period of great enlightenment, during which some of the greatest thinkers of history were examining life, nature, and the universe. Aristotle was expounding erudite philosophy, Plato had died just a dozen years before, Hippocrates forty-one years before, and Socrates just sixty-three years earlier, in 399 B.C.E.

When his brother Perdiccas was mortally wounded in battle and he became the Macedonian king in 359, Philip determined to create a mighty military machine. He built an efficient, well-disciplined army with a cavalry and infantry that were armed with long pikes. Philip soon put his army into battle, and he conquered one city after another—Pydna, Potidaea, Amphipolis, Abdera, Maroneia, and Methone among them. Some peoples, like the Pheraens, beseeched mercenaries for military assistance, but Philip eventually subjugated most of the peoples he wanted for his empire. The battles were violent; cities were sometimes destroyed, people were mutilated. In combat at Methone, Philip himself was blinded in one eye.

Over the years, Philip continued to march his army across Greece on a mission of conquest. Making an alliance with the Thebans, he defeated the Phocians at Delphi. He invaded the land later known as Bulgaria. He employed envoys to gain the support of city-states, paid mercenaries to refrain from supporting his enemies, and generally did whatever he had to do to enlarge his kingdom. But he wasn't always successful. Some cities revolted, some military actions failed. Some city-states united against him in 338 B.C.E., but Philip engaged them in battle at Chaeroneia and dealt them a severe defeat. Philip organized a convention for the city-states of Greece the next year in which he installed himself as its head and formed a League of Corinth with a voting council; the league pledged support to Philip and strove to keep peace among its constituent states. With southern Greece now under his rule, Philip was indeed at his highest moment of glory, and he covetously eyed Persia to seal his destiny as an invincible emperor.

The ornate gold larnax that contained the bones of King Philip II.

Over the years Philip took many wives, and after the quarrel in 337 at his wedding to Cleopatra, he endeavored to maintain the kingdom of Epirus as his ally. Ever the savvy statesman, Philip had the sense to keep peace in his realm, even if it meant offering his own daughter's hand in marriage. Keeping the support of his allies would be vital to Philip if he were to realize his dream of enlarging his empire. The conquest of Persia was no doubt a preoccupation on the day of his daughter's wedding, but for now he would revel in the festivities.

A royal Greek wedding was a joyous celebration that could last several days and included a feast, games, and other events. Now an excited crowd that included leaders of the various Greek city-states was enjoying the games at the amphitheater of Aigai. Accompanied by his son Alexander and his daughter's new husband, also named Alexander, King Philip II entered the theater in a procession that had commenced at his palace. But then, amid the throngs of people and soldiers, a man approached Philip and stabbed him to death.

The assassin, who tried to flee but was caught and killed by Philip's soldiers, is supposed to have murdered the king over a complaint or an alleged injustice. But some people believed that Philip's wife Olympias had played a role in the murder of her husband. Philip's newest wife, Cleopatra, was a potential obstacle to their son Alexander succeeding to the throne, but the king's death would clear the way for Alexander to become the new king of Macedonia.

Indeed, the twenty-year-old immediately replaced his father as sovereign and soon took up his father's dream of marching the invincible Macedonian-Greek army into Persia and conquering all its dominions, as well as Thebes, Asia Minor, Egypt, Babylonia, Jerusalem, Tyre, Syria, and northern India. Alexander's life and adventures were astounding: he was tutored by Aristotle and later financed the philosopher's scholarly research; he fought monumental battles against huge armies; he founded the Egyptian city of Alexandria; he disseminated knowledge and progressive ideas—indeed, he changed the course of civilizations by opening them to new ways of thinking. History would remember this conqueror of much of the known world, whose Hellenistic culture and political triumphs would reach into the future, as Alexander the Great.

But before he would march his soldiers into combat across the civilized world, before he would rule over a great empire, Alexander had a task to complete: to build a tomb for his father and give him a royal burial. In accordance with royal protocol, Philip was cremated. From a pyre that contained weapons, jewels, and other objects—possibly even horses and chariots—Philip's burnt bones were extricated, bathed in spirits, wrapped in rich purple fabric, and placed in a decorative gold chest, or larnax, along with a meticulously crafted heavy gold wreath adorned with an array of sculpted oak leaves and acorns. The larnax was placed in a marble sarcophagus and set in a chamber of the elaborate tomb. Exquisite and expertly crafted objects of gold, silver, bronze, iron, ivory, and wood were also deposited in the tomb. Then the tomb was sealed, and over it workmen piled mounds of soil.

As the years passed, the tomb sank ever more deeply into the earth. Buried three centuries before the birth of Christ and the start of the common era, the Macedonian king lay undisturbed in death through the ages.

Vergina, Greece, 1977

After a quarter-century of excavating in the area of this village in northern Greece north of Mount Olympus—a region combed by archaeologists since the mid–nineteenth century—Greek archaeologist and professor Manolis Andronicos makes a remarkable discovery: a royal tomb, with a marble sarcophagus in the funerary chamber. Inside the sarcophagus is a gold larnax containing a set of burnt human bones. Inside the chamber and in other rooms of the tomb are an array of objects including sculptures, weapons, armor, vessels, and jewelry, and in the antechamber the burnt bones of a woman in a smaller gold larnax.* Based on years of scholarly and scientific investigation and the application of historical and archaeological evidence, Andronicos later concludes that the bones in the royal tomb are those of King Philip II of Macedonia. This identification is supported by other scholars.

Murder. Mystery. Intrigue. The story of the father of Alexander the Great is one of the great tales of the ancient world, a story made all the more extraordinary with the emergence of Philip's bones twenty-three hundred years after his death. Philip's tomb and its cache of artifacts are one of the twentieth century's most important archaeological discoveries, so while his death may have been the ancient world's loss, it was the modern world's gain. With the recovery of the king's remains and royal riches that had lain hidden from human view for many centuries after their entombment, it may be said that Philip was the Greek King Tutankhamen. Like Tutankhamen's death mask, the gold larnax that contained the bones of King Philip II is the enduring symbol of an ancient king and an ancient world that shaped the destiny of much that was to come after.

LOCATION: Archaeological Museum of Vergina, Vergina, Greece.

*In his book *Vergina: The Royal Tombs,* Manolis Andronicos posits that the woman's bones are those of Philip's last wife, Cleopatra.

The Magna Carta

∾∾∾∾∾∾∾∾∾∾∾∾∾∾∾∾∾∾∾∾∾∾

DATE: 1215.

WHAT IT IS: A medieval charter that was drafted to rectify abuses in the rule of King John of England, and which demonstrated that even sovereigns must adhere to a supreme law. Several handwritten exemplifications (official copies issued under royal seal) of the 1215 charter were distributed throughout the English realm, of which four survive. The original 1215 charter was revised and reissued several times throughout the thirteenth century, and a number of these reissued exemplifications survive as well.

WHAT IT LOOKS LIKE: All the extant 1215 charters are written on parchment in Latin, are dated 15 June 1215, and have slight variations in their dimensions and wording. The text of one of the exemplifications is difficult to read as a result of damage it sustained in a fire in 1731 at the Cotton Library in Westminster, where it was stored, but it is the only extant 1215 exemplification with any vestige of the royal seal.

The Magna Carta is known as one of the great documents in the history of democracy, but in the annals of duplicitous dealings, King John's consent to the charter is almost without equal. When the tyrannical ruler acquiesced to the demand that he affix his royal seal to a document guaranteeing certain rights and liberties, made by an assembly of barons who had angrily confronted him at Runnymede (a meadow southwest of London, between Windsor and Staines) in June 1215, he pacified a group of discontented subjects and quelled a rebellion. But one can imagine what was running through his mind in view of the fact that soon after he notified the Pope of this contentious encounter, the Pope nullified the entire transaction. As a result of John's royal chicanery, civil war erupted in England. But the integrity of the realm was saved a year later by John's sudden demise, and with the new government's acceptance of the Magna Carta, the seeds of modern democracy were planted.

Many social, economic, political, ecclesiastical, and other conditions that had evolved through the centuries, not to mention the policies and events in the rule of King John, led the barons to demand a charter from their sovereign. From the fifth to the eleventh century, England was ruled by Anglo-Saxons. After William of Normandy conquered England in 1066, feudalism spread throughout England, but kings continued to rule by absolute power for the next two centuries. Over time, however, their power began to lessen. During the twelfth century, Henry II made many legal reforms, but his son John, who ascended the throne in 1199 following the death of John's brother, Richard I, ruled as a despot—albeit with many complications, including heavy taxation and contention with France, that had been passed on to him by his predecessor.

As a result of a dispute between King John and Pope Innocent III over the election of the new Archbishop of Canterbury, the Pope, forging greater strength for the Church than it had ever had, put an interdict over England, and then excommunicated John. But later, with his nobles on the brink of rebellion, John had no choice but to surrender England and Ireland to the Pope and receive back the kingdoms as fiefs.

A record of these transactions is found in an extant papal bull, that of Pope Innocent III, dated April 21, 1214, from St. Peter's in Rome (The British Library, London). In this bull the Pope describes John's letter of October 3, 1213, sealed with the royal seal, in which the king affirms the relinquishment of his kingdoms (which he had preliminarily surrendered in May 1213) and pledges to pay tributes to the Roman Church. In the bull the Pope accepts King John's vassaldom to the Roman Church and lifts the interdict of 1208.

A result of the reconciliation between King John and Pope Innocent III was John's acceptance of Stephen Langton as the new archbishop of Canterbury. Langton, in exile in Pontigny since the 1208 interdict, returned to his homeland with the aim of guiding the English monarch to renew the fair laws of previous English kings. To carry out government reform, Langton decided that a royal charter would be the most propitious vehicle and proposed this idea to some of the most powerful barons, citing the 1100 Coronation Oath of Henry as the foundation for a new charter.

After his reconciliation with Innocent III, John's popularity increased, but he still had problems with his northern barons. In early 1214 John undertook an unsuccessful military campaign against France, and while away, he angered many at home by requesting scutage (a tax levied in lieu of serving in the army).

To replenish his depleted treasury after the costly war against Philip II of France, John decided to levy new scutage. His demand elicited bitter feelings from the taxed barons, who, wanting to protect themselves from further misrule, felt they must obtain from the king a charter of liberties. At a summit in November 1214, the barons informed John they would not pay the new scutage and shortly after planned to demand a charter. Early in 1215, as they had been preparing for civil war against John, the barons proposed to John a charter based on the feudal rights of Henry's Coronation Oath that subsequent kings had largely ignored, but Archbishop Langton intervened and obtained a truce in effect through Easter. As the period of the truce ended, the barons, gathered at Stamford, once again pressed for a charter, but John continued to resist.

Although many barons, not just from the north but throughout the realm, had united to fight John, the king also had some powerful supporters. Still, while the barons were not a match for the royal army, they seized London in May 1215, encountering little resistance. Even with this crisis John at first would not concede, but finally, realizing the strength of his opposition, he gave in to the baronial demand for a charter of liberties.

On June 15, 1215, the barons and King John met at Runnymede. John agreed to their demands, which were set forth in a manuscript of forty-nine clauses that his adversaries carried with them, and he placed upon it his seal of white wax. Discussion followed, and these stipulations, which became known as the Articles of the Barons (The British Library, London), became the basis for the charter that would soon be issued with some additional revisions making it applicable to freemen rather than just barons (although freemen were then only a small part of the population, the category would eventually come to include most of the people). The assembly at Runnymede, which ended on June 23, had been successful; the barons had the seal of King John on their Articles, they had their Great Charter, and the threat of civil war was, for the time at least, abated.

In putting his seal to the Articles, John had in essence endorsed the idea that a sovereign held the same status under law as a freeman. However, even though the Magna Carta would over time become a cornerstone of democracy, it wasn't the barons' intention to acquire liberties for all people. Rather, the barons wanted the charter to safeguard the liberties of the nobles and restrict the sovereign's means to raise money. But the charter contained many democratic provisions—among them, that a freeman must have a trial by jury of his peers before he could be seized, imprisoned, out-lawed, or exiled; that rights and justice would not be sold or denied to freemen; and that the consent of a council of nobles and clergy was neces-sary for taxes to be levied—that would over time be interpreted as univer-sally applicable. The charter also provided for a council of twenty-five barons to enforce its clauses, first by warning the king of any noncompli-ance with the articles, then by forming an army under the authority of the charter to ensure compliance, without incurring a penalty for treason.

A formal charter was drafted that had been expanded to contain sixty-three clauses, and around June 24, exemplifications of what would come to be called Magna Carta (the "Great Charter") were distributed. The exact destinies of all the exemplifications are not known, but historians of the time cited their distribution to bishops and sheriffs throughout the king-dom. As many as three dozen exemplifications may have been distributed, although only thirteen are recorded to have been issued.

The Great Charters began with a preamble. Following is the preamble (translated from the Latin) of one of the extant exemplifications:

> John, by the grace of God, king of England, lord of Ireland, duke of Normandy and Aquitaine, and Count of Anjou: to the archbishops, bishops, abbots, earls, barons, justices, sheriffs, reeves, ministers, and to all bailiffs, and faithful subjects greeting.
>
> Know that we, by divine impulse, and for the salvation of our soul, and of the souls of our ancestors and of our heirs, and for the honor of God, and the exaltation of Holy Church, and the amend-ment of our kingdom, by advice of our venerable fathers . . . have in the first place granted to God, and by this our present charter, confirmed on behalf of ourselves and our heirs for ever.

This preamble was followed in basic form in reconfirmations by subse-quent kings, with the issuing king's name in place at the beginning.

Soon, probably after a communication sent by John to Innocent III, the Pope declared King John's charter invalid. In the bull of Pope Innocent III of August 24, 1215 (The British Library, London), the Pope describes John's cession of his kingdom to the Roman Church, condemns the "shameful" agreement with the barons, and declares it annulled because King John agreed to it only under threat of force:

> By force and fear, that could have assailed even the most courageous of men, he was compelled to enter into an agreement with them as

unlawful and unjust as it was base and shameful. . . . We, not wishing to close our eyes to such audacious wickedness whereby the Apostolic See is brought into contempt, the royal prerogative diminished, the English nation outraged . . . do utterly reject and condemn his agreement and under threat of excommunication command that neither the barons and their accomplices demand its observation, utterly cancelling and making void both the charter itself and any pledges or obligations that may have been made in any way concerning it, so that neither now nor hereafter shall they be of any validity.

This papal bull probably arrived in England around the end of the following month. With the charter abrogated by the Church, John caused his enemies to be excommunicated and seized their castles in the north. The barons rebelled, Stephen Langton was expelled from his position by the Church for not supporting the papal decree, and England was in upheaval until John suddenly died in October 1216 and his nine-year-old son, Henry III, succeeded him.

To help gain acceptance for the new king, who was crowned at Gloucester, the conservative regents who directed royal administrative matters issued a revised version of King John's charter on November 12, 1216, under the seal of William Marshal, the first Earl of Pembroke, who in 1215 was one of John's representatives to the barons. In the following year, 1217, the civil war came to an end, the charter was again revised and reissued, and this charter likewise omitted the clauses that were dropped in the 1216 reissue. Whenever a reconfirmation was made, copies were dispatched to counties and made known to the local people.

Even though King John in his charter bound his heirs forever, the barons became deeply concerned that royal injustices would be perpetrated again when the government in 1223 made an examination into the royal privileges enjoyed by King John. Near the end of the following year, some barons, along with Stephen Langton, who had served as a mediator during the drawing up of the 1215 charter, which he favored, sought out Henry. They asked the young king, who had by now come of age, to confirm the Great Charter of King John, which he agreed to in exchange for a mobile items tax. This last reissue of King John's Great Charter came on February 11, 1225, with the king's seal, and it was this reconfirmation that became known as the Magna Carta.

Henry's reconfirmations of the Magna Carta were not exact reproductions of the King John charters. There were certain differences, such as the

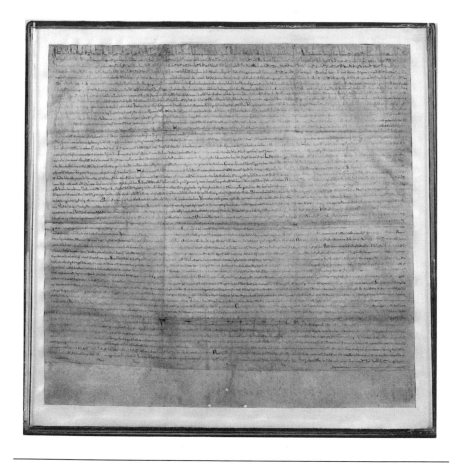

Of up to thirty-six Magna Cartas distributed around England in 1215, the Lincoln Magna Carta, pictured above, is one of only four to survive.

lack of a clause regarding the Great Council whose consent was necessary for levying taxes. But even though later sovereigns would issue the Magna Carta, Henry's 1225 charter would be the final form, with reconfirmations in later years true to its provisions. Henry III's eldest son, Edward I, confirmed the Magna Carta on October 12, 1297, and the charter's 1225 revision, the third, became entered in the Statute Roll, and was thus incorporated into English law.

Despite the considerable and admirable efforts to establish the Magna Carta in the thirteenth century, over time it became largely forgotten. The Tudor monarchs allowed Parliament to convene, but when Queen Elizabeth died in 1603 and was succeeded by her cousin, James Stuart, the King of

Scotland, a reign of Stuarts began in which the monarchy was accorded supreme power. Thus the decisions of the king were immutable; as James conceived the government, *"a deo rex, a rege le"*: "the king is from God, and the law from the king."

James's son, Charles, continued his father's autocratic rule, and after he imprisoned some subjects for refusing to bestow presents on him, Parliament compelled him to accept a petition, which, among other things, provided for tax reform. During this time, Sir Edward Coke, an outspoken authority on law who had served as privy councillor and in other legal positions under English monarchs, pulled the concepts of the Magna Carta from dormancy and contended that rulers, like common people, are bound by the law. Lord Coke elucidated the Magna Carta as a charter of rights that was applicable to all the people of a nation.

While it was a feudal instrument that addressed itself primarily to the liberties of nobles and was consequently not an ideal democratic instrument, the Magna Carta did limit the absolute power of the sovereign and criticized the oppression of the feudal classes. Although subsequently reinterpreted in ways not necessarily originally intended, the Magna Carta has served as a symbol of freedom, one held in high esteem by later generations as the foundation stone on which to build the future of democracy.

LOCATIONS:

King John's 1215 Magna Carta—four exemplifications survive:
> The British Library, London. (Two 1215 exemplifications are housed here.)
> Salisbury Cathedral, Salisbury, England.
> Lincoln Castle, Lincoln, England. (On loan from Lincoln Cathedral.)

In other locations around the world are several exemplifications of King Henry III's three revisions of 1216, 1217, and 1225, as well as his reissues or confirmations (modeled on his last revision) of 1237, 1253, and 1265 (at locations such as the Bodleian Library, Oxford; The British Library, London; and Durham Cathedral, Durham, England); and four known exemplifications of King Edward I's 1297 Magna Carta (Guildhall, London; National Library of Australia, Canberra; Public Record Office, London; and the National Archives and Records Administration, Washington, D.C., on loan from the Perot Foundation).

The Stone of Scone

DATE: 1249 (by historical record; earlier by tradition).

WHAT IT IS: The coronation throne of English monarchs, seized from the Scots in 1296.

WHAT IT LOOKS LIKE: The stone is a rectangular block of sandstone with a rough, grainy gray color. It weighs 458 pounds and measures 26¾ inches long, 16¾ inches wide, and 10¾ inches high. Two rusty iron rings are attached on top of it at the sides.

From biblical figures to ancient kings, from medieval monarchs to modern royalty, the story of the Stone of Scone is wrapped in legend and fact; it is an artifact with a long and distinguished history that symbolizes the heritage of Scotland and England and the glory of their sovereigns. Long and continuous documentation of the royal inauguration throne makes it a remarkable object of history, but its mythical background as the pillow on which a holy biblical figure rested his head and had a divine revelation inspired medieval kings, warriors, and citizens to venerate it as nothing less than a channel to God.

The oldest legend associated with the famous stone concerns the patriarch Jacob, who at Bethel dreamed of a ladder reaching from earth to heaven on which angels ascended and descended. When Jacob awoke the next morning, he took the stone on which he had rested his head and set it up as a pillar, pouring oil on top of it and vowing that if the Lord kept his promise to provide Jacob with bread to eat and raiment to wear so that he could return to his father's house in peace, then "this stone, which I have set up for a pillar, shall be God's house."

Legends continue to account for the stone's predocumented history. Called Jacob's Pillow, the stone was said to have been taken by his sons into the land of Egypt, from which it was later transported to Ireland. The ear-

By legend, the rough block of sandstone on which Jacob rested his head at Bethel was the Stone of Scone, also known as the Coronation Stone or Stone of Destiny.

liest known account of this latter trip was related around 1301 by Baldred Bissett, a commissioner dispatched to the Pope to support the cause for Scottish independence, who wrote, "Scota, the daughter of Pharaoh, king of Egypt [wife to King Gathelus, the son of the first king of the ancient Grecian district of Attica], with an armed band and large fleet sailed for Scotland, taking with her the royal seat [the Stone]. She conquered the Picts and took their kingdom and from her the Scots are named."

This legend may have been fabricated by Bissett, who wanted to establish a long line of descent for the Scots in a hearing of entitlement for the stone argued by Englishmen and Scots before the Pope. In 1527 the Scottish historian Hector Boece claimed the stone was carried from Spain to Ireland by Simon Brech, who in 700 C.E. invaded the island. On a hill known as Tara, Brech set up the stone as a throne on which kings were to be crowned. These differing accounts about the stone are still in the realm of myth, which characterizes the stone's history until the sixth century C.E.

It is about this time that the real history of the Stone of Scone (pronounced "skoon") begins. From the sixth to the thirteenth century, stories about the stone are intertwined with actual historical figures—kings and other persons of known record.

By the sixth century, there was a tradition of Irish kings being crowned on Lia Fail, the "fatal stone," a reference to the lore that if the person seated was a rightful claimant the stone would cry out, but if he were an imposter it would not utter a sound. Murkertagh, a descendant of Niall, a fifth-century Irish king and allegedly the country's first Christian ruler, bequeathed the stone to the sovereign of the Gaelic kingdom of Dalriada, which spread from Ireland to what later became known as Scotland. The stone at this time was believed to be the rock on which Jacob had dreamed of the ladder extending to heaven. It was this king of Dalriada who was said to have deposited Lia Fail (or the Stone of Destiny, as it was also known) in Dunstaffnage castle in Argyllshire.

This period precedes the formation of the nation of Scotland, which then comprised a number of different tribal kingdoms. For many years there were squabbles between the kingdoms, as well as invasions by foreigners. Unity finally came for two kingdoms, however, when in 843 Kenneth MacAlpin, the king of the Scots, conquered the Picts and became king of the united nation of Scotland. Three years later, in 846, MacAlpin conveyed the Stone of Destiny to a church on the Mote Hill of Scone, the old Pict capital, and it was from this location that it received another name, the Stone of Scone. Although no trace of any words remain on the stone, according to tradition Kenneth I engraved on it a Latin inscription, which translated into English reads:

> If fates go right, where'er this stone is found
> The Scots shall monarchs of that realm be crowned.

Exactly when the stone was first used as an inauguration throne* is not known, but it is believed to have served this function for several centuries prior to its earliest authenticated use as an inauguration stone in 1249. The account of this occasion requires some historical context.

In the mid–thirteenth century, Scotland was entering its medieval golden age. After more than 150 years of attempts to anglicize the country's crown and church—a process commenced by Margaret, the widow of Malcolm III, and continued by her sons, Edgar, Alexander, and David, who were determined to transform Celtic Scotland into a feudal state modeled after the English system—the Celtic rebellions had finally come to an end, and

---

*In medieval times the word *inauguration* was used to describe the ceremony in which Scottish kings came to power by sitting on the Stone of Scone (much later, the word came to refer to the ceremony in which presidents were inducted into office). Unlike Scottish kings, English kings were crowned, and the word *coronation* was (and continues to be) used to describe their accession to the throne. Medieval English kings looked down on their Scottish counterparts, seeing coronation as a more powerful investiture of royal authority.

English had replaced Gaelic as the national language. While attempting to seize the Hebrides from Norway, King Alexander II died of fever, leaving the Scottish realm to his son, who would lead the country into an era of stability, tranquillity, and prosperity.

Following the death of his father exactly one week earlier, Alexander III was inaugurated the king of Scotland on July 13, 1249. The inauguration took place at the monastery on the Mote Hill of Scone. In the church courtyard a cadre of the nation's most powerful noblemen escorted the new king, a mere seven-year-old boy, in a procession to the inauguration site, where a cross was set in the ground. As the Bishop of St. Andrews consecrated the boy, the men witnessing the ceremony placed gifts before their new king as he sat on a large stone covered with precious fabrics. Descriptions of Alexander's inauguration were rendered by chroniclers a century later, including by John de Fordun, who in about 1355 wrote that no king who had not been consecrated on the stone would be recognized: "This Stone is reverently preserved in that monastery [Scone] for the King of Scotland, nor were any of the Kings wont to reign anywhere in Scotland unless they had on receiving the name of King first sat upon the royal Stone at Scone." King Alexander III, almost certainly like other Scottish kings before him, was inaugurated by sitting on the Stone of Destiny, but he was not crowned like the kings of other nations.

Scotland prospered under Alexander's reign. But one night, while he was riding to join his wife, the forty-four-year-old king's horse threw him, and he died from the fall. His children having previously died, his only living descendant was his granddaughter, Margaret. An arrangement was made for Margaret to marry the king of England's son before being crowned, but she died before the marriage, leaving the successor to the crown in dispute.

Thirteen claimants vied for the throne of Scotland, most seriously among them Robert Bruce, John de Balliol, and John Hastings. Unsure which claimant's lineage most properly entitled him to the crown, Scotland's overseers asked King Edward I of England to settle the dispute. Edward agreed, but not before securing recognition from each of the royal competitors that he was Scotland's superior lord.

A judicial proceeding was held in which the royal candidates made their appeals, and Edward awarded possession of the Scottish kingdom to John de Balliol, who was made king at Scone in November 1292, where he sat on the Stone of Destiny and immediately paid homage to Edward. But during the events that followed, Balliol fell out of favor with Edward, who wanted control over all the countries of the British Isles. First, shortly after taking his oath, Balliol refused to appear in a Scottish suit before Westminster judges and was held in willful contempt of court, although he later submitted. But he was treated with disdain at Parliament and would not submit to Edward's request to serve in his army for England's impending war with France; indeed, in 1295 he became an ally of France's King Philip IV. The next year, Balliol invaded England but was captured and surrendered. To demonstrate Scottish subjugation, Edward took possession of Scotland's royal documents and seized the Stone of Scone, placing it in Westminster Abbey, next to his seat of power, the Palace of Westminster. It is possible that at this time iron rings were attached to the top of the heavy stone so poles could be inserted to carry it south to London.

In 1301 Edward I ordered a special Coronation Chair* to be made, in which the Stone of Scone could be enclosed under the chair's wooden seat. From the time Edward II was crowned in 1308, every sovereign of England has been crowned on the oaken chair containing the stone, with three exceptions: The thirteen-year-old son of Edward IV, Edward V, whose father's marriage was alleged to be invalid and who was subsequently murdered—supposedly by Richard III—in the Tower of London; Mary II, who shared the crown with William III and used another chair while William sat in the Coronation Chair; and Edward VIII, who abdicated in 1936 before he could be crowned.

These three exceptions notwithstanding, the Coronation Chair, with the Stone of Scone under the seat, since 1308 has represented the remarkable common bond among all the English monarchs who have received the crown since that time. Even a Scottish king was crowned on the Stone. In 1603, England's Queen Elizabeth died, and since she had no heirs, the monarchy passed to her nearest living male relative, her cousin, King James VI of Scotland, the son of Mary Queen of Scots. James VI became King James I of England and united Scotland and England.

Over the centuries the lofty stone was used only for coronations of English sovereigns. It was always kept encased in the Coronation Chair except on a rare few occasions. One was possibly for the installation of Oliver Cromwell in 1657 as Lord Protector, when the Coronation Chair was moved to Westminster Hall during England's Commonwealth Period (Cromwell was installed in a ceremony but rejected kingship). During

---

*The 1301 oaken Coronation Chair is still in existence today and is in relatively good shape for its great age, despite suffering some maltreatment over the years in addition to natural wear. During the seventeenth and eighteenth centuries, for example, schoolboys and visitors to Westminster Abbey defaced the chair by etching their names and other writings into it. At its highest point, the chair is seven feet tall.

The Coronation Chair with the Stone of Scone under the seat. Almost all the monarchs of England since Edward II in 1308 have been crowned sitting in the chair.

World War II the stone was hidden in a vault in Westminster Abbey, while the Coronation Chair was removed to Gloucester Cathedral.

Perhaps the stone's most remarkable absence from the Coronation Chair resulted from its theft on Christmas morning 1950.

At about two o'clock in the morning, four Scottish nationalists, ranging in age from twenty to twenty-five, broke into Westminster Abbey. Construction workers were effecting repairs on the church, and scaffolds that had been erected provided partial shielding while the nationalists carried out their crime. After exerting much labor to extract the stone from the chair, they dragged the stone along by its iron rings, only to have it break into two pieces. They placed the smaller piece in a car, and after a policeman appeared, they left, but one nationalist returned later to take the larger piece.

Dr. Alan Don, the dean of Westminster, pleaded for the return of the Stone on radio, and a massive police investigation to recover the relic ensued. The Scottish nationalists, who had hidden the stone in a wooded area, moved it to the Arbroath Abbey in Scotland. On April 11, 1951, a surprised custodian found the stone, restored to one piece now (presumably by mortar), on the altar, and two days later the medieval coronation throne was returned to Westminster Abbey. The following February, after security measures were instituted, the Stone of Scone was returned to its cavity in the Coronation Chair. The Scottish nationalist thieves were not prosecuted, perhaps out of sympathy for their belief that the Stone should be returned to its homeland.

Indeed, the stone's official return was later to take place. After seven hundred years at Westminster Abbey, the Stone of Scone, by consent of the queen of England, was returned to Scotland on November 30, 1996. The announcement of the decision was made in the House of Commons by Prime Minister John Major, and it came as a shock to authorities at Westminster. The reason the stone was removed was unclear to the Abbey authorities; conjectures in the press ranged from the fact that 1996 was the seven hundredth anniversary of the stone's seizure from Scotland in 1296 to the suspicion that its removal was a political ploy in an election year for the Conservative Party to receive votes from Scottish people. But announcement of the removal also promoted discussion over whether Scotland should gain independence.

Although the Stone of Scone is now separated from the Coronation Chair, provisions have been made to temporarily return it to Westminster Abbey to serve its traditional role when a new British monarch is crowned. With the return of the Stone of Scone to Scotland, a national treasure is home once again.

That this object has played a consistent and vital role in a national custom for centuries is in itself quite remarkable. The antiquity of the stone and its alleged use as an inauguration throne by Scottish kings of the Dark Ages conjures up romantic images of regal ceremonies with noblemen and prelates dressed in their finest garments, paying homage to the new monarch sitting proudly on the royal seat, or of warriors transporting it through the countryside, filled with awe at its reputation. With its fantastic uses and associations through the ages, the Stone of Scone, revered by many long ago as Jacob's Pillow, serves as a tangible emblem of the efforts of our long-ago ancestors to establish and maintain an orderly, harmonious society.

LOCATION: Edinburgh Castle, Edinburgh, Scotland.

The Essex Ring

DATE: Late sixteenth century.

WHAT IT IS: A finger ring with a dramatic Renaissance legend attached to it.

WHAT IT LOOKS LIKE: The ring has an outer border of gold and is set with a sardonyx cameo portrait of Elizabeth I about a half inch high and a half inch at its greatest width. Elizabeth's left profile is shown, her face a light bluish white. She wears a wig and a ruff, both auburn in color, and her dress is bluish white; there are a few auburn streaks on the shoulder of the dress. The background of the portrait is dark blue, surrounded by a border that is a very dark blue-black. There are patterns of circles on the shank of the ring (the loop around the finger). The condition of the gold is good, although Elizabeth's nose is somewhat snub, perhaps due to damage to the cameo.

English folklore is rife with tales about characters who extricate themselves from suspenseful dilemmas by using magical or divinely endowed objects. The Holy Grail, the Excalibur Scabbard, and the Bleeding Lance, for example, are mythical artifacts that supposedly protected or saved the lives of such heroes as Lancelot, Perceval, Galahad, and even King Arthur himself. Passed down through the ages in real life is a gold cameo ring whose legend tells of a venerable queen who bestowed it upon a favored soldier with the declaration that should he ever be in trouble, he was to send it back to her, and she would come to his rescue. Just a few years later the soldier, convicted of treason, faced a gruesome death by beheading and made a desperate attempt from prison to return the cameo ring to the queen and save his life. What happened next swept the nation into one of England's most compelling romantic legends, capturing the imagination and hearts of its citizens.

There are two main protagonists in this tale: Elizabeth, the queen of England from 1558 to 1603; and Robert Devereux, the second earl of Essex. They were related—Essex's mother being the queen's cousin—but it wasn't until his introduction at court in 1584 by his guardian, Lord Burghley, Queen Elizabeth's lord high treasurer and chief minister, that the handsome and genteel young Essex became a favorite of the fifty-one-year-old queen. In 1587, after Essex returned from the Netherlands—where he had fought valiantly at Zutphen in a mission to help a Spanish rebellion—he was made Master of the Horse. Many fabulous honors at court were in store for the favorite of the queen, and the future of Essex, who was born in 1566 and graduated from Trinity College in Cambridge, shone brightly.

By this time in her life, Elizabeth had established herself as a firm and intelligent sovereign, and she was on the eve of one of the greatest accomplishments of her reign: the defeat of the Spanish Armada sent by Philip II, who wanted to protect Spanish colonies in the New World from English invasion and to make England a Catholic country again by ousting the queen. Elizabeth continued the absolute monarchy of her Tudor forebears—her father, Henry VIII, who was king of England from 1509 to 1547, and grandfather, Henry VII, who ruled from 1485 to 1509 and was the son of the earl of Richmond, Edmund Tudor—as well as maintained the country's religion of Protestantism, instituted by Henry VIII.

Indeed, much of Elizabeth's reign revolved around religious conflicts stemming from the Protestant Reformation begun in Europe by Martin Luther around 1517, when her father was king and at the time an opponent of the Reformation. The Protestant Reformation, a rebellion against the Roman Catholic Church, was at least partially responsible for many of the wars in Europe during the sixteenth and seventeenth centuries. In England, ecclesiastical upheaval occurred when Henry VIII, seeking to expand his royal power, was denied by Pope Clement VII, for various political reasons, a divorce from his wife, Catherine of Aragon—a daughter of King Ferdinand and Queen Isabella of Spain, and the widow of his older brother, Prince Arthur, who had married her when he was fifteen and died shortly after. This papal refusal caused Henry to break away from Catholic Rome and the Pope's jurisdiction and establish the Church of England.

In 1533, just a year before Parliament passed the Act of Supremacy, which proclaimed the king of England the country's religious leader, Henry married Anne Boleyn, who had been his mistress while he was married to Catherine (that marriage having been declared invalid). In 1533 Anne Boleyn bore a daughter for Henry—Elizabeth—but when Anne didn't bear him a son, Henry's passion for her subsided; subsequently a jury, headed by her uncle, sentenced her to death for having sexual relations with multiple partners. Elizabeth was pronounced illegitimate in the wake of Henry's new marriage to Jane Seymour.

Despite her supposedly illegitimate status, a statute provided that Elizabeth succeed to the crown after Edward VI, the issue of her father and Jane Seymour, and her half-sister, Mary, the daughter of Catherine of Aragon and Henry VIII. Still, her accession would be marked with danger and conflict. During the reign of Mary, who was a religious Catholic, Elizabeth was imprisoned because she was seen as a threat in the wake of assassination plots and rebellions against Mary; Protestants saw Elizabeth as a future sovereign who could restore their religion to England. Both Edward and Mary had acceded to the crown, and after both died—Edward in 1553 at the age of sixteen and Mary in 1558 at the age of forty-two—Elizabeth indeed became the queen of England.

During Elizabeth's reign English trade prospered, its navy became among the most powerful in the world, and Protestantism became entrenched as the country's national religion. Elizabeth had been raised a Protestant but was tolerant of Catholics in England. Like her half-sister, she was herself the target of numerous assassination plots. Though she had several suitors, Elizabeth never married—in part, at least, to avoid relinquishing her power. But she rewarded loyalty from her soldiers and councillors.

As a favorite of Elizabeth, Robert Devereux, the earl of Essex, was enriched by Elizabeth's grants of land. But Devereux was restless with court life and sought a more adventurous course. In 1589, he banded with Don Antonio, who claimed to be the heir to the Portuguese crown. The next year he rankled the queen when, without her permission, he married Frances, the widow of Sir Philip Sidney, a statesman and poet who had died of combat wounds.

Over the next several years, Essex alternated between serving the queen in court and leading military expeditions, in the process carving out a reputation for himself as a popular soldier and war hero. As a favorite of the queen, he had open communication with her and sometimes used it to help others. For example, previous to Essex's appointment in 1593 as privy councillor, a thirty-year-old barrister named Francis Bacon sought his assistance. He became Essex's advisor but drew the ill will of the queen when in Parliament he opposed an appropriation of funds for the government's war against Spain. Still, Essex, a relentless champion of Bacon, recommended him to the queen on separate occasions for the offices of attorney general and Master of the Roll in the royal service.

In 1596, Essex embarked on a naval expedition to Cadiz against the

Spaniards. These were turbulent times when the rivalry between men for high positions was great, and according to legend, just before he left, Queen Elizabeth gave her impetuous follower the ring with the promise that should he ever commit any transgression, she would exonerate him. The English force that Essex commanded with Charles Howard defeated the Spaniards, and as a result Essex attained the status of exalted war hero, becoming, perhaps, England's most idolized soldier of the time. After Cadiz was captured, Essex wanted to press on with strategies to increase England's aggressiveness toward Spain, but he was opposed by Howard, who was backed by the war council, and the two became enemies.

Still, Essex was now a popular public figure and cast his eyes on new military achievements, heedless of the rumblings this could cause. Francis Bacon warned him that if he continued to seek fame he would turn the queen against him and beseeched his friend to eschew his ambition as a war hero and show resolve only to serve the queen. But Elizabeth's naming of Charles Howard, Essex's enemy, as the earl of Nottingham displeased Essex greatly. Essex soon embarked on his next military expedition—to seize Spanish treasure ships—and failed.

In 1598, Elizabeth's chief minister, William Cecil, Lord Burghley, who had once been Essex's guardian but became his nemesis, proposed a peace plan with Spain, which Essex opposed. The following year Essex served as chancellor of Cambridge University, but the rebellion in Ireland led by the earl of Tyrone caught his attention. Strategy meetings were held and Essex angered the queen, who now found his unbridled aspirations intolerable.

Lord Burghley wanted his son, Robert Cecil, to succeed him as chief minister, but he was opposed by Essex, now a rising star in the political spectrum, who wanted one of his own selections installed. There was constant conflict between the Cecil and Essex factions, and Elizabeth, wary of the threat an Essex faction could pose to her power, promoted Cecil, creating still greater tension with Essex. By this time, Essex was having repeated arguments and reconciliations with the queen, which sometimes played themselves out in public, and their association began to take on a very volatile aspect.

Still, after rebellion erupted in Ireland, Essex was dispatched to the country as governor-general of Ireland. The public lauded this appointment, and William Shakespeare alluded to Essex in his *Henry V* (Act V prologue):

> *As, by a lower but loving likelihood,*
> *Were now the general of our gracious Empress,*
> *As in good time he may, from Ireland coming,*

Bringing rebellion broached on his sword,
How many would the peaceful city quit
To welcome him!

With great public confidence behind him, Essex embarked on his military and political mission in Ireland, but his service there proved a disaster. In 1599 he lost the battle at Arklow, then, commanding a huge army, failed to subdue Tyrone at Ulster and was forced to enter into a truce with him.

Smarting from these fiascos, Essex left Ireland in disgrace and without permission to mollify the queen, arriving in London in September 1599. Elizabeth's reception of Essex was cordial, but an inquiry into his actions was pursued nonetheless. The following June he was condemned by the queen's privy councillors, one of whose members was his old friend and advisor Francis Bacon. Restricted to his house, Essex did not hold animosity toward Bacon. Some colleagues of Essex then tried to convince him that the queen's councillors would be ousted, which motivated him to devise a plan to march through London, seize the queen, force her to terminate her councillors, and stir the people into rebellion. Some friends such as Thomas Egerton, the Master of the Rolls and a former attorney general, advised Essex not to rebel against Elizabeth but to come to terms with her, but his mind was fixed and he organized a rebellion with citizens opposed to the government's religious politics. Hundreds of people marched with Essex, but they did not gather enough support, and the rebellion failed.

Branded a traitor, Essex was arrested at his home and brought to trial at Westminster Hall before a commission of more than thirty citizens and judges. The trial wasn't exactly impartial to Essex. Some of the commissioners were his enemies, such as the earl of Nottingham, who had participated in crushing the rebellion; Robert Cecil, the son of the late Lord Burghley; and, most prominently now, Francis Bacon, who worked vigorously and with great bitterness to convict Essex. Friends of Essex were called to give statements, and they revealed that in a secret meeting Essex had promised greater freedom for the Catholics if his rebellion succeeded. The apprehended rebels indulged in much mutual recrimination. Essex, who denied he was a Catholic, was convicted, and early in the evening of the 19th of February, 1601, was sentenced to die; he would not be the first rebel in his insurrection to be so punished. Others had already been charged with conspiracy with Essex to assassinate the queen and been executed.

Essex's execution was to take place six days later, on February 25, and it was during this time that the Essex ring legend continues, diverging from the historical record. There are variations of the legend, but according to a popular account, with his life at stake, Essex gave his royal ring to a child to deliver to one of the queen's ladies-in-waiting, Lady Scrope. The boy became confused, however, and instead delivered it to Scrope's sister, Katherine, the countess of Nottingham, whose husband, Charles, had been Essex's bitter opponent. Charles, the earl of Nottingham, withheld the ring from the queen, thus sealing Essex's fate.

Still, Elizabeth appeared disinclined to carry out Essex's death sentence. She signed his death warrant, then withdrew it. Then she signed it again. According to the legend, she was awaiting the return of the ring, which she would take as an expression of contrition by Essex and would acknowledge by commuting his sentence. Despite advice from his friends to make a direct appeal to Elizabeth, the legend continues, Essex thought the ring would suffice, not knowing it had not reached her.

Historically, efforts had been made to save Essex's life, among them a supplication from his wife to Robert Cecil. But others, most outspokenly Essex's enemy Walter Raleigh, implored the secretary of state, whom Essex had accused before the commission of disputing Elizabeth's claim to sovereignty, to sustain the death sentence. Indeed, nothing short of the queen's mercy could save Essex, but according to both legend and historical record, clemency on her behalf was not forthcoming.

The Essex Ring with its cameo portrait of Queen Elizabeth I. The left profile of the queen is shown on the gold ring.

And so, on the designated day of his execution, Robert Devereux, the second earl of Essex, attired in dark clothing, was escorted to a scaffold in the Tower of London courtyard. While Elizabeth distracted herself by playing a spinet in her privy chamber, Essex made penance before his death. He made certain declarations, including attesting to the fairness of his punishment, and prayed before a small crowd, then in three strokes was decapitated.

Essex's popularity with the masses, and some government officials, quickly became apparent. A rabble nearly lynched his executioner shortly after the beheading. Elizabeth was said to be saddened and to have been willing to exonerate Essex if he had appealed to her. Francis Bacon, who drew much negative public sentiment, disseminated an "Apologie" defending his actions. Other apologies, as well as panegyrics, songs, essays, and verses in Essex's honor were published, although some writings were censored by the government.

According to the ring legend, when the countess of Nottingham fell deathly ill, she summoned Queen Elizabeth to confess that her husband had withheld the ring. Elizabeth, distressed by the fall from grace of her once-favorite soldier, reacted with violent anger. By historical record, Elizabeth, whose health failed toward the end of her life, died two years later, in 1603, at the age of seventy.

A brief note was made by a contemporary chronicler, John Manningham, about a ring given by Essex to Elizabeth that she kept on her finger until she died, but the story of the Essex ring in a comprehensive, romanticized narrative didn't appear in print until the mid–seventeenth century, almost fifty years after the deaths of Essex and Elizabeth. It was in a history of Elizabeth and Essex that the ring legend was set forth in detail, and although the book was marred by inaccuracies, the ring story caught on with the public and became part of the lore of Elizabethan history. It continued in popularity—and in print by different authors—for many years.

For various reasons, the story of the Essex ring was not given much credibility by historians from the time the story began to appear in print. The story seemed far-fetched, contemporary accounts were lacking, and the protagonists seemed to act contrary to their typical behavior. Indeed, scholars have discounted the story of the Essex ring as a beguiling but fanciful tale. Still, there is documentation of the lineage of the so called Essex ring.

After Essex's execution in 1601, the ring, by popular account, was returned to his widow, Frances, and it stayed in the family for centuries. For several generations it was passed down the female side of the family, with each of the daughter-recipients marrying a titled Englishman. From Essex's widow, Frances (who later married William Seymour), it went to her daughter, Lady Mary Seymour (who married Heneage Finch), to her daughter, Lady Frances Finch (who married Thomas Thynne, the first Viscount Weymouth), to her daughter, Frances Thynne (who married Robert Worsley), to her daughter, Frances Worsley (who married John Carteret), and to her daughter, Lady Louisa Carteret (who married Thomas Thynne, the second Viscount Weymouth, the great-nephew of the first Viscount Weymouth and husband of Lady Frances Finch).

The so-called Essex ring continued in the family until 1911, when it was sold to Herbert, First Baron Michelham. Sixteen years later, in 1927, the ring was offered for sale by Christie's and was purchased for just over seven hundred pounds by Ernest Makower, who acquired it to donate it to Westminster Abbey and make it available for public viewing. The ring was soon given a new home, accepted by the Abbey as "traditionally the ring given by the Queen to the Earl of Essex." In the confines of its august new domicile, the ring has been in splendidly majestic company, residing near the remains of some of England's most prominent historical figures, including King Henry III, King Henry V, King Charles II, Mary Queen of Scots, poet Geoffrey Chaucer, physicist Sir Isaac Newton, lexicographer Dr. Samuel Johnson, novelist Charles Dickens, missionary and explorer David Livingstone, and Victorian prime minister William Gladstone—not to mention, ironically, Elizabeth herself.*

Posterity, then, has a ring with a fascinating legend attached to it, but whose historical authenticity is in doubt. For hundreds of years, the Essex ring has held the public imagination as the focus of a compelling Elizabethan drama. Genuine or not, several questions remain: Was the ring ever worn by Queen Elizabeth? Did she ever give it to Essex? How did the ring story start? How did Essex's widow come to have this ring, and why was it passed down in the family for so many generations with the legend attached to it? These questions and others may never be answered, but surely the Essex ring will continue to stir the hearts of those who hear its story.

LOCATION: Westminster Abbey Museum, London, England.

---

*The ring was displayed in a special case on Elizabeth's tomb before being moved to its present location.

Galileo's Middle Finger

DATE: 1642.

WHAT IT IS: The excised right middle finger of the Italian astronomer, Galileo Galilei.

WHAT IT LOOKS LIKE: The preserved finger is gray and measures 3.5 inches long and .79 inches wide at its maximum width. The finger is contained in a glass casket set on a cylindrical alabaster base on which is an inscription in Latin by the eighteenth-century astronomer Tommaso Perelli that reads: "This is the finger with which the illustrious hand covered the heavens and indicated their immense space. It pointed to new stars with the marvelous instrument, made of glass, and revealed them to the senses. And thus it was able to reach what Titans could never attain."

"E pur si muove!"
(And yet it does move!)
—*Quote attributed to Galileo Galilei
after recanting his belief that
the earth revolves around the sun*

Since ancient times, sages pondered the enigmas of the physical universe, but the idea that the earth moved in a circular orbit around the sun seemed preposterous to any logical mind. After all, people standing on the earth's surface feel no such movement, and each morning the sun is seen to rise in the east, climb to the zenith, then move west where it sets in the afternoon. Moreover, any statement to the contrary would contradict the biblical notion of the earth as the center of creation. For making precisely such a statement, the tribunal responsible for promoting the Catholic faith, the Holy Office, put the seventeenth-century scientist Galileo on trial for heresy. After weighing the evidence, the cardinals rendered their condemnation:

> We say, pronounce, sentence, and declare that you, Galileo, by reason of these things which have been detailed in the trial and which you have confessed already, have rendered yourself according to this Holy Office vehemently suspect of heresy, namely of having held and believed a doctrine that is false and contrary to the divine and Holy Scripture; namely that the Sun is the center of the world and does not move from east to west, and that one may hold and defend as probable an opinion after it has been declared and defined contrary to Holy Scripture. Consequently, you have incurred all the censures and penalties enjoined and promulgated by the sacred Canons and all particular and general laws against such delinquents. . . . We condemn you to formal imprisonment at our pleasure.

Facing life imprisonment, Galileo publicly recanted his alleged heresies and wisely avoided a lengthy sojourn in a dingy dungeon. His sentence was commuted to house arrest, carried out first at the home of his friend the archbishop at Siena and then at his villa at Arcetri, near Florence, where he died several years later, on January 8, 1642.

For the scientist who endeavored to tear down the musty curtains of antiquated beliefs and let in the light of solid mathematical reasoning, Galileo's condemnation was a fall from grace. But the great Renaissance man was a hapless victim of his times and locale; to publicly promote a scientific understanding of nature that was deemed contrary to the Bible could only invite the wrath of the Inquisition.

Galileo Galilei, the Italian astronomer, physicist, philosopher, and mathematician, was born on February 15, 1564. In 1588, at the age of twenty-four, he was appointed a professor of mathematics at the University of Pisa, then in 1592 received the same appointment at the University of Padua, where he remained until 1610. During the time he held chairs in mathematics, Galileo carried out pioneering work in mechanics, magnetism, thermometry, and astronomy. He devised the fundamental law of falling bodies, fabricated a compass, mathematically accounted for tides by applying certain concepts of Copernicus, and used a telescope he built to probe the heavens and make numerous discoveries about the planets, the Milky Way, and the moon. But around 1612, with his affirmation of Copernicus's sun-centered universe, he began to stir the anger of philoso-

An artist's rendition
of Galileo in prison.

phers and theologians and provoke a response that would culminate in a personal crisis.

Galileo lived during an era when reasoning and independent inquiry were beginning to supplant traditional religious dogma and superstition. With humanists, inventors, writers, artists, explorers, and scientists of the likes of Erasmus, Gutenberg, Shakespeare, da Vinci, Michelangelo, Columbus, and Copernicus carrying out important and revolutionary work, the Western world was aflame with invigorating ideas, exciting discoveries, and pioneering achievements. During this time of reawakening, known as the Renaissance, which began in Florence at the start of the fourteenth century and lasted through the end of the seventeenth century, people began to look at life in different ways, to question old sacrosanct doctrines of faith and attempt to comprehend nature in ways that seemed to blaspheme the Bible. Whereas the teachings of the Church had previously been accepted without question, the rebirth of free inquiry led people to question the Church's teachings and search instead for truths based on empirical observation. After the long intellectual and creative dormancy that had characterized the Dark Ages, the free-thinking spirit that had animated ancient Rome and Greece was reinvigorated.

As a free-thinking and autonomous scientist, Galileo ran into problems through his investigations. He contradicted conventions such as the Aristotelian notion that bodies of different weights fall at a speed in proportion to their weight in favor of the conclusion that all bodies, no matter what their weight, fall to the ground at the same speed. His probing of the heavens—in which he observed sunspots, noted that the planets showed phases, and found that moonlight was not emitted by the heavenly body itself but was the reflection from its surface of the sun's light—led him to affirm Copernicus's heliocentric hypothesis.

The idea of a sun-centered world in which the planets revolve around the bright celestial body was actually a Pythagorean doctrine that the Polish astronomer Nicolaus Copernicus had taken up in his posthumously published *De revolutionibus orbium coelestium* (Concerning the Revolutions of the Heavenly Bodies). After Galileo embraced the sun-centered hypothesis, it spread through the Western world. Proponents of the Aristotelian system, in which a fixed earth stood as the center of the universe, were now in danger of being discredited, and they conspired to condemn Galileo as a promulgator of blasphemy. Galileo warned that if people were made to feel that belief in the laws revealed by science was sinful, it would ultimately be harmful, and he zealously attempted to convince Church authorities that his theories did not endanger ecclesiastical beliefs because they were only theories. Acting in his own best interests, however, he denounced Copernicus's writings, which the Holy Office put on the list of prohibited material until its "errors" could be removed. Galileo continued to devote himself to further scientific study though, and in 1632, his *Dialogue Concerning the Two Chief World Systems* was published, which was in effect a renewed argument for the Copernican heliocentric system. Although the Roman Catholic censors gave Galileo their consent to publish the book, its support of the Copernican system caused an uproar. The Pope charged that he had been deceived into allowing its publication, and this accusation ultimately led to Galileo's prosecution by the Inquisition. The Inquisition held that a 1616 decree forbade Galileo from expounding on the theories of Copernicus, and it produced a document (whose authenticity has been the subject of debate) stating the proscription. The Inquisition banned all Galileo's works and ordered him imprisoned. Forced to betray his own knowledge and acknowledge a false truth, Galileo formally recanted:

I, Galileo, son of the late Vincenzo Galilei of Florence, being seventy years old . . . swear that I have always believed, believe now, and with God's help, will in the future believe all that the Holy Catholic and Apostolic Church doth hold, preach, and teach. But since, after having been admonished by this Holy Office entirely to abandon the false opinion that the Sun is the center of the universe and immovable, and that the Earth is not the center of the same and that it moves, and that I was neither to hold, defend, nor teach in any manner whatsoever, either orally or in writing, the said false doctrine; and after having received a notification that the said doctrine is contrary to Holy Writ, I wrote and published a book in which I treat this condemned doctrine and bring forth very persuasive arguments in its favor without answering them. I have been judged vehemently suspected of heresy, that is of having held and believed that the Sun is at the center of the universe and immovable, and that the Earth is not at the center and that it moves. Therefore, wishing to remove from the minds of your Eminences and all faithful Christians this vehement suspicion reasonably conceived against me, I abjure with a sincere heart and unfeigned faith all these errors and heresies, and I curse and detest them as well as any other error, heresy, or sect contrary to the Holy Catholic Church. And I swear that for the future I shall neither say nor assert orally or in writing such things as may bring upon me similar suspicions; and if I know any heretic, or one suspected of heresy, I will denounce him to this Holy Office, or to the Inquisitor or Ordinary of the place in which I may be.

Although his voice in scientific matters continued through his writing—his treatise on solid bodies and accelerated motion, *Discourses and Mathematical Demonstrations Concerning Two New Sciences,* was published in Holland in 1638—Galileo Galilei was physically set apart from the world, symbolically banished from civilization in the commutation of his prison sentence to house arrest. After eight long years of confinement at his Arcetri villa, Galileo died on January 8, 1642, at the age of seventy-seven. For a scientist who was instrumental in vanquishing antiquated ideas about the world and supporting scientifically based theories that attempted to explain the world rationally, Galileo's last years were a sad chapter in a great life. His body was placed in a small room in the Chapel of Saints Cosmas and Damian, but a quirky fate awaited the corpse.

The ecclesiastical condemnation precluded Galileo from having a proper funeral in the main chapel of the church where he was buried, and this later,

The middle finger of Galileo's right hand set in a glass bowl mounted on an alabaster stand.

evidently, caused some of his compatriots to feel remorseful. Vincenzo Viviani, who as a teenager attended Galileo in the last few years of his life and went on to become an engineer, provided in his will for a tomb to be built in the main chapel as a fitting sanctuary for the ostracized scientist, and on March 12, 1737, Galileo's remains were moved to the more appropriate spot for reinterment. During the transport a scholar, Anton Francesco Gori, severed the right middle finger of Galileo. The corporeal relic, which became an object of veneration, was later displayed at the Laurenziana Library, then, for a period of time beginning in 1842, in a Galilean rotunda inside the Museum of Physics and Natural History along with other artifacts related to Galileo's life and work.

Galileo had led a very distinguished and troubled life. He made numerous extraordinary scientific contributions, among them discovering four of the satellites of Jupiter and improving the telescope. But for defying convention, for favoring science over Scripture, he was persecuted and made to suffer, isolated from society in his advanced years when he was debilitated and blind.

That Galileo did not see justice served upon him in his own lifetime is historically moot. A papal apology for the Holy Office's condemnation of the scientist was offered in 1992. Although official vindication for the brilliant Renaissance physicist did not come until three centuries after his death, he didn't have to wait so long for payback.

It is crudely apropos that nearly a century after his death, when his writings were gaining credence and stirring the imaginations of other bright successors, he had plucked from him a particular anatomical vestige. For his allegedly radical ideas and discoveries, Galileo's contemporaries gave him a hard time. In return, the esteemed and exonerated scientist gave history his middle finger.

LOCATION: Institute and Museum of the History of Science, Florence, Italy.

George Washington's Schoolboy Copybooks

DATE: 1744–1748.

WHAT THEY ARE: Three bound journals containing learning exercises written by George Washington when he was between the ages of twelve and sixteen.

WHAT THEY LOOK LIKE: The cover of the "School Copybook" is dark blue with gold tooling and measures 15⅛ inches long by 10⅝ inches wide; its folios measure 14⅞ inches long by 10 inches wide. The cover of George Washington's "Second School Copy Book" is red and measures 12⅛ inches long by 9 inches wide; its folios measure 11⁷⁄₁₆ inches long by 7⁵⁄₁₆ inches wide. The front cover of the "Forms of Writing" copybook is black with gold tooling and measures 10³⁄₁₆ inches wide by 14¹³⁄₁₆ inches long; its folios measure 8³⁄₁₆ inches wide by 12½ inches long. The pages of the "School Copybook" and "Forms of Writing" copybook are inlaid (set inside cutout pages that are overlaid by sheer silk glued on both sides); those of the "Second School Copy Book" are hinged (attached with a folded piece of paper to a support sheet). Much of the print in the journals appears faded, and some of the words are no longer visible on the leaves.

He trekked through the wilderness, braved the harsh elements, met nature head-on in carrying out missions of vital importance to his fledgling nation in the New World, the mostly uncharted land on which English settlers had first set foot little more than a century earlier. But before he thrashed through the frontier, trained soldiers in the art of warfare, led militias over mountains and across rivers, engaged in fierce battles, and took the reins of a newly independent nation—indeed, long before, as he was developing his emotional and intellectual character while a raw lad—George Washington set himself to becoming a colonial gentleman and wrote out exercises that addressed such vexing social issues as these:

Is it proper to clean one's teeth with a tablecloth? Speak out loud while yawning? Drum one's fingers in the presence of others? Rinse one's mouth in company? Point one's finger when talking? Use reproachful language? Touch any part of one's body that is not usually observed?

Welcome to George Washington's "Rules of Civility & Decent Behavior In Company and Conversation," a fascinating, if sometimes amusing (at least by our modern frame of reference) guide to good manners, etiquette, and moral behavior. Occupying the last several pages in Washington's "Forms of Writing" copybook, "The Rules of Civility" were derived from ethical precepts formulated by sixteenth-century French Jesuits. The influence of the rules on young George is apparent in the character of his later life.

There are three surviving compilations of what are referred to as George Washington's schoolboy copybooks. Many writings of the first U.S. president exist, such as letters, notes, instructions, and ledgers, but the schoolboy copybooks are special for various reasons: little is known about George Washington's early years, so they shed light on his youth; they open a window on colonial education and social etiquette; and they show young Washington to be meticulous and hard-driven, traits evident in the man who led the American Army to victory over the British Redcoats in the Revolutionary War, presided over the Constitutional Convention, and was unanimously voted by electors to be the first president of the United States of America. In his adult years Washington was conscientious in his personal life and professional career, and consequently he was a prolific writer of letters, messages, accountings, and other items. He wrote lucidly and eloquently, and his schoolboy copybooks evince the man who would become such a fastidious, careful, and dignified individual.

Like his "Forms of Writing," George Washington's "School Copybook" and "Second School Copy Book" contain a potpourri of writings, but these latter volumes concentrate more on learning exercises, particularly in the areas of mathematics and geography. The "School Copybook," dated 1745, contains numerous exercises with titles such as "Geometrical Definitions," "Geometrical Theorems," "Surveying," "Solid Measure," "Gauging," and "Geographical Definitions." On one page of this volume young George wrote out the definitions of such geometric concepts as straight and obtuse angles, as well as drawing a variety of geometrical shapes to illustrate the definitions. On other pages he worked out geometrical problems such as "How to measure a piece of land on the form of a circle."

There are pages headed "Memorial Verses" that are divided into several boxes with definitions and mathematical exercises related to the calendar. Mathematical exercises in the "Memorial Verses" pages include "What is the golden number for the present year 1746," "What was the cycle of the sun for the year 1707," and "What will be Easter Day Anno 1749." On other pages of the "School Copybook," Washington wrote out definitions of geographical terms such as *island, peninsula, isthmus, promontory, sea, strait, creek,* and *bay,* named the bodies of water surrounding Africa and America, and listed the provinces of North and South America.

Much of Washington's "Second School Copy Book" is devoted to mathematical exercises. For instance, the first entry is entitled "Multiplication of Feet, Inches & Parts." Other entries include "Notation of Decimals," "Addition of Decimals," "Subtraction of Decimals," "Multiplication of Decimals," "Division of Decimals," "Reduction of Decimals," "Concerning Simple Interest," "Plain Trigonometry Geometrical and Logarithmetical," "Plain Trigonometry Oblique," and "Surveying of Land."

Here are examples of actual entries:

Notation of Decimals: Example: This decimal fraction 25/100 may be written thus .25; its denominator being known to be a unit with two cyphers [zeroes] because there are two figures in it. Numerator in . . . like manner 125/1000 may thus be written .125; and 3575/10000 thus .3575 and 75/1000 thus .075 and 65/10000 thus .0065.

Another entry reads:

Concerning Simple Interest: 1st. When money pertaining or belonging to the person is in the hands, possession or keeping, or is lent to another, & the debtor payeth or alloweth to the creditor, a certain sum in consideration for forbearance for certain time; such consideration for forbearance is called interest, loan, or use money; & the money so lent, & forborne . . . is called the principal. 2. Interest is either simple or compound. 3. When for a sum of money lent there is a loan or interest allowed. And the same is not paid, when it becomes due; & if such interest doth not then become a part of the principal it is called simple interest.

There are also many mathematical computations the young Washington carried out, such as 3.1252×2.75, or the interest on a sum of money for one year at 6 pounds.

•   •   •

The entries in the "Forms of Writing" copybook begin with a promissory note dated March 12, 1744/45, and a Bill of Exchange dated May 27, 1745, and end with "The Rules of Civility." In between are entries with titles such as "An Arbitration Bond," "Form of a Servants Indenture," "A Bill of Sale," "Deed or Conveyance for land by a man and his wife," "Lease of Land," "Form of a Virginia Patent for land," "Form of a Virginia warrant," "To Keep Ink from Freezing or Moulding," and "Christmas Day" (a poem).

"The Rules of Civility & Decent Behavior In Company and Conversation," the best-known entry in Washington's school copybooks, consists of 110 numbered maxims written on ten pages. The handwriting is in the old style, in which the letter *s* looks like an *f*, so that the word *presence* seems to be spelled *prefence,* and *discourse, difcourfe.* Not all the rules concern manners; many concern religious and moral behavior. Here are some of the rules Washington wrote out (with their designated numbers):

2. When in company put not your hands to any part of the body not usually discovered.

4. In the presence of others sing not to yourself with a humming, noise, nor drum with your fingers or feet.

5. If you cough, sneeze, sigh, or yawn, do it not loud but privately, and speak not in your yawning, but put your handkerchief or hand before your face and turn aside.

7. Put not off your cloths in the presence of others, nor go out your chamber half dressed.

58. Let your conversation be without malice or envy, for 'tis a sign of a tractable and commendable nature.

76. While you are talking, point not with your finger at him of whom you discourse nor approach too near him to whom you talk especially to his face.

100. Cleanse not your teeth with the table cloth, napkin, fork, or knife but if others do it let it be done with a pick tooth.

101. Rinse not your mouth in the presence of others.

108. Honour and obey your natural parents altho they may be poor.

110. Labour to keep alive in your breast that little spark of celestial fire called conscience.

"The Rules of Civility" contain some precepts that might now seem outdated, but many of the rules hold up well. People of any age can take a les-

The first page of the "Rules of Civility & Decent Behavior In Company and Conversation" in Washington's hand. The printing is faded but still legible.

son from "In visiting the sick, do not presently play the physician if you be not knowing," and can surely apply the admonition not to dispense advice if one is not an authority on a particular subject. Indeed, as archaic as the language in which the rules are couched may sound, their content makes the point that good manners never become outdated.

In his copybooks, George Washington's script is neat and flowing, almost calligraphic; his drawings of geometrical shapes are precise and artistic. Although his education was limited, Washington's penmanship and drawings show a student who took care and pride in his work.

The original order of the pages is not known; in the mid–nineteenth century, the U.S. government purchased the exercise pages from a Washington family descendant, and sorted and bound the leaves into copybooks.

Little is known about George Washington's education. He once indicated that he had been principally instructed by a private tutor. On the other hand, he may have had some institutional schooling in the last years of his

A nineteenth-century illustration of George Washington playing as a youth. While young Washington was becoming acquainted with the vast wilderness, he was also studying to become a proper colonial gentleman.

education, as fellow Virginian George Mason, in a mid-1750s letter to Washington, noted that he had run into an "old schoolfellow" of Washington. In any case, whether by private tutor or in school, Washington's academic education ended when he was about sixteen years old.

While the original documents from which "The Rules of Civility" were derived may have been intended for use in the schooling of aristocratic children, George Washington's education in itself was weak by standards of the day for children from families of means. With the inheritances he received at a young age, however, George Washington had financial subsistence, at least in terms of property.

Washington's father, Augustine, had four children by his first wife and six by his second. George was the first offspring of his father's second marriage, to Mary Ball in 1731. Augustine Washington died in 1743, but George, who was eleven at the time, was close to some of his half-siblings, including Lawrence, with whom he traveled to the West Indies and whose Mount Vernon estate eventually passed to George. But it was while living with Lawrence, who became his guardian after his father died, that young George was introduced to the profession of surveying. Lord Fairfax, the cousin of Lawrence's wife, had massive landholdings in Virginia and dispatched parties to survey his land so squatters could pay taxes. As a teenager, George would sometimes accompany these expeditions, receiving land as compensation for his services. By the time he was seventeen, he was appointed a county surveyor, learning much as he journeyed into the wilderness of the westward land. His youthful experience in the wilderness no doubt aided him later when he commanded the Continental Army and, along with his men, endured great hardships in fighting the British, from fiercely cold winters to meager supplies of food.

Washington's lack of formal education by no means impeded him from gaining an elevated station in life, which he achieved via his self-confidence, physical strength, natural intelligence, curiosity, and ability to absorb information from people, nature, and the totality of his outside world. While contemporaries like Thomas Jefferson, who became the third U.S. president, and John Adams, Washington's vice president and presidential successor, were known as great intellects, Washington's self-determination, resoluteness, and practical abilities no doubt not only allowed him to excel at whatever endeavors he undertook, but enabled him to lead a fledgling nation to heights greater than those to which it might have risen under a genuine scholar. He did make grave military blunders on occasion, and there were bleak times when his armies came close to falling apart, but his strong nature kept his soldiers together.

Washington heeded well his early lessons on etiquette, because he did indeed grow into a proper colonial gentleman. He was courteous and possessed of great integrity, although he may have been a little too straitlaced. Charles Biddle, the acting chief executive of Pennsylvania, said of him, "He was a most elegant figure of a man, with so much dignity of manners that no person whatever could take any improper liberties with him."

As a soldier during the Revolutionary War, Washington was naturally itinerant and was known to have accepted hospitality in many a dwelling in the northeast United States; the familiar phrase "George Washington slept here" derives from his nomadic military life. And through it all Washington maintained his propriety. One might even hazard a guess that in his frequent intercourse with colonial folk, the hero of the emerging nation never took out his false teeth at the dinner table to clean them with the tablecloth, never spoke while he yawned or rinsed his mouth in the company of others, and never put his hands to a part of his body not usually observed. Washington seemed to carry for life the honorable precepts he set down in the 1740s in his schoolboy copybooks.

LOCATION: Library of Congress, Washington, D.C.

John Harrison's Fourth Marine Timekeeper

~~~~~~

DATE: 1759.

WHAT IT IS: The first mechanical device to successfully and practicably measure longitude at sea.

WHAT IT LOOKS LIKE: The timekeeper resembles a stopwatch; a silver case encloses the inner mechanism. Its face is white, and it has delicate filigree designs around the hands and numbers.

Out of desperation, a beleaguered eighteenth-century government offers a fortune to anyone who can solve a seemingly impossible scientific problem that is plaguing the kingdom. A front-runner emerges—not from among the realm's most brilliant minds, such as Isaac Newton, John Flamsteed, or Edmond Halley—but in the person of the son of a carpenter who is himself unschooled in the ways of natural philosophy.

This man of undistinguished background toils for many years to perfect an apparatus that solves the intractable problem, rejecting one attempt after another until finally his latest mechanism, radically different from his previous efforts, is demonstrated to be effective and to meet the criteria of the competition. But the jurors, some of whom favor an entirely different solution, fault the apparatus on various grounds, and he receives only half the reward. The man, old now but determined as ever, builds yet another instrument and appeals to the king, finally receiving the balance of the reward money, and the long-awaited and coveted credit for having formulated a solution that will enable the country to dominate the seas and become one of the most powerful nations on earth. His is a story of struggle and determination, hardship and conviction, and ultimately of triumph, a tale with all the makings of a riveting historical novel save for one significant element: it is unequivocally true.

Even in ancient times people took to the seas, seeing the expansive waters as a path to other lands and cultures. But getting from one point to another in a vast ocean was a problem that persisted through the centuries. Although navigators could determine latitude by calculating a star's (including the sun's) altitude at the time it crossed the meridian, longitude—the vessel's position east or west of a particular point—was also needed for sailors to know where they were. The trouble was, there was no known way to measure longitude.

Over time, people navigated the seas using a variety of aids. These included everything from observation of the sun, stars, and constellations to sailing directions, landmarks, and charts. Magnetic compasses were in wide use by the fourteenth century, by which time people commonly recognized that the earth was not flat but round. After Columbus, seamen began to use more sophisticated equipment such as quadrants, cross-staffs, astrolabes, and sextants, as well as almanacs and lunar tables calculated with painstaking effort.

The probing of the heavens by the Italian scientist Galileo aided navigation. After his discovery of four of the satellites of Jupiter, announced in 1610, Galileo studied the moons' motions and was able to determine with precision when they would appear from and disappear into the giant planet's shadow, and in this way Jupiter's moons functioned as a natural clock for mariners. But the determination of longitude still proved elusive, and the difficulties it posed to European seafarers are evident in the fact that even Galileo embraced the challenge, while the Netherlands offered a sum of 30,000 florins to the person who could successfully devise a method to resolve the problem.

During the great age of exploration, mariners such as Dias, Columbus, Cabot, da Gama, Balboa, Cortés, Magellan, Cartier, Drake, La Salle, and Hudson successfully sailed to far-off lands and claimed for their countries newly discovered areas, but their voyages were difficult and often perilous. The inability to determine longitude made for poor navigation and frequently resulted in mishaps on the seas. One such terrible disaster galvanized a country into finding a solution.

On the 22nd of October, 1707, the English seamen on the deck of the *St. George* watched in horror as their sister ship, the *Association,* having smashed into rocks near the Isles of Scilly, sank rapidly beneath the waves, taking all eight hundred men aboard to their deaths. The inability to determine longitude made such tragedies all too common, and the English government decided once and for all to do something about it. A 1714 act of Parliament established a Board of Longitude for the purpose of administering a competition—the then-vast sum of 20,000 pounds would be awarded to any person who could devise a useful and practical means of determining longitude to within thirty miles, to be demonstrated by a vessel sailing on the ocean for a month and a half.

The two mainstream approaches were to construct a lunar table, using calculations of the distance of the moon at different times, and to devise a timepiece—that is, a clock or watch—that could withstand the ship's motion, as well as weather and temperature variations that could cause it to lose or gain seconds. This timepiece would give longitude based on the difference between the time at a known location (to which the timepiece would be set) and the actual time it was for the navigator wherever he was on the water.

People from all walks of life responded to the parliamentary act. Over the years many solutions were submitted, but none held up to the board's rigid requirements. More than ten years after the 1714 act was announced, a clockmaker named John Harrison began to ponder the longitude dilemma and how he could solve it. Harrison, born in 1693, was creative in his work, having invented a gridiron pendulum around 1726, about the time he approached the longitude challenge.

The Yorkshire native was to devote the next forty-seven years to the longitude question. For almost ten years he labored on his first timepiece, a large spring-driven mechanism using rolling balances and a grasshopper escapement with dials representing seconds, minutes, hours, and days. Given a trial run on a frigate sailing to Lisbon, it proved to be a marvelous piece of machinery that efficiently told time and could be used to give the longitude of a vessel, but Harrison thought he could build a better, more accurate mechanism and spent the next five years working toward this end. Containing a few modifications over the first device, the second timekeeper worked well also, but Harrison was again displeased with what he thought were construction problems and commenced working on yet a third timekeeper. As it had previously done, the Board of Longitude, which recognized Harrison's accomplishments and his potential to create a workable device, granted him a stipend that would enable him to carry out further work.

The third timekeeper contained an important innovation—a bimetallic strip to correct changes in temperature—as well as other new features, but like its predecessors, it failed to comply with the stringent requirements for accuracy set by the board. This was a blow to Harrison, who had devoted nearly two decades to the construction of this timepiece.

Harrison, however, was dauntless and even obsessive in his pursuit of the longitude problem; he didn't retire from the competition but passionately continued his efforts. For the design of his fourth timekeeper, he chose to go in a different direction.

Rather than create an elaborately constructed piece of machinery with long rods and bar balances and large wheels, Harrison opted for a dramatically different design, one that resembled an ordinary pocket watch. Because of its small size, this timepiece contained miniaturized parts based on those in his previous models, such as the bimetallic strip. After numerous tests of his fourth timekeeper, Harrison was ready for it to undergo a trial sponsored by the board. The trial was carried out in the West Indies early in 1762, with Harrison's son, William, making the trip and taking the readings. The timepiece worked exceptionally well, with a very small rate of error, but because the Harrisons did not establish the clock's rate (its daily loss or gain of time) beforehand, the trial was discounted.

The Board of Longitude allowed another test of Harrison's fourth timepiece, but by this time the once-sympathetic board had begun to look upon Harrison with disfavor. The board's membership had changed over the years, and, by now, good progress had been made with the lunar method, which had considerable appeal. Once lunar distances had been calculated, this method was much less expensive than producing a mechanical timekeeper, and was even deemed by some to be more accurate.

There was friction between Harrison and the board, but both parties managed to persevere in the project. A retrial was held back in the West Indies, and the fourth timepiece once again performed remarkably well, far surpassing the accuracy requirements set out for the competition.

Still, the reward eluded Harrison, as the board was not convinced he had met the stipulations of the competition. The board decided to grant Harrison the difference between the sums it had previously granted him and ten thousand pounds, to make up half the award, but it would not give him the balance unless he could fulfill a number of conditions. The purpose of the competition was to devise a practical method to determine longitude, and the board insisted Harrison construct and test two additional timekeepers to make sure his original was not a one-of-a-kind anomaly.

But this was problematic for Harrison. First, his fourth timekeeper was not accessible, as it had been turned over to the board to be copied by another craftsman; and second, he needed more money to construct the additional watches. The board denied Harrison any additional grants, and another defeat occurred when Harrison's fourth timekeeper underwent a clinical test and did not fare well, owing in part to its poor maintenance at the Royal Observatory where testing was conducted. Nevertheless, the indomitable Harrison was already building another mechanism.

After devoting many years to constructing intricate devices that could successfully measure longitude at sea, John Harrison built a different kind of device, the watch pictured above, which finally earned him the acclaim and prize money he sought.

With the aid of his son, he succeeded in constructing a fifth timekeeper, but because he could not build yet another one to meet the board's requirement, and because he was disillusioned with the board, he sought help from a higher authority—the king of England, George III. At a demonstration of the timekeeper, the king was wildly impressed. The board was moved once again to conduct an investigation of Harrison's timekeepers, but it went nowhere; Harrison's son, William, became agitated by the board's persistent questioning and walked out. However, in 1773 Parliament and King George recognized John Harrison's invention and granted him the balance of the reward. Not only was Harrison vindicated, he became venerated.

Harrison's timekeeper was not the only practical means to determine longitude at this time, as the lunar method was also used, tables predicting the motion of the moon having been available since 1767. And as Harrison's timekeeper could not easily be reproduced, later devices more closely became the model for modern marine chronometers. Still, John Harrison, after a lifelong pursuit, introduced with his fourth marine timekeeper a watch that showed longitude could be measured accurately at sea with a mechanical instrument and was an important contributor to the practice of making sea travel safer and more efficient.

LOCATION: National Maritime Museum, London.

The Virginia Declaration of Rights

C~~~~~~~~~~~~~~~~~~~~~~~~~~~~~

DATE: 1776.

WHAT IT IS: A document that sets forth the basic and fundamental natural rights of citizens of colonial Virginia.

WHAT IT LOOKS LIKE: It is a paper folio written on both sides in brown ink. Pages one, two, and three (except for the last several lines) are badly faded, but page four is legible. The two-leafed paper folio, which is permanently housed in an oxygen-free stainless-steel and Plexiglas case, measures 12½ inches high; its folded width is 7½ inches and its open width is 15 inches. Early in the twentieth century, the paper folio was laminated between two layers of silk to strengthen it. The document, which is in poor condition, is permanently stored in a temperature-controlled vault.

That all men are born equally free and independant, and have certain inherent natural Rights . . . among which are the Enjoyment of Life and Liberty . . . with the Means of . . . pursueing . . . happiness . . .

The source of this sublime quote? Many people would say it bears an eerie similarity to the Declaration of Independence. But no, Thomas Jefferson's hallowed manifesto, a timeless doctrine championing freedom and liberty, came *after* the Virginia Declaration of Rights, from which the above quote is taken. And there are more lines inked by Jefferson that bear a striking resemblance to the earlier document. But while the Virginia Declaration, which was written chiefly by statesman George Mason, has been acknowledged by scholars as the basis for other documents, such as the U.S. Bill of Rights and France's Declaration of the Rights of Man, the substantial similarities between the Declaration of Independence, which launched Thomas

Fame eluded George Mason, but the colonial statesman's Virginia Declaration of Rights was an important document of early American history.

Jefferson to immortal fame, and the Virginia Declaration of Rights, whose author has languished in relative obscurity over the years, poses an intriguing question: What's going on here, plagiarism or influence?

The genesis of the Declaration of Independence, America's most venerable instrument of democracy, is well known. With the New World colonists desiring to terminate their allegiance and political ties to Great Britain because of King George III's repeated injustices, a committee was formed to express the resolution of Richard Henry Lee, the senior delegate from Virginia, that the united colonies become "free and independent states." Between the 11th and 26th of June, 1776, Thomas Jefferson, a Virginia lawyer and statesman, drew up the bulk of the draft, to which committee members made only minor changes. On June 28, the committee presented its draft to the Continental Congress, which read it and debated Lee's resolution, then added some words and deleted others before adopting the final draft. Jefferson was unsettled by the revisions made by the Congress, but the Declaration of Independence was essentially still his, and over the years his reputation as its primary author was rightfully handed down.

Shortly before Jefferson commenced writing his first draft, his fellow Virginian George Mason was carving out his own manifesto of liberty for his colony. Pursuant to the Continental Congress's May 10, 1776, recommendation that the colonies "adopt such government as shall . . . conduce to the happiness and safety of their constituents," the Virginia Convention convened and called for a committee to draft a bill of rights. A twenty-seven-man committee was formed, and Mason, a respected political thinker who for more than a decade previously had been writing about human rights, emerged as the chief architect. Mason began writing the first draft of his declaration around the 20th of May and completed it within a week. He produced in his own hand a set of articles that provided a bill of rights for the citizens of Virginia, reflecting the political goals of the convention. A number of clauses were tacked on by Thomas Ludwell Lee—a brother of Richard Henry Lee—in his hand, as well as by other committee members.

On May 27 the committee draft was read to the Virginia Convention; then it was printed and distributed so it could be discussed. Beginning on May 29, over the next ten days or so delegates criticized and debated the wording and meaning of the articles. The delegates wrangled, sometimes acrimoniously, over propositions such as whether there should be "the fullest Toleration in the Exercise of Religion," and whether the words "that all men are born equally free and independant" would lead to a rebellion by the slaves, but finally the debates came to an end, and on June 12 the final draft was ratified in Williamsburg. Meanwhile, newspapers in other colonies printed drafts of the Virginia Declaration of Rights, not only bringing it into wide circulation but enabling it to serve later as an exemplar for state constitution preambles. By the time Jefferson sat down to write his draft, Mason's document was well known.

Plagiarism is the taking of words and ideas of another writer and passing them off as one's own without attribution. It is alleged to occur when the literary purloiner's work is substantially similar to the earlier work, and when the alleged infringer had access to the original work. To determine plagiarism, lines from the original work and the allegedly copied work are compared. Similarity of words as well as ideas should be observed.

Here follows a comparison of lines from the first publicized draft of George Mason's Virginia Declaration of Rights and Thomas Jefferson's "original Rough draught" of the Declaration of Independence:

Mason: That all Men are born equally free and independant.
Jefferson: That all men are created equal & independant.

Mason: And have certain inherent natural Rights.
Jefferson: That from that equal creation they derive rights inherent & inalienable.

Mason: Among which are the Enjoyment of Life and Liberty, with the Means of acquiring and possessing Property, and pursueing and obtaining Happiness . . .
Jefferson: Among which are the preservation of life, & liberty, & the pursuit of Happiness.

Mason: That power is, by God and Nature, vested in, and consequently derived from the People. . . . That Government is, or ought to be, instituted for the common Benefit and Security of the People, Nation, or Community.

Jefferson: That to secure these ends, governments are instituted among men, deriving their just powers from the consent of the governed.

Mason: That whenever any Government shall be found inadequate, or contrary to these Purposes, a Majority of the Community had an indubitable, inalienable and indefensible Right to reform, alter or abolish it.

Jefferson: That whenever any form of government shall become destructive of these ends, it is the right of the people to alter or to abolish it.

Mason: Of all the various Modes and Forms of Government, that is best, which is capable of producing the greatest Degree of Happiness and Safety.

Jefferson: To institute new government, laying it's foundation on such principles & organising it's powers in such form, as to them shall seem most likely to effect their safety & happiness.

It is clear from the above examples that some of the words, phraseology, and thoughts in Jefferson's Declaration of Independence are strikingly similar to those in George Mason's Virginia Declaration of Rights. The line-by-line comparison reveals an expression of the same ideas. Jefferson uses similar phraseology, and while there is no verbatim reproduction of words, there is often replication of key words.

Mason's "certain inherent natural Rights" is a key point in his manifesto, which was essentially duplicated by Jefferson in his. Another vital point is Mason's "Among which are the Enjoyment of Life and Liberty, with the Means of . . . pursueing and obtaining Happiness." Jefferson echoes this point, with his "Among which are the preservation of life, & liberty, & the pursuit of Happiness." Jefferson's duplication of Mason in these and other instances is obvious, but to his credit it can be said that he expressed the same sentiments more succinctly, if not more lyrically.

But of the total number of words and ideas in each document, how much duplication is there? Mason's first draft consists of sixteen paragraphs (including articles written by others), each a sentence or two long. The body of the text of Jefferson's original document begins with two expository paragraphs, then follows with more than two dozen articles listing the colonists' grievances against the king of Great Britain, and concludes with a few expository paragraphs.

Pages two and three of the Virginia Declaration of Rights. Page two is faded and difficult to read.

It is the second paragraph of Thomas Jefferson's Declaration of Independence that seems to infringe on Mason, specifically his first three propositions. Jefferson's Declaration begins with the well-known phrase, "When in the course of human events . . ." The phrase commences a long, eloquent sentence, and its language and ideas are not contained in Mason's thesis. The second paragraph begins with "We hold these truths to be self-evident." This phrase isn't contained in Mason's document either, but the similarities begin immediately after it, with Jefferson's "That all men are created equal & independant." And it is here that there is similarity not only in words and thoughts, but in thought patterns and the sequence of thoughts.

It is this last element that casts the most suspicion on Jefferson. That manifestos of liberty would share ideas is not unreasonable or unusual, even if there is a commonality of words; after all, there may be only a limited number of ways to express a particular idea. But a document that duplicates the thought pattern and sequence of thoughts of another, especially when it contains much the same language, strains credibility as to the subsequent writer's originality.

It may be said that the similarities, as substantial as they are, are limited to a handful of sentences. Indeed, there is ample difference in the ideas and language in the remainder of the two documents, which is to be expected since they each address a different, albeit related, purpose, as their titles state: one a bill of rights for citizens (as a basis for establishing the principles of government), the other a declaration of independence or dissolution of political connections (as a basis for rebellion). The remainder of Jefferson's document is a list of the colonists' grievances against the king of Great Britain. But even here there is some commonality of ideas. Mason proclaims, "Man hath a right . . . to a speedy Tryal by a Jury," while Jefferson rebukes the king "for depriving us, in many cases, of the benefits of trial by jury."

A case can easily be made that there would be a natural overlap of ideas, given the similarity of the theses, but in the end it can be asserted that some of the most famous principles of Jefferson's Declaration include to a large degree thoughts and words that resemble Mason's. "That all men are created equal" is perhaps the most memorable point of Jefferson's Declaration, and it imparts virtually the identical thought (not to mention some of the same words) as Mason's "That all Men are born equally free and independant." A comparison of the two documents indeed shows the apparent influence of the Mason document on Jefferson.

But did Jefferson deliberately plagiarize from Mason? That is a very difficult call to make and, given the stature of Jefferson in American history, not an accusation one would make lightly.

It is highly improbable that Jefferson was not aware of Mason's document. The two men were political representatives from the same state, they were friends, and they traveled in the same political circles. It is possible that Mason had given a copy of his Declaration to Jefferson, but even if he hadn't, Mason's Virginia Declaration was published between June 6 and 12 in three newspapers in Philadelphia, the same city in which Jefferson resided while writing his Declaration. How could Jefferson *not* have been familiar with Mason's document?

While the Declaration of Independence may in part be based on the Virginia Declaration of Rights, Mason's doctrine itself has literary antecedents dating back to the Middle Ages and extending through the eighteenth-century philosophical movement known as the Enlightenment. Indeed, the long and noble line of charters of freedom, many derived in part from their antecedents, are like members of a family chain who have received genetic material from their ancestors. Among the illustrious members of this "family" of freedom documents is the 1215 Magna Carta, the 1689 English Bill of Rights, and John Locke's 1690 *Second Treatise of Government.*

The *Second Treatise* contains phrases that may be recognized in Mason's and Jefferson's declarations, for example: "life, liberty and estate," "free, equal and independent," and "all men, however born, are free." But these and other similar Lockeian phrases are used in essentially different contexts. Mason and Jefferson embrace many of the same ideas set forth by Locke, but it is doubtful that a strong case could be made that they plagiarized him. Still, the influence of Locke is apparent.

The doctrine of natural rights sets forth that human beings are equal and free by nature and have many natural rights including the right to act of their own free will, the right not to be subordinated to political control without their permission, and the right to be secure from injury by others in their lives, liberty, and property. Locke masterfully set forth natural rights theories, but the doctrine was also effectively expounded by other philosophers, such as Thomas Hobbes and Samuel Pufendorf. Locke embraced other political tenets in such works as his *Essay on Toleration,* whose lengthy thesis was concisely taken up by Mason, who proclaimed in his Virginia Declaration "that all Men shou'd enjoy the fullest Toleration in the Exercise of Religion . . . unpunished and unrestrained by the Magistrate. . . ."

There are undoubtedly various examples of ideas and words written by Mason that were set down by others before him. And like Mason, who may have borrowed from those who preceded him, Jefferson wasn't the only one to take such a literary cue. James Madison dipped into the literary and philosophical riches of Mason's Virginia Declaration in formulating the U.S. Bill of Rights, the U.S. Constitution's first ten amendments. The Declaration of the Rights of Man and of the Citizen, France's constitutional preamble issued in 1789 by the National Assembly, embodied many of the same precepts as the Declaration of Independence, including that citizens have certain sacred rights, that "men are born and remain free and equal," that humans have the inalienable rights of "liberty, property, security, and resistance to oppression," and that "every man is presumed innocent until he has been declared guilty." That France's declaration should closely mirror America's was no surprise, since it was drafted by the Marquis de Lafayette after visiting America, where he passionately embraced the U.S. doctrine. (Ironically, the demand for a constitution from the French monarchy, which led to limited powers for the king and eventually to Louis XVI's beheading, grew partially out of the debts incurred by France in assisting American citizens win independence from England.)

Both Mason and Jefferson received input from their peers on their preliminary and final drafts. But each document became the child of its chief architect. Still, Jefferson himself disavowed claims to originality in his declaration. In a letter to Henry Lee dated May 8, 1825, from his home at Monticello, Jefferson took up the intent of the Declaration of Independence. Recalling the days a half century earlier when the British government had contravened the Americans' rights and the colonists were forced to wage war to cast off the despotic English government, he wrote that "an appeal to the tribunal of the world was proper for our justification. This was the object of the Declaration of Independence." Indeed, the Declaration of Independence was printed in a variety of publications and in this way disseminated to the world.

According to Jefferson, the declaration was not intended to set forth fresh doctrines of a united people under the oppressive tentacles of a foreign power, but to express to the world a people's mutual pledge to levy war to protect their lives and honor. "Not to find out new principles, or new arguments, never before thought of, not merely to say things which had never been said before," Jefferson wrote, "but to place before mankind the common sense of the subject, in terms so plain and firm as to command their assent, and to justify ourselves in the independent stand we are compelled to take."

Jefferson continued, delineating how the document was to be the product of American thinking: "Neither aiming at originality of principle or sentiment, nor yet copied from any particular and previous writing, it was intended to be an expression of the American mind, and to give to that expression the proper tone and spirit called for by the occasion. All its authority rests then on the harmonizing sentiments of the day, whether expressed in conversation, in letters, printed essays, or in the elementary books of public right, as Aristotle, Cicero, Locke, Sidney, &c."

In January 1777, broadsides of the Declaration of Independence were printed and distributed. It was on these copies that citizens first saw the names of the signers, which until then had not been publicly revealed. At the end of the month John Hancock, the Continental Congress's president and the declaration's first signer, distributed the broadsides with a letter in which he wrote:

> As there is not a more distinguished Event in the History of America, than the Declaration of her Independence—nor any, that, in all probability, will so much excite the Attention of future Ages, it is highly proper, that the Memory of that Transaction, together with the Causes that gave Rise to it, should be preserved in the most careful Manner that can be devised.

That may be true, but history would be remiss in not honoring a beacon of freedom, one whose literary flourishes were grafted onto the more celebrated document whose legacy remains the quintessence of manifestos championing the right of individuals to be free from political tyranny. Indeed, in the interests of scholarship, the historical record, and propriety, future generations would do well to heed the debt owed by the Declaration of Independence and its framers, chiefly Thomas Jefferson, to George Mason and his noble charter of freedom, the Virginia Declaration of Rights.

LOCATION: Library of Congress, Washington, D.C.

The Rising Sun Chair

CRECRECRECRECRECRECRECRECRECRECRECRECRECRECRECRECRECRE

DATE: 1787.

WHAT IT IS: The chair on which presiding officer George Washington sat during the Constitutional Convention, whose fame was further enlarged by a propitious remark made about it by one of the convention's most esteemed delegates.

WHAT IT LOOKS LIKE: It is a mahogany Philadelphia Chippendale armchair with a high back and partially covered armrests that measures 60¾₆ inches from top to bottom, 29¹¹⁄₁₆ inches at its greatest width, and 22¹⁵⁄₁₆ inches at its greatest depth. Its seat is covered in red morocco leather (which traditionally was dried goatskin). The chair's open-worked splat is composed of vertical and horizontal rails on which are engraved designs of wheat and cornucopiae. At the top of the splat is a horizontal crest rail whose center area forms an artistic elevated shape. In the center of this shape is a gold-painted carving of a half sun with carved facial features of eyes, eyebrows, and a nose that is surrounded by a semicircular pattern of carved lines denoting sun rays. Standing on the center ray is a carved pole on which rests a Liberty cap that resembles an umbrella.

It was merely an artistic carving on a mundane object, but the ups and downs of the political convention in which the object played a role seemed to be reflected in the ambiguous design, as observed by one of the convention's most prominent participants. In its metaphorical essence, ultimately the design—like the convention itself—auspiciously reflected the destiny of a nation.

•   •   •

The year was 1787 and the place was Philadelphia, where fifty-five dele-gates from the thirteen sovereign states had come to decide the political future of the United States of America. With so many different political interests present, the convention—whose ostensible goal was to revise the nation's legal framework—promised healthy debate, if not downright dis-cord. Yet the stakes for this loose confederation of thirteen states separated by internal political turmoil were high: their future as a united country.

Since their settlement, the thirteen British colonies along the Eastern seaboard of America had functioned under the strong arm of their mother country. Their individual governments were monitored by the British monarch's royal governors, and English soldiers in the colonies enforced the onerous burdens imposed upon them by the mother country, including the restrictions on trading with any other country save England, the forced importation of English goods, taxes on sugar and tea, and much more. Despite the colonies' many common obstacles and hardships—the wilder-ness, unfriendly Indians, the threatening presence of imperialistic Spain with its territories to the south and west—they still maintained separate political structures. It was only after they united and formed the First Continental Congress in 1774, and had their subsequent pleas for partial autonomy rudely ignored, that they banded together to once and for all rid themselves of the oppressive British monarchy.

On November 15, 1777, sixteen months after representatives of the thir-teen American colonies formalized their intention to be free and indepen-dent states and dissolve all political connection to Great Britain with the Declaration of Independence (National Archives Building, Washington, D.C.), they drew up a set of articles that unified them under one central gov-ernment. It wasn't until 1781, after the Americans (with the help of a French army) defeated the British at Yorktown, Virginia, and claimed victory in the war, that all the states approved the articles, but even then the states con-tinued to look upon themselves as separate nations in their own right.

For eight years, until 1789, the Congress governed the new country under the Articles of Confederation (National Archives Building, Washington, D.C.), but as James Madison declared, the articles were "nothing more than a treaty of amity and alliance between independent and sovereign states." Indeed, under the weak Articles of Confederation, the Congress did not have the authority to levy taxes, regulate interstate and foreign commerce, establish a uniform currency, or gather an army; in effect, with the require-ment to have votes of nine of the thirteen states, the Congress could hardly enact laws. The states acted as individual sovereign entities, issuing their own currency (which was not honored reciprocally), and many even maintained their own navies.

Several leading statesmen decided the situation had to be remedied. After the Virginia state legislature passed a resolution calling for the states to appoint commissioners to consider a uniform system of commerce throughout the country, the governor of Virginia requested a session to discuss the trade measure. On September 11, 1786, twelve delegates from five states convened at the so-called Annapolis Convention in Maryland. A committee was formed to draft a report, which was adopted. But the delegates determined not to proceed with it because the representation at the convention was insubstantial (more delegates were on their way but didn't make it by the time the session ended on September 14). Some of the delegates took up the subject of the need to revise the Articles of Confederation, calling for state delegates to convene at a session "to devise such further provisions as shall appear to them necessary to render the constitution of the Federal Government adequate to the exigencies of the Union." The report, containing the announcement that the session would commence in Philadelphia "on the second Monday in May next," was distributed to the states. The following February, Congress affirmed that on the scheduled date delegates would meet "for the sole purpose of revising the Articles of Confederation."

On May 14, 1787, the appointed state delegates began converging on Philadelphia for the convention. Seventy-four delegates were supposed to attend, but only fifty-five showed up, and they wouldn't all arrive until July. Furthermore, delegates attended from only twelve states—Delaware, Maryland, Virginia, North Carolina, New Hampshire, Massachusetts, Connecticut, New York, New Jersey, South Carolina, Georgia, and Pennsylvania; Rhode Island declined on the grounds that the real intention of the convention was to empower the central government by diminishing the powers of the state governments. But the gravity of the convention was apparent, and the participants comprised many colonial luminaries, including George Washington, Benjamin Franklin, Alexander Hamilton, Gouverneur Morris, Charles Pinckney, Roger Sherman, James Madison, and James Wilson.

From May 25 to September 17, 1787, the delegates gathered (though never all together at once) in the Assembly Room at the Pennsylvania State House (later Independence Hall), a two-story redbrick building with a tower and a basement, to decide their country's future. And it was in the first-floor Assembly Room where the delegates met that one of the chairs in the room was immortalized.

As often is the case, it was the random intersection of time, location, and past and current events that caused this mundane object to be transformed into a relic for the ages. As a general rule, an ordinary object may become renowned through its association either with a celebrated person or a famous event of history. William Penn's seventeenth-century secretary (The Library Company, Philadelphia), for example, would undoubtedly have been consigned to a New World rubbish heap had it not been associated with the English founder of Pennsylvania. The Northwest Ordinance of 1787 (National Archives Building, Washington, D.C.) providing for territorial legislatures for settlers west of the Ohio River was preserved because of its historic importance. But what is particularly fascinating about this eighteenth-century Assembly Room speaker's chair is that it was used in a seminal event of American history and is intimately associated with not one but two legendary figures of the time.

During the British occupation of Philadelphia in the winter of 1777–78, the Redcoats had used the Pennsylvania State House on Chestnut Street to house American prisoners of war. It was during this time that the original speaker's chair disappeared; presumably it was broken into pieces with all other loose wood in the building to be used as firewood to warm the British soldiers on the first floor (the American prisoners were lodged on the second floor). After the war, Philadelphia cabinetmaker John Folwell was selected to build a new speaker's chair, and he made it in 1779 in the Chippendale style.

At the top of his ornate chair, Folwell carved a half-sun design. He was a member of the St. John's Masonic Lodge, and it is possible that his association with this organization had some influence on his design of the chair. Folwell knew he was making the Assembly's speaker's chair and perhaps tried to reflect the power of the speaker in his design, since Masonic tradition equates a rising sun with the supreme authority of the lodge's grand master. As for the carved wheat and other designs on the open-worked splat, these may be associated with Masonic ceremonies held to consecrate lodge halls, and may also refer to Pennsylvania's agricultural bounty as it is represented on the state seal.

Folwell was commissioned to make the speaker's chair while the Pennsylvania State House was being refurbished in 1779, and the funds to finance it came from the sale of confiscated property. During the British occupation of Philadelphia in the Revolutionary War, some local residents were loyal to the English king. When the British left Philadelphia, some of these people, who did not support the American war effort, were afraid to remain in the city for fear of being punished, perhaps even hanged. They

LEFT: *A full view of the "Rising Sun Chair."*

ABOVE: *A close-up view of the "rising sun" crest that inspired Benjamin Franklin to make his famous remark that immortalized the chair.*

took what belongings they could and fled (many went to England or Nova Scotia), often leaving behind their homes and assorted property. Members of the Assembly of the State of Pennsylvania knew who the Crown Loyalists were and confiscated the estates of these fugitives. This seized property was sold off, and its revenues were used to refurbish the State House.

On December 7, Pennsylvania state treasurer David Rittenhouse remitted two hundred pounds to Folwell to pay for the chair, which probably took a few months to make. It was initially placed on the State House's second floor during the repairs occasioned by the British occupation, but it is unclear where the chair was located in the State House for the next six years. However, by 1787 it was in the Assembly Room on the first floor. It was in this very same room that representatives of the colonies had met to begin signing the newly engrossed Articles of Confederation in 1778 and to debate and sign the Declaration of Independence before that in 1776.

Now, eleven years later, this chair would find itself in the same room for another monumental event of American history: the creation of the United States Constitution. And during the convention the chair would be occupied by the greatest American hero of the day.

He was retired and reluctant to attend the convention, but George Washington came as a delegate of Virginia and was unanimously appointed president of the Constitutional Convention. As president, or presiding officer, Washington, the former commander in chief of the Continental Army, sat in Folwell's speaker's chair, which was set on a platform above the others in the room.

The various delegates had their preconceived agendas. Debate began as Virginia governor Edmund Randolph introduced a series of fifteen resolutions calling for a strong national government comprised of executive, judicial, and legislative branches; these resolutions were collectively known as the Virginia Plan (four copies are known to survive, including three at the Library of Congress, although Randolph's original handwritten plan is not extant). The New Jersey delegates opposed the states' loss of powers under a strong central government and supported a revision of the Articles of Confederation that merely gave more powers to Congress (six handwritten

In this illustration of the 1787 Constitutional Convention, presiding officer George Washington is seated on the platform on what became known as the Rising Sun Chair.

texts related to the New Jersey Plan are known to exist; these are associated with James Madison, David Brearly, George Washington, Luther Martin, and two documents in the hand of William Paterson). Still other delegates offered other plans for government, some even supporting the idea of a government headed by a king. A proposal for a plan of government based on the British form was presented in the Hamilton Plan (four to six variously annotated copies are known to exist*). There was also the Pinckney Plan[†] presented by South Carolina delegate Charles Pinckney, which Pinckney proffered years later as the model for the last draft of the Constitution.

Many issues were debated during the Constitutional Convention, including state representation in the legislative branch and the counting of slaves for purposes of taxation. There was tremendous discord among the delegates, and at times it appeared that the session would fall apart. Pennsylvania delegate Gouverneur Morris later recalled, "The fate of America was suspended by a hair." Were it not for the presence of the man who had led the Americans to victory over the British in the Revolutionary War, George Washington, with his venerable reputation and authority, the convention might never have reached a successful conclusion.

But the issues were eventually worked out in favor of a central government with numerous powers, and a five-man Committee of Detail was formed to create a draft for a constitution on July 26. A first draft (Historical Society of Pennsylvania, Philadelphia) in James Wilson's hand was submitted on August 6, but renewed attention was focused on several specific issues. Slavery, trade regulation, and the method of electing the president were among the matters occupying the delegates' attention.

A third copy of the committee's report was made at the convention on August 6 (sixteen copies are known to survive at institutions such as the Library of Congress, The Library Company, Historical Society of Pennsylvania, National Archives, and The Pierpont Morgan Library). After more revisions were made by the Committee of Style and Arrangement a revised document was presented in convention on September 12 (this document does not survive); the committee's plan was ordered to be printed and furnished to the delegates (of the approximately sixty copies printed, fifteen are known to survive).

The delegates were eventually able to settle on suitable compromises, and in September revised and voted on different articles of the Constitution. On September 15 the final vote came, and the delegates approved the document

---

*Some historians disagree as to the number of extant Hamilton Plans.
[†]The original Pinckney Plan was lost, but at the Historical Society of Pennsylvania, there is an outline written by James Wilson that contains summaries of the original plan.

establishing the central government's powers. It delineated the composition of the House of Representatives and the Senate of the United States; provided for Congress to have the power to collect taxes, borrow money on the credit of the nation, regulate trade between the states and with foreign countries, coin money, establish post offices, declare war, raise armies and a navy, and make laws necessary for carrying out the powers vested by the Constitution in the United States government; and described the executive powers of the president. An engrossed (official and stylized) copy of the new Constitution was ordered.

Two days later, on September 17, thirty-nine delegates, a majority of those who attended the convention, signed the new engrossed United States Constitution (National Archives Building, Washington, D.C.). It would prove to be one of the outstanding manifestos of government in history, and it began with the immortal preamble:

> We the people of the United States, in Order to form a more perfect Union, establish Justice, insure domestic Tranquillity, provide for the common defence, promote the general Welfare, and secure the Blessings of Liberty to ourselves and our Posterity, do ordain and establish this Constitution for the United States of America.

But the making of the Constitution was painful for those who attended the sessions, which were closed to the public. Indeed, it was a heated and shaky convention, filled with obstacles, philosophical dissension, and political minefields. Benjamin Franklin, at eighty-one the elder statesman of America, took notice of the half-sun design on Washington's speaker's chair. Throughout the convention, with all its ups and downs, Franklin was intrigued by the meaning of this half sun; indeed its symbolism was too great to escape notice by the witty author of the *Poor Richard's Almanacs*.

We bear a debt of gratitude to the venerable James Madison, who took copious notes on the proceedings (Library of Congress, Washington, D.C.), for recording for posterity Franklin's remark immortalizing Washington's chair. Here's Madison on the momentous conclusion of the convention:

> Whilst the last members were signing [the Constitution] Doctor Franklin looking towards the President's Chair, at the back of which a rising sun happened to be painted, observed to a few members near him, that Painters had found it difficult to distinguish in their art a rising sun from a setting sun. I have, said he, often and often in the course of the Session, and the vicissitudes of my hopes and

fears as to its issue, looked at that behind the President without being able to tell whether it was rising or setting.

The metaphor in the carved design was now clearly manifest. The outcome of the contentious proceedings could have gone either way; the convention could well have dissolved into chaos, aborting the birth of the fledgling nation. But with the signing of the convenant binding the states together as an entity under one central government, Franklin had his answer:

> But now at length I have the happiness to know that it is a rising and not a setting Sun.

Franklin's prognosis was of course right on target, though the bright denouement he suggested would take some time to actualize. Before the Constitution could become "the law of the land," it was necessary, as the delegates provided, for nine states to ratify it. After the Constitution was signed, anti-Federalists vociferously expressed their opposition to the document's provision for a powerful central government—one that could potentially be dominated by wealthy people—in newspaper essays, with demonstrations, and through other means. From December 7, 1787, through January 9, 1788, Delaware, Pennsylvania, New Jersey, Georgia, and Connecticut ratified the Constitution, but the other states were undecided. However, one by one the rest of the states began to ratify; and finally, when New Hampshire became the ninth state to ratify on June 21, 1788, the Constitution could be put into operation, and at last the states could be formed into a true union.

It was a hot and grueling few months, that summer of 1787 in Philadelphia when fifty-five state delegates gathered to plot out a legal map, a political course for the citizens of the United States. Midwives to a nation that would over time rise to become a global superpower, the delegates held destiny in their hands as they struggled to hammer out its legal foundation.

And with his propitious remark, Benjamin Franklin not only captured the spirit of the historic proceedings, and prophesied a young nation's ascendance, but immortalized a chair as well—the only piece of furniture known to have survived the Constitutional Convention of 1787.

LOCATION: Independence National Historical Park, Philadelphia, Pennsylvania.

The Louisiana Purchase Treaty

DATE: 1803.

WHAT IT IS: The agreement between the United States and France providing for the latter to sell its New World territory of Louisiana to the former.

WHAT IT LOOKS LIKE: The American originals include a "Treaty Between the United States of America and the French Republic, April 30, 1803" (in separate French and English documents), the Senate ratification of October 20, 1803 (signed by an official of the Senate), and President Thomas Jefferson's proclamation of October 21, 1803 (signed by Jefferson). All are handwritten manuscripts.

Europeans of the Renaissance era thought of their enlightened realm as the "civilized" world, and considered the New World—a vast terrain of wilderness stretching from the Atlantic to the Pacific Ocean—to be inferior; because the land had bred only savages, they assumed, it was therefore not of the same quality as that in the Eastern Hemisphere.

The major European powers of England, France, and Spain dispatched soldiers to colonize the New World, but holding on to the land they claimed became a test of their strength. During the power struggles of the sixteenth, seventeenth, and eighteenth centuries, countries entered into numerous treaties and ceded and retroceded land like chess pieces. In some cases the language of the treaties was ornate, befitting the sovereigns of the countries, as in this brief passage from the introduction to the treaty of San Ildefonso of October 1, 1800, between France and Spain: "His Catholic Majesty having always manifested an earnest desire to procure for His Royal Highness the Duke of Parma an aggrandizement which would place his domains on a footing more consonant with his dignity. . . ."

Although its land was considered inherently inferior, the New World still offered much opportunity to Europe, and colonization was an important European activity during these centuries. Eventually the European colonizers lost their New World land, but they surely never envisioned that two centuries down the line the seeds they sowed in the New World would grow into great and prosperous societies playing major roles on the stage of world affairs.

It was a time of international unrest, during which the major European nations of England, France, and Spain engaged in bloody war, fearful that a superior enemy might gain control over their valued possessions in North America. It was also a time of great hope, with the fledgling United States eager to stretch its boundaries westward and grow into a strong and independent nation. But two nations, the United States and France, similar in many ways yet also very different, would come together as parties to a treaty that was to have important consequences not only for them but for the rest of the world as well.

The American colonists had a quarter century earlier fought their way to freedom from the British, who under King George III had controlled the thirteen New World colonies; the French working class, fed up with the prodigal and oppressive reign of King Louis XVI, had likewise rebelled and overthrown their king. With America's Declaration of Independence and France's Declaration of the Rights of Man, the common people in both countries made it clear that liberty and equality were the ideals they wanted their countries to embrace. But now, at the dawn of the nineteenth century, with Thomas Jefferson the president of the United States of America and Napoleon Bonaparte the first consul of France, each nation had divergent interests that were brought together by a single parcel of land. What happened as a result of this common bond is the story of the growth of one nation, the near-destruction of a continent across the ocean, and the dramatic transformation of many lives in an epic era of history that would reverberate for many years to come.

Paris, 1803

James Monroe, as President Thomas Jefferson's plenipotentiary, had arrived in the French capital. A growing concern back in the young American republic motivated the president to send the esteemed Virginia statesman to Europe to assist the American minister at Paris, Robert R. Livingston, in negotiating a deal with the French to buy New Orleans and the Floridas so western American settlers would have a port from which to ship their goods.

A Frenchman cruising down the Mississippi River from Canada in 1682 claimed the valley of the Mississippi River in honor of the king of France,

Louis XIV, naming it Louisiane. Forts were built to establish colonies, and except for a brief period of fourteen years when the territory was turned over to a private company because it was too costly for the French government, the area was controlled by France. Over the years French colonists poured into Louisiane; in 1718 hundreds arrived, some settling in New Orleans.

The Mississippi River at this time was an important route and was also used by American settlers in the West. America was largely an agricultural nation at the time of its declared independence from Great Britain, and some of its citizens settled to the west of the thirteen original colonies. Farther west stretched the huge territory known as Louisiana, extending from the Gulf of Mexico all the way up to Canada. With the Appalachians preventing land transport of their products to eastern markets, American farmers west of these mountains instead transported them down the Mississippi River to New Orleans, where the products were transferred to boats that hauled them across the Gulf of Mexico to the eastern American seaboard and abroad. The 1795 Pinckney Treaty with Spain provided Americans with the right to transport their goods on the Mississippi River and to store their goods at New Orleans after having paid a duty, a privilege called the right of deposit.

Within a few years, Americans began to fear that the rights granted them by the Pinckney Treaty would be denied by Spanish authorities in Louisiana. Some of their anxieties would be realized due to momentous events occurring across the Atlantic.

Leading a coup d'état in 1799, Napoleon Bonaparte extirpated the French Directory and took control of France as its first consul. Charles-Maurice de Talleyrand-Périgord, the French minister of foreign affairs, hatched a plan for the country to establish an empire in North America, which Napoleon approved. In a secret treaty of October 1, 1801, Napoleon coerced the Spanish king, Charles IV, into ceding back to France for a consideration the territory which it had conveyed to Spain some forty years earlier, Louisiana. This transfer was upheld in another treaty signed almost six months later.

The British got hold of the treaty and passed on the agreement to the American minister in England, who in turn forwarded it to Thomas Jefferson. The president responded by sending a letter dated April 18, 1802, to the American minister in Paris, Robert R. Livingston, in which he discussed the dilemma now presented to the United States and implied a threat that was probably more rhetoric than a realistic promise of action, since it involved America's old nemesis:

The cession of Louisiana and the Floridas by Spain to France works most sorely on the U.S. On this subject the Secretary of State has written to you fully. Yet I cannot forbear recurring to it personally, so deep is the impression it makes in my mind. It compleatly reverses all the political relations of the U.S. and will form a new epoch in our political course. Of all nations of any consideration France is the one which hitherto has offered the fewest points on which we could have any conflict of right, and the most points of a communion of interests. From these causes we have ever looked to her as our *natural friend*, as one with which we never could have an occasion of difference. Her growth therefore we viewed as our own, her misfortunes ours. There is on the globe one single spot, the possessor of which is our natural and habitual enemy. It is New Orleans, through which the produce of three-eighths of our territory must pass to market, and from its fertility it will ere long yield more than half of our whole produce and contain more than half our inhabitants. France placing herself in that door assumes to us the attitude of defiance. Spain might have retained it quietly for years. Her pacific dispositions, her feeble state, would induce her to increase our facilities there, so that her possession of the place would hardly be felt by us, and it would not perhaps be very long before some circumstance might arise which might make the cession of it to us the price of something of more worth to her. Not so can it ever be in the hands of France. The impetuosity of her temper, the energy and restlessness of her character, placed in a point of eternal friction with us, and our character, which though quiet, and loving peace and the pursuit of wealth, is high-minded, despising wealth in competition with insult or injury, enterprising and energetic as any nation on earth, these circumstances render it impossible that France and the U.S. can continue long friends when they meet in so irritable a position. They as well as we must be blind if they do not see this; and we must be very improvident if we do not begin to make arrangements on that hypothesis. The day that France takes possession of N. Orleans fixes the sentence which is to restrain her forever within her low water mark. It seals the union of two nations who in conjunction can maintain exclusive possession of the ocean. From that moment we must marry ourselves to the British fleet and nation.

Jefferson opted for diplomacy instead and requested Livingston to work out a settlement with the French. But Talleyrand avoided negotiating, and the situation became more desperate when in 1802 the Spanish governor of Louisiana suspended the vital right of deposit. With their livelihoods at stake, as well as the growth of the West, the western American settlers became incensed, and their concerns soon reached the nation's capital. Through American agents at the French capital, Jefferson heard rumors that King Charles of Spain hadn't yet ceded Louisiana to France by written treaty, although he was about to. With the situation at once crucial and uncertain, Jefferson dispatched to Paris James Monroe, George Washington's minister to France who had recently retired as governor of Virginia, to join Livingston in negotiating.

President Jefferson had wanted Livingston to request France not to take back Louisiana from Spain, but if it had already done this, he wanted to purchase New Orleans and the Floridas from France. But now, after a temporary halt to fighting between England and France, the Peace of Amiens had collapsed and war was on the verge of breaking out again. With Livingston threatening that America might ally itself with Great Britain, the Louisiana territory perhaps seemed to Napoleon to be a pivotal possession now. On the one hand, with French forces engaged in war in Europe, it could be lost in an Anglo-American attempt to wrest control of it. On the other hand, disposing of it for a good sum could enrich the royal treasury and help finance France's wars in Europe.

In 1803 Talleyrand shocked the American minister Robert Livingston by asking what the United States would offer for the entire Louisiana territory. James Monroe soon assisted him in negotiating a price for the 828,000-square-mile territory. The agreed-upon sum was $11.25 million.

Napoleon's decision to sell Louisiana troubled President Jefferson. A strict adherent to the U.S. Constitution, Jefferson knew the Constitution did not authorize the government to buy territory. Jefferson wanted to enact a constitutional amendment to provide authorization, but he was warned that protracting the arrangement might cause Napoleon to rescind his offer. So making a vague interpretation of the Constitution, Jefferson went forward in purchasing Louisiana by formal provision of a treaty.

On April 30, 1803 (the eleventh year of the French Republic), French and American envoys signed the treaty for the cession of Louisiana at Paris. The treaty, which was originally drafted and agreed to in the French language, contained ten articles.

The treaty confirmed France's ownership of the colony of Louisiana as per the treaty of San Ildefonso of October 1, 1800, between the first French consul and the king of Spain, and ceded the territory to the United States. Other provisions of the treaty specified that residents of Louisiana be

The *"exchange copy,"* or French ratification of the Louisiana Purchase Treaty, signed by Bonaparte and Talleyrand. A skippet and two tassels are attached to the binding by cords. It has regal blue velvet covers adorned with gold ornamentation; at the center of the front cover of the volume are the letters "P.F.," standing for "Peuple Français."

granted all the rights of U.S. citizens; that all French military posts in the ceded territory be remitted to commissaries of the U.S. president; that for a twelve-year period ships coming directly from France or Spain or their colonies into the port of New Orleans and other Louisiana ports would not be subject to higher duties than those paid by U.S. ships; and that the treaty be ratified within six months from the date of signing.

The signatories to the treaty were, for the United States, Robert R. Livingston, Minister Plenipotentiary, and James Monroe, Minister Plenipotentiary and Envoy Extraordinary; and for France, Barbé Marbois, Minister of the Public Treasury.

On the same date as the treaty, two conventions were held providing for the payment by the United States to France of sums to cover the purchase of Louisiana. One convention provided for the U.S. government to pay France 60 million francs ($11,250,000), the other for the United States to assume the debt owed by France to United States citizens. The negotiating parties agreed on an amount of $3.75 million, bringing the total purchase price of the Louisiana territory to $15 million. However, interest payments would boost the final payment much higher. The cession treaty and the two conventions composed one transaction and were all signed at the same time.

The Louisiana Purchase Treaty provided that the land ceded to the United States was, as Jefferson wrote on July 15, 1803, "according to the bounds to which France had a right," but the boundaries of Louisiana were in fact not clear. Talleyrand, in response to Livingston's question about the boundaries, replied that he did not know and could not offer any direction, but that "you have made a noble bargain for yourselves, and I suppose you will make the most of it." Spain continued to claim that it owned the Floridas, a dispute that wouldn't be settled until the United States purchased the territory in 1819. In the meantime, Jefferson was concerned that the purchase of Louisiana might not have been constitutionally valid and expressed his desire for an amendment to the Constitution, but on October 21, 1803, the U.S. Senate voted to ratify the Louisiana Purchase.

With the treaty signed, America more than doubled its size, and it could send scouts to explore its vast new terrain, have its citizens settle the untamed land, form new states, and strengthen its union. Napoleon, whose royal treasury was enriched by the purchase agreement, could now embark on a dream of conquest in which he would march his armies across Europe and attempt to seize nations with which to build a powerful French empire over which he would be the supreme ruler. Two very different goals, on two different sides of the world, yet each country a catalyst—via its desire to acquire or dispose of the Louisiana Territory—for the other's goal.

The Louisiana Purchase Treaty was not just a real estate transaction but a reflection of the world political situation at the dawn of the nineteenth century. Behind it were the goals and dreams of powerful men, and in its aftermath came a plethora of momentous events it hastened. From the Lewis and Clark expedition to the Napoleonic wars, this land paved the way for important actions to come over the following years. Between the lines of the Louisiana Purchase Treaty, one may read the desires of eager statesmen and a despotic sovereign, and ultimately the fates of legions of people and the destinies of nations on both sides of the Atlantic Ocean.

LOCATION: National Archives and Records Administration, Washington, D.C. The French-held Louisiana Purchase Treaty documents are located at the Archives Nationales, Paris, France.

The Lewis and Clark Journals

DATE: 1804–1806.

WHAT THEY ARE: The journals in which the co-leaders of the first expedition through the American Northwest recorded their experiences and observations, and the information they gathered about the inhabitants, animals, and plant life in the country they passed through.

WHAT THEY LOOK LIKE: There are numerous journals, field books, and loose manuscript sheets that collectively comprise the so-called Lewis and Clark journals. The principal set of journals, a collection of eighteen, all housed at one institution (the American Philosophical Society), are basically of three bindings and sizes: thirteen volumes are bound in red morocco and have dimensions of 8¼ inches high by 5 inches wide; four are bound in marbled cardboard with leather spines and measure 6¾ inches by 4 inches; and one is bound in brown leather and is 8¼ inches by 5 inches. Another set (at the Missouri Historical Society) consists of four volumes bound in red morocco, each measuring 8¼ inches by 5 inches, and one volume bound in elkskin that is 6¾ inches by 5½ inches.

At the dawn of the nineteenth century, a band of explorers led by Meriwether Lewis and William Clark became the first U.S. citizens to cross the vast wilderness of the unknown and uncharted American Northwest and reach the Pacific Ocean. They traversed valleys and plains, ascended mountains, floated over rapids, communicated with natives they encountered, and endured bitter winters, as they went along diligently recording their interactions and observations, which Americans eagerly awaited in order to see whether the trans-Mississippi West offered the potential for commerce and settlement. Out of this journey came the famous Lewis and Clark journals, but there is a mystery attendant on their writing. President Thomas Jefferson assumed the entries were written daily, as the expedition co-leaders wended their way to the Pacific coast and carried on their myriad surveys. Yet noted scholar Elliott Coues, who investigated many of the journals in the early 1890s, found the condition of these journals too pristine and the penmanship too good and too uniform for the entries to have been recorded regularly during an arduous transcontinental odyssey.

Neither Lewis nor Clark revealed how their frontier documents were written, leaving later investigators to scour the extant original records of the expedition to determine whether the journals were written on a daily basis, or at some later date and place and were not actually on-the-scene accounts of events as had previously been believed. Do the journals offer posterity a distorted view of the original celebrated expedition through the northwestern United States? What is the solution to this mystery surrounding the writing of the immortal journals of Lewis and Clark?

After years of deliberation and a few failed attempts to launch explorations of the American Northwest, Thomas Jefferson, as president of the United States in 1803, finally had the power to obtain funds for and dispatch such an expedition. On June 20 he informed his private secretary, Meriwether Lewis, by letter (Library of Congress, Washington, D.C.), that the objective of this mission was "to explore the Missouri river, & such principal stream of it, as, by it's course & communication with the waters of the Pacific Ocean may offer the most direct & practicable water communication across this continent, for the purposes of commerce. . . ."

Though such exploration was a goal long envisioned by Jefferson and others, the recent purchase of the Louisiana Territory had made the American public eager to learn about the resources of the newest addition to their nation. Other exploratory expeditions would follow, including Zebulon Pike's two-year journey into the Southwest beginning in 1805, but Lewis and Clark were the first to venture into the Northwest.

The preparations for the Lewis and Clark expedition were varied and complex, requiring the leaders to recruit capable men, outfit the expedition with food and supplies for some indeterminate length of time, and become learned in several areas, as a vital part of the mission would be to gather information on the country they passed through. To the latter end Lewis spent some time in Philadelphia, home of the American Philosophical Society. Some of the society's members, the leading scientists in the young republic, tutored Lewis in the natural sciences, celestial navigation, and other areas.

On July 5, 1803, Lewis left Washington for Pittsburgh, where he arrived eight days later and waited for his keelboat, a fifty-five-foot flat-bottomed boat, to be built. On August 30 Lewis and a party of eleven men moved down the Ohio River, at different points stopping to pick up volunteers for the expedition. Clark joined them at Louisville, and they made their way to the Missouri River. The expedition had wanted to camp for the winter high on the Missouri, but was prohibited from doing so. The territory of Louisiana had been ceded by Spain to France, whose minister issued a passport to provide the explorers with protection, but the Spanish head of the province had not yet received official word of the cession to France (and France's subsequent cession to America), and as a matter of his government's policy had to deny the foreigners permission to encamp there.

Looking for a new base, the expedition party in the fall set down a camp at the mouth of the Rivière Dubois, or Wood River, in Illinois, then part of the Indiana Territory. Here, across from the mouth of the Missouri River, they would wait for the cold weather to break and for the Louisiana Territory to officially pass from France to the United States before beginning their journey. In the interim, the men were put through military drills and disciplined when necessary for various military infractions such as drinking and fighting. Lewis spent much time in St. Louis, less than twenty miles away, where he gathered even more supplies, questioned local people about the Indians who lived along the Missouri, and witnessed in March 1804 the Louisiana Territory transfer. Finally spring arrived, and the expedition was ready to be launched.

On May 14, 1804, the Lewis and Clark expedition officially began at the mouth of Wood River. At 4:00 P.M., as local inhabitants looked on, some forty-five men in high spirits departed Camp Dubois on the keelboat and in two smaller pirogues, or dugout canoes. The craft were laden with food, weapons including flintlock rifles and an airgun, medical supplies, scientific apparatus, gifts for the Indians, and many other accouterments and supplies—including, of course, journals, manuscript papers, and writing implements. The Corps of Discovery, as the explorers called themselves, crossed the Mississippi and then began their journey up the Missouri. Near the end of October they arrived at the country of the Mandan Indians (in what is now North Dakota), where they built Fort Mandan to spend the winter. The winter months were bitterly cold, and during this time several members of the expedition actively wrote about the land, its inhabitants, and their experiences there.

On the 7th of April 1805, sixteen men, the escorting party, returned east on the keelboat with a collection of material gathered on the expedition, including animal skins, stuffed animals, elk and ram horns, Indian clothing, plant specimens, and live animals, as well as some written records. The rest of the group, the permanent party, resumed their penetration into the western frontier. They continued climbing the Missouri (now with a young Shoshone woman, Sacagawea, the wife of their translator, Toussaint Charbonneau), crossed the Continental Divide and the Bitterroot Mountains, descended the Clearwater, and proceeded along the Snake and Columbia Rivers to the Pacific coast. In his entry for November 18, 1805, Clark wrote that his party sighted the Pacific Ocean with "estonishment."

The Corps of Discovery built Fort Clatsop (near what is now Astoria, Oregon), where they camped for the winter before heading back east from the Pacific Northwest on March 23, 1806. In July the party decided to break into two groups so more information could be gathered. Taking different routes—Lewis's group crossed the Rockies to the Missouri, Clark's descended the Yellowstone—the factions converged in mid-August and proceeded down the Missouri to St. Louis, which they reached on September 23, 1806, officially bringing the eight-thousand-mile expedition to an end two years and four months after it began.

President Jefferson directed the mission's leaders, Lewis and Clark, to record details of their journey. In his June 20, 1803, letter to Captain Lewis, Jefferson wrote:

> Your observations are to be taken with great pains & accuracy, to be entered distinctly, & intelligibly for others as well as yourself, to comprehend all the elements necessary . . .

Solicitous of the need for other written records in the case of loss or damage to theirs and to have additional frameworks to draw upon, the commanders ordered their sergeants and encouraged others on the expedition "to keep a separate journal from day to day of all passing occurrences, and such other observations on the country &c as shall appear to them worthy of notice."

After returning to St. Louis at the end of September, Clark made his last journal entry. In an entry dated September 26, 1806, he wrote that it was "a fine morning we commenced wrighting &c."

"Commenced wrighting"? Was he referring to their journals? If so, hadn't Lewis and Clark been writing in their journals as they traveled across the country? A few editorial touch-ups would be reasonable and expected, but what was the need now to spend months "wrighting" if that was something they had been doing all along?

Certainly that was the impression the president had. In early January 1807, Lewis delivered the journals to Jefferson, who was anxious to read them. Jefferson wrote of the journals:

> Ten or twelve such pocket volumes, Morocco bound . . . in which, in his own handwriting, he [Lewis] had journalised all occurrences, day by day, as he travelled. They were small 8vos and opened at the end for more convenient writing. Every one had been put into a separate tin case, cemented to prevent injury from wet. But on his return the cases, I presume, had been taken from them, as he delivered me the books uncased.

Indeed, Jefferson noted that the journal entries had been recorded on a daily basis. How later scholars came to analyze the journals and arrive at a different conclusion has to do with their provenance.

Jefferson rewarded Lewis and Clark for their successful mission by giving them public land and commissions; he appointed Lewis governor of the Louisiana Territory and Clark brigadier general of the Missouri militia and superintendent of Indian affairs for the Upper Louisiana Territory. But Lewis delayed taking office as governor so he could ready the journals for the printer's shop. He spent four months in Philadelphia, and when it was incumbent upon him to return to the new territory in the autumn of 1807, he took the journals with him.

His sundry official responsibilities as governor left Lewis little time to further prepare the journals, and when he set out for Washington in the fall of 1809 for an inquiry into his expenditures, he brought with him the expedition journals and some unrelated government documents. Lewis was accompanied by an Indian agent, James Neelly, but unfortunately the trip turned out tragically. While the two were staying at an inn along a route called the Natchez Trace near Hohenwald, Tennessee, shots blasted early one morning, and Lewis was found with chest and head wounds. The celebrated thirty-five-year-old leader of the famous American expedition died on October 11. Lewis's death appeared to be a suicide, but later speculation that he had been murdered surfaced.

Agent Neelly took Lewis's two trunks containing the invaluable journals and conveyed them to Washington. William Clark and President James

Madison's private secretary, Isaac Coles, pored over the contents of the trunks; Clark took possession of the journals and field books and brought them with him to Fincastle, Virginia.

In April 1810, Philadelphia litterateur Nicholas Biddle, whom Clark had recruited to put the journals in book form, joined him in Virginia, where he reviewed the documents, queried Clark about the journey, and made notes about their discussions in a notebook (American Philosophical Society, Philadelphia), which he later used to write his book. Biddle took nearly all the expedition journals back to Philadelphia with him, as well as Sgt. John Ordway's 1804–1805 journal of the expedition (American Philosophical Society) that he and Captain Lewis had purchased from Ordway for $300 shortly after they returned to St. Louis. While he worked on the famous Lewis and Clark journals, Biddle, somewhat imprudently, made annotations in them in red ink.

Biddle was to write only a narrative of the expedition, and so he turned over some of the journals to Dr. Benjamin Smith Barton, an eminent physician, naturalist, and author, who was going to prepare a book on the scientific aspects of the expedition. Biddle finished writing in mid-1811. Some three years later, in 1814, Biddle's *History of the Expedition under the Command of Captains Lewis and Clark to the Sources of the Missouri* was published (three copper plates engraved with maps from the book are at the American Philosophical Society), essentially a pared-down and paraphrased narrative of Lewis and Clark's journals, excluding the scientific aspects of the venture. Barton's planned book was never published. He died at the end of 1815 with three journals in his possession, sparking the concern of former president Thomas Jefferson and prompting him to have a colleague retrieve them from Barton's widow. This was accomplished, and the three journals were conveyed from Philadelphia to Washington.

About eighteen months after they arrived, Jefferson had the journals returned to Philadelphia again, where they were deposited at the American Philosophical Society, founded in 1743 to foster, as Benjamin Franklin noted, "the common stock of knowledge." The Barton journals were soon joined by the Biddle journals to bring the majority of the epic Lewis and Clark journals under one roof.

For seventy-four years, from 1818, when the fourteen Biddle volumes plus another journal on celestial calculation were added to the three Barton volumes, until 1892, the Lewis and Clark journals languished more or less in obscurity in their Philadelphia sanctuary. But they were not totally forgotten. In 1837 the U.S. secretary of war, on behalf of artist John James Audubon, petitioned for the journals to be loaned to Audubon, who was then in Europe. But the society denied the request because of the potential perils of an ocean voyage. Then, in 1888, following the publication of the society's minutes through 1838, which revealed the location of the Lewis and Clark journals, individuals began to inquire about using the journals for various scholarly pursuits.

In 1892 scholar Elliott Coues, who had been asked by a publisher to revise the 1814 *History of the Expedition,* turned his attention to the original journals and was granted his request to examine them at his home in Washington, D.C., their first time there since former President Jefferson had gathered them. Coues was a multitalented man who was a physician, anatomy professor, ornithologist, mammalogist, editor, and author of important books on animals. Coues perused the journals and arranged them chronologically by giving them codex identifications with letters of the alphabet. According to this system, Clark was the author of journals A, B, G, H, I, M, N, and P; Lewis the author of journals D, E, F, J, K, L, and O; and Lewis and Clark together of journals C, Q, and R.

But in his close inspections of the journals, Coues noticed that their condition belied books that could have served as diaries on such a long trek. "The covers are too fresh and bright," he wrote, "the paper too clean and sound." Coues noted the pristine legibility of the penmanship and concluded that the red morocco-bound journals "were certainly written after the return of the Expedition, and before Lewis's death in October 1809— that is, in 1806–9."

Such a conjecture was tantamount to blasphemy! To say that the renowned Lewis and Clark journals, supposedly day-by-day eyewitness accounts of actions and observations feverishly inscribed by the two explorers on their epic journey, had in fact been transcribed, edited, and rewritten from original documents was a tacit admission that they may have contained observations and comments whose accuracy had been distorted by the passage of time.

The main Lewis and Clark journals left Philadephia one final time when Ruben Gold Thwaites of the Historical Society of Wisconsin needed the journals to prepare a comprehensive publication of them. From October 1902 through November 13, 1902, the journals were shipped a few at a time to Thwaites, who made his own discoveries and conclusions about the writing habits of Lewis and Clark. Simply stated, Thwaites believed that the co-commanders each day made rough notes in small field books and when encamped for an extended period developed their notes "into more formal records," with both Lewis and Clark often borrowing "freely from the other's notes," although Clark "not infrequently copied Lewis practically verbatim." "Upon returning to St. Louis," Thwaites speculated, "these individual journals were for the most part transcribed into neat blank books—bound in red morocco and gilt-edged—with the thought of preparing them for early publication. After this process, the original field-books must have been cast aside and in large measure destroyed. . . . There have come down to us, however, several note-books which apparently were written up in the camps."

In the introduction to his eleven-volume *Journals of the Lewis & Clark Expedition,* scholar Gary Moulton refutes this notion and takes up the improbability of Lewis and Clark composing a massive amount of words in the red journals during their three-month stay in St. Louis. According to Moulton, Lewis and Clark were busily engaged at this time: "The captains were traveling; visiting relatives; seeing to other business; and attending public ceremonies, welcoming celebrations, and banquets. During that period Lewis was also escorting the Mandan chief Big White (Sheheke) to the capital."

An examination of the Lewis and Clark field notes and journals reveals certain things about their writing habits. The field notes may have been transcribed into formal journal entries soon after they were written, or after ample time had passed, perhaps as long as months later. Field notes may have been copied into the journals virtually verbatim or been revised and expanded, as the field notes and journals do not always match. Journal entries often contain material of which no mention is made in the field notes, indicating that the diarist had inserted information not originally set down in the field notes. Lewis and Clark did not always write field notes first; sometimes they wrote directly into their journals without first making rough notes. Torn pages were inserted into the journals. Clark makes mention of his "private journal," but it is not clear whether this was his field notes or his formal journal. In the early part of the expedition, water damage may have occurred to some of the journals and other manuscripts when a boat had a mishap and took on water.

In addition to the question of whether the entries were written as the events were happening or after the fact, other mysteries attend the journals. Why are there large gaps in Lewis's journals, particularly from the start of the journey on May 14, 1804, for almost a year—that is, until the following April—when he almost certainly would have kept a journal during that important time? After Lewis died his possessions were accounted for, and it was found that he had sixteen red morocco journals. He supposedly had all the journals—both his and Clark's from the expedition—

but why are there seventeen red journals in total that survive? Why are there blank spaces and numerous consecutive blank pages between journal entries? Why are there insertions in one or the other's journals by the other co-leader?

Deciphering the daily and postexpedition field notes and journals is an endeavor that leaves attempts to reconcile their composition unsatisfied. There are mysteries that may never be definitively solved but only intelligently approached by logical deductions. Indeed, the writing is very even and was obviously done under controlled circumstances and environments, not on bended knee examining a new plant species or being chased by a grizzly or toiling away in rain or snow. Through the years people have commonly assumed that the journals were rough notes, jotted down as the expedition

A page from one of Meriwether Lewis's journals. From an entry dated March 16, 1806, the page features a drawing of a white trout salmon.

moved from spot to spot. The general impression has been that the co-leaders kept these journals in their pockets or traveling bags, and as they made an observation would simply take them out and begin scribbling away. But the literal cleanliness of the writing suggests that Lewis and Clark wrote in their journals when they had a chunk of time on their hands, such as during the long, cold months they spent in their winter camps. Because of the voluminousness of the journals, it is hardly conceivable that they could have been written after Lewis and Clark returned to St. Louis and were waiting to go to Washington, although it is possible that some writing could have taken place during that time. Nevertheless, some scholars have postulated that Lewis and Clark wrote out all their journals in the window of three months that they spent in St. Louis.

In his *Journals of the Lewis & Clark Expedition,* Gary Moulton concluded:

> There is little reason to accept the theory that the red notebook journals were all written after the return from subsequently discarded field notes. Considering the great amount of extant material and the labor involved in writing it, we need not imagine extensive sets of field notes paralleling the notebooks when the existence of such notes is neither known nor required by the evidence. Whatever Clark's "we commenced wrighting" in his last journal entry refers to, it was probably not the task of writing all the red books covering a year and a half of travel. Most of the material we now have was written by the captains in the course of the expedition.

Indeed, the course of scholars' thinking has changed. Thwaites believed that it was possible that the Lewis and Clark journals were not real-time eyewitness accounts of their journey, but were, rather, written at a later time during the expedition. Consequently, he thought that most of their original notes, written in field books as they went along, were probably discarded after they were transferred to the formal journals.

But modern scholars believe that what we have today are the field books, notebooks, journals, and manuscript sheets in the hands of Lewis and Clark, written before, during, and after the expedition. And they *do* serve as firsthand accounts of the two-year epic journey that began in 1804 and which both hastened the development of commercial trade in the American Northwest and fostered an understanding of a vast wilderness that led to the settlement of the region.

The historic importance and uniqueness of the journals is self-evident. The northwestern United States has over the years evolved with the burgeoning of society and technology into an area with numerous bustling metropolises that are major centers of industry in the world. Although white adventurers such as the English navigators James Cook and George Vancouver and the Canadian fur trader Alexander Mackenzie explored the American Northwest before Lewis and Clark, the journals are especially valuable in that they are the diaries of the first nonnatives to sweep through the entire region, prior to the subsequent stampede by white men into the Northwest that transformed it into an evolved region of interconnecting paved roads and concrete cities.

The information about the Northwest passed on by Lewis and Clark revealed a land with abundant natural resources and potential. The commanders did not find a water passage through the northwest to the Pacific Ocean,* but their expedition was nevertheless a resounding success. It stirred the minds of Americans and prompted many to turn west and settle the area; as well, it gave America a claim to Oregon. The reader of the journals can vicariously experience the thrilling journey of the first American transcontinental overland expedition as the explorers followed their senses and encountered Indians and strange animals and many glorious wonders of nature. The reader can, along with the explorers, observe new species of animals and plants, feel their frustrations, sense their curiosity, and revel in their courage.

Seven years after the epic mission ended, Thomas Jefferson wrote that Meriwether Lewis possessed "a fidelity to the truth so scrupulous that whatever he should report would be as certain as if seen by ourselves." Though scholars over the years have doubted that the journals were the "scrupulous" truth, in all probability they were written soon after the events, so they are essentially genuine diaries of what happened, and as such future generations may sense the same awe and excitement that the co-commanders Meriwether Lewis and William Clark did from 1804 through 1806 as they boldly stepped into a new world and reported on it for posterity.

LOCATIONS:

American Philosophical Society, Philadelphia, Pennsylvania, has eighteen bound journals, thirteen of which are bound in red morocco, four in marbled cardboard, and one in brown leather. These are considered the principal set of surviving journals from the Lewis and Clark expedition.

The Missouri Historical Society, St. Louis, has four red morocco journals; Clark's elkskin field book covering the journey from Traveller's Rest Creek, Montana, to Fort Clatsop, Oregon; and numerous other manuscript material and documents written by Lewis and Clark or related to the expedition.

Beinecke Rare Book and Manuscript Library, Yale University, New Haven, Connecticut, has Captain William Clark's field notes covering the expedition's stay at Camp Dubois, journey up the Missouri, and winter encampment at the Mandan villages (the notes, written on

---

*President Jefferson had instructed Lewis to find a water communication from the mouth of the Missouri River to the Pacific Ocean "for the purposes of commerce." Lewis and Clark instead traveled over land and mountains, not finding, as they expected, a connection between the Missouri and the Columbia Rivers.

individual sheets, were returned with the escorting party in April 1805), as well as fifty-four maps of the journey route and Clark's detailed map of northwestern America.

Western Historical Manuscript Collection, Columbia, Missouri, has Lewis's 1805 astronomy notebook, and Lewis and Clark's 1809 memorandum book listing debts due by Clark and a list of Lewis's private debts.

Other members of the Lewis and Clark expedition kept journals, and these survive as follows: John Ordway (American Philosophical Society), Joseph Whitehouse (Newberry Library, University of Chicago), and Charles Floyd (State Historical Society of Wisconsin). It should also be noted that while many other Lewis and Clark artifacts from the expedition survive at different locations, there are, prominently, numerous plant and mineral specimens at the Academy of Natural Sciences, Philadelphia; a significant collection of maps and Jefferson's correspondence with Lewis at the Library of Congress, Washington, D.C.; Lewis's telescope at the Missouri Historical Society; and Clark's pocket compass at the National Museum of American History, Washington, D.C.

ℬeethoven's Ear Trumpets

DATE: circa 1812–1813.

WHAT THEY ARE: Two pairs of "listening tubes" that were designed to improve the composer's hearing.

WHAT THEY LOOK LIKE: The hearing aids consist of long tubes connected to funnels and are made of brass.

Of all the musical sounds ever produced by humans, from the first babbled melody to the latest chart-topper's catchy chorus, the most famous, enduring, and universally recognizable motif is arguably the simple but arresting sequence of notes that opens Ludwig van Beethoven's Fifth Symphony. Indeed, the sublime genius of Beethoven, with his oeuvre of nine symphonies, thirty-two piano sonatas, and numerous orchestral, chamber, choral, and other works, has been recognized for two centuries both by common folk and by celebrated musicians alike. But fate dealt a cruel hand to the prodigious composer when he was a young man by robbing him of a vital sense. Before 1800, when he was not yet thirty, the maestro began losing his hearing and eventually became deaf, unable to hear any piece of music he wrote except in his mind. As the outside world fell silent to the musical genius, Beethoven withdrew from society and plunged into his work, immersed in his own private torment.

When Beethoven realized his ability to hear was fading—noticing that he had to draw his head closer to the piano to hear when he played—he tried everything he could think of to ameliorate his condition, from visiting physicians to applying salves and other remedies, all to no avail. The composer despaired at his lack of success and was embarrassed by his condition, letting few of his friends know at first. Despite his growing deafness, he still carried on his life as best he could. "To give you an idea of this curious condition," he wrote to a friend, "I must tell you that in the theater I must get close to the stage in order to hear the actors. If I am at a slight distance then the high notes of instruments and singers I do not hear at all. I can often hear the low tones of a conversation but I cannot make out the words. It is strange that in conversation people do not notice my lack of hearing but they seem to attribute my behavior to my absence of mind. When people speak softly I hear tones but not the words. I cannot bear to be yelled at. Heaven knows what will come of this."

But as the sounds of life faded over the years, Beethoven (who was born in Bonn, Germany, in 1770 but spent most of his professional life in Vienna) even contemplated suicide. He agonized over his hearing loss and became more impatient and short-tempered with those around him. "For me there can be no recreation in the society of my fellows, refined intercourse, mutual exchange of thought," the composer wrote in 1802. "Only just as little as the greatest needs command may I mix with society. I must live like an exile."

It is not known whether it was at the composer's behest or the maker's initiative, but around 1812 or 1813, Johann Nepomuk Mälzel made four brass "Horinstrumente," or listening instruments, for the maestro. Beethoven was acquainted with Mälzel (1772–1838), having composed his op. 91, "Wellington's Victory," for Mälzel's mechanical musical instrument, the Panharmonikon, in 1813; in later years Beethoven used a metronome developed by Mälzel for tempo markings.

Mälzel intended that as sounds passed from the funnel through the tubes of his ear trumpet, their volume would increase, and when they made direct contact with the listener's ear on the other end, the person would be able to hear them more clearly. Unfortunately, Mälzel's ear trumpets didn't help Beethoven much, if at all, and the composer's hearing continued to worsen. By 1818 Beethoven was totally deaf and could not communicate orally. Visitors to his home used "con-

Beethoven hoped that Johann Nepomuk Mälzel's ear trumpets, pictured above, might enable him to better hear the music he composed. But the primitive hearing aids did not help Beethoven and the composer's hearing loss continued to grow worse over time.

versation books" to write their communications to him. When he could no longer hear, Beethoven relied on his auditory memory to compose. The composer, whom Mozart praised and Vienna's nobility embraced admiringly, was condemned to an existence of external silence.

Poor Beethoven! His music was timeless, but the technology of his day was too primitive to remedy his physical impairment. But his condition gives rise to an intriguing question: If Beethoven had lived at a later time, say the late twentieth century, would technology have been able to help him hear, or even to cure his deafness?

Whether Beethoven's condition could have been improved or cured would have depended on the etiology of his deafness, which is uncertain. However, from a description of his condition written to his friend Karl Amende, it appears that he had a progressive sensorineural hearing loss (a hearing loss derived from a problem in the inner ear). Initially, Beethoven experienced a "whistle and buzz continually" in his ears. This tinnitus may have been due to the degeneration of hair cells in the cochlea. High-frequency sounds were lost first, and then the low tones.

Modern technology probably could have improved Beethoven's condition. Once his deafness was diagnosed, he would have been fitted with hearing aids. These would have made sounds louder, so he would not have needed to get so close to his piano keys to hear. He could also have utilized an FM system in the concert auditorium so that sounds from the orchestra would be delivered into his hearing aid directly, like a personal radio station. This system would have also eliminated the distracting background mumble of the audience. With special frequency-transposing hearing aids, his speech discrimination would have been improved, so in conversations he would have been able not only to detect voices but also to discriminate some spoken words as well.

With modern developments in assistive technology, he might have been a candidate for a cochlear implant when his hearing loss became profound. With his excellent auditory memory, the implant would have allowed him to hear with an internal coil inserted into his cochlea to substitute for the missing hair cells. This coil would receive sound information from an external ear-level microphone and speech processor Beethoven would have worn at his waist or behind his ear.

The speech processor, a tiny computer, would have had several programs to choose from. The composer could have selected the best one depending on the environment he was in. One setting would allow him to hear better in conversation, one at a noisy gathering, and another when listening to music. He would have needed to relearn sounds, however, because the new

In this nineteenth-century painting by A. Grafle, Beethoven plays for a small but appreciative audience.

signals he received would have sounded different from what he had heard in the past. Once his brain had made the switch, he probably would not have lapsed into the despair he felt at the end of his life.

One can only dream of what music the highly original Beethoven, who diverged from Mozart's and Haydn's pure classical form and initiated the Romantic period, might have composed had he had access to modern hearing-device technology. Then again, it could have been his deafness that drove him to create the masterpieces he did once he became isolated in the sanctum of his own inner voices.

Beethoven didn't even complete his famous Symphony no. 5 in C Minor with its stirring opening theme until around 1808, when his hearing loss was marked and he was well acquainted with despondency.* Had they worked, the ear trumpets Mälzel made for Beethoven could have spared one of history's greatest musical geniuses the physical and emotional torment that ravaged his life; perhaps they could have enabled him to give to the world an even more glorious body of music. But besides the immortal music he did compose, among the items Beethoven left to posterity are two sets of ear trumpets, which, in their futility, demonstrate that despite a debilitating physical handicap, Beethoven's genius and determination prevailed, enabling the great maestro to enrich the ages.

LOCATION: Beethoven House, Bonn, Germany.†

---

*The first four notes of Symphony no. 5 were used during World War II as the station identification signal by the BBC European Service and as an Allied signal meaning "Victory"; in Morse code, the sequence of three shorts and a long stands for V.
†Beethoven's hearing aids came into the possession of his clerk, Anton Schindler, probably as an inheritance from the composer. Schindler donated the hearing aids to the Königliche Bibliothek in Berlin, which in 1889 presented them to the Beethoven House on the recommendation of the king of Prussia.

Harrison's Peace Pipes

~~~~~~

DATE: 1814.

WHAT THEY ARE: Two of the three surviving peace pipes presented by Major General William Henry Harrison to the Delaware, Shawnee, and Wyandot Indian tribes at the Second Treaty Council of Greenville, Ohio, on behalf of President James Madison.

WHAT THEY LOOK LIKE: The pipes are made of sterling silver and have an S-shaped stem and an urn-shaped bowl with a hinged cover with beaded edges and acanthus leaves in Federal style engraved at the base. The bowls are 2 inches in diameter. From the mouthpiece to the bowl the overall length of the Delaware pipe is 16 inches, the Shawnee pipe 20 inches. The bowls have four oval medallions adorned and engraved as follows: a scene of a Native American and an American general shaking hands; an eagle derived from the Great Seal of the United States; two hands clasped above the inscription "Peace and Friendship"; and the legend, for the Delaware pipe, "Presented by Maj. Gen. Harrison to the Delaware Tribe of Indians 1814," and for the Shawnee pipe, "Presented by Maj. Gen. Harrison on behalf of the U.S. to the Shawanoese Tribe of Indians 1814." The pipes were originally identical, but the stem of the Delaware pipe was broken and the repair altered the angle of the stem, which perhaps accounts for its stem being shorter than that of the Shawnee pipe.

His name was Wabozo, or Snowshoe Hare, but he was commonly called the Mysterious One because he could change his appearance to any shape he desired, just as the hare can metamorphose from brown to snowy white during the winter. Born to a mortal mother and an immortal father countless ages ago, the young man headed west over prairies and plains and mountains in search of the Creator—his father—because of his growing concern that his people were becoming self-absorbed and losing their spiritual identity. And when Wabozo found the Creator, his eternal father gave him a pipe for his people to smoke so that their thoughts and prayers and words would become visible to the Creator in the form of tobacco smoke, and the Creator would be able to give the people proper guidance. Over time the peace pipe born of this Native American legend became not just a holy object, a tool of prayer, but a sign or offering of friendship.

In 1814 the U.S. government presented three peace pipes to indigenous tribes as gifts of thanks for their pledge to fight on America's side against the British in the War of 1812. While these frontier pipes were strictly items of diplomacy, compositionally and structurally inconsistent with an authentic peace pipe—a sacred instrument of prayer—they nonetheless represented the amity between the two groups and their evolving relations. But for the Indians, who entered into a second treaty at Greenville, Ohio, in the wake of disastrous defeats and the death of the Shawnee warrior Tecumseh, the agreement more or less meant the beginning of their end. Weakened until they could no longer significantly resist the Americans, who usurped and settled their land, the Indians faced the dawn of a new era, and the pipes became tangible symbols of their reluctant acquiescence to the new order.

Some historical context will shed light on the circumstances that led up to the presentation of the silver pipes in 1814. The Revolutionary War brought independence to America but left Americans anxious to push the country's borders westward, even if such settlement encroached on the natural rights of the native inhabitants of the lands. For its part, the U.S. government had tried to prevent Americans from settling on Indian land. When war with England broke out in 1775, the Continental Congress had ordered Americans not to settle on Indian land out of fear that the Indians, who were fierce and powerful fighters, would side with the British in their fight against the colonists. The Continental Congress's policy was only moderately successful. Although force was sometimes used to keep colonists from moving onto Indian land, the settlers were resolute in their determination to live, hunt, and work on lands to the west. This resulted in fierce Indian attacks on colonial settlements in Kentucky, Ohio, New York, and Pennsylvania, where the Iroquois and other tribes lived.

The Native American tribes were still viable after the Revolutionary War, so it was in the interests of the new American government to keep relations between the Indians and American citizens cordial and peaceful. It was the position of the American government that Indian land belonged to the Indians, and the government's War Department set up posts in Indian country not only to maintain cordiality but to establish a system of fair trade with them through recognized agents and prevent unscrupulous white traders from swindling the natives.

Still, Americans turned their backs on government policy and continued to settle lands not ceded. In defiance of the encroachment, the Indians, despite the treaties they negotiated with the U.S. government, menaced the settlers. American troops were sent to impose peace, and one such expedition, led by General Arthur St. Clair, resulted in a clash with Indians on the Wabash River during the summer of 1791 and ended in the loss of six hundred soldiers.

With Indian raids in the west endangering American settlement, President George Washington ordered General Anthony Wayne in the spring of 1792 to lead troops in the Northwest Territory against the frontier Indians. The following year Wayne commenced a campaign against the Indians, who were receiving encouragement from British troops in the area. As they moved north, building forts along their line of progress, Wayne's troops were attacked by Indians, but on August 20, 1794, "Mad Anthony" brought about the defeat of the united Northwest Indians at Fallen Timbers in Ohio, and then continued to harass them and destroy their villages without interference from the British. Wayne finally called a meeting, and from mid-June through early August 1795, delegates from the Delaware, Shawnee, Wyandot, Kaskaskia, Miami, Pottawatomie, Chippewa, Wea, Kickapoo, Ottawa, Eel River, and Piankashaw met at Fort Greenville, Ohio. The defeated and demoralized chiefs were compelled to comply with Wayne's demands, and in the Treaty of Greenville, signed on August 3, 1795, they ceded Indian claims to the Ohio Valley, involving some 25,000 square miles.

On August 7, General Wayne announced to the gathering of tribes: "Listen! All you Nations present. I have hitherto addressed you as brothers. I now adopt you all, in the name of the President and Fifteen Great Fires of America, as their children, and you are so accordingly. The medals which I shall have the honor to deliver to you, you will consider as presented by the hands of your father, the Fifteen Fires of America. These you will hand down to your children's children, in commemoration of this day—a day in which the United States of America gives peace to you and all your Nations, and receives you and them under the protecting wings of her eagle." The next day the medals were distributed to the tribes, and some time after this first Greenville treaty engraved silver peace medals were distributed to

signers of the treaty, including Chief White Swan of the Wea tribe, a sub-
tribe of the Miami (Kansas City Museum, Kansas City, Missouri), and
Chief Tarhe (also known as "The Crane") of the Wyandot (Historical
Society of Pennsylvania, Philadelphia).

Soon, Americans settled the Ohio Valley and moved on further—to lands
inhabited by the dislodged Indians. Tecumseh, a brilliant chief of the
Shawnee tribe who envisioned an Indian nation separate from that of the
white men, traveled far and wide in an attempt to unite the many Indian
tribes in resisting American attempts to take still more of their land, but he
was successful only to a limited extent. Some Indian chiefs such as the
Miami chief Little Turtle instead advocated peace and continued to enter
into treaties with the U.S. government.

The governor of the territory of Indiana—later the states of Indiana,
Michigan, Wisconsin, and Illinois, and a small part of Minnesota—William
Henry Harrison, was concerned by the Shawnees' disruption of peace in the
Wabash Valley and angered by Tecumseh's refusal to recognize the Indian
land cessions. Harrison made it his goal to expel the Indians from the
Northwest Territory, from which the Indiana Territory had been carved,
and which now consisted essentially of the land that later formed the state
of Ohio. Harrison gathered an army at the Tippecanoe River, near the village of Tecumseh's brother, Prophet. The Native Americans, alarmed,
advanced on the white soldiers, but they were repelled and their village
torched.

During the War of 1812 Tecumseh joined forces with the British, hoping
that a Redcoat victory would enable him to realize his dream of a separate
Indian nation. But the British were defeated, and in the Battle of the Thames
in Canada, the Shawnee Indian leader was killed while fighting off the
advancing Americans. Debilitated and now further set upon by encroach-
ing settlers, the Indians were compelled through additional treaties to cede
more lands. The Second Treaty Council of Greenville, Ohio, was held on
July 8, 1814, and not only provided for the Indians to give up more land
but served to formally uphold the cessions made over the years and to recognize the Indians' support of the United States in its fight for independence
from England. Here, on behalf of President James Madison, Major General
William Henry Harrison presented silver peace pipes to the Delaware,
Shawnee, and Wyandot Indian tribes that attended the treaty council.
Representatives from each tribe received a pipe from Harrison; for the
Shawnee, it was Blackhoof, one of his tribe's delegates to the U.S. govern-
ment; for the Wyandot it was Chief Tarhe.

Over the years the U.S. government had bestowed gifts on Indian tribes when they ceded land to the government, but the Harrison peace pipes were the most elegantly adorned pipes it ever commissioned for the Indians. They were not meant to be smoked—their silver composition and the shape of their bowls would have made that difficult—but were rather "presentation pieces," made to symbolize the cordial relations between the giver and the recipients, and at the treaty Harrison expounded on the meaning of the pipes. Authentic Indian pipes, those smoked for religious purposes, were usually made of stone and wood. Harrison's long, slender pipes with their engraved silver bowls were all in one piece as opposed to the normal *pwagan,* or peace pipe, which comprised separate bowls and stems joined together to form one piece. As most of the Indian language was (and remains) verbs, or action words, so too was the peace pipe considered a tool of action, as it created a link to the Creator.

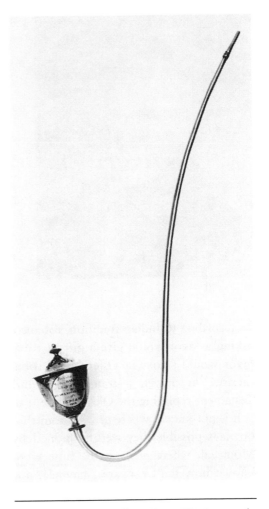

The pipe given by William Henry Harrison to the Shawnees in 1814. Its stem is intact, unlike the surviving Delaware pipe, which has a repair made on its stem.

But a peace pipe was also a religious action tool, in that its *pwag ne,* or rising smoke, made the smoker's thoughts and words and prayers visible to the Creator. The Creator in the Indian concept was not an entity on whom was bestowed worship and praise, as in the Judeo-Christian concept, but was rather considered an egalitarian being, having created the earth equal to heaven. Different Indian tribes have different traditions about the origin of their pipes. For several tribes in the Ohio Valley, it derived from Wabozo.

William Henry Harrison's defeat of the Indians in November 1811 led to great popularity, an 1840 campaign slogan with running mate John Tyler of "Tippecanoe and Tyler too!" and a decisive election to the office of president of the United States.

According to Indian tradition, tobacco is the means of prayer. A person asking a favor would give a gift of tobacco, and the person fulfilling the favor would smoke it. Offerings of tobacco had long ago replaced blood sacrifice in prayer, a transition in Indian theology akin to the New Testament replacing the Old Testament in Christianity.

It is not known where or by whom the Harrison treaty pipes were made, but it is possible they were fashioned by a silversmith in Philadelphia or Montreal, where pipes at the time were sometimes made. It is also not known how the Delaware, Shawnee, and Wyandot pipes were used after their receipt from Harrison, since they were not smoking pipes (later testing of the pipes revealed that the Shawnee pipe was never smoked, but there was some evidence of smoking in the Delaware pipe); presumably the pipes were kept wrapped and brought out on special occasions. The Wyandot pipe seems to have disappeared from history, and its whereabouts are unknown.

The injustice of Americans exacting cessions from Indians whose land they trespassed and settled on is manifest. Indeed, the first colony in North America was founded by the English navigator Sir Humphrey Gilbert, whose 1578 charter authorized him "to discover and to take possession of such remote, heathen and barbarous lands as were not actually possessed by a Christian prince or people." Unwittingly, perhaps, the spirit of this haughty notion was aggressively embraced by Americans in their newly independent republic in the late eighteenth century. But the acquisition of land from the North American Indians was actually nothing new at this time; the French, British, Dutch, and Spanish over the course of a few hundred years had all colonized North America, trading for land or seizing it in battles.

The peace pipes presented to the Indian tribes at the Second Treaty Council of Greenville played an important role in the negotiation of the treaty in which the Delaware "ceded to the U.S. all claim to the thirteen sections [a section is 640 acres] of land given to them by an act of Congress March 3, 1807." The Delaware, Shawnee, and Wyandot were granted a nine-square-mile tract of land with unrestricted rights.

Today Harrison's peace pipes are not just reminders of the treaties early-nineteenth-century American Indians were compelled to enter into, but of the natives' spirit of willingness, if not forced resignation, to live in harmony with white men even when they had to give up their land to do so. Indeed, besides being symbols of the establishment of relations between Indians and early Americans, the pipes are emblematic of the early evolution of the midwestern United States. At the time, the pipes testified to the United States' appreciation of the concessions made by the Indians and its hope for renewed friendship, a bond which would unfortunately be stained by further bloodshed on both sides as the rest of the century unfolded.

LOCATIONS:

Delaware peace pipe: National Museum of Natural History, Washington, D.C.

Shawnee peace pipe: The Kansas City Museum, Kansas City, Missouri.*

---

*The Delaware peace pipe came to the National Museum of Natural History, which is part of the Smithsonian Institution, as a private gift from Victor Evans. The Shawnee peace pipe was acquired by a Civil War veteran named Daniel Dyer, who, with his wife, Ida, collected Indian relics. Daniel Dyer became an Indian agent, first at the Quapaw Agency in Kansas, where he appears to have been respected by Native Americans, then at Fort Reno, Oklahoma, where his habit of requesting soldiers every time he thought the Indians were ready to go on the warpath caused Generals Nelson A. Miles and Philip Sheridan to come to investigate; after one summer at Fort Reno, Dyer was removed from his post as agent. Although most of the artifacts, particularly the quality pieces, in the "Dyer Collection" were acquired by Ida, the Dyers divorced in 1897 (for the second time; they first divorced in 1876 and then remarried the same year) and the entire collection became the property of Daniel. In 1898 the Dyer Collection went on loan to the Kansas City Board of Education, and it became the board's property in 1910. In 1939, several small museums and historical societies merged into the Kansas City Museum, and the Dyer Collection, along with the Kansas City Board of Education's collection of artifacts, became one of the museum's founding collections.

John Adams's Pigtail

‫ᄋᄂᄋᄋᄂᄋᄋᄂᄋᄋᄂᄋᄋᄂᄋᄋᄂᄋᄋᄂᄋᄋᄂᄋᄋᄂᄋᄋᄂᄋᄋᄂᄋᄋᄂᄋᄋᄂᄋᄋᄂᄋᄋᄂ‬

DATE: 1829.

WHAT IT IS: The pigtail of the last *Bounty* mutineer to survive on Pitcairn Island.

WHAT IT LOOKS LIKE: The hair is braided and bound at one end, and is 7½ inches in length. It is a light sandy color.

It is a quaint relic of a man whose lifespan encompassed the American Revolution, the French Revolution, Horatio Nelson and the Battle of Trafalgar, the Napoleonic Wars, and the War of 1812, but whose own life was imbued with adventure and romance half a world away from those momentous events. One can imagine that this relic, a pigtail, imparted a distinctive look to the man, John Adams—the seaman, the mutineer, the fugitive, the compatriot, the progenitor, the last survivor, the teacher, the missionary, the New World paterfamilias—who in his remote world struggled from the depths of fear to the peak of sublime happiness. Evoking the man, the pigtail of John Adams opens the storybook of history to one of the most compelling chapters of human drama and pathos on the high seas, and its extraordinary aftermath.

Pitcairn Island, the South Pacific, January 1790. The *Bounty* sailed cautiously along the rocky coast of the island, its crew apprehensive about dangers lurking beyond the shores. After more than one hundred days at sea, the men and women aboard the 215-ton ship were anxious to disembark and settle into a refuge they could make their home. But it would have to meet their peculiar needs. They had been searching for an island that was uninhabited and fertile, and which ships cruising the South Pacific would probably not draw near. This seemed the ideal choice. Fletcher Christian, who had led the mutiny aboard the *Bounty*, read about this island in a travelogue of the South Seas he found in Lieutenant Bligh's quarters after Bligh and eighteen crew members were put out to sea in the ship's launch, but the island's position was charted incorrectly, and it had proved difficult to find.

The occupants on board this pirated vessel were nine of the *Bounty* mutineers—Fletcher Christian, Edward Young, Matthew Quintal, John Mills, Alexander Smith, John Williams, William Brown, Isaac Martin, and William M'Koy—and twelve women and six men from the South Pacific islands of Otaheite and Tubuaï. The crew of the *Bounty* was coming to start a new life, to stake a claim in paradise and isolate themselves from the rest of the world. None on board could have imagined the events that would unfold, what fate lay in store for them as the *Bounty* cruised in, ready to launch an exploratory party to survey this Eden before stepping into it.

How these men and women came to arrive on Pitcairn is a vital component of the tale. It had all begun in England with the government-ordered botanical mission of the *Bounty*, an exploring ship that was to obtain breadfruit plants on Otaheite, or Tahiti, and transport them to the West Indies, where they would be introduced as food to the native slaves there. England, by the late eighteenth century, was the strongest colonial empire in the world, and it sought lands unclaimed by European powers that could be of benefit to its commerce. English explorers such as James Cook and Samuel Wallis sailed the Pacific and visited many islands in the 1760s, but it was on July 2, 1767, on Lieutenant Philip Carteret's worldwide voyage aboard the *Swallow*, that a young midshipman named Robert Pitcairn was the first to spot the uninhabited island that was named for him.

The *Bounty*, fitted in 1787 at Deptford, England, for its mission, had more than forty men aboard when it left for the South Pacific. Lieutenant William Bligh, who had sailed with James Cook in his second expedition around the world—during which the breadfruit plant was discovered on Otaheite—was the commander of the ship, with Fletcher Christian serving as the master's mate. The vessel set out in December 1787 and soon incurred heavy damage from a storm and rough waters, making it necessary to lay over in the Canary Islands for a refitting before continuing.

The ship picked up the breadfruit plants in Otaheite, but its crew remained on the island for half a year making further collections. On this tropical island, no doubt more than a few of the crew members were captivated by its charms—the breathtaking landscape, the simple, peaceful lifestyle, and, not least, the beauty of the women.

Finally the *Bounty* left Otaheite for the West Indies with its breadfruit cargo, but when it was about three hundred miles out to sea, several members of the crew mutinied. Over the years various dramatizations of the revolt have villainized Lieutenant Bligh for treating his crew harshly. But while he was irascible, he was not as tyrannical as were other contemporary ship commanders: for example, flogging on board the *Bounty* was substantially less frequent than on other vessels. The cause of the mutiny has been examined and debated, but most likely it was a combination of Bligh's vituperative language and the sensitivity of Fletcher Christian, who inspired some of the crew to revolt early in the morning of April 28, 1789.

Sometime after four A.M., Christian and three men—John Mills, Thomas Burkitt, and Charles Churchill—burst into Bligh's cabin, yanked him out of bed, and tied his hands tightly behind his back. The mutineers, armed with muskets, machetes, and bayonets, led Bligh to the deck. One of the men following with a loaded firearm was a seaman who went by the name Alexander Smith, but whose real name was John Adams. While this sedition was transpiring, other crew members were forcibly restrained below. The bo'sun was brought up on deck, and under the threat of immediate death was ordered to raise a launch. Christian had decided that Bligh and his party would be put to sea in the ship's cutter, which was in a deteriorated condition and meant to hold no more than ten persons, but the frantic appeals of the bo'sun and some others persuaded him to use the longboat instead. As this whole drastic enterprise was proceeding, Bligh was urging his captors to come to their senses and importuned the other crew members not to participate in it. He was repeatedly warned, "Hold your tongue, sir, or you are dead this instant."

Some men were forced into the longboat immediately; others were permitted to collect food, supplies, and navigational instruments before leaving the ship. The ship's officers were ordered into the boat while Christian gripped Bligh's hand rope. Bligh dared the armed mutineers to shoot, but instead they uncocked their weapons. Still others of the crew had to be prevented from leaving the ship with Bligh, and they cried out to the captain to remember that they were not participants in the mutiny. Others followed into the twenty-three-foot launch, including, finally, Bligh, who was untied just before he climbed in. Bligh, who had made two previous voyages with Christian, asked him if his action was a proper restitution for the friendship he had shown him, and Christian replied in an agitated tone, "That, Captain Bligh, that is the thing. I am in hell. I am in hell!" It was an answer that was to bring a degree of satisfaction to the commander during the perilous voyage he was to make. By means of the rope that tied the

This 1851 lithograph by Royal Navy Lieutenant Conway Shipley depicts a view of Pitcairn Island showing Fletcher Christian's house.

Bounty and the launch together, the mutineers moved the launch astern, threw some additional provisions out to them, including scraps of pork, and then taunted the nineteen unfortunate men aboard the launch before setting it adrift.

The men in the launch were then faced with the terrifying prospect of having to navigate their way a great distance in the vulnerable open boat with a meager supply of food. They were near Tofoa, so they decided to stop off at the island to build up their food reserves. They collected some coconuts and breadfruit, but as they were casting off they were attacked by a group of natives, who hurled stones at them. One man was killed before they cast off, and even afloat they weren't safe from the natives' hostility. The natives pursued the fleeing Englishmen in canoes. It was only after the occupants of the open boat threw articles of their clothing in the water that the natives' attention was diverted and they could get away.

The difficulties the men in the open boat encountered in trying to return to England were substantial, and it is a testament to the excellent navigational skills and foresight of Lieutenant Bligh that the boat did not capsize during any of the storms it encountered, nor did the men starve, despite the scant provisions aboard. In this small boat the eighteen remaining men had scarcely room to move their limbs, were constantly wet, and continually felt the chill of the night "with nothing to cover them except the heavens." Amazingly, without any catastrophes or other fatalities, the open boat reached the Indonesian island of Timor, some four thousand miles from where they started, and the displaced *Bounty* crew finally returned to England in another vessel.

Bligh's reception in England was sympathetic and positive, and the government set out to punish the mutineers and demonstrate that such a reprehensible act would not be tolerated. Mutiny was punishable by death according to the 1749 Articles of War, and the mutineers were undoubtedly aware of this. With a capital crime committed and the pride of the Royal Navy at stake, a ship of war, the *Pandora*, with 160 men aboard, was sent to Otaheite to pick up the mutineers. If they had left the island, the *Pandora* was to search every other island in the South Pacific until as many mutineers as possible could be found, captured, and returned to England to stand trial in the king's court.

During the time of Bligh's struggle to return to England and the subsequent launch of the *Pandora*, the mutineers in the *Bounty* had been trying to carve out a new life for themselves as fugitives in the Pacific. The *Bounty*, under the leadership of Fletcher Christian, sailed to Tubuaï, a nineteen-square-mile island that is part of a huge chain of islands extending eight hundred miles, where the natives proved unfriendly. In need of food sources and companionship, the Englishmen sailed back to Otaheite to obtain animals and to try to convince women, including those they had known while previously on the island collecting the breadfruit plants, to return with them to Tubuaï. Several women did go, but once they were back in Tubuaï, discontent flourished among the mutineers. It was finally decided that those who desired would be dropped off at Otaheite, and the remainder, with their women and any additional women and manservants they could acquire at Otaheite, would move on to another destination.

After a stop on Otaheite, they arrived at Pitcairn early in 1790, almost nine months after the mutiny. Some men from the *Bounty* took a small boat to the island to survey it. After they found the island much as described in Bligh's travelogue, the rest of the party was allowed to go ashore. All the ship's stores were soon unloaded, which probably included John Adams's sea chest (National Maritime Museum, London).

Christian apportioned the island to the nine mutineers; each would have land to build a home and a future. Each Englishman had a woman, and a few women who were left over went to live with the Otaheitan man-servants.

A few days after the settlers' arrival, the *Bounty* was run into rocks so her contents could be taken out and the animals on board landed. The ship was then torched on Christian's command—no doubt so that no one could leave and reveal the fugitives' whereabouts, and so the ship itself would not signal their presence. But the destruction of the *Bounty* also had the effect of marooning the pilgrims.

Despite the constraints and stresses under which they carved out new lives on the island, the residents of Pitcairn Island enjoyed an auspicious beginning. The island was livable and met their needs. They were in a sanctuary of isolation and security even if Bligh should make it back to England, which would assure a sentence of death for each one of them. But then the male inhabitants of the island began to quarrel.

According to Sir John Barrow, who in 1831 wrote what may be the definitive account of the entire *Bounty* affair, *The Eventful History of the Mutiny and Piratical Seizure of H.M.S. Bounty: Its Causes and Consequences,* Fletcher Christian's remorse over his actions on board the *Bounty* began to get the better of him. Barrow quoted a statement that John Adams was later to make: "It was clear enough that this misguided and ill-fated young man was never happy after the rash and criminal step he had taken; that he was always sullen and morose; and committed so many acts of wanton oppression, as very soon incurred the hatred and detestation of his companions in crime, over who he practised that same overbearing conduct, of which he accused his commander Bligh." But then again Barrow was to report another comment Adams made subsequently that painted a diametrically opposite account of the lead mutineer, wherein Christian is seen as having a constantly happy disposition.

In any case, with the native women as their wives, the Englishmen started families. But approximately two years after their arrival, a series of tragic events occurred to ignite the simmering ill will.

While gathering birds' eggs on a cliff, the wife of John Williams fell and died, and subsequently Williams usurped the wife of one of the native servants to be his new wife. The servant, clearly wronged, was understandably upset by this action. With his fellow natives, who sympathized with him and like him were angry at the Englishmen for other forms of maltreatment, he planned revenge—not just on the culprit Williams but on all the white men, who might otherwise repeat the same action under similar circumstances.

The Englishmen found out about the assassination plot of the native men with the help of the women, who, in a little ditty they composed, suggested the bloodletting yet to follow: "Why does black man sharpen axe?/ To kill white man," the women chanted. With the mutineers after them, the wronged Otaheitan husband and a male companion tried to hide, but their fellow natives killed them as a means of pacifying the Englishmen and perhaps of saving their own lives. The peace would only be temporary, unfortunately.

England, 1792. Life-and-death court trials were held for those mutineers apprehended by the crew of the *Pandora.* The mission had been calamitous, exacting a toll in lives far greater than the number of people who were to be brought to justice.

The *Pandora* had sailed to Otaheite, where it found and seized sixteen of the twenty-five mutineers. A search for the remaining mutineers, including Fletcher Christian, the ringleader, was fruitless. So the *Pandora* headed back to England, but on its way, on August 28, 1791, in the Santa Cruz Islands, the ship suffered a horrible wreck in which thirty-five men aboard were drowned, including four of the shackled *Bounty* prisoners. The voyage was completed in launches, and the harshness of famine, cold, and fatigue suffered by Bligh and his men in their open boat was ironically repeated. The commander of the *Pandora,* Captain Edward Edwards, had dispensed severe and unpitying treatment to the captured mutineers, whose misery was compounded by the prospect of having to stand trial upon their return. Aboard the *Pandora,* before returning to England, one prisoner was murdered by another, and the victim's friends exacted retribution in kind. After their court trial in 1792, of the surviving ten *Bounty* prisoners who returned from Otaheite, three were hanged, three were sentenced to die but received a royal pardon, and four were acquitted.

Pitcairn Island, 1793. For more than a year there had been peace on the island, but the abusive treatment the surviving Otaheitans received from the Europeans continued to gnaw at them until they resolved to do away with the former seamen altogether. One day in October, while the white men were working on their land, the Otaheitans gathered muskets and hammers and proceeded to the Englishmen's homes. They killed John Williams, Fletcher Christian, John Mills, William Brown, and Isaac Martin. Matthew Quintal and William M'Koy fled to a mountain. Edward Young, whom the Otaheitan women favored, was hidden by them, and John Adams was shot in the shoulder but negotiated a peace for himself.

With five of the mutineers dead and the Otaheitans now in command of the island, the natives planned to seize the widows of those they killed. But the women, incensed at this notion, struck back. With the participation of Edward Young, all the Otaheitan men were killed. This left four of the Englishmen and ten women. For the next five years there was peace on the island.

But the downfall of paradise seemed to be the order of things. William M'Koy, who had been employed in the making of alcohol before becoming a seaman on the *Bounty,* successfully applied his knowledge to produce spirits on Pitcairn, becoming a heavy drinker often subject to raging alcoholic bouts. During one such rage he killed himself by hurling himself from a rock. Matthew Quintal was the next to cause his own demise, although his death left the stain of blood on Adams and Young. Quintal's wife had been killed in an accident while hunting birds' eggs, and now Quintal wanted to appropriate another woman. Despite the abundance of Otaheitan females on Pitcairn, and despite the previously fatal example, Quintal insisted on having the wife of one of his compatriots. He then tried to kill both Adams and Young but was stopped. However, the two latter men, surmising that Quintal had murder on his mind and might well be successful the next time, felt he was too grave a threat to their lives and used a hatchet to eliminate him.

Now, of all the men to come to Pitcairn, only Young and Adams were left. Sick of the bloodshed, they set themselves on a religious path of repentance, holding "regular church services" and instilling a sense of piousness and devotion into the island's children, who now numbered nineteen. But Young's days were numbered also, as he succumbed to an asthma condition not long afterward.

This left John Adams with eight or nine women and the numerous children of the dead *Bounty* mutineers. The little band of survivors assiduously applied themselves to working the land, growing bananas and yams. But could they stay alive? And would Adams continue to escape capture? He was consumed with the dispiriting notion that England would send a ship to bring him home and hang him.

But Pitcairn being cut off from civilization, Adams could not have known that with international wars and other dramatic national and world events transpiring, little thought would be given to the *Bounty* mutineers who had mysteriously vanished. With no word about them as time passed, some assumed they had been swallowed by the sea or slaughtered by natives. In any case, the price paid for the capture of the other mutineers was too high, and the national affairs of England too frenetic, to devote money and resources to hunting down the nine men who might or might not be alive in another part of the world.

Pitcairn Island, 1808. The *Topaz,* an American trading ship on a sealing expedition commanded by Captain Mayhew Folger, happened on the island. It was the first contact the residents of Pitcairn had had with the outside world in more than nineteen years. Of course it was of concern to Adams whether the officers aboard this ship might try to convey him back to England to stand trial.

Folger's acquaintance with the people on Pitcairn was a mutually satisfying one, and his discovery of John Adams, the *Bounty* mutineer who went by the name of Alexander Smith, was passed along and reached the English Admiralty in May 1809. As related by Sir John Barrow, an English officer's report of Folger's experience on Pitcairn read:

> Captain Folger, of the American ship *Topaz,* of Boston, relates that upon landing on Pitcairn's Island, in lat. 25° 2' S., long 130° W., he found there an Englishman of the name of Alexander Smith, the only person remaining of the nine that escaped in his Majesty's late ship *Bounty,* Captain W. Bligh. . . . There are now some grown-up men and women, children of the mutineers, on the island, the whole population amounting to about thirty-five, who acknowledge Smith as father and commander of them all; they all speak English, and have been educated by him (as Captain Folger represents) in a religious and moral way. . . . Smith gave to Captain Folger a chronometer made by Kendall, which was taken from him by the Governor of Juan Fernandez.

With this report, the outside world would not only learn for the first time what had happened to the missing *Bounty* mutineers, but would discover an unknown society on a remote South Seas island.

Pitcairn Island, September 1814. At a distance of about half a dozen leagues, two British ships of war, the *Briton* and the *Tagus,* spotted the island. The captains did not know quite what to make of this, since Pitcairn, the only island charted in the area, had a supposed longitude of 133° 24' W, and the *Tagus* observed this island as having a latitude of 24° 40' S and a longitude of 130° 24' W. The next morning the frigates moved in, and to their crews' surprise, they sighted huts. The surprise increased when two youths dressed in nothing but loincloths suddenly appeared and descended a hill carrying canoes over their shoulders. The two natives set their canoes in the water and paddled out to the ships. On reaching the vessels, one asked, in English no less, "Won't you heave us a rope now?"

When the older of the two youths was asked who he was, he identified himself as Thursday October Christian, and then without hesitation proceeded to offer details about himself and the island. He was the son of Fletcher Christian, he said, one of the *Bounty* mutineers, who was now dead. Thursday had taken as a wife one of the Otaheitan women that the mutineers had brought with them, and she was much older than he. Christian was twenty-four years old and a strapping six feet tall. His friend was George Young, son of the late *Bounty* midshipman, Edward Young. Sir Thomas Staines of the *Briton* invited the two islanders below deck for a meal, and was surprised once again when, with the meal set before them, the two young men stood up and recited a prayer.

The two youths surveyed the ship with wonder. Of this John Barrow wrote, "The youths were themselves greatly surprised at the sight of so many novel objects—the size of the ship—of the guns, and everything around them. Observing a cow, they were at first somewhat alarmed, and expressed a doubt whether it was a huge goat or a horned dog, these being the only two species of quadrupeds they had ever seen. A little dog amused them much. 'Oh! what a pretty little thing it is!' exclaimed Young. 'I know it is a dog, for I have heard of such an animal.'"

The two youths also told the captains that there was one last Englishman surviving on Pitcairn. He was known on the *Bounty* as Alexander Smith, but his real name was John Adams. Intrigued by the whole episode and the youths' stories, Staines and Captain Pipon of the *Tagus* decided to visit the island and have a look about for themselves.

The two boys took the captains back, whereupon they were greeted by John Adams and his old, frail, and nearly blind Otaheitan wife. The sight of the king's uniform initially made Adams think his freedom was in danger, but the fact that the officers were alone and unarmed convinced him that they were not a threat. On the island the two captains found about forty-six inhabitants, and they were immediately struck by the physical attributes of the young people born there, as Barrow was to note: "The young men all born on the island were finely formed, athletic and handsome—their countenances open and pleasing, indicating much benevolence and goodness of heart, but the young women particularly were objects of attraction, being tall, robust, and beautifully formed, their faces beaming with smiles, and indicating unruffled good humour; while their manners and demeanour would have done honour to the most enlightened people on earth."

Back in his hut, Adams expressed his fears to the two captains that they were going to take him back to England. He had surmised correctly that the British government had been out to capture him along with the other mutineers, but was not aware that its pursuit of the missing mutineers had been largely abandoned.*

Both Staines and Pipon allayed Adams's fears. Staines said that he had never even heard of John Adams, and Pipon's sentiment echoed the remark he would shortly make, which was that although legally "they could only consider him in the light of a criminal of the deepest dye, yet that it would have been an act of the greatest cruelty and inhumanity to have taken him away from his little family, who, in such a case, would have been left to experience the greatest misery and distress, and ultimately, in all probability, would have perished of want."

Adams lied about his prominent role in the *Bounty* mutiny, saying that he was ill in bed when he was awakened by a disturbance and forced to participate in the rebellion. But he said he would return to England to face justice. Hearing this, one of his daughters nearly became hysterical; the other women present began to weep, and all the other inhabitants were shocked and extremely upset. When Pipon said that Adams would not have to go back to England, all the natives were visibly elated and grateful for the captains' great humanity.

Adams assured his visitors that morality of the highest standards existed on the island. He advised all the young women, who called him their father, to delay marriage until they acquired enough property to ensure the proper upbringing of children. By Adams's decree, a boy on the island had to be twenty to marry, a girl eighteen.

Sir Thomas Staines, who served under Horatio Nelson and had been knighted in 1809, transmitted to the British Admiralty in Valparaiso the following month a report of his accidental discovery of Pitcairn:

---

*When the government sent the *Pandora* to the Pacific to capture the *Bounty* fugitives, it had issued descriptions of the wanted men. Adams's description, which of course was unknown to him, read:

Alex: Smith 22 (age) Ab. 5ft. 5 in. High. Brown Complexion. Brown Hair, Strong Made, very much pitted with the Small Pox, and very much tatowed on his Body, Legs Arms and Feet, and has a Scar on his Right Foot where he has been cut with a Wood Axe.

I fell in with an island where none is laid down in the Admiralty or other charts, according to the several chronometers of the *Briton* and *Tagus*. I therefore hove to, until daylight and then closed to ascertain whether it was inhabited, which I soon discovered it to be, and, to my great astonishment, found that every individual on the island (forty in number), spoke very good English. They proved to be the descendants of the deluded crew of the *Bounty*, who, from Otaheite, proceeded to the above-mentioned island, where the ship was burnt.

Christian appeared to have been the leader and sole cause of the mutiny in that ship. A venerable old man named John Adams, is the only surviving Englishman of those who last quitted Otaheite in her, and whose exemplary conduct, and fatherly care of the whole lot of the little colony, could not but command admiration. The pious manner in which all those born on the island have been reared, the correct sense of religion which has been instilled into their young minds by this old man, has given him the pre-eminence over the whole of them, to whom they look up as the father of one and the whole family.

. . . The island must undoubtedly be that called Pitcairn, although erroneously laid down in the charts. We had the altitude of the meridian sun close to it, which gave us 25° 4' S. latitude, and 130° 25' W. longitude, by the chronometers of the *Briton* and *Tagus*.

. . . I cannot, however, refrain from offering my opinion, that it is well worthy the attention of our laudable religious societies, particularly that for propagating the Christian religion, the whole of the inhabitants speaking the Otaheitan tongue as well as the English . . .

Pitcairn Island, 1825. During this year the last of only a handful of major ships that would visit Pitcairn in John Adams's lifetime came upon it. Other smaller vessels may have happened upon the island. One that did was a whaling vessel, from which a man named John Buffet was so taken with the inhabitants of Pitcairn that he decided to remain as a teacher and integrate himself with the community as a full-fledged member. But now the *Blossom*, a warship exploring Pitcairn's neighborhood in the South Pacific, sighted the island and ran in for a visit. Before the *Blossom* could venture close in, a boat carrying John Adams and some of the island's youths came out to greet her. Adams was in his early sixties now and portly. His youthful brown hair had disappeared on top and was white on the sides.

Probably for most of his adult life, John Adams had worn his hair long in the back. At the time of the *Bounty* mutiny in 1789, seamen commonly plaited the back of their long hair into pigtails; it was not their custom to wear wigs. Short hair became fashionable some time after the mutiny, but in his isolation in the South Pacific, Adams would not have been aware of this.

The last surviving mutineer on Pitcairn related the *Bounty* affair to Captain F. W. Beechy and his crew, although his story was laced with inaccuracies. A party from the *Blossom* was taken in pairs by the young natives to the island because of the difficult landing conditions. They were led to the village on the island, which was in an elevated area hidden under trees.

The *Blossom* landing party was made to feel they were welcome and honored guests on Pitcairn. They were given comfortable sleeping accommodations, and their rests were smooth save for certain interruptions. As John Barrow noted, "After the lights [torches made of *doodoe* nuts strung upon the fibers of a palm leaf] were put out, the evening hymn was chanted by the whole family in the middle of the room. At early dawn they were also awaked by their morning hymn and the family devotion; after which the islanders all set out to their several occupations."

There was a sense of unaffectedness and purity on Pitcairn that outsiders from the civilized world would have some difficulty getting accustomed to. But in this regard, if modesty proved to be an obstacle it was only temporary, as one *Blossom* guest reported:

> On looking around the apartment, though it contained several beds, we found no partition, curtain, or screen; they had not yet been considered necessary. So far, indeed, from concealment being thought of, when we were about to get up, the women, anxious to show their attention, assembled to wish us good morning, and to inquire in what way they could best contribute to our comforts. Many persons would have felt awkward at rising and dressing before so many pretty black-eyed damsels, assembled in the centre of a spacious room; but by a little habit we overcame this embarrassment.

With the proper opportunity now presenting itself, Adams, who performed wedding ceremonies for the young people of the island as well as christenings, now importuned Captain Beechy to perform a wedding ceremony for him and his wife. Indeed, a marriage ceremony took place with Beechy officiating.

Sir John Barrow, who was born of poor parents and rose to secretary of the Admiralty, was moved by the moral and righteous path Adams had taken:

If the sincere repentance of Adams, and his most successful exertions to train up the rising generation in piety and virtue, can be considered as expiating in some degree his former offences, this survivor is fully entitled to every indulgence that frail humanity so often requires, and which indeed has been extended to him by all the officers of the navy who have visited the island. They have all strongly felt that the merits and redeeming qualities of the latter years of his life have so far atoned for his former guilt, that he ought not to be molested, but rather encouraged, in his meritorious efforts, if not for his own sake, at least for that of the innocent young people dependent on him.

Still it ought never to be forgotten that he was one of the first and most daring in the atrocious act of mutiny and piracy, and that, had he remained in Otaheite, and been taken home in the *Pandora,* nothing could have saved him from an ignominious death.

Barrow also noted the moral and legal dilemma that those officers who visited Pitcairn must have weighed in their minds on learning the identity and crime of John Adams. Of Sir Thomas Staines, who visited the island in 1814, Barrow wrote that the British naval commander "had to struggle, on this trying occasion, between duty and feeling. It was his imperative duty to have seized and brought him a prisoner to England, where he must have been tried, and would no doubt have been convicted, though he might, and probably would, from length of time and circumstances in his favour, have received the king's pardon. Perhaps, however, on the whole, it was fortunate, that in balancing, as it is known this gallant officer did, between the sense of duty and the sense of feeling, the latter prevailed, and justice yielded to mercy."

In March of 1829, John Adams passed away. It was a custom of the times to cut off the hair of deceased loved ones for mementos, and Adams's family severed his pigtail to save as a keepsake. On Adams's grave the islanders placed a handmade fourteen-by-twenty-seven-inch wooden tombstone (National Maritime Museum, London). A lead sheet, attached to the board by nails and its edges bent around the wood, contained a punched inscription that read: "Sacred to the memory of Mr. John Adams who died March 5, 1829 Aged 65 years." Adams's death left his New World society without a leader. But having been concerned about the welfare of the islanders, he had implored them before he died to select someone to guide them.

Indeed, Adams had expressed his concern to Captain Beechy that with the growing population on Pitcairn, the island would not be able to support

The pigtail of the last surviving Bounty mutineer on Pitcairn Island, John Adams.

its inhabitants, and the captain said he would help, although that could mean resettling the people elsewhere. Disturbed by this prospect, John Barrow wrote in his 1831 book, "It is hoped, however, that no such interference will take place; for half a century at least, there is no danger of any want of food."

One year after Adams's death, in 1830, a British ship arrived with clothes, tools, and other supplies as presents from the king of England for the people of Pitcairn Island. Thursday October Christian and others rushed out in boats to greet the visitors and were invited on board HMS *Seringapatam*, where they received the hospitalities of the British; their only disappointment was that no clergyman was going to be dropped off permanently to lead them. On the island the British guests were treated to the full amenities of the natives; the visitors took note of the grace recited before each meal and the amens at their conclusion.

"Captain Waldegrave, like all former visitors," wrote Sir John Barrow, "bears testimony to the kind disposition and active benevolence of these simple islanders. The children, he says, are fond and obedient, the parents affectionate and kind towards their children. None of the party ever heard a harsh word made use of by one towards another. They never slander or speak ill of one another."

But Barrow also noted his concern about the future of the New World of

Pitcairn. He wrote, "It is impossible not to feel a deep interest in the welfare of this little society, and at the same time an apprehension that something may happen to disturb that harmony and destroy that simplicity of manners which hitherto characterised it."

By now, the children of the mutineers had not only grown into adults, but they too had children who were young men and women. This "little society" had indeed been touched from the outside, as two others, after John Buffet, decided to stay behind on the island after their vessels passed by. Barrow noted that one of them, George Hunn Nobbs, who was born in 1799 and began service in the navy in 1811, came to Pitcairn in 1828, married Fletcher Christian's granddaughter, and introduced a legal code specifying various crimes such as adultery and their punishments.

After Captain Beechy alerted the British government of the islanders' risk of food shortage, attempts were made to remove the group, but for one reason or another the plans were never carried out. HMS *Seringapatam* had come for this purpose, but Captain Waldegrave, finding the people comfortable and happy in their surroundings and not desiring any sort of change, let them stay.

John Barrow was so concerned about the future of the Pitcairn natives and the preservation of their innocence that he concluded his book with this thought:

> Happy, thrice happy people! May no improper intruders thrust themselves into your peaceful and contented society! May that Providence which has hitherto protected you, still continue to pour down those blessings upon you, of which you appear to be so truly sensible, and for which you are justly thankful! May it throw round the shores of your enviable little Eden, "cherubim and a flaming sword," to guard its approaches from those who would endanger your peace; and above all, shield you from those, who would perplex and confuse your unsophisticated minds, by mysterious doctrines which they do not themselves comprehend! Be assured that, so long as you shall adhere to the line of conduct you have hitherto pursued, and be contented with your present lot, your happiness is secure; but once admit ignorant or false teachers among you, and from that period you may date the commencement of misfortunes and misery!

Pitcairn Island, 1852. Rear Admiral Sir Fairfax Moresby, who was born just three years before the *Bounty* mutiny and who in 1870 would become admiral of the Royal Naval fleet, visited Pitcairn in HMS *Portland,* the first admiral of the Royal Navy to do so. He discovered that the island's pastor, George Hunn Nobbs, was not officially vested, so he left on the island his ship's chaplain, the Rev. W. H. Holman, so Nobbs could return to England to become ordained, which he was later that same year.

Reverend Holman returned to England in 1853, nine months after his arrival on Pitcairn, and brought back with him John Adams's pigtail and other artifacts he had purchased on Pitcairn. John Adams had never returned to England after he left in 1787 on the *Bounty,* spending some forty years of his life living as a fugitive in the South Pacific. But twenty-four years after his death, his pigtail found its way back to his motherland.

The population on Pitcairn continued to increase after John Adams's death, and in 1856, many of the islanders were evacuated to Norfolk Island. Three years later, in 1859, Pitcairn was gradually resettled, and a new stone tombstone for John Adams was erected with the same inscription as the original, except for a wistful two words tacked on at the end: "in hope." Some of the Pitcairn colony that was evacuated died on Norfolk Island, such as George Hunn Nobbs, who passed away in 1884. In 1891 John Adams's original wooden tombstone was displayed at the Royal Naval Exhibition in Chelsea, courtesy of Admiral Moresby's son-in-law.

The men and women who first settled on Pitcairn no doubt realized that in their remote paradise, they would become latter-day Adams and Eves. Unfortunately some of the roguish Englishmen could not maintain the civility necessary to achieve harmony. Incurring the wrath of the natives, they destroyed the innocence of their new world. But finally the dust of malice cleared and good prevailed. And so today, and for posterity, we have a relic of one of the original Adamses of Pitcairn Island—a plait of hair that, for all its quaintness, represents the spirit of repentance, virtue, and redemption that shaped this little Garden of Eden, settled in desperation in 1790.

LOCATION: National Maritime Museum, London.

The Doubleday Ball

DATE: 1839 (by tradition).

WHAT IT IS: A ball associated with the alleged inventor of baseball, Abner Doubleday.

WHAT IT LOOKS LIKE: It is a small baseball stuffed with compressed fabric. Its cover is a single piece of brown leather cut into "petals," which are sewn together around the stuffing; some of the seams are coming apart.

America loves a good myth. Among its most venerable apocryphal stand-bys are that the young George Washington declared "I cannot tell a lie" when asked by his father if he had chopped down the cherry tree; and that Abraham Lincoln composed his famous address on the train to Gettysburg. Curiously, these nineteenth-century fabrications (which have their origins, respectively, in Mason Locke Weems's 1800 *The Life and Memorable Actions of George Washington,* and spurious eyewitness accounts of pas-sengers on the same train on which the sixteenth president rode to Gettysburg) have stubbornly persisted to the present. The story of the invention of America's national pastime, baseball, also has a fanciful prove-nance, crafted not to honor a *real* early architect of the sport but to meet the needs of a later time. But what do the Spanish-American War, a deranged wife killer, a six-year-old boy, and a ragged old ball found in an attic trunk have to do with the fabrication that the sport of baseball was invented by Abner Doubleday?

The story of the origin of baseball has for generations been wrapped in the legend that Abner Doubleday conceived the sport in Cooperstown, New York, some eleven years prior to the midpoint of the nineteenth century. The myth received its substantiation not from any records or eyewitness accounts of the day, but in the tenuous findings of a committee formed in the first

Civil War general Abner Doubleday may have been an authoritative commander on the battlefield, but he didn't invent the baseball field.

decade of the twentieth century, validated and sanctioned years later by a somewhat mysterious discovery. Consequently, people have commonly accepted the notion that while baseball evolved from previous forms of ball games, it was Abner Doubleday, the nineteenth-century West Point cadet who went on to become a general in the American Civil War, who formulated the rules by which modern-day baseball is played. The Doubleday creation myth says much about how falsehoods enter the history books and deserves examination.

As a game played with simple equipment, essentially just a bat and ball, modern-day baseball indeed has antecedents that stretch back to some of the earliest human societies. The sport's evolution through the centuries was influenced by many factors, including culture and social mores.

The basic physical elements of baseball are throwing, hitting, catching, and running. These elements were constituents of some of the earliest human games. The Greeks, Romans, and Egyptians, among other societies, are all known to have had stick-and-ball games; later, the Mayans, in the Western Hemisphere, also played such games.

References to stick-and-ball games can be found in written sources of the Middle Ages, including the 1086 Domesday Book. In France in the thirteenth and fourteenth centuries, it was an Easter tradition to play stick-and-ball games, but it is not clear why.

On the family tree of stick-and-ball games, cricket, which developed in the Middle Ages, is a near relative to baseball. It is a field game with eleven players on each side, using bats (with a blade), a ball, and two wickets (each formed by three stumps and two bails, or pieces of wood, across their top); runs are scored when the batter, standing at a wicket, hits the ball thrown to him by the bowler and dashes to the wicket across from him before any of the fielders spread out on the field can return the ball to the wicket. Cricket itself is a descendant of ancient games, and although a national sport of England, its origins are in dispute; some say it developed in France.

Because under its old rules a cricket match required a great deal of time to play, in the British tradition the sport was an aristocratic pastime. Indeed, by the early 1800s, a proper cricket match could take a good three days to play.

By the early eighteenth century another stick-and-ball game called "baseball" was played in England, but its rules are not clear. It was undoubtedly played by children; in 1744, England's first specialized children's publisher, John Newberry, issued a collection of rhymed poems accompanied by woodcut illustrations about children's games, including base-ball, entitled *A Little Pretty Pocket-Book*. The first of two publications of the book in America occurred in 1762, when Hugh Gaine, a New York printer, published the book with the title *A Little Pretty Book, Intended for the Instruction and Amusement of Little Master Tommy and Pretty Miss Polly*. Under a woodcut picturing young players wearing hats, standing at posts spaced apart in the form of a triangle, was a quatrain, titled "Base-Ball," that described how the game was played:

> *The* Ball *once struck off,*
> *Away flies the* Boy
> *To the next destin'd Post*
> *And then Home with Joy.*

A feature of many of these games was that runners were not tagged but put out by defensive players who threw the ball at them, an action called "plugging" or "stinging." These games were sometimes referred to as baseball, and they certainly do represent the beginnings of American baseball.

For the most part, stick-and-ball games were the domain of children in colonial America, but beginning in the late 1700s older teenagers and young adults took up playing ball from time to time. George Ewing reports in his diary that as a soldier at Valley Forge, Pennsylvania, in 1778, he "exercised in the afternoon in the intervals played at base." Princeton College students played "baste ball" in 1786, and enthusiasm for the sport only seemed to grow from there. In what may have been the first American college campus craze, from about 1810 to 1830, students at Brown, Bowdoin, and other eastern colleges couldn't get enough of baseball-type games.

What's remarkable about this phenomenon in these pre-Victorian times in class-conscious America is that men felt comfortable playing the game. In many localities, the notion that adults would spend considerable time playing a game like baseball would have seemed childish or odd, and while the players would not have been arrested or punished, they did risk being

A nineteenth-century illustration of the "New York Game," as established by the Knicker-bocker Base Ball Club in 1845. The picture shows the configuration of the field and the position of the players (note the second and third basemen standing on the bases). The pitcher is shown throwing underhand; it wasn't until 1884 that pitching was changed to overhand.

castigated by their peers. Stick-and-ball games were banned at Princeton on the grounds that they were "dangerous as well as beneath the propriety of a gentleman."

Small towns also banned ball playing. In 1816 the towns of Cooperstown, New York, and Worcester, Massachusetts, both passed ordinances prohibiting the playing of ball in the streets (at Cooperstown the ban applied to specific streets). Ball playing could result in horses being frightened or a window being broken, but it may also be said that sometimes when youths do things that annoy adults, the latter find ways to make them illegal.

Illustrations of baseball-type games continued to feature children even as late as the 1830s, which may indicate that mainstream adults continued to view stick-and-ball games as children's games. There was rounders, for instance, a children's game popular in England in which a person would throw a ball to a side of three or four batters, and whoever hit the ball would try to run to a base and then return home before a fielder could retrieve it and throw it at him. If he succeeded, he earned a run; if not, he exchanged places with the fielder who hit him. There were many variations of this involving more bases, but this was the basic format of the game. There was also One o'Cat (with its variations) and its offshoot, town ball. In One o'Cat, Two o'Cat, Three o'Cat, and Four o'Cat, players hit the ball, ran to bases, then tried to return to the original batter's base to score runs, the particular game played determining the number of bases used. In town ball, players divided into teams and used a small bat to hit the ball to opponents waiting in the playing field. There were other games too, such as barn ball and goal ball, in which balls, bats, and sticks were often makeshift objects, and the rules and playing fields varied according to the players. A feature of many of these games was that runners were "plugged."

Although children's books about stick-and-ball games continued to be published in America, men began to organize into clubs to play town ball and other precursors of modern baseball. Players were sometimes hungry for a challenge, as evidenced by this newspaper article that appeared in the July 12, 1825, edition of the *Delhi* (New York) *Gazette:*

> The undersigned, all residents of the new town of Hamden, with the exception of Asa C. Howland, who has recently removed into Delhi, challenge an equal number of persons of any town in the County of Delaware, to meet them at any time at the house of *Edward B. Chace*, in said town, to play the game of BASS-BALL, for the sum of one dollar per game. If no town can be found that will produce the required number, they have no objection to play against any selection that can be made from the several towns in the county.

The names of nine men were printed under the article. Most were relatively young British émigrés who had come to the United States after the War of 1812, some quite recently.

Baseball remained a local pastime until September 1845, when a group of town ball players organized the New York Knickerbocker Base Ball Club. The team sprouted from some of the members' previous association with a volunteer fire department. The volunteer firefighters were middle-class men in their twenties and thirties who worked in Manhattan in such professions as customs brokering, pharmacy, medicine, legal services, and banking. The fire department was a way for these young men to offer community service, but it also provided a social outlet. After meetings the men would pursue some form of amusement, such as playing ball, and then dine.

The fire company disbanded in the early 1840s, but some of the members continued to play ball, and over time others joined them. The men met regularly to play ball at different sites in the New York City area, and around 1844 they even started taking a horse ferry (in which a horse on deck turned the wheel to move the ferry) across the Hudson River to Hoboken, New Jersey, where they would walk along the shore for about a mile to the Elysian Fields to play. A rules committee later formed, and on September 23, 1845, the New York Knickerbocker Base Ball Club adopted twenty rules for the playing of baseball.

In June 1846, the New York Knickerbockers played their first match. They suffered a humiliating defeat—according to one account the pitcher on the opposing team was an experienced cricket bowler—and did not play another team until five years later. But other teams formed in the interim, and by the mid-1850s there were more than twenty-five clubs, many founded by former New York Knickerbockers, which played in Manhattan, Brooklyn, Staten Island, and the Bronx, using the New York Knickerbocker rules. Some of these clubs were proficient ball teams and drew crowds of a thousand or more people. The New York Knickerbockers reemerged as a competitor around 1851, and while their record was not outstanding, they left an enduring legacy: their 1845 set of twenty rules became the basis for modern-day baseball.

Among the rules that became known as the "New York Game" were:

- the bases shall be from "home" to second base, forty-two paces; from first to third base, forty-two paces equidistant;
- a ball knocked out of the field, or outside the range of the first or third base, is foul;
- three balls being struck at and missed and the last one caught, is a hand out; if not caught is considered fair, and the striker is bound to run;
- a player running the bases shall be out, if the ball is in the hands of an adversary on the base, or the runner is touched with it before he makes the base;
- three hands out, all out.

The Knickerbocker rules contained certain innovations, such as creating foul territory, and were important in another respect: they made baseball more advanced by eliminating plugging.

In May 1858 ten clubs playing town ball in and around the Boston area met at Dedham, Massachusetts, to draw up a set of rules. There was disagreement in a number of areas, and the players discussed meeting at a later date to address them, but apparently never did. Still, they adopted twenty-one "town base ball" rules that became known as the "Massachusetts Game," among them:

- four bases or bounds shall constitute a round;
- the distance from each base shall be sixty feet;
- the bases shall be wooden stakes, projecting four feet from the ground;
- the catcher shall not enter within the space occupied by the striker, and must remain on his feet in all cases while catching the ball;

- the ball must be thrown—not pitched or tossed—to the bat on the side preferred by the striker, and within reach of his bat;
- players must take their knocks in the order in which they are numbered, and after the first inning is played, the turn will commence with the player succeeding the one who lost on the previous inning;
- the ball being struck at three times and missed, and caught each time by a player on the opposite side, the striker shall be considered out;
- should the striker stand at the bat without striking at good balls thrown repeatedly at him, for the apparent purpose of delaying the game or of giving advantage to players, the referees after warning him, shall call one strike, and if he persists in such action, two and three strikes;
- if a player, while running the bases, be hit with the ball thrown by one of the opposite side, before he has touched the home bound, while off a base, he shall be considered out;
- a player, after running the four bases, on making the home bound, shall be considered one tally;
- in playing all match games, when one is out, the side shall be considered out;
- in playing all match games, one hundred tallies shall constitute the game, the making of which by either club, that club shall be judged the winner.

The Massachusetts version of baseball was very popular in the Boston area, but as the New York Game spread and increased in popularity in the Civil War period, town ball essentially fell by the wayside, and the Massachusetts Game disappeared. To the people of mid–nineteenth-century America, the New York Game was superior because it was a more orderly game, and the ball was not thrown at the runner.

In America's pre–Civil War era, baseball continued in popularity, and its rules became more refined. In New York City, a group of clubs met and decided that games would be played for nine innings, instead of the seven innings proposed by the members of the New York Knickerbocker club. In 1859 the first intercollegiate baseball game took place: Amherst College faced Williams College on neutral territory at Pittsfield, Massachusetts. The game was played under the rules adopted the previous year at Dedham.

Baseball almost from the beginning of its evolution as a professional sport seemed to be cast as an American game, as something that expressed American ideals and values and was uniquely American. The notion that baseball had evolved from British rounders was by the 1870s and 1880s rejected by some American authorities, who seemed determined to believe that somehow an American had brought the game into being.

In the late 1850s, Henry Chadwick, an English expatriate who wrote for the *Brooklyn Eagle,* helped form the National Association of Ball Players. Chadwick, who was a cricket player and covered cricket matches, made many contributions to baseball, including creating the box score and publicizing the sport as it was taking shape. Here's Chadwick conveying the popularity of the game in an article published in the *New York Clipper* on October 26, 1861, about a ball game played five days earlier in Hoboken, New Jersey:

> The game of base ball is, as our readers are for the most part aware, an American game exclusively, as now played, although a game somewhat similar has been played in England for many years, called "rounders," but which is played more after the style of the Massachusetts game. New York, however, justly claims to being the originators of what is termed the American Game, which has been so improved in all its essential points by them, and its scientific points so added to, that it does not stand second either in its innate excellencies, or interesting phrases, to any national game of any country in the world, and is every way adapted to the tastes of all who love athletic exercises in this country.

Chadwick's enthusiasm for baseball being an "American Game" would diminish over time, and he would later figure prominently in the debate over whether baseball was in fact English or American in origin. Chadwick and two others of his time, Alexander Cartwright, who spearheaded the founding of the New York Knickerbockers, and Harry Wright, a world-class cricket player who was one of the leading members of baseball's first professional team, the Cincinnati Red Stockings, would become known as "the three fathers of baseball."*

As America was undergoing a vast change in the last quarter of the nine-teenth century, baseball—in the New York style—became established as the country's national pastime. In 1874 American baseball players went on an exhibition tour to Great Britain, and in 1889 embarked on a worldwide tour. The latter was organized by Albert G. Spalding, the sporting goods executive who had been a star pitcher for the Chicago White Stockings and helped establish the National League.

---

*Abner Doubleday and Albert G. Spalding have also been referred to as "fathers" of modern baseball.

Spreading the national pastime was the American thing to do, and Spalding, during the 1888 global tour, drove the concept home. In masterful public relations stunts, baseball players competed in front of the Egyptian pyramids and posed on top of the Sphinx. Boys on the streets in Morocco were photographed holding baseball bats just like red-blooded American kids. Indeed, Spalding dispensed bats to young street urchins with missionary zeal (of course, as a sporting goods manufacturer, Spalding had something to gain personally by popularizing baseball). As Spalding would later write in his high-spirited baseball book:

All America has come to regard Base Ball as its very own, to be known throughout the civilized world as the great American National Game. . . . Ever since its establishment in the hearts of the people as the foremost of field sports, Base Ball has "followed the flag." It followed the flag to the front in the sixties, and received then an impetus which has carried it to half a century of wondrous growth and prosperity. It has followed the flag to Alaska, where, under the midnight sun, it is played on Arctic ice. It has followed the flag to the Hawaiian Islands, and at once supplanted every other form of athletics in popularity. It has followed the flag to the Philippines, to Porto Rico and to Cuba, and wherever a ship floating the Stars and Stripes finds anchorage today, somewhere on a nearby shore the American National Game is in progress.

The last quarter of the nineteenth century was an exciting period in America, with many revolutionary American inventions altering the very fabric of society. Beginning with Alexander Graham Bell's invention of the telephone in 1876, Americans over the next twenty-five or thirty years introduced to the world the phonograph, the incandescent lamp, the motion picture, the gasoline automobile, and the airplane. America even had its own indigenous music in ragtime, the jaunty, syncopated tunes that swept the country. Political tensions were simmering in Europe, but that was too far away to be of much interest.

On February 15, 1898, an event happened that would bring American nationalism to a fever pitch. In the harbor of Havana in Spanish-controlled Cuba, the U.S. battleship *Maine* blew up. More than 250 American sailors were killed,* and their countrymen refused to consider the explosion an

---

*Among the *Maine*'s casualties were members of its championship baseball team. Only one of the team's members, an outfielder, was not killed in the blast.

accident. They turned their wrath on Spain, incited in part by Spain's oppressive treatment of Cubans and driven by the strident yellow journalism of some influential American newspapers that had been clamoring for war.

Despite Spain's willingness to reform its policies in Cuba, the United States sent its troops into action. In Cuba and the Philippines, the Americans swiftly wiped out the Spanish naval fleets. The Spanish-American War wasn't much of a war, but it created a newly fervent patriotism. The last time Americans had been at war, it was among themselves; now they had a common enemy and couldn't get enough of the war. They showed their support by parading through city streets with the Stars and Stripes held high, and their passion rescued a new entertainment medium called moving pictures (by this time the novelty had worn off) as they flocked to theaters to view footage of American soldiers shellacking the Spanish villains. It didn't matter that many of the battles were staged on sets and in water tanks in New York City and New Jersey.

Americans took pride in their victory over an Old World power. Spain had attacked an American ship in Cuban waters—and even if it hadn't, it was still the enemy. An attack on an American institution caused outrage. An attack on an American institution on American soil would surely draw the unbridled wrath of the country. Such an "attack" came some years later from Henry Chadwick.

Chadwick, the British expatriate sportswriter, penned a piece about the origin of baseball that ran in the 1903 *Baseball Guide* published by Albert Spalding. In his essay, Chadwick traced the history of modern baseball to the British game of rounders. The piece set off a firestorm of discontent among baseball's elite, and the next year Spalding in his annual guide countered Chadwick's assertion and proposed a commission to investigate and report on the origin of baseball.

Known as the Mills Commission after its head, A. G. Mills, who in the 1880s had served as president of the National League, the committee consisted additionally of two U.S. senators, Arthur Gorman of Maryland and Morgan Bulkeley of Connecticut, both former baseball executives; two businessmen, Bostonian George Wright and Philadelphian Alfred Reach, both former ballplayers (George Wright was the brother of famous baseball player Harry Wright); James Sullivan, the president of the Amateur Athletic Union; and Nicholas Young, a longtime secretary of the National League. All baseball insiders, the members of the Mills Commission were not well suited to conduct a scholarly investigation, and in fact did not go about their inquiry with great precision. The commission ran advertisements in sports publications inviting anyone who knew anything about the early days of baseball to write in. The most significant correspondence received was deemed to be from a mining engineer from Colorado named Abner Graves.*

Graves wrote that Abner Doubleday had invented baseball at Cooperstown, New York, in 1839. The Mills Commission asked him to provide additional details, and Graves responded. According to Graves, Doubleday had sketched out a diamond-shaped playing field and introduced certain rules that had altered the game of town ball to create the new game that became known as baseball. Graves gave the impression that he and a bunch of boys had engaged in disorderly games of ball (played with bats, balls, and bases) at Cooperstown, and that one day Abner Doubleday had shown up with rules for their field—a ninety-foot playing field shaped like a diamond with the bases set out at different positions. Graves's testimony did not offer much in the way of concrete proof; it was the recollection of one man some sixty-five years after the game's alleged inception.

The trouble was, Graves assumed that the Abner Doubleday who came to Cooperstown was the same Abner Doubleday who had become a famous major general in the Civil War. Graves did go to school in Cooperstown with an Abner Doubleday, who was about the same age as Graves. However, this Abner Doubleday, the son of a Bruce Doubleday and a cousin of the major general, was an unlikely inventor of baseball in 1839, as he was only about six years old at the time.

Abner Doubleday the major general was born in 1819 in Ballston Spa, New York, near Schenectady, about a two-day ride at the time from Cooperstown. Abner's father was a bookseller, and when Abner was young his family moved to Auburn, New York, about eighty miles west of Cooperstown.

Abner grew up in Auburn, and then attended the U.S. Military Academy at West Point, New York. No records have surfaced of this Abner Doubleday ever having been in Cooperstown, and indeed he probably never visited the town. Doubleday was a student at West Point in 1839, and it is unlikely that he would have been able to take time off from his studies at the military academy to invent and play baseball. Doubleday graduated from West Point in 1842, and then his military career went into full gear; he entered the Civil War as a major and became famous for firing the first cannon shot in the Civil War on the Union side at Fort Sumter. There are no known contemporary accounts of Doubleday having played baseball or invented rules for it.

Graves offered testimony to the Mills Commission but provided no

---

*Researchers have never been able to review the correspondence received by the Mills Commission or other paperwork it had, as its records were destroyed in 1911 when the New York City building they were in caught on fire.

concrete evidence supporting his assertions. When the Mills Commission asked for more information, Graves provided precise details almost seven decades after the event. It is possible that Graves, seeking attention, embellished his story for the fame he would earn from his purported association with the inventor of baseball, or even that he was manipulated to a degree by the Mills Commission. Graves may have initially referred to the younger Abner Doubleday as the inventor of baseball. Six years old is certainly too young to have invented sophisticated rules for a game like baseball, but not to have played it. So many years removed, Graves may have thought someone he played ball with had provided rules for the game, the name of his boyhood acquaintance Abner Doubleday then popping into his mind. When the Mills Commission members heard the name Abner Doubleday, of course they would think it was the famous major general of the Civil War and seize upon it being that Doubleday.

The Mills Commission accepted Graves's testimony of Doubleday as baseball's inventor. What could have been more American than baseball, a game played during the Civil War, invented by a soldier in the war, and even the soldier who fired the cannon shot that began the war? As Albert Spalding would later write about Doubleday:

> The founder of our National Game became a Major General in the United States Army! The sport had its baptism when our country was in the preliminary agonies of a fratricidal conflict. Its early evolution was among the men, both North and South, who, during the war of the sixties, played the game to relieve the monotony of camp life in those years of melancholy struggle.

Lending support to Graves's claim was a man named Curry, a past president of the original New York Knickerbocker Base Ball Club, who stated that one day one of the team's members, a man named Wadsworth, had brought a diagram showing the layout of the ball field. It so happened that Wadsworth had family from upstate New York, and A. G. Mills conjectured that Wadsworth had learned to play baseball the Doubleday way upstate and then taught Doubleday's version of the game to the Knickerbockers. Wadsworth presumably worked in a customs house, and Mills tried unsuccessfully to track down Wadsworth's records, which, he believed, would have shown him to have lived in Cooperstown.

Abner Graves's account was the Mills Commission's best case for American authorship of the game. The mining engineer seemed to the Mills

Commission to be a reliable witness, but not much was known about him—or his mental stability. Of course it couldn't be known at this time that some two decades later Graves would have a dispute with his second wife over the sale of their house. He wanted to sell it, she didn't. She owned the house, but that didn't matter to Graves. He murdered his wife and spent the rest of his days in an insane asylum.

At the end of 1907, the Mills Commission declared in a report (published in the 1908 *Baseball Guide*) that baseball was a sport indigenous to the United States with no ties to other games; and that Abner Doubleday, the American major general, had invented the sport of baseball in Cooperstown, New York, in 1839. Although the findings were bolstered by an alleged witness, Graves, they still lacked conclusive evidence that would confirm Doubleday as the originator of the sport. That evidence would come (in tenuous form) twenty-seven years later, in 1934.

Indeed, the Mills Commission was the final arbiter in the debate over the origin of baseball. In a letter of December 30, 1907, to James E. Sullivan, Secretary of the Special Base Ball Commission, A. G. Mills wrote:

I cannot say that I find myself in accord with those who urge the American origin of the game as against its English origin, as contended for by Mr. Chadwick, on "patriotic grounds". In my opinion we owe much to our Anglo-Saxon kinsmen for their example which we have too tardily followed, in fostering healthful field sports generally, and if the fact could be established, by evidence, that our national game, "Base Ball", was devised in England, I do not think that it would be any the less admirable nor welcome on that account. . . .

Until my perusal of this testimony, my own belief had been that our game of Base Ball, substantially as played today, originated with the Knickerbocker Club of New York, and it was frequently referred to as the "New York Ball Game".

. . . In the last analysis, [Chadwick's] contention is based chiefly upon the fact that, substantially, the same kind of implements are employed in the game of Base Ball as in the English game of "Rounders" to which he refers; for if the mere tossing or handling of some kind of a ball, or striking it with some kind of a stick, could be accepted as the origin of our game, then Father Chadwick would certainly have to go far back of Anglo-Saxon civilization,—beyond Rome, beyond Greece, at least to the palmy days of the Chaldean

Empire! Nor does it seem to me that he can any more successfully maintain the argument because of the employment, by the English school boy of the past, of the implements or materials of the game.

. . . In the interesting and pertinent testimony for which we are indebted to Mr. A. G. Spalding, appears a circumstantial statement by a reputable gentleman, according to which the first known diagram of the diamond, indicating positions for the players was drawn by Abner Doubleday in Cooperstown, N.Y., in 1839. Abner Doubleday subsequently graduated from West Point and entered the regular army where, as Captain of Artillery, he sighted the first gun fired on the Union side (at Fort Sumpter [sic]) in the Civil War. Later still, he was in command of the Union army at the close of the first day's fight in the battle of Gettysburg, and he died full of honors at Mendham, N.J., in 1893. . . . In the days when Abner Doubleday attended school in Cooperstown, it was a common thing for two dozen or more of school boys to join in a game of ball. Doubtless, as in my later experience, collisions between players in attempting to catch the batted ball were frequent, and injury due to this cause, or to the practice of putting out the runner by hitting him with the ball, often occurred.

I can well understand how the orderly mind of the embryo West Pointer would devise a scheme for limiting the contestants on each side, and allotting them to field positions, with a certain amount of territory; also substituting the existing method of putting out the base runner for the old one of plugging him with the ball.

I am also much interested in the statement made by Mr. Curry, of the pioneer Knickerbocker Club, and confirmed by Mr. Tassle, of the famous old Atlantic Club of Brooklyn, that a diagram, showing the ball field laid out substantially as it is to-day, was brought out to the field one afternoon by Mr. Wadsworth. . . . From that day to this, the scheme of the game described by Mr. Curry, has been continued with only slight variations in detail. It should be borne in mind that Mr. Curry was the first President of the old Knickerbocker Club, and participated in drafting the first published rules of the game.

It is possible that a connection more or less direct can be traced between the diagram drawn by Doubleday in 1839 and that presented to the Knickerbocker Club by Mr. Wadsworth in 1845, or thereabouts, and I wrote several days ago for certain data bearing on this point, but as it has not yet come to hand I have decided to delay no longer sending in the kind of paper your letter calls for,

promising to furnish you the indicated data when I obtain it, whatever it may be.

My deductions from the testimony submitted are:

First. That Base Ball had its origin in the United States.

Second. That the first scheme for playing it, according to the best
evidence obtainable to date, was devised by Abner Doubleday at
Cooperstown, N.Y. in 1839.

The Mills Commission report was published in the spring of 1908. The
commission, which in its report stated that it had relied on "a circumstantial statement by a reputable gentleman," determined that baseball was
American in origin and had been invented by Abner Doubleday, who had
been a major general in the Civil War.

Henry Chadwick, whose article about the origin of baseball had sparked
the Mills Commission investigation, was appalled by the commission's findings and immediately fired off a note of protest to Spalding. But the opinion of Chadwick, who died five weeks later, or anybody else who concurred
with him, wouldn't matter. Baseball was now certifiably an American game,
created by an American. The findings of the Mills Commission were duti-
fully reported in the press. The *New York World* filed this story:

> The commission appointed to determine where base ball originated
> has reported, after a painstaking investigation covering three years,
> that the game was first played at Cooperstown, N.Y. under the
> direction of Abner Doubleday in 1839. . . . Their report settles an
> old controversy and is entitled to respect of all investigators of the
> origin of the horse or discoverers of "missing links." Base ball is
> thus proved to be, like poker, a genuine American product. It did
> not come "out of the mysterious East," like our religions and lan-
> guages, like chess and cards, peaches and sherbert. It was not played
> in ancient Rome, like hop-scotch and jackstraws. It is native, indige-
> nous, all our own, and the fact is a just subject for pride.

On March 26, 1908, the citizens of Cooperstown, New York, learned
possibly for the first time that their village had been the birthplace of
America's national sport when the *Freeman's Journal* ran a front-page arti-
cle with these headlines: "Home of Baseball," "Game Originated in
Cooperstown," and "Abner Doubleday, Afterward Major General, Its
Originator—A Monument Suggested."

The news no doubt surprised the residents, and they had to have been taken aback by the timing of the announcement. The previous year, 1907, had been the village's hundredth anniversary. Townspeople had tried to draw tourists by touting the village's literary heritage—it had been founded by William Cooper, the father of famed novelist James Fenimore Cooper—and held a summerlong celebration. If only they had known that Abner Doubleday had invented baseball on their fields sixty-eight years earlier, surely they could have attracted more visitors!

With baseball codified as the invention of an American, the timing was ripe for Albert G. Spalding's book, *America's National Game: Historic Facts Concerning the Beginning, Evolution, Development and Popularity of Base Ball with personal reminiscences of its vicissitudes, its victories and its votaries.* The book reflected Spalding's overflowing pride in America's national pastime being a homegrown sport, but it also provided much information about the early days of baseball that would probably have been lost to posterity had Spalding not taken the time to write his book.

How American is baseball? This is an issue Spalding addressed, and it would be hard to accuse him of being shy about expressing himself in this regard:

> I claim that Base Ball owes its prestige as our National Game to the fact that as no other form of sport it is the exponent of American Courage, Confidence, Combativeness; American Dash, Discipline, Determination; American Energy, Eagerness, Enthusiasm; American Pluck, Persistency, Performance; American Spirit, Sagacity, Success; American Vim, Vigor, Virility.
>
> Base Ball is the American Game *par excellence,* because its playing demands Brain and Brawn, and American manhood supplies these ingredients in quantity sufficient to spread over the entire continent.

Spalding didn't miss an opportunity to mock British gentility. Noting that cricket matches can sometimes take two or three days to complete, Spalding wrote that "cricket would never do for Americans; it is too slow." But the Englishman "is so constituted by nature" to play such a "genteel game" for such a long time. Spalding continued:

> Our British Cricketer, having finished his day's labor at noon, may don his negligee shirt, his white trousers, his gorgeous hosiery and his canvas shoes, and sally forth to the field of sport, with his sweetheart on one arm and his Cricket bat under the other, knowing that

he may engage in his national pastime without soiling his linen or neglecting his lady. He may play Cricket, drink afternoon tea, flirt, gossip, smoke, take a whisky-and-soda at the customary hour, and have a jolly, conventional good time, don't you know?

Baseball, of course, was not a "genteel" game. Winning is what mattered, and, unlike the British, Americans didn't mind getting down and dirty. Here's Spalding on the difference between baseball and cricket:

Cricket is a gentle pastime. Base Ball is War! Cricket is an Athletic Sociable, played and applauded in a conventional, decorous and English manner. Base Ball is an Athletic Turmoil, played and applauded in an unconventional, enthusiastic and American manner.

Baseball at the time was of unchallenged popularity as an American sport, lapped up by kids across the country, and this fact also did not escape Spalding. He wrote:

In every town, village and city is the local wag. He is a Base Ball fan from infancy. He knows every player in the League by sight and by name. He is a veritable encyclopædia of information on the origin, evolution and history of the game. He can tell you when the Knickerbockers were organized, and knows who led the batting list in every team of the National and American Leagues last year. He never misses a game. His witticisms, ever seasoned with spice, hurled at the visitors and now and then at the Umpire, are as thoroughly enjoyed by all who hear them as is any other feature of the sport. His words of encouragement to the home team, his shouts of derision to the opposing players, find sympathetic responses in the hearts of all present.

The Doubleday invention story was widely accepted after the Mills Commission report and received validation in 1934 when an old baseball with its seams torn apart was said to have been found in a trunk in an attic of a farmhouse in Fly Creek, New York, a hamlet about five miles west of Cooperstown. According to the story, a farmer from Fly Creek came to Cooperstown one day with a ball he had found in his house—the same house in which Abner Graves had once lived. Stephen C. Clark, a scion of a very wealthy local family who had an ownership interest in a local newspaper, purchased the ball for the sum of five dollars.

Clark decided to display the ball—soon dubbed the "Doubleday Ball" by a newspaper editor—with other baseball memorabilia in a Cooperstown club room. Then a man named Alexander Cleland, a top administrator for Clark, conceived the idea for a full-fledged national baseball museum. Indeed, the time was ripe, if not overdue, for such a venture. By the mid-1930s, baseball was a classic sport that had grown in America from a national pastime to a national obsession, and as such it needed its own full-blown shrine. Current players such as Babe Ruth, Dizzy Dean, Lefty Gomez, and Pie Traynor had captured the public's imagination, while stars of past eras like Cap Anson, Kid Nichols, Nap Lajoie, and Ty Cobb were already part of the folklore of the sport. When plans were being made for a centennial celebration of baseball in Cooperstown, National League president Ford Frick suggested a hall of fame to fete the sport's most illustrious participants. The two ideas became intertwined, and with Clark's resources, the concept came to life. On June 12, 1939, one hundred years to the day after the alleged invention of the sport by Abner Doubleday, a ceremony was held for the dedication of the National Baseball Hall of Fame and Museum in Cooperstown.

The Doubleday Ball was the most important of the Hall of Fame's artifacts, its Holy Grail, but some mystery attended its acquisition. The ball was presented almost from the start as an artifact that demonstrated the link between Doubleday and baseball by virtue of its discovery in the house of Abner Graves. But neither the name of the person who had found the ball nor the location of the farmhouse where it was discovered were ever publicized.

Still, the story of the discovery of the Doubleday Ball may be true, and the ball could have been found in a house in which Abner Graves once lived. The Graves family did live in the Fly Creek area for several generations. And the ball was old, obviously from the nineteenth century, and indeed offered exciting possibilities for speculation about who had played with it.

The Doubleday Ball is small and is stuffed with cloth or cotton. From what is known about early balls, it is consistent with an early townball or early baseball. But it could also have been a toy. Many of these early balls were homemade and not sold at local stores. Farm families of the time had to be self-sufficient in many ways, and making a child's ball would not have been uncommon, nor would it have been difficult.

The Doubleday Ball has a sewn leather cover and has no component of rubber, which wasn't readily commercially available until the 1840s. Based on its stuffing and other characteristics, the ball could have been made in the 1820s or 1830s. A child may have used the ball to play catch with. It is also possible that the Doubleday Ball is the oldest extant baseball in the United States, but such a claim cannot be made conclusively without knowing exactly when the ball was crafted.

In any case, all conjecture about the ball is just that. The ball's history cannot be known for certain, but one thing can be deduced: there is no demonstrable connection between the ball and Major General Abner Doubleday. Even if Abner Graves did own or play with the ball, that fact does not prove that Abner Doubleday of Civil War fame played with the ball, much less that he invented modern baseball.

Who played with this nineteenth-century baseball? Its origins are uncertain but the so-called Doubleday Ball is symbolic of the beginning of the sport of baseball.

It had long been believed that Abner Doubleday never wrote about baseball or even mentioned it in any of his writings. For years researchers scoured Doubleday's articles, correspondence, and other writings, but could not find any discussion of baseball to substantiate the claim that he had invented the sport. In 1989, however, a letter written by Doubleday in which the term *baseball* is used was brought to light by Mrs. William B. Thomas of Wayne, New Jersey, who was searching records of the National Archives for information on Moses Hunter, her husband's great-great-grandfather, who had served in the I Company of the Twenty-fourth Colored Infantry under Colonel Doubleday.

Abner Doubleday served in the Union army at the battle at Gettysburg, Pennsylvania, which commenced on July 1, 1863, and ended two days later, with heavy casualties on both sides. On the third day Doubleday ordered an attack on Confederate lines at nightfall. But General George Meade countermanded Doubleday's order, which might have resulted in the capture of the main enemy force, including General Robert E. Lee himself, and ended the Civil War. A cloud hung over Doubleday's name for a time after the war as military analysts suggested that it was his indecision that cost the Union a total victory. Although years later it became known that Doubleday had wanted to pursue battle, after the war Doubleday was returned to the rank of colonel and sent to Texas to command an African-American unit of soldiers. At the time this was considered an undesirable assignment, but Doubleday nevertheless took the demotion in stride, a true and loyal soldier above all.

In a letter dated June 17, 1871, from regimental headquarters at Fort McKavett, Doubleday requested funds from the U.S. Army adjutant general in Washington, D.C., to purchase portraits and statues that could inspire his troops, as well as items of recreation. Doubleday wrote:

> I have the honor to apply for permission to purchase for the Regimental Library a few portraits of distinguished generals, Battle pictures, and some of Rogers groups of Statuary particularly those relative to the actions of the Colored population of the south.
>
> This being a colored regiment ornaments of this kind seem very appropriate. I would also like to purchase baseball implements for the amusement of the men and a Magic Lantern for the same purpose. The fund is ample and I think these expenditures would add to the happiness of the men.

That Doubleday ordered baseball equipment for his troops does nothing to bolster the claim that he is the sport's inventor, but the letter is of significance in that it is the only piece of extant writing in which the supposed inventor mentions the name of the sport with which he is associated.

Since its beginnings, baseball, arguably the ultimate, best-loved stick-and-ball game of all time, has come to mean many things for both fans and players. Played as an organized sport before the Civil War, baseball was proudly construed by Americans to be wholly American, a recreation devised, altered, guided, evolved, sparked, promoted, played, and passionately enjoyed on the shores of the New World, a lively diversion with an American historical tradition like Old Glory or ragtime or log-splitting.

As the twentieth century commenced—with the phonograph, telephone, automobile, and moving pictures already wondrous realities of everyday life; and radio, airplane, and television soon to become permanent fixtures in the tapestry of society—America had a glorious national pastime: baseball, the game that evoked the carefree spirit of summer, unbridled merriment, a sense of timelessness, idyllic charm, and oh, yes, an ethos of friendly competition.

The spirit of American nationalism at the end of the nineteenth century as brought out by the Spanish-American War set the climate for acceptance of the claim that an American had invented baseball. It was Abner Graves, a mining engineer who later murdered his wife, who made this claim, confusing Abner Doubleday the soldier with Abner Doubleday, the six-year-old boy in Cooperstown in 1839, when Graves alleged Doubleday invented the rules of baseball. The Mills Commission accepted Graves's testimony, and the finding of a ball in 1934 that Abner Doubleday had purportedly played with at Cooperstown when he "invented" baseball substantiated the myth. The Mills Commission worked in an era when "invention" was the buzz-word of the day, and every good idea had to have a progenitor. The Doubleday creation myth of baseball is a splendid tale that fills this bill, but it is, unfortunately, untrue.

The Doubleday creation myth was a patriotic construction that was con-venient for its time and serves several other purposes as well. With its pastoral setting in Cooperstown, New York, and its war hero, Abner Doubleday, the myth fills Americans' need for the genesis of their national pastime to have a bit of romance to it. It might even be argued, on a more philosophical level, that despite baseball having evolved over a long period, people are more emotionally satisfied with the notion of a single creator, even if it is a legend. Furthermore, the Doubleday creation myth has been beneficial for baseball and Cooperstown. Unlike the case with basketball, whose inventor and time of invention are known—James Naismith in 1891—the controversy over baseball's origins and attempts to debunk the Doubleday myth over the years have given baseball an element of mystery that heightens awareness of the sport. Why go to all the trouble of digging out the truth when the myth serves so well? Indeed, the perpetuation of the Doubleday creation myth is in many ways undoubtedly healthy for baseball.

Still, debunking a myth does not, and should not necessarily, expunge the importance of a spurious relic, as the relic's symbolism and what it means to people may sometimes be more important than its authenticity. Indeed, the world is full of artifacts that are not what they purport to be.

Learning the facts behind the baseball creation myth does nothing to diminish the symbolism of the Doubleday Ball. Like the romantic images conjured up by the sport, the Doubleday Ball, a quasi-validation of the Mills Commission's conclusion, has become a symbol of the myth that Abner Doubleday created the sport, which is part of the tradition of baseball.

The Doubleday Ball is by tradition a vestige of the early days of baseball, fittingly shredded from use. Limned with the fingerprints of people who lived during baseball's first days, it could have been a child's toy, but it also just possibly could have been a ball that was gripped, tossed, and smacked by mid–nineteenth-century players in the game's infancy. The Doubleday Ball handily fills the need for a crown jewel of the sport.

LOCATION: National Baseball Hall of Fame and Museum, Cooperstown, New York.

Vendovi's Head

CICICICICICICICICICICICICICICICICICICICICICICICI

DATE: 1842.

WHAT IT IS: The skull of a nineteenth-century Fiji Islands cannibal chief wanted for masterminding the trapping of an American merchant crew that was subsequently eaten.

WHAT IT LOOKS LIKE: The skull has a mix of Melanesian and Polynesian characteristics and is of average size for its population group. The condition of the teeth shows that the person had good dental health when he was alive.

This is a story about a strange set of events that is reported to have happened in a remote part of the world a long time ago. It involves a group of people whose customs and practices may seem bizarre, if not repugnant, to us today, but it should be remembered that these people were the product of their own unique civilization, and that as savage as they may appear, they could also demonstrate sensitivity and warmth. Although this story may be shocking, it is a real story about real people and an undeniable part of the heritage of humankind.

While en route to Kantavu from the island of Viti Levu in the Fiji Islands, Paddy Connel warned Captain Bachelor that while in Rewa he had heard that the natives coveted what they believed to be a valuable cargo aboard the American merchant brigantine *Charles Doggett,* and that the captain and his crew were in great danger from the treacherous contrivances of the natives. Connel, an Irish vagabond who years earlier had settled in the Fiji Islands and by his own account had married some one hundred women there and sired dozens of children, was acquainted with many of the islanders and should be privy, Bachelor assumed, to such conspiratorial activities. Captain Bachelor had hired him and some other men to help the Americans obtain bêche-de-mer, a kind of sea cucumber used in oriental trade, and for further assistance Bachelor had engaged on Viti Levu two chiefs, Vendovi and Vasu, for their help in collecting the marine animal.

Shortly after, the *Doggett* arrived at her destination, an island off the eastern tip of Kantavu, where there was a hut for processing the bêche-de-mer, and a local chief came aboard the visiting vessel as a token of security. This was a customary practice, but the next day the special visitor complained of illness and returned to the island. One day later, Vendovi, the Rewan chief whose assistance had been previously obtained, came on board the *Doggett* to importune Captain Bachelor to bring medicine to the ailing chief on the island. The captain was willing to comply with the request, but Paddy Connel, having observed that the chief's manner when departing the vessel was a bit too cheerful for someone who was ailing, warned Captain Bachelor that stepping ashore was tantamount to a death sentence, as surely with his presence there the natives would carry out some egregious offense.

Captain Bachelor was faced with a difficult decision this day in August 1834. He had entered into an agreement with the natives to obtain their help in a matter of commerce, and he didn't want to insult them or withhold medicine that could help the allegedly ailing chief, who had specifically requested the captain as the purveyor of his needed medication. On the other hand, could the chief's illness and the request for the captain to bring medicine be part of an elaborate plot to murder him and his men already working on the island? Could the natives be so treacherous? What should he do?

Contemporary accounts of the Fijian natives' customs and society provide a clearer understanding of the dilemma faced by Captain Bachelor and his crew. Let us draw on the reports of U.S. Navy Rear Admiral Charles Wilkes, who visited the Fiji Islands six years after this incident and wrote about it in his five-volume *Narrative of the United States Exploring Expedition During the Years 1838, 1839, 1840, 1841, 1842.* Wilkes's visit to Fiji was a stop on an expedition to chart oceans and lands and collect samples of plant and animal specimens, as well as objects belonging to the different cultures the voyagers encountered. In the summer of 1838, a small fleet left Virginia to commence the expedition, with Wilkes its commander.

According to Wilkes, the Fijians had volatile personalities; they could be jovial one minute and fly into "demon-like anger" the next. They were prone to stealing and lying, he asserted, the latter being such a respected accomplishment that they preferred to tell lies even when honesty would serve them better.

To gain a woman's hand in marriage, Wilkes noted, the consent of her parents and brother was required, though if the mother and father refused, the woman could still marry if her brother consented. Sometimes marriages were arranged, and in the lower classes a wife could be exchanged for some object, the result being that she was regarded as the husband's property. "The usual price is a whale's tooth, or a musket," wrote Wilkes, "and this once paid, the husband has the entire right to the person of the wife, whom he may even kill and eat if he feels so disposed." Polygamy was a common practice, the number of wives a man might have limited only by his desire and means of subsistence.

Wilkes reported that when a husband died, it usually meant the end for his wife or wives too, for it was the practice for a woman to be slain at her husband's funeral. She would either be strangled or buried alive, and if she resisted, her relatives would be eager to assist her in this ritual—not so much, Wilkes suggested, to bring her into spiritual union with her husband as to obtain her property and possessions. Unfortunately for the Fijian women, one man's death could spell doom for more than one female. Here's Wilkes on the fate of some women after the death of a king:

> At the funeral of the late king, Ulivou, which was witnessed by Mr. Cargill, his five wives and a daughter were strangled. The principal wife delayed the ceremony, by taking leave of those around her; whereupon Tanoa, the present king, chid her. The victim was his own aunt, and he assisted in putting the rope around her neck, and strangling her, a service he is said to have rendered on a former occasion, to his own mother.

People who were born with a physical deformity or were chronically ill were commonly put to death, according to Wilkes, and those descending into a state of decrepitude invited their friends to end their lives. Even a physical injury where there was a complete recovery could have fatal repercussions if the family felt disgraced, as in the case of the boy who lost a leg to a shark, then was nursed back to good health by a white resident, only to be strangled because of his appearance.

Human sacrifice was a common custom of the Fijians, Wilkes reported:

> The victims are usually taken from a distant tribe, and when not supplied by war or violence, they are at times obtained by negotiation. After being selected for this purpose, they are often kept for a time to be fattened. When about to be sacrificed, they are compelled to sit upon the ground, with their feet drawn under their thighs, and their arms placed close before them. In this posture they are bound

so tightly that they cannot stir, or move a joint. They are placed in the usual oven, upon hot stones, and covered with leaves and earth, where they are roasted alive. When the body is cooked, it is taken from the oven, and the face painted black, as is done by the natives on festal occasions. It is then carried to the mbure, where it is offered to the gods, and is afterwards removed to be cut up and distributed, to be eaten by the people. Women are not allowed to enter the mbure, or to eat human flesh. . . . When a new mbure is built, a party goes out and seizes the first person they meet, whom they sacrifice to the gods. When a large canoe is launched, the first person, man or woman, whom they encounter, is laid hold of and carried home for a feast. When Tanoa launches a canoe, ten or more men are slaughtered on the deck, in order that it may be washed with human blood. Human sacrifices are also among the rites performed at the funerals of chiefs, when slaves are in some instances put to death. Their bodies are first placed in the grave, and upon them those of the chief and his wives are laid.

Unlike in some cannibalistic societies, where human flesh was eaten only as a part of a ritual, there was, said Wilkes, no such restriction among the Fijians. Here is Wilkes again, on the Fijians' practice of cannibalism:

The eating of human flesh is not confined to cases of sacrifice for religious purposes, but is practised from habit and taste. The existence of cannibalism, independent of superstitious notions, has been doubted by many. There can be no question that, although it may have originated as a sacred rite, it is continued in the Feejee Group for the mere pleasure of eating human flesh as a food. Their fondness for it will be understood from the custom they have of sending portions of it to their friends at a distance, as an acceptable present, and the gift is eaten, even if decomposition have begun before it is received. So highly do they esteem this food, that the greatest praise they can bestow on a delicacy is to say that it is as tender as a dead man. Even their sacrifices are made more frequent, not merely to gratify feelings of revenge, but to indulge their taste for this horrid food.

. . . The cannibal propensity is not limited to enemies or persons of a different tribe, but they will banquet on the flesh of their dearest friends, and it is even related, that in times of scarcity, families will make an exchange of children for this horrid purpose.

If the Fijian natives indeed had no reservations when it came to eating the bodies of their families, friends, and neighbors, obviously there would be no moral impediment to consuming those of strangers. Returning to Captain Bachelor's dilemma, he weighed the decision of whether he should go ashore to administer medicine to the "sick" chief or stay aboard. He had received multiple warnings from Paddy Connel but perhaps wasn't fully convinced of their accuracy. He may not have wanted to believe the natives would have no compunctions, if they thought they could be successful at it, about murdering the whole crew of a visiting ship for its cargo and a hearty meal.

As it turned out, Captain Bachelor heeded Paddy Connel's warning and stayed aboard the *Charles Doggett,* but after foolishly dispatching men to the island a few days earlier, compounded his error by sending one of his officers to bring the medicine to the allegedly ill chief. Vendovi expressed disappointment at Bachelor's decision but returned by boat to the island with the officer. Not long after their arrival, the bêche-de-mer hut was ablaze, and what was left of the crew on board the American brig, guessing what was taking place, gazed helplessly at the shore, then fired futile volleys from the ship's carronades.

The Americans were able to negotiate for the return of the bodies. Seven bodies, Charles Wilkes wrote in his *Narrative,* "were brought down to the shore much mutilated, in consideration of a musket. The eighth, a negro, had been cooked and eaten. Captain Bachelor had the bodies sewed up in canvass, and thrown overboard, in the usual manner. They however, floated again, and fell into the hands of the savages, who, as [Paddy Connel] afterwards understood, devoured them all. They complained, however, that they did not like them, and particularly the negro, whose flesh they said tasted strong of tobacco."

Six years after this debacle, Charles Wilkes, on his South Pacific information-gathering naval expedition, spoke with Paddy Connel, who told him of the mass killings of the Americans from the *Charles Doggett.* Incensed by Connel's report, Wilkes felt this heinous crime could not go unpunished and resolved to bring the main culprit to justice. Connel told him that person was Vendovi, although his brothers, also chiefs, had been party to the murderous scheme.

Through Connel, Wilkes requested Captain William Hudson— commander of the man-of-war *Peacock,* which was part of his expedition, then anchored off Viti Levu—to effect the capture of Chief Vendovi. Coincidentally, an artist from the ship had recently drawn a portrait of Vendovi at Rewa, a settlement on Viti Levu, so it was known that their target was around. They hatched a plan to invite the islanders aboard the vessel for a festive reception. Soon, the king and queen, chiefs, servants, and other natives, numbering more than seventy, were visitors on board the *Peacock,* and Vendovi himself was expected to join the gathering. The visitors sensed something strange was happening, as Wilkes wrote: "There was an evident constraint in the manner of the visitors, which was apparent from their not expressing the usual astonishment at everything they saw." But after some time had passed and it was obvious Vendovi would not be showing up, Captain Hudson, through a translator, informed the king, a brother of Vendovi, and the chiefs that they and their party were

This representation of cannibal chief Vendovi comes from a drawing by A. T. Agate that was engraved by J. W. Paradise. Vendovi's face is soft and expressive, in contrast to other illustrations that survive, which show Vendovi with a harsh, if not fierce, countenance.

prisoners on the ship and that the Americans' purpose was to apprehend Vendovi for slaughtering their countrymen several years before.

The islanders feared their captors were going to kill them, but they were assured that it was Vendovi, the mastermind of the murder of the *Charles Doggett* crew, who was the target, and that it was necessary to hold them hostage to effect his capture. The royal party was sympathetic to the American position, saying that Vendovi should be punished and that he in fact was troublesome to them as well. But they did make it a point that although others had been involved in the slayings, Vendovi alone should be punished.

One of the royal visitors, a man named Ngaraningiou, who proclaimed Vendovi to be his enemy, was sent to Vendovi's home to take him prisoner, if possible, and bring him to the vessel. Ngaraningiou had had many difficulties with Vendovi and was glad to be the instrument that would undoubtedly lead to Vendovi's death, even if he, like the king, was Vendovi's brother. Perhaps any remorse over turning in his brother for such a purpose was lessened by his recollection that Vendovi had taken the life of their oldest brother. For their part, the Americans still harbored some concern that the natives, as a matter of revenge, would attack the missionaries on the island, but they were assured that this would not happen and furthermore had taken the precaution of alerting them to what was occurring.

Despite the dangers of his mission, Ngaraningiou did make it to Vendovi's home and embarked on his plan to seize him. He sat next to Vendovi, placed his hand on his arm, and explained that he was wanted for the murder of the *Doggett* crew some years back. He told Vendovi that the king and queen, as well as others, were being held hostage aboard a foreign vessel and that the chief's surrender was a condition of their release. Although he probably knew his surrender was tantamount to a death sentence, Vendovi agreed to go, an honorable act on his part in deference to the royal rulers. When Ngaraningiou did not return with Vendovi later that day, however, the *Peacock* crew became worried about the emissary's safety. In fact, while Vendovi was willing to leave immediately for the *Peacock*, Ngaraningiou himself delayed the trip until the next day. During the evening, on board the *Peacock*, the natives entertained the crew with dances.

The next day Vendovi, in a canoe with Ngaraningiou, arrived at the *Peacock* and came on board. "He was a model of a man, very tall and erect and of a proud bearing, scrupulously clean in his habits," Wilkes wrote of Vendovi in his autobiography. Vendovi carried on board with him a Jew's harp he had obtained and which he liked to play, being very fond of music. With his crew and royal guests present, Captain Hudson interrogated Vendovi about the crime for which he was sought, and Vendovi, according to Wilkes, "acknowledged his guilt in causing the murder of part of the crew of the Charles Doggett, and admitted that he held the mate by the arms while the natives killed him with clubs." Satisfied that Vendovi was guilty of murder, if not the architect of the whole macabre plot, Captain Hudson resolved to take Vendovi to America to be rehabilitated in the manners of a civilized society. The Fijians surmised they would never see Vendovi again, and their farewells to him were quite a spectacle. As Wilkes described it:

> All the party were now much affected. Kania, the king, seated himself on the right of Vendovi, taking hold of his arm, while

Navumialu placed himself on the left. .... All shed tears and sobbed aloud while conversing in broken sentences with their brother. The natives shed tears also, and none but Ngaraningiou remained unmoved. The king kissed the prisoner's forehead, touched noses, and turned away. The inferior chiefs approached and kissed his hands, whilst the common people crawled up to him and kissed his feet. One young man who belonged to the household of Vendovi, was the last to quit him; he wished to remain with his master but was not permitted. In bidding farewell to the chief, he embraced his knees, kissed his hands and feet, and received a parting blessing from Vendovi, who placed his manacled hands on his head. The young man retreated backwards towards the ladder, sighing and sobbing as though his heart would break.

The royal party was released and given gifts before their departure. As the *Peacock* took off, Vendovi—a much-feared chief with the reputation of having killed many innocent people in his lifetime and to have feasted often on human remains—wept aloud. Before bringing Vendovi to America, Captain Hudson intended to bring his man-of-war to Kantavu to find the other guilty chiefs who had participated in the *Charles Doggett* crew killings—and torch their villages, if necessary—but strong winds steered his vessel so far away as to make returning time-consuming and difficult, considering he was to rendezvous with another vessel.

Vendovi was taken off the *Peacock* and placed on the USS *Vincennes*, another ship on Wilkes's expedition. The voyage to America would not follow immediately. This was, after all, a scientific expedition, and it was not finished; plant, animal, archaeological, geological, and ethnographical specimens in different geographical areas had to be collected. Wilkes allocated different reconnaissance missions to the vessels under his command; the ship bearing Vendovi was to explore the North American coastline from Canada to northern California. This afforded the chief of Rewa a glimpse at how Native Americans lived, and he responded with a bit of snobbery. According to Wilkes, Vendovi felt it was beneath him to talk to people of color, thinking them primitive, and was amiable only toward the white men. As Wilkes wrote in his autobiography, "He was a splendid picture of a Savage, very proud & very haughty in his bearing and evinced much disgust at the natives of the Northwest coast and those of the Sandwich Islands and would never condescend to keep any intercourse with them, applying to them all the strong epithets the Feejee language offered of his contempt for the colored race. With the whites he was more on a par and many of our men he became attached to and accepted kindnesses from them." The *Vincennes* met up with the other ships in Wilkes's fleet in Hawaii and took an eastern route, first to California, then to Hawaii, Singapore, and around Africa to return to the United States.

On the trip to America, Vendovi was friendly, jovial, and kind, in contrast to the personality he had exhibited in his homeland. No doubt he aroused the sympathy of the mates on board, who knew that on Vendovi's arrival he would again be clapped in chains, that he would draw the wrath of Americans whose countrymen he had murdered, and that he would face a trial. But the voyage proved fatal for Vendovi. He became ill, and after an elderly sailor on board who spoke his language and with whom he had developed a friendship passed away, his condition deteriorated. On the day in June 1842 that his vessel sailed into the New York City harbor, some two years after leaving his South Pacific home, the ailing Chief Vendovi was carried off the boat and taken to a naval hospital. He died shortly thereafter. Had he lived, this exotic chief who had killed and purportedly devoured many human beings would surely have caused a stir in New York City, not to mention the whole of America; and likewise, the sight of a large civilized city would probably have amazed the Fijian chief. But with his death, none of this was to come to pass.

After Vendovi's death, physicians at the hospital made a death mask of his head with plaster and then removed the head; the remainder of the Fijian chief's corpse was buried in the cemetery by the hospital. Vendovi's skull was sent to the National Institute for the Promotion of Science, a recently formed repository for artifacts acquired on exploratory missions, and later, after its termination in 1861, to the Smithsonian Institution. Without a physical anthropology section, however, the Smithsonian wasn't deemed the right home for this specimen, and seven years later it went to the Army Medical Museum, also in Washington, D.C. But in the early 1900s, after the Smithsonian's creation of a physical anthropology division, Vendovi's skull was returned to its former home.

Vendovi's remains have scientific relevance for numerous reasons. Foremost, the skull is of a known individual: there is an accurate account of when he lived, his tribal affiliation, his age, and his cause of death. Additionally, at the time Vendovi was alive there was little or no Caucasian admixture in the Fijian population. Therefore, his cranial morphology reflects a more accurate representation of the Fijian population, especially of the Fijian people from the late eighteenth century. Because of this factual record of Vendovi's background, the morphology and cranial measurements from Vendovi's skull have been used for comparison purposes to evaluate and hypothesize population migrations in the South Pacific through other crania from Oceanic (South Pacific) archaeological investigations and to help in the classification of historical Oceanic skeletal collections in museums throughout the world. Vendovi's craniometric data are part of the International Forensic Data Bank, which is used to help identify people involved in mass fatalities or in questionable deaths.

On a broader scale, human skeletons are, in a way, like a diary. Retained in the morphology of the hard tissue are the effects of diet, disease, trauma, and aging that the individual sustained during life. From these discernible markers and from bone chemistry such as mineral and isotope compounds retrieved by biochemical analysis, nutritional and environmental influences to bone formation and maintenance can be determined. Vendovi's skull is such a storehouse of information, curated in its holding institution for today's ongoing research and available for future generations of researchers and new research technologies that may easily answer questions not even thought of yet.

Fijians today remember Vendovi with pride, and some Fijians living in New York City and other parts of America visit the memorial grave to Vendovi in Brooklyn as an annual tradition. Representatives of the Fijian people have indicated that they are honored that one of their ancestors and former chiefs is part of the Smithsonian Institution, and that by his being there, he continues to contribute to the research and understanding of the Fijian people and is an integral part of the institution's purpose to make all information available for dissemination throughout the world.

The story of the murder of the *Charles Doggett* crew by Fijian natives in 1834 is, on the surface, one of deceit, murder, and mayhem. Looking deeper, one sees that it is also a poignant tale of human redemption. Vendovi, the fearsome cannibal chief, having perpetrated a horrible massacre, willingly gave himself over to justice to keep his own people from being punished; wept when he left his kinsmen, knowing he would never see them again; marveled at the worldly sights he saw on his voyage to judgment; and thoroughly charmed his captors. And the ultimate irony is that Vendovi the cannibal, after his own untimely death, gave back something to civilization by contributing to the study of physical anthropology with his own severed skull.

LOCATION: National Museum of Natural History, Washington, D.C.

The Battle Sword of Colonel Najera

CRRRRRRRRRRRRRRRRRRRRRRRRRRRR

DATE: 1846.

WHAT IT IS: A sword used in a famous duel of the Mexican War.

WHAT IT LOOKS LIKE: The sword measures 41½ inches; all its mountings, including the hilt and sheath fittings, are made of sterling silver. There are inscriptions on either side of the sheath's upper ring, one side reading "Worn by Lt. Col. Nagera [sic], of the Mexican Lancers who fell in personal combat with Col. John C. Hays of the Texas Rangers," the other side reading "Captured in the battle of Monterey/Septem.r 21st 1846." The blade contains an engraving in Spanish (whose view is partly obstructed by the scabbard), which, roughly translated, reads, "Draw me not with anger, sheath me not without honor."

Adventure-movie aficionados everywhere would immediately recognize this tense one-on-one battle scene: amid a throng of excited onlookers, an American swashbuckler faces off against an intimidating foreigner wielding a sharp saber. With his nemesis preparing to deliver a fatal blow, the American, empty-handed and apparently defenseless, simply reaches for his holstered pistol and pumps one fatal round into his challenger, felling him instantly.

The confrontation between Indiana Jones and the black-robed thug in *Raiders of the Lost Ark*? Well, let's just say that history in all its sundry dramas has an uncanny way of anticipating fictionalized entertainment. Try the mid–nineteenth-century duel between the cool and intrepid Texas Ranger Jack Hays and a bold and little-known Mexican Army colonel!

It was the Mexican War that provided the setting for this real-life derring-do on an open range in Mexico in 1846. The war had its roots in the expansionist fever that began to sweep America around the turn of the nineteenth century. In 1803 the United States doubled its size with the purchase of the Louisiana Territory from France, and while the War of 1812 interrupted U.S. plans to absorb northeastern Florida after its agents stirred Americans there into rebellion against the Spanish, America finally acquired Florida from Spain in 1819 with the Adams-Onis Treaty.

In the 1840s, the concept of Manifest Destiny—the idea that it was the natural course for the United States to expand its westward boundary all the way to the Pacific Ocean, so that the country's borders would extend "from sea to shining sea"—emerged in full bloom. There were many provinces to the west that could be added to the United States, and Texas seemed a good first acquisition.

During the first half of the nineteenth century, major changes were also taking place in Mexico. Since Christopher Columbus had opened up the New World for Europe in 1492, Spain had mined its colonial empire in the Western Hemisphere, and Mexico had been added to that empire less than thirty years later, when Hernán Cortés conquered the Aztecs through campaigns that sometimes employed cruel tactics.

Spain's grasp on Mexico and its other New World colonies had been firm for almost three hundred years, until the Napoleonic Wars of the early 1800s weakened Spain, and France invaded Mexico (around 1808). With Spain's power now eroded, Mexicans saw a chance to gain their independence and in 1810 began a revolution that culminated eleven years later, in 1821, with independence from Spain. Texas, once a province of Spain, became absorbed into the new Republic of Mexico, which invited Americans to settle in its new northern territory.

Indeed, efforts had already been mounted to attract Americans to this vast area when Moses Austin, in 1820, tried to create an Anglo-American colony there by obtaining a land grant from Spain. Following Austin's death in 1821, his son, Stephen, continued his mission to bring in settlers, an effort so successful that in 1830 Mexico tried to curb further immigration. But the settlers desired their own independence—not to mention a continuation of slavery, which Mexico wanted to end—and the Texans eventually rebelled against the Mexicans. In the first major battle, on October 2, 1835, the Americans defeated Mexican soldiers at the Guadalupe River; but the next year, after Texas had declared its independence, the Mexican Army defeated the Texans at the Alamo in San Antonio.

With the Alamo massacre burning in their minds, the Texans retaliated at San Jacinto and drove the Mexican Army out of their territory. The Texans formed the Lone Star Republic, an independent political entity that became a focal point of interest for many countries. European powers wanted it

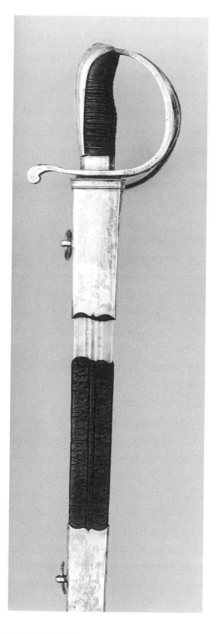

Najera's battle sword. Engraved on the upper section of the sheath on one side is the legend: "Worn by Lt. Col. Nagera, of the Mexican Lancers who fell in personal combat with Col. John C. Hays of the Texas Rangers."

to remain independent to prevent America from expanding. For the United States, the Texas Republic was controversial; southern and western states favored its annexation, while northern states resisted, not wanting to add another slave state. In early 1845, however, after an unsuccessful attempt in the Senate to establish a treaty providing for Texas's annexation, Texas was finally admitted to the Union when Congress passed a joint resolution.

Mexico's outrage at this action was further exacerbated by the United States' claim that the Rio Grande was the international border between the United States and Mexico (Mexico contended the Texan border was the Nueces River) and by American intentions to claim more northern Mexican lands. After John Slidell, who had been dispatched to Mexico by President James Polk in November 1845 to try to purchase New Mexico and California and settle the border dispute, failed in his mission, Polk sent soldiers to the area of the border dispute.

On April 25, 1846, a battle erupted between forces of the two countries when a Mexican regiment crossed the Rio Grande to engage a waiting American cavalry led by General Zachary Taylor. President Polk asked Congress to declare war, arguing that Mexico had "shed American blood on American soil." Within a few weeks Congress authorized the president to recruit volunteers into the army and granted $10 million for the United States to attack Mexico. The southern states embraced the war, while the northern states opposed it on the grounds that Mexico, which had become an independent country only twenty-five years previously, was a weak country, and that annexing Texas would inflame the slavery issue.

Meanwhile, on May 8, 1846, another battle erupted at Palo Alto, Texas, in which Zachary Taylor led the Americans to their first major victory in the then-undeclared war. War officially came shortly after, however; the United States made its declaration on May 13, and Mexico reciprocated against its northern neighbor ten days later. Thus the Mexican War was official, with many new battles to be fought and much more blood to be spilled.

In the early morning hours of September 21, 1846, Zachary Taylor received a note from General W. J. Worth recommending that the enemy be diverted at the eastern end of Monterrey. Taylor concurred. While it was still dark, Colonel John Coffee Hays, a Texas Ranger who had received a commission in the army, led a scouting party to determine if the enemy was preparing to ambush Worth's camp. Through the night it had been raining, and Hays's rangers had had to sleep on the wet ground without blankets to protect them from the cold air. After riding about a mile, Hays stopped his unit, deciding to wait until dawn broke; his men dismounted and made camp, some falling immediately to sleep.

When sunlight broke through the darkness, it revealed a stunning sight— a Mexican cavalry brandishing lances with flapping pennons six hundred feet away. The Mexican cavalry's leader ordered his men into formation. Colonel Hays issued an order for his rangers to prepare themselves for battle, then mounted his horse and headed out to meet the enemy.

After riding a couple of hundred feet, Hays, an experienced Indian fighter, confronted the Mexican leader, also on horseback. Hays bowed. The Mexican colonel, whose name was Juan N. Najera, returned the gesture by removing his headgear. Hays, wearing a bandanna and holding a saber, challenged his counterpart to a duel, and Najera accepted. Hays's men, now awake and watching, wondered about their leader's intentions, since he was not known to be an adept swordsman.

In moments the duel was ready to commence. The Jalisco cavalry (part of General Manuel Romero's brigade) and the Texas Rangers, situated on opposite sides, fixed on the two combatants. As Hays slowly advanced, without warning the Mexican colonel suddenly charged, swinging his sword. Hays swerved, losing his grip on his own sword, which fell to the ground. But Najera had turned and was bearing down on his now-unarmed adversary. Before his nemesis could cut him down, Hays drew one of his pair of six-shooters and fired a shot into Najera, dropping him from his horse and killing him instantly.

Hays bolted toward his men, who were now on their horses, and shouted for them to get off and take cover behind their mounts. The Mexican cavalry charged, but the rangers held them off, killing dozens but losing only one of their own men. The Americans knew their death toll would have been much higher save for the order by Hays to dismount and take cover.

The Americans continued to defeat the Mexicans in battle after battle until even the American pioneers in California forced Mexican officers out. In 1848, the Treaty of Guadalupe Hidalgo provided for settlement of the war, with Mexico to cede California and New Mexico to the United States and recognize the Rio Grande as Texas's southern border, in return for a U.S. payment of $15 million to Mexico.

When the Mexican War finally ended in 1848, John Coffee Hays decided to pursue a career outside the military. But he was to be no ordinary civilian. The reputation of the Texas Rangers from the Mexican War had spread far and wide, with Hays perhaps the most famous of this stalwart bunch.

Hays's fame is a typical example of the larger-than-life esteem in which mid–nineteenth-century easterners held their western heroes. In 1853, for example, Hays wanted to attend the presidential inauguration of his old friend and fellow Mexican War officer, Franklin Pierce, in a bid to be appointed California's surveyor general. Before arriving in the nation's capital he stopped off in New York, where one day he was recognized by a man talking in the street with an acquaintance. The man remarked to his friend, "That's Colonel Jack Hays, the famous Texas Ranger," whereupon his friend shouted, "My God, hurry up and catch him. I'd rather be introduced to him than any man in the world."

The man accosted Hays and introduced his friend. The man later wrote, "After the interview I had hard work convincing my friend that the modest, unpretentious, mild, quiet-toned gentleman he talked with was the world-renowned Jack Hays, the Texas Ranger. He had expected to see a man breathing fire and with the war over look conspicuous and overpowering in every feature."

Hays's presence at Pierce's inauguration and at the celebration that followed drew the attention of the public and the newspapers. One reporter wrote that of all the people in the capital for the inauguration, the center of interest was the Texas Ranger, Jack Hays, about whom "it may be safely asserted that no man in America . . . since the great John Smith explored the primeval forests of Virginia . . . has run a career of such boldness, daring and adventure. His frontier defence of the Texas Republic constitutes one of the most remarkable pages in the history of the American character." Needless to say, Hays was awarded the federal surveyor-general post that he had come to Washington to seek.

While he was a ranger, Hays had befriended a Comanche chief named Buffalo Hump, and one day he had idly promised to name his first son after the Native American. When his first son was born in California, Hays made good on his promise. Hays's uncle sent word to Buffalo Hump that his old friend from Texas had a son, and that Hays had given his son the chief's name for a nickname. Buffalo Hump promptly purchased two gold-washed silver spoons (one is engraved "Buffalo Hump Hays," the other "BHH") and a matching cup, and had a friend deliver these items to the Hays family in San Francisco.

After the duel in which Hays shot and killed Najera, either Hays recovered the Mexican colonel's sword from the battlefield as a souvenir or one of his men retrieved it to present to him as a gift. It stayed in Hays's family until about 1989, when John Hays, a direct descendant and namesake of the celebrated "Captain Jack," and his mother donated the sword along with other original John Hays artifacts, including the Buffalo Hump Hays silver spoons, to its present home. Today the sword serves as a symbol not only of gallant duels fought with pride and courage in the interests of national ambition, but of a historic struggle in which Texans fought hard for their independence.

LOCATION: Autry Museum of Western Heritage, Los Angeles, California.

*C*harles Dickens's Prompt-Copy of *A Christmas Carol*

ᘓᖱᕤᘝᖱᕤᘝᖱᕤᘝᖱᕤᘝᖱᕤᘝᖱᕤᘝᖱᕤᘝᖱᕤᘝᖱᕤᘝᖱᕤᘝᖱᕤᘝᖱᕤᘝᖱᕤᘝᖱᕤᘝᖱᕤᘝᖱᕤᘝᘓ

.

DATE: 1849.

WHAT IT IS: The novelist's specially prepared copy of his famous novel that he used for reading in public, containing alterations of the text, stage directions, and other annotations.

WHAT IT LOOKS LIKE: It is a bound volume in which the 166 pages cut from a copy of the twelfth edition of the novel are affixed to larger cream-colored sheets. In the wide margins and on the inlaid pages are alterations, comments, directions, and editorial symbols made by the author in ink and pencil. The text contains many crossed-out passages; examples of stage directions include "cheerful narrative," "tone to mystery," "tone down to pathos," "up to cheerfulness," "stern pathos," and "tone to Tiny Tim." The cover measures 6½ inches wide by 8⅞ inches long by 1 inch deep. The pages are 5½ inches wide by 8½ inches long; the inlaid pages measure 3¼ inches wide by 5½ inches long. The book has marbled paper-covered boards and a red morocco leather spine that is stamped in gilt.

At eight o'clock on the evening of March 15, 1870, a bearded gentleman dressed in formal attire with a red geranium sprouting from his lapel walked onto the stage of St. James's Hall in London. He carried with him the prompt-copies of the two works he was to perform that night, *A Christmas Carol* and *The Trial from "Pickwick,"* but having recited them scores of times before, he would during the course of the night turn their pages only perfunctorily, without needing to refer to them. Having captivated audiences on both sides of the Atlantic with his public readings over the years, this was to be the very last of his Farewell Readings series.

Charles Dickens, the century's most famous and popular novelist, was ill and exhausted, his public readings having exacted a serious toll on his health, and he resolved that after this last show he would devote his full energies to completing his novel-in-progress, *The Mystery of Edwin Drood.*

Dickens set down his prompt-copies on his wooden reading table at the center of the stage, which had a little shelf on which rested a flask of water. His main reading piece of the evening was the *Carol,* and he was ready to bring the story to life, with all its animated, colorful characters. He drew a deep breath as his adoring audience waited, aware that Dickens ("The Inimitable," as he was nicknamed) was an ill if not dying man.

Charles Dickens had embarked on a secondary profession of delivering public readings of his works almost inadvertently after the publication of his second Christmas book, *The Chimes,* in 1844. For reasons of frugality, Dickens, along with his family, had been living in Italy since the summer of that year, but he had corresponded with his friend John Forster about celebrating the book's publication by doing a reading for their close friends. Forster agreed to host such a gathering, and Dickens returned to London, where on December 3 he delivered a reading of *Chimes*—his first reading of any of his works—to about a half-dozen people. It was a cozy little affair that would through time take on an aura of legendary proportions. As Dickens read his holiday story, he brought some of the men seated around him to tears, an effect the author would have on audience members throughout his lecture career, and one he would delight in.

Thereafter, it became Dickens's practice to stage readings of portions of a new or in-progress literary endeavor. It was a couple of readings to a circle of friends in Lausanne, Switzerland, in 1846 that gave Dickens the idea that there was money to be made in what he had previously been doing for free. Dickens at the time had been preoccupied with the impending publication of his *Dombey and Son,* and on September 12 he held a soiree in which he read the novel's first chapter. It was such a success that shortly after Dickens gave another reading to the same group. So enthused was the author by the reception that he wrote a letter to Forster in which he expressed his satisfaction at making audiences laugh and declared that "in these days of lecturings and readings, a great deal of money might possibly be made (if it were not infra dig*) by one's having Readings of one's own books."

Some friends would advise the illustrious author that it was in fact beneath his dignity to read for profit, but the idea nonetheless held a powerful appeal

---

*Meaning "beneath one's dignity."

A page from Charles Dickens's prompt-copy of A Christmas Carol. Dickens marked the pages of his prompt-copy to edit the story and help him bring it to life when he recited it to audiences.

for Dickens. That Dickens was naturally suited to appear onstage before an audience was consistent with his restless character. As a young man he had an avid interest in theater and over the years had written and acted in plays, and he sometimes even performed duties as a stage manager for various productions.

It wasn't until eight years later, however, that Dickens actually delivered his first public reading—and it was not for profit but for charity. A writer whose works commented penetratingly on the social ills of his day, Dickens decided that his readings would be for the benefit of particular causes. Perhaps Dickens's compassion for the unfortunate developed partly as a response to his own youthful poverty.

Born on February 7, 1812, in Landport, Charles John Huffam Dickens was the second of eight children. His father, John, was a government clerk who was locked up in the Marshalsea, a debtors' prison, and when Charles was ten his mother had opened a school that failed to attract students. Charles was forced to go out and earn money himself, and he went to work in a factory where he mounted labels on blacking pots. This was a painful part of young Charles's life, "an evil hour for me," he called it, that no doubt provided inspiration for such themes as cruelty to children and inhumanity to the poor that he would bring out later in his stories. It was the plight of uneducated male laborers that first drew Dickens's philanthropic attention, however, and for the benefit of the Birmingham and Midland Institute, a free educational institution, on December 27, 1853, he gave his first charity reading. For some three hours Dickens riveted the audience's attention at the Birmingham Town Hall with his animated storytelling of his beloved *Carol*.

By this time his book was on its way to becoming a classic. Dickens had begun to write *A Christmas Carol. In Prose. Being a Ghost Story of Christmas* in early October 1843 and had completed the novella by the end of November. He submitted his original manuscript (The Pierpont Morgan Library, New York City) to his publisher, Chapman & Hall, and it was published on December 17, 1843. The title page was printed in two colors, and the book contained illustrations by John Leech.

One can imagine the Victorian audience enthralled as the author acted out his tale of a miser being taken on eye-opening excursions by the Ghosts of Christmas Past, Present, and Future, which lead him to discover the true spirit of Christmas. Onstage Dickens infused life into his *Carol* characters: Ebenezer Scrooge, Bob Cratchit, Tiny Tim, the ghost of Jacob Marley, Mr. and Mrs. Fezziwig, and others. A review from the *Portland Transcript* of February 4, 1868, gives a vivid picture:

> His power of facial expression is wonderful; it is as much what he does as what he says that constitutes the charm of his performance. He gives a distinct voice to each character, and to an extraordinary extent assumes the personality of each. At one moment he is savage old Scrooge, at the next, his jolly nephew, and in the twinkling of an eye little timid, lisping Bob Cratchit appears. All this is effected by the play of features as well as the varying tones of voice. It is the comical or the savage twist of the mouth—the former to the right, the latter to the left—the elongation of the face, the roll or twinkle of the eyes, and above all the wonderful lift of the eyebrows, that produce such surprising and delightful effects. And then he not only personates his characters, he performs their actions. This he does by means of wonderfully flexible fingers, which he converts at pleasure into a company of dancers, and makes to act and speak in a hundred ways. He rubs and pats his hands, he flourishes all his fingers, he shakes them, he points them, he makes them equal to a whole stage company in the performance of parts. But then the man is also there. Dickens, the author, comes in at intervals to enjoy his own fun; you see him in the twinkle of an eye and the curve of the mouth. When the audience laughs he beams all over with radiant appreciation of the fun.

Dickens's fame as a reader instantly spread, and he was soon besieged by invitations to recite his works. Under the mistaken impression that he had turned professional, many of those requesting a performance offered to pay him. Over the next few years offers poured in from all over Great Britain—

and elsewhere—so many, in fact, that Dickens couldn't even begin to consider all of them. He resisted the temptation, albeit with reluctance, to read professionally because of the belief that it would compromise his higher calling as a writer, and he continued to speak for the benefit of charities. Dickens customarily drew large audiences of between two and four thousand people at a single reading. A *Christmas Carol* was an audience-pleasing favorite and a staple of his repertoire.

As time passed, however, his own emotional and financial difficulties caused the novelist seriously to consider making a career out of reading for profit. By 1857 his marriage was dissolving, and he would find that he had a deep need to be around people; the tremendous outpouring of admiration and affection bestowed on him at readings lifted some of his despondency. In 1857 Dickens had also moved into a new home, Gad's Hill, and doubtless this had drained his resources while elevating his lifestyle. Just before he separated from his wife Dickens remarked, "I must do *something*, or I shall wear my heart away." The allure of being surrounded by ardent admirers, as well as of the potential financial gain, was obviously too great to pass up.

On April 29, 1858, Dickens made his professional debut as a reader at London's St. Martin's Hall. For his performance he chose not his vastly popular *Christmas Carol*, as he had originally planned (the spring was the customary "season" for public readings in London at the time), but another Yuletide tale, *The Cricket on the Hearth*. Only a few weeks later, however, Dickens installed *Carol* in his professional repertoire.

Dickens prepared special annotated copies of the works he read in public in which he wrote performance instructions and cut out passages. Though his dependence on these prompt-copies would wane through the years, he would nevertheless continue to carry them onstage. Dickens was a diligent rehearser and had memorized his better-received works like *Carol*, but he kept his prompt-copy near in case of a lapse.

Over time Dickens shortened *A Christmas Carol* in half-hour increments until he had it down to under ninety minutes, in order to fit another item into his program to entertain audiences for about two hours. But the *Carol*'s reading time was always approximate, as Dickens never gave the same performance twice, including more or less text depending on his own mood and the audience reaction, and sometimes improvising on his own printed words. Dickens was by no means a mechanical reciter and improvised lines and mannerisms to try to amuse his audience. If any new material received a very positive response, Dickins would be apt to include it in future readings.

By the schedule of speaking engagements written on its flyleaf in the author's hand, it is known that the extant prompt-copy of *A Christmas Carol* was used by Dickens in his readings by 1859; it may well have been used in his first charity reading in December 1853, although no proof of this exists; and it was undoubtedly used through his last professional readings in 1870. Dickens made his *Carol* prompt-copy by pasting the smaller pages from the 1849 twelfth edition, printed by Bradbury & Evans, onto a bound volume of larger sheets, but such a cut-and-paste method wasn't the only way he made his prompt-copies; sometimes the author had small special printings made that contained his annotations.

In the first seven months of his career as a professional reader, Dickens gave a series of lectures in London and toured the provinces, Ireland, and Scotland, delivering scores of readings. The admission to watch a Charles Dickens reading varied, but some indication may be obtained from the broadside of his December 29, 1858, reading of *Little Dombey* and *The Trial from "Pickwick"* at the Chatham Lecture Hall. The terms of admission for the evening performance are given as: "To the Gallery Stalls, 3s. Body of the Hall, Reserved Seats, 2s. Unreserved, 1s." (The abbreviation "*s.*" denoted shillings, a monetary unit in use at the time.)

Traveling from city to city on his reading tours and delivering emotion-filled performances was no doubt strenuous. Dickens would go out on the road for a few weeks or a few months at a time, sometimes lecturing several times in a single week. Drawing enormous crowds virtually wherever he went, the engagements were lucrative and the money too tempting for him to give up or even slow down. After resting less than two weeks after his first London season, he embarked on his first provincial tour. Dickens traveled with a small entourage comprising a manager, who handled the business arrangements for the tours, and a few stagehands.

While Dickens energetically pursued his career as a professional reader, he had by no means forsaken his profession as a writer. In 1850 Dickens had started a weekly periodical, *Household Words,* and put in it installments of such works as *Hard Times.* In the periodical's successor, *All the Year Round,* Dickens included installments of his 1859 French Revolution romance, *A Tale of Two Cities,* which he thought would have wide commercial appeal. And for eight months beginning in December 1860, the author published in *All the Year Round* weekly installments of *Great Expectations,* his novel about the need for people to set themselves free from the past in order to build the future. His literary output was prodigious, and delivering public readings did not seem in any way to hamper his genius.

It seemed that writing fiction had almost always been part of Dickens's aspirations. In 1831 Dickens became a reporter in Parliament, but he was soon to begin more creative literary pursuits. He wrote articles for newspapers and magazines, many of which were compiled in *Sketches by Boz* in 1836. Due to the success of *Boz,* in the same year he began writing *The Pickwick Papers,* stories that were published monthly, as well as adapting a *Boz* sketch for the stage. His remarkable literary career followed. Many of his novels were published in serial form and provided a critical look at social ills. So popular was Dickens, first nicknamed "Boz" and later "The Inimitable," that lines from some of his books—such as "It was the best of times and the worst of times"—would become embedded in popular culture.

After his manager, Arthur Smith, became ill in mid-1861 (he died a few months later), Dickens retained Smith's associate, Thomas Headland, to handle his bookings, but Dickens wasn't happy with the way Headlands conducted the business aspects of his readings and did not renew the contract. From March through June 1863, Dickens delivered a series of readings in London, his last for a few years. Dickens soon began work on a new novel, *Our Mutual Friend,* which was published in installments over a year and a half beginning in May 1864. During the first six months of 1865, a debilitating illness and an injury from a train accident took their toll on Dickens, now approaching his mid-fifties. But the author relished the adventure and excitement of traveling and performing before the public, and so, in early 1866, he signed with the efficiently run firm of Chappell to book his future reading tours.

Dickens developed a repertoire that eventually reached about sixteen pieces. Not all the items that Dickens prepared went over successfully, and those that did not he scrapped from his programs. Dickens even sometimes rehearsed pieces that he never actually read, such as *Mrs. Lirriper's Lodgings, Great Expectations,* and *The Haunted Man.* As he embarked on a tour under his new theatrical manager, Dickens prepared new items including *Doctor Marigold.* Among the items he performed through the years as a professional reader included *Sikes and Nancy* (a dramatic episode from *Oliver Twist*), *Nicholas Nickleby, Boots at the Holly-Tree Inn, Mr. Bob Sawyer's Party, The Poor Traveller,* and *Mrs. Gamp.*

Invitations to do public readings came from foreign countries with offers of extravagant fees. Dickens found that even language wasn't an obstacle; in France many audience members didn't understand English but seemed to relish his performances nonetheless.

Over the years invitations came to Dickens to speak in America, some for quite substantial amounts of money. He fielded these offers cautiously, especially in light of U.S. political turmoil in the 1850s and 1860s. In 1867 he finally sent his business manager to appraise firsthand his prospects for drawing crowds and making money in America. Dickens had actually visited America before, in 1842, during a trip that also included Canada. This journey had a political tone: he spoke out against slavery and an inadequate American copyright statute that resulted in many of his stories being illegally reproduced in the States.

With his manager reporting that he would be very well received in America, Dickens decided to go ahead and tour the country, despite the physical hardships he would have to endure. A farewell dinner was held in his honor in London on November 2, 1867, at which the attendees, who included many prominent people in the arts, saluted him emotionally, and a week later Dickens set sail for America. On November 19 he arrived in Boston, where almost two weeks later he delivered his first reading. Dickens's reading tour took him to some seventeen cities in the East, including New York City, Washington, Buffalo, Rochester, Providence, and New Haven. The presence of Dickens in America excited many—his fame was so great now that even the ill feelings inflamed by his earlier visit were forgotten—and people turned out in droves not just to hear him read but to catch a glimpse of the world's most popular novelist. Dickens's last reading in the States took place on April 20, 1868.

Dickens wanted to retire from touring but felt the financial benefits from one last reading series would help secure his future. On October 6, 1868, the author commenced what was billed as his "Final Farewell Series of Readings." His tour took him to numerous cities in England, as well as to Scotland. His readings encompassed many audience favorites, including, of course, the *Carol.*

As he commenced this series, Dickens was not just tired but afflicted with a variety of debilitating medical conditions. By February he literally could not stand on his feet, and his dates in Glasgow and Edinburgh had to be canceled. But he recuperated and continued his readings, despite serious physical impairments. In mid-April 1869 he lost all sensation in his left side while in Preston, and he notified his doctor, who rushed to see him from London. Dickens's physician insisted the author return with him to London for further diagnosis; there doctors advised Dickens to cancel his readings for the next several months, which the author did reluctantly.

Within a few months Dickens had recovered sufficiently to obtain his physician's permission to resume his readings. His theatrical managers had been so devoted to him that he felt compelled to read as a way of making up to them the engagements he had had to cancel. His doctor limited his engagements to London, and in July 1869 an announcement was made that the author would "resume and conclude his interrupted series of Farewell Readings."

At St. James's Hall on January 11, Dickens delivered the first of a handful of farewell readings; the last took place there on March 15. Dickens's poor physical condition was well known at this time, and the public sadly realized that they might be seeing the celebrated novelist onstage for the last time.

For his last reading, he chose the two selections that constituted his most popular program, *A Christmas Carol* and *The Trial from "Pickwick."* While not as vigorous as in past years, as always he rendered an excellent performance (a critic would note that he read his *Carol* "with marvellous pathos, and in the reading discriminates the characters with wonderful tact and evidently well-practised ability"). Dickens lamented that after many years—and by some estimates more than 450 performances—this would be his final reading, and he closed the evening with these words:

> Ladies and Gentlemen,—It would be worse than idle, for it would be hypocritical and unfeeling, if I were to disguise that I close this episode of my life with feelings of very considerable pain. For some fifteen years, in this hall and in many kindred places, I have had the honour of presenting my own cherished ideas before you for recognition, and, in closely observing your reception of them, have enjoyed an amount of artistic delight and instruction which perhaps it is given to few men to know. In this task, and in every other I have undertaken as a faithful servant of the public, always imbued with a sense of duty to them, and always striving to do his best, I have been uniformly cheered by the readiest response, the most generous sympathy, and the most stimulating support. Nevertheless, I have thought it well at the full floodtide of your favour to retire upon those older associations between us which date from much further back than these, and henceforth to devote myself exclusively to the art that first brought us together. Ladies and Gentlemen, in but two short weeks from this time I hope that you may enter, in your own homes, on a new series of readings at which my assistance will be indispensable; but from these garish lights I vanish now for evermore, with one heartfelt, grateful, respectful, and affectionate farewell.

Those were Dickens's last words onstage, though there might have been hope for more one day. The novelist was only fifty-eight and still vigorously embraced life, loving the interaction of his public readings, even if he overexerted himself to the point where it impaired his health.

Still, the end came unexpectedly soon. On June 9, 1870, almost three months after his final reading, Charles Dickens passed away. Having grown up in need, he never seemed able to shake that insecurity, and the compulsion to work himself to the bone to ensure himself an income no doubt hastened his demise.

Though he was a very public person, people came to realize that they knew surprisingly little about the private Charles Dickens. *A Christmas Carol,* one of his favorite works to recite onstage—and certainly the most popular of his readings with the public— is a heartwarming and hopeful tale about the redemption of the human spirit and gives us a glimpse into the soul of this very private person. By the end of the story Scrooge has changed his stingy ways;

This illustration of Dickens giving his last public reading ran in the Illustrated London News on March 19, 1870, four days after the acclaimed novelist read A Christmas Carol and the trial scene from Pickwick Papers at St. James's Hall in London.

performing many acts of kindness, he comes to understand the true spirit of Christmas. *Carol* concludes with Tiny Tim crying out the now-famous words, "God Bless Us, Every One!" The prompt-copy of this perennial classic reminds us that the earthly manifestation of divine blessing, for Dickens, lay in the sharing of one's heart with others.

LOCATION: New York Public Library (Berg Collection), New York City.

The First American Flag Raised in Japan

≈≈≈≈≈≈≈≈≈≈≈≈≈≈≈≈≈≈≈≈≈≈≈

DATE: 1853.

WHAT IT IS: The U.S. flag displayed by Commodore Matthew Perry's seamen on the first official American diplomatic visit to Japan.

WHAT IT LOOKS LIKE: The flag measures 41 inches by 64 inches and has 13 red and white stripes and 31 stars. It is made of wool bunting and has a canvas hoist.

On a summer day in 1853, the arrival of a squadron of foreign vessels in the heretofore inviolate waters of the Land of the Rising Sun signaled a fateful turn of events for that closed nation. With entry forbidden to outsiders for centuries, Japan had maintained an isolation policy that had kept it firmly entrenched in a feudalistic state. The repercussions of this unwelcome intrusion could not have been foreseen by the denizens of the island nation, but as the foreigners marched ashore, determined and resolute, carrying with them a thirty-one-star American flag that symbolized the unprecedented visitation, their arrival heralded a drastic change in policy that would extricate Japan from its dark ages and launch the country onto a path of monumental technological and commercial growth in the emerging industrial world.

To Commodore Matthew Calbraith Perry's disappointment, a squadron of only four vessels was available to leave the southwest Okinawa Islands port and coaling station of Naha for Japan on July 2, 1853. With the importance of the great mission ahead, a show of a dozen warships would have been more impressive, and perhaps even necessary, but the vessels that would have rounded out the fleet had not yet arrived. As impediments had already delayed the expedition too many times, the smaller force would have to do.

The abbreviated fleet consisted of two steamships, the *Mississippi* and the *Susquehanna* (the flagship), and two sailing ships, the *Plymouth* and the *Saratoga*.

The commodore's mission was a diplomatic one, but how the island dwellers would perceive it was difficult to predict, making the venture inherently perilous. Japan fiercely enforced its isolation; outsiders who tried to penetrate the country's borders were subject to attack.

In 1637, following its massacre of thousands of Japanese converts to Christianity, the Japanese government had feared that its islands would be invaded by new missionaries from Europe. The ruling shoguns ordered all missionaries to leave the country and banned foreigners from entering. While hunting whales and other sea life in Japanese waters, or in traveling from California to China, American sailors had been fired on by the Japanese. Indeed, Japan was so hostile to outsiders that seamen shipwrecked on its shores were known to have been slaughtered.

In the mid–nineteenth century, the American government determined to remedy this danger to its mariners and in the process establish relations with the mysterious island nation. To carry out this objective, the government chose the country's most able seaman, Matthew Calbraith Perry, younger brother of the famed War of 1812 hero Oliver Hazard Perry. Matthew Perry's mandate was to employ persuasion if possible but force if necessary. Approximately eight months after his selection, during which time he studied his mission and determined that it could be accomplished only by a show of force, meeting the Japanese on their own assumed level of superiority, Perry departed from Norfolk, Virginia, on November 24, 1852, and sailed by way of the south Atlantic around the Cape of Good Hope. Perry carried letters signed by President Millard Fillmore, as well as a document (U.S. Naval Academy Museum, Annapolis, Maryland) affixed with the Great Seal of the United States and signed by President Fillmore that authorized to Matthew Perry "Five Full Powers in Blank."*

Unsure of how the Japanese would greet them, but knowing the islanders' enmity toward outsiders and history of fighting off any attempts to establish relations, the Americans spent their voyage to Japan filled with heavy anticipation. The crews regularly mustered, practiced military

*The president's authorization of "Five Full Powers in Blank" conferred on Perry the power of plenipotentiary for negotiating a treaty. The Great Seal of the United States, most commonly affixed to treaties, proclamations, and instruments investing authority in American emissaries, is by law under the custodianship of the Secretary of State, has limited uses, and may only be affixed to a commission that bears the signature of the president.

exercises, and prepared their weapons in the event they should be engaged in battle.

On the 8th of July, the American vessels were sighted by several fishing junks as the small fleet cruised up the coast of one of the Japanese islands. Alarmed by the arrival of strangers, some of the junks immediately turned back to shore. As the ships proceeded toward Uraga (located near the modern city of Yokohama), Japanese fishermen on boats and others along the shore watched in amazement as the steamers—belching out smoke—moved against the wind and tide with sails furled. It was clearly the first time the Japanese had seen a large vessel other than a sailing ship.

On the verge of making contact with the Japanese, Perry ordered the crews to take their positions on deck and the guns readied for action. The commodore called the squadron's captains to his cabin for a conference as the ships rounded Cape Sagami. Cruising into Yedo (later Tokyo) Bay, the American vessels were approached by several Japanese boats filled with men, but the steamers, moving counter to the wind, continued on their way and left the sailboats trailing.

The commodore wanted to show the Japanese from the outset that their visitors were firm and resolute, strong and serious. Other foreigners before him had failed to negotiate with the Japanese, and Perry was determined not to repeat the mistake of misunderstanding the Japanese psyche. Aware of the Japanese people's conviction of their inherent superiority, Perry knew he had to meet them on their own level and hold himself in the most dignified manner to earn their respect. Relations would be cordial but formal, and no one but authorities of the appropriate rank would be admitted on board the American vessels. Armed confrontation was the last resort and diplomacy the first.

The American squadron passed Cape Sagami and entered the Uraga Channel, with the Sagami Peninsula to the west and Awa Province to the east. The waters were filled with fishing boats, which scurried out of the path of the oncoming flotilla and then at an ample distance paused to allow their occupants to contemplate the alien fleet.

In the late afternoon the four American ships anchored in designated positions in Yedo Bay near the city of Uraga as guns from native forts boomed and guard boats filled with soldiers approached. The Japanese tried repeatedly to climb aboard the visiting vessels, casting towlines and mounting chains, but they were repelled by the American sailors who brandished firearms, cutlasses, and pikes.

A boat in which stood a man holding an official-looking document was rebuffed by the *Susquehanna*, then pulled alongside the *Mississippi*; the man read in French from his paper that the visitors should leave the area. Soon another boat came abreast of the *Susquehanna,* and one of its occupants proceeded to converse in Dutch with the interpreter on board the ship. After asking many questions about the foreigners, he implored them to let him on board, but he was told that the vessel's commander was of the highest rank in his branch of service, the "Lord of the Forbidden Interior," who could meet only with the highest-ranking official of the city. The Japanese man responded that the vice governor was in his company and that he was of the highest rank, but when asked why the governor himself had not come, he replied that the governor was by law not allowed to board visiting ships. The man offered an intelligent compromise: if the rank of Perry as Lord of the Forbidden Interior was too high to permit him to meet with a mere vice governor, a lesser personage with a rank equivalent to that of the vice governor might receive the Japanese delegation aboard ship. After deliberately stalling a bit, Commodore Perry agreed.

The Japanese interpreter and vice governor climbed the *Susquehanna*'s gangway ladder and were led to a private cabin; Perry, closeted in adjoining quarters, conducted the exchange by way of a subordinate. The commodore made it known that he carried a letter from the United States president addressed to the emperor of Japan and that he would permit an appropriate official to come on board to see a translation of the document as a prelude to the commodore personally delivering the letter to the empire's highest-ranking official. The vice governor interjected that they faced the immediate problem of the strictures of Japanese law, which mandated that matters of foreign affairs be conducted only at Nagasaki. Perry stood his ground and adamantly refused to budge from Uraga. To move his ships to Nagasaki, where the Dutch had a post,* might, Perry knew, subject the Americans to the same restrictions the Japanese had imposed on the Dutch; and the latter, having warned the Japanese about the coming American expedition, might view the Americans as rivals and even try to subvert their mission. The commodore preferred to remain in Uraga because of its proximity to Yedo, which he believed to be the home of the emperor.

The following morning a boat bearing a group of Japanese artists drew

---

*Japan's relationship with the government of the Netherlands was so minor that the island nation was still effectively isolated from the Western world. Japan permitted the Dutch to maintain a post so it could acquire European products it needed, and so the Dutch could transport Japanese goods out of the country. But Japan imposed rigorous restrictions on their trade, and the shoguns treated the Dutch in the most degrading manner. Even Japanese who worked for the Dutch were required to profess anti-Christian sentiments.

The "Five Full Powers in Blank," signed by President Millard Fillmore, that authorized Commodore Matthew Perry to negotiate treaties with Japan as he deemed appropriate.

near the visiting vessels so that the artists might make detailed sketches. Later in the day a delegation of high-ranking officials approached the *Susquehanna*. An interpreter communicated that the governor of Uraga wished to board the ship (contrary to the vice governor's notice the previous day that his superior could not do this), and permission was granted. The governor was shown President Fillmore's letter and Commodore Perry's commission, both reposing in stately gold containers, by Perry's highest-ranking officer. The governor offered his American counterpart some Japanese delicacies he had brought with him. Then he once again raised the issue of moving the site of the Americans' business to Nagasaki, but the commodore refused, stating through his officer that, if necessary, he would take a force of men on land to personally present the American president's letter to the emperor. The governor, whose name was Kayama Yezaiman, had no other recourse but to say that he would make the appropriate inquiry to the court at Yedo to see how to proceed, and departed the American ship.

For three days the American squadron remained in Yedo Bay. During the wait, Perry dispatched survey boats to make observations of the shores and record scientific soundings of the harbor's depths so ships entering the bay in the future would not run aground on rocks, all under the careful watch of the Japanese in boats and armed soldiers onshore who appeared ready to engage in confrontation.

A reply came on the morning of Tuesday, July 12—or at least it seemed it would, when sailors aboard the American ships spotted three boats departing from Uraga, with one boat, set apart from the others by a special flag, eventually pulling out from the others to approach the *Susquehanna*. On the boat was Kayama Yezaiman, who climbed aboard the American flagship with his entourage, including two interpreters. A conference was held once again between the governor and two of Perry's top officers, the commodore cloistered in his cabin and participating through an aide. The Japanese governor began by explaining that there had been a misunderstanding regarding the conveyance of the translated documents. The commodore, though doubting the misunderstanding, rejected the governor's offer of a high-ranking Japanese official to receive the papers with transmission to Nagasaki via either a Chinese or Dutch agent. Perry repeated by written message that he would not go to Nagasaki or receive communication via a Chinese or Dutch agent and would deliver the letter from the president of the United States to none other than the emperor of Japan or his foreign affairs secretary.

The governor took leave of the ship to return to Uraga to confer with a city court official and came back later in the day to continue the negotiations. After much discussion of the delivery of the translated copies and originals, the specific Japanese official who would receive the communications, and the place of reception, it was agreed that a person of the necessary rank, whose authority must be affirmed in a document signed by the emperor, would receive the original letters and the translated copies not on board any American ship but on land; and that the commodore would not wait for the emperor's reply but would return months later for it.

The meeting concluded with the Americans offering their distinguished guests the hospitality of the ship. The governor spent several enjoyable hours on board, consuming so many spirits that his face turned red.

The next day the governor returned to the *Susquehanna* in the afternoon with the documents required by the commodore: a letter from the emperor of Japan, to which a seal was attached, addressed to Toda, the prince of Idzu, first counselor of the empire, authorizing him to receive the letter of the American president, along with a certificate of authenticity in the governor's hand and a Dutch translation.

Fine details of the exchange were worked out. Perry's survey boats had determined that the ships could be placed within firing distance of the site of the colloquy onshore, for protection in case the Japanese planned a betrayal. The commodore's men now informed the governor that it would not be appropriate to the commodore's rank for him to travel a great distance from the ship in a boat, so the Japanese were forced to agree to allow the Americans to bring their squadron in closer to shore.

In the evening, after the visiting dignitaries had left the *Susquehanna,* Perry met with the captains of his fleet to work out security and other details for the parley. From the shore could be heard the clattering sounds of construction, and the bay was busy with boats preparing for the event.

The occasion that was the object of all the negotiation, planning, and

Commodore Perry and his crew deliver President Millard Fillmore's letter addressed to the emperor of Japan requesting that Japan and America develop friendly relations and commence commercial trade with one another. The Japanese erected a special building for the formal reception of the letter.

activity was finally realized on Thursday, the 14th of July, a day that began with haze but that cleared into bright sunshine. Before eight in the morning, the *Susquehanna* and the *Mississippi* began to edge nearer the shore, several Japanese boats following in close proximity. Spread out on the beach ahead were ornamental screens of cloth stretched over beams of wood and numerous colorful banners, along with several divisions of Japanese soldiers.

At a signal from the American flagship, boats were launched from the other vessels of the squadron filled with officers, marines, sailors, and musicians wearing the full-dress uniforms of their service, who were to precede the commodore to the ceremony. A flotilla of more than fifteen boats plus two Japanese vessels, one carrying Kayama Yezaiman, proceeded down Yedo Bay accompanied by lively music. When the party was halfway to its destination, the cannons on board the flagship were fired to proclaim that Commodore Matthew Perry, Lord of the Forbidden Interior, would now leave his vessel to proceed to the ceremony.

When the flotilla reached shore, the crews disembarked and formed into lines according to their ranks. The assemblage was impressive: three hundred Americans and at least five thousand armed Japanese soldiers, many on horseback, arrayed across the beach.

As Perry stepped onshore, his accompanying staff formed a double line through which he passed. Then the procession began. The governor of

Uraga and his interpreter led the way, followed by American seamen, a pair of boys carrying the imposing boxes containing President Fillmore's letter and Commodore Perry's commission, and then the commodore himself, flanked by tall, armed Negro seamen. Two of the most muscular of the American sailors, carefully chosen from among the crews, bore a ceremonial banner and the American flag. The latter was a thirty-one-star wool bunting ensign with thirteen red and white stripes—the first American flag ever to be officially carried onto Japanese soil.

The Americans found that for residents of such an isolated country, the Japanese were surprisingly well informed about the United States. Earlier, when a globe had been placed before some Japanese dignitaries aboard the *Susquehanna,* without hesitation they pointed out New York City and Washington, D.C. The people of Japan had heard many stories about the vast country that lay across the Pacific, but with Perry's mission they were first seeing up close its flag, the red, white, and blue symbol of unity revered by the people of the United States of America half a world away, now proudly carried to an official meeting between the two nations.

The procession wound its way around a path to the wooden building specially erected for the occasion in the small village of Gori-Hama. A decorated canvas tent formed an entranceway connected by a carpet to an anteroom. Following this was the reception hall, which was raised off the ground, its floor covered by red cloth and its walls adorned with purple silk ornaments.

When Commodore Perry entered the room, the two imperial counselors, Prince Toda of Idzu and Prince Ido of Iwami, stood up to greet their guest with a bow, but they made no utterance and indeed remained silent throughout the ceremony. The commodore and his entourage were seated, and after several minutes of dignified silence a Japanese interpreter told his American counterpart in Dutch that Prince Toda was ready to receive the letters, inquiring whether they were ready for conveyance. The American interpreter imparted the request to the commodore, who motioned to the boys to proceed with the delivery. The boys walked to the front of the room, followed by the Negroes, who took from their hands the gold boxes, withdrew the letters, which were adorned with silk cords, and placed them on a varnished scarlet chest set on a table.

Of the four documents—Fillmore's letter, Perry's commission, and two letters from the commodore to the emperor—the president's letter was of greatest historical importance. Fillmore proposed to the emperor that America and Japan "should live in friendship and have commerical intercourse with each other." Aware that "the ancient laws of your imperial majesty's government

This thirty-one-star American flag was officially carried into Japan in July 1853 during Commodore Perry's expedition.

do not allow trade, except with the Chinese and the Dutch," Fillmore observed that as "the state of the world changes and new governments are formed, it seems to be wise, from time to time, to make new laws," and suggested that free trade between the United States and Japan "would be extremely beneficial to both." The president also asked that the Japanese treat Americans who were shipwrecked on Japanese shores with kindness. Finally, he requested that American steamships be allowed to stop in Japan to replenish their stores of coal and other necessary provisions. The president ended his letter urging the emperor to accept some presents made in the United States and intended "as tokens of our sincere and respectful friendship."

After the delivery Yezaiman, who had been kneeling, arose and then fell to his knees before the prince, who handed him an imperial receipt for the American documents. In a similar fashion the governor transmitted the receipts to the commodore.

With the delivery concluded, the commodore communicated through his interpreter that in a few days the American squadron would leave Japan, to return the following spring for a response to the president's letter. Those present filed out in formal silence, and the procession returned as it had come to the landing area, which was filled with Japanese government vessels on the water and soldiers on the shore. With Perry's boat in the lead, the flotilla headed toward the American ships, the musicians aboard performing patriotic tunes.

Because he had heard of the arrival in Japan of a Russian emissary, Commodore Perry returned to Japan earlier than planned, on March 8, 1854, with an augmented squadron of ships, arriving in Yedo Bay. The Japanese emperor seemed reluctant to sign a pact of amity, but may have realized that the country's isolation policy was becoming outmoded and could create serious problems for Japan. Several weeks later, on March 31, he agreed to sign the Treaty of Kanagawa with the United States, providing for the opening of two Japanese ports to U.S. vessels with an American consul at one of them. Perry signed the treaty with a brown-painted bamboo pen that he had acquired in China and carried home the treaty in a rectangular cardboard box with a lift-off top, also from China (both items at the U.S. Naval Academy Museum, Annapolis, Maryland). As tokens of appreciation and to demonstrate the potential for commercial enterprise between the two nations, the commodore bestowed numerous gifts on the Japanese, including scientific and communications instruments, agricultural tools, liquor, books, swords, firearms, and a miniature railroad.

The effects of the pact were astounding, bringing Japan out of the past and opening the country to trade and interaction with foreign nations. Within a few years Japan opened ports for American ships to put in to for protection in bad weather as well as for trading, and soon other countries signed agreements with Japan similar to its treaty with America. With Japan's education, manufacturing, banking, and other enterprises updated and improved, and its feudal system soon eliminated, Japan entered the modern world.

Much that followed for Japan in the ensuing years was the result of Commodore Perry's insightful diplomatic negotiation. Japan's relationship with the United States—and ultimately with the rest of the world—had its formal birth in the ceremony of July 14, 1853.

For the United States, the flag raised in Japan symbolized its national and commercial interests in the Pacific; to Japan, the flag was emblematic of the pressures from the outside world to shed its isolation. The success of this enterprise demonstrates that relations between alien nations may be accomplished peacefully and graciously, that diplomacy can triumph over fear and hostility, that force should be used only in self-defense. The flag represents not just the desire of a free and independent nation to expand its trade and diplomatic relations, but the yearning of a people to seek out other civilizations and forge bonds with different races in the spirit of a common humanity.

LOCATION: United States Naval Academy Museum, Annapolis, Maryland.*

---

*Dr. Ninian Pinkney, an Annapolis naval surgeon who served under Matthew Perry during the Mexican War, presented the flag on behalf of the commodore to the U.S. Naval Academy during graduation exercises on June 12, 1855.

The Emancipation Proclamation

~~~~~~

DATE: 1862 (for the First and Preliminary drafts); 1863 (for the Final Proclamation).

WHAT IT IS: President Abraham Lincoln's decree outlawing slavery in the rebel states of America.

WHAT IT LOOKS LIKE: There are four surviving Emancipation Proclamations—two original manuscripts in Lincoln's hand and two engrossed (formally scripted) copies. The first draft (read by Lincoln to his cabinet in July 1862) is on standard blue-lined paper and is one-and-a-half pages long, with each sheet measuring 11½ inches long by 7¾ inches wide. The Preliminary Proclamation of September 22, 1862, also in Lincoln's hand, is on four pages that each measure 13¹¹⁄₁₆ inches long by 8³⁄₁₆ inches wide and contain some words that are crossed out as well as two blocks of printed material that were pasted on. There is an engrossed copy of the Preliminary Proclamation that consists of seven pages with dimensions of 16⅝ inches long and 10⅝ inches wide. The engrossed "final" Emancipation Proclamation of January 1, 1863, with Abraham Lincoln's signature, is a document comprising two large sheets of paper folded into a folio format and subsequently separated so the writing fills five of the eight pages of the folded paper (with three pages blank); its dimensions (like those of the engrossed Preliminary Proclamation) are 16⅝ inches long by 10⅝ inches wide.

The Emancipation Proclamation, President Abraham Lincoln's hallowed manifesto of liberty and freedom, is a curious anomaly. After the states of the South seceded from the United States to form the Confederate States of America, the North was faced with a vexing political question: Should the overriding goal of the Civil War be to abolish slavery, or to preserve the Union? Even many opponents of slavery in the North believed preservation was the more crucial issue, and the president had to walk a careful line between the two factions so as not to alienate either the preservationists or the abolitionists; he needed the support of both groups to preserve the Union and end slavery.

Indeed, Lincoln was adamantly opposed to slavery, but he was also a pragmatist. In his August 22, 1862, letter (Wadsworth Atheneum, Hartford, Connecticut) to Horace Greeley, editor of the *New York Tribune,* Lincoln wrote:

> My paramount object in this struggle *is* to save the Union, and is *not* either to save or to destroy slavery. If I could save the Union without freeing *any* slave I would do it, and if I could save it by freeing *all* the slaves I would do it; and if I could save it by freeing some and leaving others alone I would also do that. What I do about slavery, and the colored race, I do because I believe it helps to save the Union; and what I forbear, I forbear because I do *not* believe it would help to save the Union. I shall do *less* whenever I shall believe what I am doing hurts the cause, and I shall do *more* whenever I shall believe doing more will help the cause.

Lincoln clearly understood that he had to save the Union before he could help the slaves; the preservation of the Union was his top priority.

With military and political considerations dictating caution, Lincoln's Emancipation Proclamation went through various drafts, from an initial working paper in which he expressed some ideas on the subject to a Preliminary Proclamation, which essentially functioned to serve notice to the people engaged in rebellion against the United States, to a final proclamation in which, political considerations notwithstanding, he called for an end to slavery in the rebel states. Ironically, although in theory the final proclamation severed the chains of bondage that enslaved the American Negro in rebel states, in reality it did not free a single slave. Still, the Emancipation Proclamation transformed the Civil War into a battle for liberty and democracy and became an enduring symbol of freedom. It was a written affirmation of the Union's dedication to the cause of freedom and liberty, a message to the entire world that human subjugation would not be allowed.

Slavery had been an integral part of American society since colonial times. Ships transported Negroes from Africa, captured mostly from the western section of the continent, and by the beginning of the eighteenth century, their import composed a thriving trade made up of mainly American and British concerns.

Over time those who saw slavery as immoral and wrong became more outspoken, and a movement for reform reached its peak near the mid-nineteenth century. Abolitionists in the North had been making their views known more forcefully and radically since the early 1830s, while pro-slavery factions sometimes mounted vicious attacks against their opponents. The slavery question became a thorny political issue. In 1850, Congress passed the Fugitive Slave Act, which provided for owners of slaves to reclaim runaways. The election in 1860 of Abraham Lincoln enraged many people in the South, who had derided the future president as a "black Republican." On December 20, 1860, South Carolina became the first state to secede from the Union, followed the next month by Mississippi, Florida, Alabama, Georgia, Louisiana, and Texas, forming the Confederate States of America. Virginia, Arkansas, North Carolina, and Tennessee seceded and joined the Confederacy in the six months that followed. On April 12, 1861, Confederate soldiers attacked Fort Sumter, and the War Between the States began.

When Lincoln gave his inaugural address on March 4, 1861, the United States was a divided nation. Although slavery was a major factor in this disunion, other conditions, such as the rivalry and economic differences between the agricultural South and the industrial North, the slave states being in jeopardy of losing control of Congress because of the projected admission of free states from the western territories, and social differences in Southern and Northern societies, played contributing roles. In his inaugural speech Lincoln endeavored to quell apprehension among the Southern states regarding the security of property by making the oft-quoted declaration: "I have no purpose, directly or indirectly, to interfere with the institution of slavery in the States where it exists."

For many years Lincoln had wanted to abolish slavery in the nation's capital, but he did not press the issue. On April 16, 1862, as he was beginning his second year as president, Lincoln signed "AN ACT For the release of certain persons held to service or labor in the District of Columbia." An anti-slavery group had pressed for passage of this bill, which established a commission to determine the value of slaves, whose masters, if loyal to the United States, could receive a maximum of $300 per slave. The slaves in the District of Columbia were set free by the new law, while slaves in other parts of the country were not affected by it and continued eagerly to await emancipation.

Just a few months later, Lincoln would make his first formal attempt at freeing the slaves in the South. In May and June of 1862, Lincoln sketched out a decree outlawing slavery in the rebellious states, much of it written in the War Department's telegraph office, where he spent time almost every day following the Union Army's progress; these writings of Lincoln do not survive. Soon, however, he wrote a more formal document, the initial draft of the Emancipation Proclamation. It is not known when Lincoln wrote this initial draft, but an analysis of Lincoln's itinerary points to July 13, 1862. The president had returned to Washington three days earlier, on July 10, from a visit to General George McClellan's headquarters on the James River. Various matters consumed his time over the next two days, and then in a carriage ride to the funeral of Secretary of War Edwin McMasters Stanton's infant son on July 13, Lincoln surprised Secretary of the Navy Gideon Welles and Secretary of State William H. Seward with a reading of his preliminary draft.

Lincoln presented the first draft of his Emancipation Proclamation on July 22, 1862, to his cabinet, which then consisted of Secretary of State Seward, Secretary of War Stanton, Secretary of the Treasury Salmon P. Chase, Secretary of the Interior Caleb B. Smith, Postmaster General Montgomery Blair, Attorney General Edward Bates, and Secretary of the Navy Welles.

In the first paragraph of the two-paragraph document, Lincoln warned "all persons . . . to cease participating in, aiding, countenancing, or abetting the existing rebellion, or any rebellion against the government of the United States, and to return to their proper allegiance to the United States." At the end of the second paragraph, the president declared: "And, as a fit and necessary military measure for effecting this object, I, as Commander-in-Chief of the Army and Navy of the United States, do order and declare that on the first day of January in the year of our Lord one thousand, eight hundred and sixtythree, all persons held as slaves with in any state or states, wherein the constitutional authority of the United States shall not be practically recognized, submitted to, and maintained, shall then, thenceforward, and forever, be free."

Welles and Chase described the reactions of the cabinet members to Lincoln's first draft of his Preliminary Proclamation in their diaries (Library of Congress, Washington, D.C.). From them we learn that Chase and Stanton advocated the proclamation's release; Bates offered only measured support (he opposed Negroes having equal rights with whites); and Blair thought the proclamation would cause harm in the upcoming congressional elections.

*The first page of the Emancipation
Proclamation of January 1, 1863.*

Lincoln withheld this proclamation on the
counsel of his secretary of state, William H.
Seward. The Union armies were dispirited,
having suffered many defeats, and Seward
believed that issuing a proclamation would
appear to be a desperate gesture on the president's behalf. It made more sense, Seward
reasoned, for the president to publicly
change his earlier position of noninterference
with slavery when the war picked up for the
Union.

Lincoln seized the opportunity to do so
immediately after the Battle of Antietam in
Maryland. A Confederate army under General
Robert E. Lee tried to drive an assault into the
North in mid-September but was repelled by a
Union army under McClellan. Thousands of
soldiers died on both sides, but there were far
more fatalities in the Southern army. While
neither side actually "won" the battle, the North had successfully held back the
Southern advance, and it was enough of a victory for the president to put forward the Emancipation Proclamation from a position of strength.

And so Lincoln presented the Preliminary Proclamation to his cabinet on
September 22, 1862. (This contained substantial revisions from his initial
draft; Lincoln himself wrote the Preliminary Proclamation, and Secretary of
State Seward made many corrections on the manuscript.) Lincoln declared
that in one hundred days, on January 1, 1863, "all persons held as slaves
within any state or designated part of a state, the people whereof shall then
be in rebellion against the United States shall be then, thenceforward and
forever free."

Indeed, on January 1, 1863, one hundred days after the Preliminary
Proclamation, the "final" Emancipation Proclamation was issued. Lincoln
signed the document in midafternoon, after hundreds of government officials and citizens who had come into the White House over the past few
hours for New Year's Day festivities had left. The document signed by
Lincoln contained all the corrections he had made or requested to be made
earlier in his handwritten draft, with alterations made right up through the
morning of January 1.

Lincoln's final Emancipation Proclamation of January 1, 1863, begins
with a summing up of his Preliminary Proclamation of September 22, 1862,

and follows with an enumeration of the states and parts of states in rebellion against the United States. Lincoln went on to declare that by virtue of the power vested in him as commander in chief of the United States Army and Navy in time of actual armed rebellion against the authority and government of the United States, "all persons held as slaves within said designated States and parts of States, are, and henceforth shall be free; and . . . the Executive government of the United States, including the military and naval authorities thereof, will recognize and maintain the freedom of said persons." Other statements Lincoln made include enjoining the freed slaves to abstain from violence except in self-defense, and that when allowed, the freed slaves, "labor faithfully for reasonable wages." Finally, Lincoln asserted that freed slaves "of suitable condition, will be received into the armed services of the United States to garrison forts, stations, and other places, and to man vessels of all sorts in said service." This invitation for slaves to serve in the armed forces was not contained in the Preliminary Proclamation.

For all its good intentions, the final Emancipation Proclamation failed to address completely the liberation of American slaves. It applied only in areas controlled by the Confederacy, over which the president had no actual control, and so it did not immediately free any slaves. It did not declare slaves in loyal states to be free, although it indirectly offered slaves their freedom if they would join the Union Army and allowed them to fight for a preserved Union in which slavery was outlawed. Four lithographic copies were made of Lincoln's handwritten final proclamation, and this would prove fortunate, since the fate of this priceless original document was to be catastrophic.

An engrossed copy was made of Lincoln's final Emancipation Proclamation of January 1, 1863.* Written on two large sheets of paper folded to make eight pages, the engrossed Emancipation Proclamation was signed by President Lincoln and Secretary of State Seward.

In the early evening of this New Year's Day, the Emancipation Proclamation was telegraphed around the country from the office of the War Department. News of the Emancipation Proclamation was greeted in some places with jubilance, while in some areas of the North radicals

---

*A variety of official and unofficial copies of the Emancipation Proclamation were published, and some of these were signed by President Lincoln as well as by members of his cabinet or staff. In 1864, about forty-eight commemorative copies of the Emancipation Proclamation were printed for the Philadelphia Sanitary Fair, one of a number of sanitary fairs, and signed by Lincoln and Seward, to be sold to help soldiers injured in the Civil War. Approximately half of these documents survive, and some have been sold over the years for relatively large sums of money.

In this 1864 lithograph a Union soldier reads the Emancipation Proclamation to slaves in hiding, possibly at an Underground Railroad location. A young woman, with two children holding on to her, kneels in prayer, while older Negroes listen hopefully in the shadows. The work was widely printed during the Civil War and many viewers tried to determine its symbolism.

complained that Lincoln had issued it only to strengthen the military. Still, over the next several days there were joyous celebrations and ceremonies in Northern cities, many with speeches and singing.

Lincoln retained the first draft of his proclamation (it later passed to his son Robert Todd Lincoln), but due to his beneficence, the Preliminary Proclamation fell into private hands, then became the property of a state government. During the Civil War the U.S. Sanitary Commission provided care for injured Union soldiers. To help raise money for this purpose, the commission held bazaars in many states, and sometimes requested President Lincoln to donate important manuscripts so they could be auctioned, sold, or raffled off.

Lincoln realized the importance of this cause and parted with his manuscript. The original draft of Lincoln's Preliminary Proclamation was sent to Emily W. Barnes of the Army Relief Bazaar in Albany, New York, by Assistant Secretary of State Frederick W. Seward, who in a letter dated January 4, 1864, noted that "the body of it is in his own handwriting, the pencilled additions in the hand of the Secretary of State, and the formal beginning and ending, in the hand of the Chief Clerk." In February and March 1864, the Army Relief Bazaar was sponsored to collect money for the U.S. Sanitary Commission, and a raffle was held in which the well-known abolitionist Gerrit Smith won the document. Smith donated it to the Sanitary Commission to help it raise additional funds. On April 28, 1865, two weeks after Lincoln was assassinated, the New York State Legislature purchased it for the state library for $1,000.

While four handwritten and engrossed Emancipation Proclamations by, or contemporary to, Lincoln are known to exist, unfortunately the version that might be considered the most valuable of all these documents, the final proclamation in Lincoln's hand, does not survive. The president sent the working copy of his final Emancipation Proclamation to the Northwestern Sanitary Fair in Chicago. This original draft was sent to the fair managers with a letter dated October 26, 1863. The document was purchased for $3,000 by Thomas Bryan, who donated it to the Soldiers' Home in Chicago, where it was destroyed in the 1871 Great Chicago Fire.

The engrossed Emancipation Proclamation is considered the official document, but it was actually copied from other versions.

Lincoln was an ardent believer in democracy, impassioned about the founding of America on the principle "that all men are created equal." Slavery was the antithesis of this premise, and would, he believed, only lead to a weakening of the structure of democracy. In a speech at Edwardsville, Illinois, on September 11, 1858, Lincoln made the point that if the people of a nation had the inclination and opportunity to take away the liberty of their fellow human beings, they would "become the fit subjects of the first cunning tyrant" who rose among them.

In December 1865, eight months after Lincoln was assassinated, the Thirteenth Amendment was ratified, outlawing slavery in the United States and freeing the slaves in the North who had been untouched by the Emancipation Proclamation. With this action, the degrading manacles of human bondage were finally sundered, and the passionate advocate of freedom whose proclamation led the way became immortalized as the Great Emancipator.

LOCATIONS:

First draft (July 22, 1862): Library of Congress, Washington, D.C.

Preliminary Proclamation: *Lincoln's draft* (September 22, 1862): The New York State Library, Cultural Education Center, Empire State Plaza, Albany, New York. *Engrossed copy* (September 22, 1862): National Archives and Records Administration, Washington, D.C.

"Final" Proclamation: *Engrossed copy* (January 1, 1863): National Archives and Records Administration, Washington, D.C.

Slices of Tom Thumb's Wedding Cake

DATE: 1863.

WHAT THEY ARE: Pieces of cake preserved from the wedding of the famous nineteenth-century dwarf.

WHAT THEY LOOK LIKE: Small slices were given to the guests and were typically a few inches long by a couple of inches wide and an inch or two deep.

On February 10, 1863, Charles Sherwood Stratton, better known to the world as General Tom Thumb, publicly formalized the great love of his life by marrying Mercy Lavinia Warren Bump, professionally dubbed Queen Lavinia.* The wedding was one of mid–nineteenth-century New York's great "fairy tale celebrations," capturing the imaginations of poor and rich folk alike. As *The New York Times* began its coverage of the ceremony:

> Those who did and those who did not attend the wedding of Gen. Thomas Thumb and Queen Lavinia Warren composed the population of this great Metropolis yesterday, and thenceforth religious and civil parties sink into comparative insignificance before this one arbitrating query of fate—Did you or did you not see Tom Thumb married?

Helping to orchestrate the wedding of the two Lilliputians was the renowned showman and master of humbug, Phineas Taylor Barnum.

---

*Lavinia was working for P. T. Barnum only a few months before she was married, and in many of the early advertisements she was referred to as the "Little Queen of Beauty." She tended not to be called by this title after she was married. Indeed, she had a long career and was not really referred to as Queen Lavinia, although the title occasionally popped up in advertisements.

Having made exorbitant amounts by exhibiting the two at the American Museum on Broadway, his Gotham gallery of sideshow attractions and curiosities, Barnum tried to induce the couple to postpone their wedding, but the two were deeply in love, and it is a testament to their commitment to each other that they forged ahead without deference to Barnum or concern over financial incentives. Accepting the inevitable, Barnum, who had a flair for the dramatic and for spectacles, saw the publicity value of the wedding and helped put on the best event he could. With Tom, twenty-five years old, always having an affinity for women and the women an affinity for him, the wedding seemed especially to intrigue the female population.

According to the story filed by the *Times* reporter,

> No one need be surprised that two little matters should create such a tremendous hullaballoo, such a *furore* of excitement, such an intensity of interest in the feminine world of New York and its neighborhood, as have the loves of our Lilliputians. We say "feminine world" because there were more than twenty thousand women in this City yesterday morning up and dressed an hour and a half before their usual time, solely and simply because of the approaching nuptials. . . . They didn't all have cards of admission, oh no, but it wasn't their fault. Fathers were flattered, husbands were hectored, brothers were bullied and cousins were cozened into buying, begging, borrowing in some way or other *getting* tickets of admission to the grand affair.

Grace Church on Broadway was the site of the matrimonial ceremony, and on the big day the excitement was palpable. The streets were jammed with carriages, the sidewalks clustered with spectators, windows and doorways filled with onlookers. Colorful streamers and other decorations brightened the streets, reporters jockeyed through the crowd to get a close-up view, police officers labored to keep order, vehicles were detoured. Carriages drove up to the church and let out their passengers, then promptly left so the next vehicle could pull up and deposit its guests, all under the careful supervision of the police, all the details arranged by Barnum himself. So voluminous was traffic for the blissful event that part of Broadway essentially closed down.

The fame of the couple was so great that craftsmen and merchants sought to capitalize on the little people's marriage. They desired to have guests purchase their goods as gifts, and even directly contributed to the parade of presents for the publicity. As the *Times* said of the union: "The marriage of Gen. Tom Thumb cannot be treated as an affair of no moment—in some respects it is most momentous. Next to Louis Napoleon there is no one person better known by reputation to high and low, rich and poor, than he."

The wedding was the social event of the New York season and the guest list exclusive. As a longtime performer, Tom knew and invited many in the upper crust of New York society, but invitations also went out to other notable people such as the president of the United States, government officials, and war heroes. Some citizens offered to pay large amounts of money for admission, but the couple adamantly refused to put them on sale; Tom and Lavinia wanted to ensure that their wedding was not just a public spectacle but a legitimate affair.

Throngs of spectators stood in the wintry cold outside the church as guests clutching the coveted admission cards filled the church. The women were dressed to the nines. As the *New York Herald* noted, the chapel of Grace Church was "indeed . . . the show . . . the true 'vision of fair women.' Here was the carnival of crinoline, the apotheosis of purple and fine linen. Never before was the scarlet lady seen to such advantage. Babylon was a rag to it. . . . There were silks of every possible hue, and thus a rich variety of colors in the picture. There was, too, every possible species of toilet—dainty headdresses, delicate bonnets, and whatever can make the sex beautiful and lead everybody else into temptation."

In the church an organist played the *William Tell* Overture and the *Tannhauser* march. The guests were filled with anticipation, and police officers were omnipresent. Seated among the guests were common folk and distinguished Americans alike.

The guests waited for the arrival of the wedding party with such impatience that several times they thought the bride and groom had arrived, only to be disappointed. Finally, the famous P.T. joined the throng along with members of the couple's family. Soon a commotion in the rear signaled everyone in the church that the bride and groom, having made their way through the crowd outside, were about to make their grand entrance. Preceding the pair down the aisle were a couple even more diminutive in size, other Barnum stars, Commodore Nutt and the sister of the bride, Huldah Pierce Bump, known to many as Minnie Warren.

More than a thousand people had jammed into the church, all yearning to witness the delicious spectacle, and they finally saw the couple walk to the altar. How was the bride and groom's stroll down the aisle greeted by the spellbound audience? The *New York Herald* offered this account:

Everybody was on the cushions at once and eager to see, though none could do so, save the few who sat along the middle aisle. But the murmur of voices and little exclamations marked their very slow progress up the aisle until they reached the open space and ascended the steps of the little dais prepared for them in front of the chancel rail.

And now, the lives of two loving people would become linked in holy matrimony. The groom, Charles Stratton, had been born on January 4, 1838, in Bridgeport, Connecticut. At birth he weighed nine pounds, six ounces, so it seemed that his growth would be normal, as it was for his two older siblings (there would be four Stratton children altogether), but he stopped growing at about a year, and it soon appeared that he would be different. In his autobiography, *Struggles and Triumphs*, Barnum recounts how he met Stratton:

> In November 1842 I was in Albany in business. As the Hudson River was frozen over I returned to New York by the Housatonic Railroad stopping one night at Bridgeport, Connecticut to see my brother Philo F. Barnum, who at the time kept the Franklin Hotel. I heard of a remarkably small child in Bridgeport, and at my request my brother brought him to the hotel. He was not two feet high, he weighed less than sixteen pounds, and was the smallest child I ever saw that could walk alone. But he was a perfectly formed bright-eyed little fellow with light hair and ruddy cheeks and he enjoyed the best of health. He was exceedingly bashful but after some coaxing he was induced to talk with me and he told me that he was the son of Sherwood Stratton and that his own name was Charles S. Stratton. After seeing him and talking to him I at once determined to procure his services from his parents.

Little Charles's mother accompanied the boy to New York City, where they took up residence in an apartment and she chaperoned the boy in his new profession. Providing instruction in a variety of entertainment forms to the four-year-old boy—who was naturally talkative, energetic, and clever, not to mention handsome—Barnum transformed Charles Stratton into General Tom Thumb, the elfin raconteur, mimic, crooner, and child hoofer "newly arrived from England." In addition to giving the boy a new country of origin, Barnum shrewdly added seven years to Charles's age: a tiny eleven-year-old was much more of a novelty than a tiny four-year-old. Barnum advertised his new discovery as being twenty-two inches tall; in truth the lad was closer to twenty-six inches. Over the years Tom Thumb earned a vast amount of money for Barnum—estimated at one-quarter of the impresario's earnings—and performed before Queen Victoria of England and other royal sovereigns in Europe, as well as endearing himself to the gentry of New York society.

The bride, Lavinia Warren Bump, was born on October 31, 1841, in Middleboro, Massachusetts. Her siblings who preceded her were of normal height, but she grew very slowly, and it soon became apparent that she was a dwarf. Like her future husband, she too began working in show business at an early age, performing for a time in floating carnival shows that cruised up and down the Mississippi River. By most accounts, Lavinia, a bright, vivacious, pretty young woman, was reluctant when Barnum first asked her to work for him, but he met with her parents and convinced them that it would be in her interests to do so. In working for Barnum, Lavinia performed vaudeville routines and short plays written for her, sang, danced, told stories, and recited poetry. Performers who worked for Barnum entertained in his New York museum as well as in his traveling shows.

Charles Stratton met Lavinia around December 1862, before she had begun to work in Barnum's American Museum in New York. He was immediately smitten with her, pursued her, and soon asked her to marry him. She accepted.

As a woman of twenty-one years on her wedding day, Lavinia was a pleasing sight. In its coverage of the marriage, the *New York Herald* described Lavinia as "a little lady of very fair proportions, decidedly of the plump style of beauty, with a well rounded arm and full bust. . . . Her countenance is animated and agreeable complexion decidedly brunette, black hair, very dark eyes, rounded forehead and dimpled cheeks and chin." Despite the favorable description, the reporter perhaps rankled Lavinia by adding, "Her little sister is to our heretical taste the prettier of the two." According to *The New York Times,* Minnie Warren, who was thirteen, was "the smallest woman in the world."

Lavinia's wedding dress was made by the famous Madame Demorest, and it was the quintessence of elegance. Here's how the *Herald* described the gown:

> The material is a superb quality of taffeta, changing from pale amber to a silvery white and producing a peculiarly rich and deli-

cate tint. The skirt . . . is ornamented to represent the emblems of different nationalities on each separate breadth, connected in each seam by . . . feathers and lace—altogether forming an elegant border around the skirt.

The design in front of the dress represents growing corn for America; on the right a rose for England adorned by buds and leaves; on the left a laurel for France; and on the remaining breadths are exhibited an acorn in the leaves for Germany, a shamrock for Ireland, a thistle for Scotland, and a vine with clusters of grapes for Italy. The designs are lined in very narrow folds of white satin, their effect being heightened . . . with narrow point appliqué over a petticoat of white glace silk covered with . . . fine tulle, the divisions being traced with seed pearls.

Shortly after 12:30 P.M. the formal ceremony began, what the *Herald* called "the great moment of the great show." The pocket-sized quartet stood at the altar, the bride and bridegroom flanked by Commodore Nutt and Minnie Warren. *The Lives of Tom Thumb and Wife,* a pamphlet published around 1881, describes what happened next:

Irrepressible exclamations of delight and astonishment tinkled all over the house. Ladies stood on tiptoe, some daring ones of small stature actually mounting the seats so eager in their pleasurable excitement to see that they overlooked the possibility of being seen and masculine necks were stretched as far as white neckties would permit. And yet no sooner had the four tiny mites arranged themselves in the prescribed form for the marital ceremony than the voice of the Reverend Mr. Willey of Bridgeport, Connecticut secured perfect silence and reverent attention. While in the hearts of all the "goodlie companie" of "fair women and brave men" gathered there arose a prayerful wish for the perfect peace and prosperity of the fairy-like pair. The bride was given away at the request of her parents by the Reverend Dr. Putnam of Middleboro and the words of the service were repeated in audible distinctness by both the bride and groom. . . . The benediction was pronounced by the Reverend Dr. Taylor, rector of Grace Church, whereupon the General saluted his wife with an honest kiss, the last of the *three millions* pressed in public upon the lips of his lady admirers.

Tom Thumb and his bride Lavinia, flanked by Commodore Nutt and Minnie Warren, greeting guests at Tom and Lavinia's wedding.

The ceremony was poignant and joyous; the *Herald* characterized it as "one of the most remarkable marriages ever celebrated in a civilized community."

The wedding guests then headed over to the Metropolitan Hotel, where a reception was to be held for the newlyweds. Police officers were stationed around the area to keep order, but mobs of excited people flocked to the hotel, and if this in itself didn't make it difficult for the party to reach the Metropolitan, there was yet another diversion: scores of people ran through the streets shouting and chasing after the carriage. Eventually the bridal party made it through the hubbub and into the hotel, ready to commence their party. The *Herald* described how the guests were greeted: "As Thumb and his bride and Nutt and Miss Warren stood on the piano, the visitors filed past and paid their respects, and so it went on and went over."

The wedding gifts, displayed in glass cases, were extravagant and plentiful. They included silver cups, a gold necklace, a diamond ring, coral jewelry, a silver watch, a small billiard table, an easy chair, a miniature set of parlor furniture, a miniature sewing machine, a miniature silver horse and chariot, and a porcelain-and-gold dinner set.

The immense wedding cake was made by William H. Barmore Confectioners. In *The Lives of Tom Thumb and Wife,* the cake was described thus:

> The bridal cake, furnished by Barmore, of Broadway, weighed eighty pounds, the base gracefully ornamented with leaves of the forest, surmounted with shells of the ocean, with scrolls neatly entwined, on which rested a magnificent Egyptian Temple of Fame, each column bearing cupids and angels, with scrolls and harps, recording the nuptial vows of the youthful couple standing beneath

its splendid arches, while the reverend doctor pronounces the blessing. On the extreme top is seen the Angel of Fame, proclaiming to the scattering flowers from horns of plenty as they glide along Life's voyage. In point of beauty and workmanship, it was the nonpareil of bridal cake.

Slices were meted out to all in attendance. As noted in *Tom Thumb and Wife,* "Upon leaving the hotel, the guests were supplied with wedding-cake, over two thousand boxes being thus distributed."

After the reception the newlyweds retired to their suite, but the guests refused to end the merriment. Outside the hotel, an eight-piece band performed in honor of the newlyweds, and a large crowd gathered around. About a half hour later, at half past ten, General and Mrs. Tom Thumb came to the balcony to greet the gaggle of people below. The couple were tired and it was their first night of wedded bliss, but Tom Thumb was diplomatic. He said, "I will make this speech like myself. Short." After some brief remarks he bade the crowd good night, Lavinia blew a kiss, and they both disappeared into their suite.

Though displayed as spectacles for public diversion, Tom Thumb and Lavinia amassed a good sum of money in their employment with P. T. Barnum. Little people in their day were looked on as freaks, but their exploitation could earn them a good living and was thus often welcome. The fate of such diminutive folk could have been worse, of course. In previous centuries in Europe, for instance, dwarfs would sometimes be employed as "fools" in royal courts, homes, and inns for the fun and amusement of their keepers and their company. Charles and Lavinia had fame, money, and an estate in Middleboro, Massachusetts.

In July 1883, Tom Thumb, at his Middleboro home, died of a stroke. He was forty-five years old; at the time of his death he was about forty inches tall and weighed around seventy pounds. Tom and Lavinia never had any children, but about a year after they married a story circulated that Lavinia had given birth. Photos of the pair with various children, none of which was theirs, reinforced the rumor.

An illustration of Tom Thumb and Lavinia Warren Bump's wedding cake. At the top an "Angel of Fame" proclaims the happiness of the newlyweds on an Egyptian Temple of Fame, which graces angels and cupids with harps and scrolls. Designs of forest leaves and ocean shells decorate the base.

Lavinia later married a dwarf from Italy who claimed a royal title. Count Magri asserted that the Pope had bestowed the title (his brother, also a dwarf, was Baron Magri), but there never seemed to be any concrete evidence of such an official title.

The pieces of wedding cake from the marriage of Charles Stratton and Lavinia Warren Bump would surely have disappeared from history had not Lavinia and others seen fit to save them. Perhaps Lavinia saved her piece not just as a keepsake but because of the tradition that it was good luck to save pieces of wedding cake and would result in a fruitful, successful marriage.

Lavinia bestowed one vestige of the cake to Harrison Grey Fiske, a theater manager who was married to the famous stage actress, Minnie Maddern Fiske. In a letter to Fiske dated February 16, 1905, the former Mrs. Tom Thumb, now Countess Lavinia Magri, wrote about the enclosure:

> Allow me to present you with a piece of my Wedding Cake which was made when I was married to Charles S. Stratton known as the only Original Genl. Tom Thumb—Feb. 10th 1863 at Grace Church New York City. My anniversary was the 10th of Feb 1905. This Cake is now Forty two years old. The public are under the impression that I am not living. I was married the second time to Count Primo Magri April 6th 1886 at Italy Trinity Church forty second St. New York City.

The countess's quaint present to Harrison Grey Fiske was preserved privately until it was donated along with many other pieces in the Minnie Maddern Fiske collection to the U.S. government. Another piece of wedding cake was purchased in the early 1930s from a private dealer by Harry Hertzberg, a prominent Texas collector of circus memorabilia.

To the naked eye, the pieces look like dark fossilized masses. To imaginative and romantic souls, however, the unsightly slices of cake from the 1863 wedding of Tom Thumb and Queen Lavinia are a glorious reminder that physical limitations are no barrier to true love.

LOCATIONS: Library of Congress, Washington, D.C.

The Hertzberg Circus Collection and Museum, a division of the San Antonio Public Library, San Antonio, Texas. (Other slices of cake from Tom Thumb's wedding may exist at other locations.)

Thomas Edison's Original Tinfoil Phonograph

ᘓᘓᘓᘓᘓᘓᘓᘓᘓᘓᘓᘓᘓᘓᘓᘓᘓ

DATE: 1877.

WHAT IT IS: The first machine in history to play back recorded sound.

WHAT IT LOOKS LIKE: The device consists of a grooved cylinder with a crank running through its center and two diaphragms with recording and playback needles at opposite sides of the cylinder. The mechanism is mounted on a metal base.

It was one of those fantastical contraptions that people through the centuries could only imagine. For instance, in his posthumously published 1657 novel, *A Voyage to the Moon*, the French writer Savinien de Cyrano de Bergerac described a fictitious voyage to the moon and told how he came upon "a box—somewhat of metal . . . it was a book, indeed, but a strange and wonderful book . . . made wholly for the ears and not the eyes, so that when anybody has a mind to read in it, he winds up the machine with a great many little springs . . . and straight, as from the mouth of man or a musical instrument, proceed all the distinct and different sounds."

Ah, the phonograph—translated from the Greek, the word means "sound writer"—the dream of countless generations. But how impossible it must have seemed!

A device that could grab sounds out of the air, preserve them, and then re-create them in all their varied and rich timbres, pitches, tones, textures, and nuances? A device that could, in essence, bring the past to life?

Today, the phonograph already represents outdated technology, but to those of long ago the idea of a machine that could capture and reproduce sounds seemed downright preposterous. And yet while the phonograph is one of those landmark human achievements that changed the landscape of everyday life forever, its discovery was actually made by accident.

It was while trying to make an improvement on the telegraph and telephone that Thomas Alva Edison stumbled on the idea for a phonograph. The telegraph was developed in the United States primarily as a means of communicating across the expanding nation, as pioneers and others moved out west during the first half of the nineteenth century. The telephone came along later, credited to Alexander Graham Bell after he spoke over a wire to his assistant Thomas Watson in March 1876.

When the telephone first came into use, it was thought that it would be used like the telegraph—that is, a person would go to an office and give a message to an operator, who would then make a connection to a remote line and speak into the phone; the message would be transmitted to an operator at the other end, who would in turn take down the message and deliver it to its intended recipient.

In Edison's day, inventors were constantly looking for ways to store telegraph and telephone messages so that they could be played back and delivered to the recipient at a later time. In the course of trying to build a device that could record telegraph and telephone messages, Edison observed that when a telegraph stylus read inscriptions by moving very rapidly over paper, "light, musical, rhythmical sound," resembling indistinct human talk, seemed to emanate from the telegraph. Knowing that in the telephone a diaphragm's vibrations are converted into electricity and then back to sound so they may be heard, Edison thought that by placing a stylus over a lead-based surface, he could record vibrations as impressions that could be changed back to their original sound. From this idea, Edison realized that a talking machine was a possibility.

Even at this stage, Edison's utilitarian vision for the talking machine was as a device that could record telephone messages. The telephone was a recent invention that only the rich could afford; if he could invent a talking machine, anybody could record a message that could be transmitted from a telephone in one office to another, where the recipient could listen to the message.

It was during the second half of 1877 that Edison began his scientific investigation and conducted experiments to build a workable prototype. On July 18 he conducted an experiment and sketched on paper illustrations of a person conveying air through a telephone tube, the wind sounds and hisses producing vibrations that resulted in a diaphragm powerfully vibrating. The experiment apparently promoted his confidence and excitement; Edison concluded, "Just tried experiment with a diaphram having an embossing point & held against parafin paper moving rapidly the spkg vibrations are indented nicely & theres no doubt that I shall be able to store up & reproduce automatically at any future time the human voice perfectly."

The next day Edison provided some technical explanation for his work in a British patent document for a sound telegraph:

> The vibrations of the atmosphere, which result from the human voice or from any musical instrument or otherwise, are made to act in increasing or lessening the electric force upon a line by opening or closing the circuit, or increasing or lessening the intimacy of contact between conducting surfaces placed in the circuit at the receiving station; the electric action in one or more electro magnets causes a vibration in a tympan, or other instrument similar to a drum, and produces a sound, but this sound is greatly augmented by mechanical action. I have discovered that the friction of a point or surface that is in contact with a properly prepared and slowly moving surface, is very much increased or lessened by the strength of the electric wave passing at such point of contact, and from this variation in the friction a greater or less vibration is given to the mechanism or means that produce or develope the sound at the receiving station, thereby rendering clear and distinct the sound received that otherwise would not be audible.

Over the next few months Edison continued to give thought to transmitting sound vibrations via diaphragms, but he wasn't the only one to endeavor to create a recording-and-playing device. In October 1877, an article appeared in a French publication that told about a conception of Charles Cros, a dabbler in scientific inventions. Advancing on the work of E. L. Scott de Martinville, who some twenty years earlier had developed a contraption that made indentations corresponding to sound vibrations, Cros had the previous April written a treatise about a procedure in which inscriptions were made on a flat lampblacked glass that was caused to vibrate, the inscriptions then being used to reproduce the vibrations and recreate the sounds originally reproduced. Cros's idea for a phonograph was similar to Edison's, but unlike Edison he was unable to build a working prototype.

On November 29, Edison sketched a diagram of his conception for a phonograph and turned it over to one of his assistants, John Kruesi, to build. Sometime during the first week of December 1877, Kruesi, apparently under his boss's watchful eye, built the mechanism in accordance with the diagram. Edison immediately tried it out. At this phase of his life—often

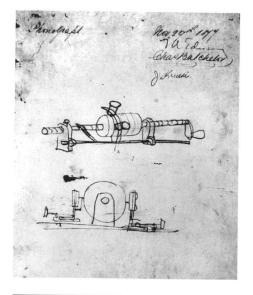

Thomas Edison's sketch, dated November 29, 1877, for his original tinfoil phonograph. Edison had his associates, Charles Batchelor and John Kruesi, sign the sketch for patent protection.

considered his creative peak—he worked out of a laboratory in Menlo Park, New Jersey. In what was to become a legendary story about the invention of the phonograph, Edison began his immortal experiment by shouting into a recording horn, "Mary had a little lamb / its fleece was white as snow / and everywhere that Mary went / the lamb was sure to go."

As Edison spoke into the horn, he turned a crank, setting the mechanism in motion. The air waves of his voice caused a recording needle to move and make indentations on a piece of tinfoil wrapped around a cylinder. After he finished speaking, Edison turned the crank in the opposite direction, which rewound the cylinder and brought the tinfoil back to its starting point. The recording needle was then reset down on the tinfoil, the crank turned again—and this time the sound of Edison reciting the well-known nursery rhyme was heard coming out of the recording horn. Voilà! This demonstration marked the first time sound had ever been preserved and re-created, and history had just been made!*

Edison wasted little time in revealing his remarkable achievement to the world. On December 7, with a couple of his assistants in tow, he offered a public demonstration of his new talking machine at the New York City office of *Scientific American* magazine. On the same day Edison's assistant Charles Batchelor wrote the following letter to the editor of *English Mechanic*, announcing and explaining his boss's new invention:

> Mr. Thos A Edison of New York a well known Electrician has just devised a method of recording and reproducing the human voice. It

*The recording horn and tinfoil used in this famous trial are not known to exist anymore, the latter doubtless discarded as trash.

had the merit of extreme simplicity and is entirely a mechanical device.

A sheet of tinfoil is made to move in front of a diaphragm provided with an embossing point in its centre, at a uniform speed. When the diaphragm is vibrated by the human voice the ever varying rate of vibration is accurately recorded by indents in the tinfoil; this indented sheet is made to move at the same speed in front of, and in contact with, a delicate spring which is connected to another diaphragm and to which it transmits the same rates of vibrations under the same conditions and in consequence gives forth the same sounds as those spoken in the first place. It has been exhibited for the last few days in New York and has excited the admiration of many scientific men.

Also on the same day Edward Johnson, a Menlo Park employee, sent Edison's Washington, D.C., business associate, Uriah Painter, a brief but cogent telegram: "Phonograph Delivered to me today. Complete success. Talks plainer than telephone. . . ."

With his invention now realized, and excitement about it beginning to spread feverishly, Edison set out to profit from it. In 1878 he licensed the Edison Speaking Phonograph Company to exploit the new machine. In these Victorian times, public lectures were a popular form of entertainment, and the phonograph was set on a path to become a kind of stage performer in its own right. The company manufactured hundreds of machines and dispatched trained demonstrators to travel around to theaters, country fairs, and other venues and entertain audiences with the talking machine that could reproduce sounds. Onstage people would whistle, play musical instruments, deliver speeches, recite poems, sing songs, all while the newfangled machine, with a fresh piece of tinfoil, captured the sounds. Then the demonstrator would crank the cylinder and, to the audience's delight, play back the sounds just heard. Crowds flocked to hear the new talking machine. The demonstrators kept a percentage of the gate, forwarding the rest of the receipts to the Edison Speaking Phonograph Company, which in turn remitted a portion to the inventor.

But public interest in the phonograph faded as the novelty wore off. Although an enthusiastic Edison predicted his "baby" would be an important medium for making music and literature available and would also be useful as a dictating machine, it had no practical application at the time. The sound it produced was harsh, sibilants were missing, and the tinfoil sheet lasted no more than a handful of plays. Edison's machine seemed to

Using Thomas Edison's drawing as a blueprint, John Kruesi constructed the first workable tinfoil phonograph, pictured above.

have much potential, but it just wasn't ready for the commercial marketplace. While Edison's attention would be diverted by his work on an incandescent lamp, others sought to realize the phonograph's potential.

In 1880 Alexander Graham Bell hired technicians to improve on Edison's phonograph, and in 1885 he had several applications for a machine that was somewhat different, replacing Edison's tinfoil cylinder with a machine that used a wax-coated cardboard tube. This machine became known as a "graphophone."

Edison renewed his attention to the phonograph around 1886, and developed his own wax cylinder. The inventor continued to refine his improvement as others—such as Ezra Gilliland, who developed an electrical machine to play the cylinders—endeavored to make the phonograph commercially viable. Soon an investor purchased several companies in the field, including Edison's, for the purpose of making and selling dictating machines.

Still, neither the phonograph nor the graphophone could gain a foothold in the commercial world. Machines installed in offices performed erratically, and the parts were not interchangeable. Perhaps the greatest reason for their defeat was the enormous resistance of office stenographers (almost all men in those days), who feared technological displacement! The neophyte sound-recording industry appeared doomed, although other entrepreneurs would not be discouraged. Recognizing the vast potential of the talking machine, they not only made further technological improvements but envisioned other commercial applications for it as well.

In 1890 an enterprising businessman changed the destiny of the crippled phonograph business. Louis Glass installed a battery-powered model of Edison's phonograph in the Palais Royal saloon in San Francisco. The machine had several listening tubes, and patrons paid a nickel to open up a tube. The machines—each with four sets of tubes—could earn twenty cents a play. Glass's idea caught on, and there were eager lines waiting to deposit a nickel.

Entrepreneurs across the nation began installing the machines, grouping several of them at one location, and thus was born the "phonograph parlor." What people wanted to hear most were vaudeville and musical comedy songs, band arrangements of marches and concert pieces, comic monologues, and virtuoso whistling solos.

Improvements in recordings were constantly being made. Emile Berliner, a German immigrant, developed a flat disc and in 1901 formed with Eldridge Johnson the Victor Talking Machine Company, issuing recordings of Russian stars on its "red label" for five dollars each. The year 1906 marked the introduction of the Victrola, the first record player to incorporate the reproducing horn into the body of the player (thus eliminating the external horn, which had been a dust-gathering eyesore for housewives). Soon the two-sided record came along, and records became the most popular form of home entertainment. In 1927 the Automatic Music Company began manufacturing coin-operated record players that could play many selections. These machines came to be called jukeboxes. The 1933 repeal of Prohibition sparked the opening of thousands of nightclubs and bars, almost all equipped with jukeboxes, which stimulated millions of record sales and saved the record industry. Musical artists such as Bing Crosby, Louis Armstrong, and the Mills Brothers developed cult followings via jukeboxes.

From 1946 to 1958, the record industry grew further, technologically and economically. Magnetic tape was introduced as a recording medium, facilitating the recording process when mistakes were made. In 1948 the Columbia Record Company introduced the twelve-inch long-playing record (LP) with a playing time of up to twenty-three minutes on each side, and in 1949 RCA offered a seven-inch vinyl record playable at 45 revolutions per minute. Each company produced turntables with speeds designed to play its records.

It was probably the development of the LP and the 45 that saved the phonograph industry from the competition of another new home entertainment industry around this time—television. As people bought TV sets, both the radio and recording industries suffered. Because radio could no longer afford live entertainment, it had to program records in a format to be played by disc jockeys. Ironically, not only did radio begin to prosper again, but it aided the record industry by playing (or promoting) its records.

In 1958, stereo recordings were introduced, but it was almost ten years before enough consumers had acquired compatible playback equipment that the old mono recordings could be phased out.

In the mid- to late 1960s, cassette and eight-track recordings caught on with the public, and in the early 1970s quadrophonic ("surround") sound was introduced. Video discs and CDs soon followed, the latter eventually becoming enormously popular. New and improved technologies will undoubtedly continue to be introduced for the singular purpose of enhancing the pleasure of listening to music.

Thomas Edison's original tinfoil phonograph is a surviving piece of history, the progenitor of a new technology that launched the sound-recording age. All that has followed, from later phonographs to cassettes to today's compact discs, and all that will follow as new technologies are developed, are descendants of the device that Edison created to demonstrate that sound could be preserved and reproduced. In retrospect, the invention by the Wizard of Menlo Park seems inevitable, the product of thousands of years of human progress. But the debt to Edison's genius is immense, for with his technology, humankind has been able to record for posterity the sounds of life.

LOCATION: Edison National Historic Site, West Orange, New Jersey.

Jesse James's Stickpin

◠◡◠◡◠◡◠◡◠◡◠◡◠◡◠◡◠◡◠◡◠◡◠◡◠◡◠◡◠

DATE: 1882.

WHAT IT IS: An ornamental pin, used like a tiepin, that was owned by the nineteenth-century outlaw.

WHAT IT LOOKS LIKE: The stickpin now exists in separate pieces—a small diamond-shaped stone measuring less than one-quarter inch across made of black obsidian, or volcanic glass, which has a small piece of its original brass mounting on one side; and pieces of the pin, each less than a quarter-inch long.

Jesse James dreamed up many crazy schemes, but never could the notorious bandit of the Old West have imagined that the commonplace stickpin he inserted through his cravat on the last day of his life would resurface more than a century later to help settle a long-standing dispute about whether his alleged remains were actually his.

In 1881, the year before he died, Jesse James had a price on his head. The Wanted posters blared in large bold print: "Proclamation of the Governor of Missouri! Rewards for the Arrest of Express and Train Robbers," and then in fine print offered a reward of $5,000 for the arrest and conviction of each person who had participated in the train robberies near Glendale in Jackson County on October 8, 1879, and near Winston in Daviess County on July 15, 1881. But Jesse and his brother Frank were set apart from the rest of their gang. While the proclamation offered the reward "for the arrest and conviction" of unnamed parties, in the closing paragraphs Jesse and Frank were specifically named, along with a reward of $10,000 "for the arrest and delivery" of "each or either of them to the sheriff of Daviess County." Governor Thomas T. Crittenden set the higher bounty for the James brothers because one of the train robberies wasn't just a robbery. In the Daviess County holdup, the conductor, William Westfall, and a train company employee, John McCulloch, were murdered, in the same county where Jesse and Frank had already been indicted for the murder of John W. Sheets.

These Glendale and Winston misdeeds were only two in a long streak of crimes committed by Jesse Woodson James, who had devoted his adult life to sticking up banks and trains. Born in Clay County, Missouri, on September 5, 1847, to Robert and Zerelda James, Jesse knew his father only for a short time. Robert James, a Baptist minister who was one of the founders of William Jewel College in Liberty, Missouri, took off to join the California gold rush when Jesse was just a toddler and died in 1850 at a Placerville, California, gold camp, leaving Jesse and his siblings to be raised by their mother, who was widowed once more before marrying her third husband, Dr. Reuben Samuel, with whom she had four more children.

It was the American Civil War that drew Jesse and his brother Frank into a life on the lam. Frank James had become a member of the guerrilla forces of William C. Quantrill that roamed the country pillaging and terrorizing Union forces and citizens. Quantrill's guerrilla band had formed years before the start of the Civil War, in the course of the bloody Missouri-Kansas border skirmishes between slave-owning farmers in Missouri and abolitionists in Kansas. Mostly farmers, Quantrill's men took every opportunity to search out and harass Union forces and citizens in the area but had no interest in joining the Confederate militia and being sent away to fight far from home.

But Jesse's world changed one day when, around mid-1863, as the North and South were locked in battle, a local Union militia came to the Samuel-James home, whose inhabitants they suspected of aiding Confederate guerrillas by passing information to them. Union soldiers strung Dr. Samuel from the backyard bean tree, although they were not able to make him confess, and put a rope around young Jesse's neck while prodding him with swords, warning him that if he ever aided the guerrillas in any way he would be killed. Jesse's sister and his mother, the latter pregnant at the time, were arrested shortly afterward and incarcerated in the most horrific prison conditions.

Jesse was just a boy of fifteen at the time. But these incidents were so egregious that they seemed to have resonated harshly in him, leading him to ignore authority and view himself as an outsider. He joined the guerrilla forces of Bloody Bill Anderson, who had split off from Quantrill and risen to supremacy as one of Missouri's strongest guerrilla commanders. Young Jesse sustained harsh wounds in some of the guerrillas' ferocious attacks on federal garrisons but recovered enough to participate in the brutal Centralia massacre, in which some thirty guerrillas torched parts of the town, robbed incoming stagecoach passengers, and otherwise tormented the citizens. In their most heartless exploit they forced a train to stop, lined up more than two dozen unarmed federal soldiers aboard, and cold-bloodedly executed all but one of them. (A quick retaliation by Union soldiers was a fiasco; the guerrillas wiped out about a hundred of the troops.) Soon Union attacks on the guerrillas in Missouri killed their leaders and weakened their forces, but the ruthless executions festered in the memories of Union soldiers.

On May 21, 1865, as the Civil War drew to an end, Jesse and a small band of guerrillas, carrying a white flag, were on their way to Lexington, Missouri, to surrender when a band of drunken Union soldiers saw them approaching and opened fire. Jesse was severely wounded in the chest; he crawled into some bushes and hid until the soldiers wandered off, then managed to make it to his nearby home in Kearney. Friends took him to Nebraska to keep him out of the hands of the authorities, but he was convinced his wound was fatal and insisted on being brought back to Missouri to die. In a home in the Harlem section of Kansas City, he was nursed by his first cousin, Zerelda (named for his mother, but whom he called Zee), who was to become his wife. Recovered somewhat but still terribly debilitated, he traveled to California to visit an uncle, Drury James, who operated a mineral springs resort. It was said that the sulfur in the mineral springs probably helped him regain his health.

The wanton treatment of the Confederate guerrillas and the tempestuous politics in Jesse's home state catalyzed the descent of some men into banditry. In 1866 Jesse and Frank began their own personal plunge into a life of crime when they committed their first stickup, of a bank, in which one person was killed. From that time on Jesse James blazed a trail of stickups over a wide area of the United States, including Missouri, Nebraska, Minnesota, Iowa, Kansas, Arkansas, Alabama, Texas, and California. Lurid press reports made him a legend, if not a folk hero, in his own time. But in the eyes of the law he was a wanted man.

In 1875, for instance, two men, said to have been Pinkerton detectives, were hunting for him in connection with his train stickups. Arriving at the Samuel-James farm, where they thought Jesse and Frank were hiding, the detectives reputedly threw either a flare pot or a bomb into the farmhouse. Whatever it was, someone inside the house kicked the object into the fireplace, where it exploded, blowing off the right arm of Jesse's mother and fatally wounding Archie Peyton Samuel, his eight-year-old half brother, who died within hours.

Jesse, who with his brother Frank was probably not at home that night, was no doubt incensed by this bloody intrusion into his mother's domain, and he continued holding up trains and banks. On the 25th of July, 1881, Governor Tom Crittenden issued a proclamation for the arrest of the James gang members.

For more than fifteen years some of the best lawmen in the country had been doggedly on Jesse James's trail, but to no avail. Jesse led a circumspect life, rarely taking off his gunbelt, trusting few, and divulging his true identity only to his gang members. He moved around a lot, used numerous aliases, and gave out multiple cover stories as to what he did for a living.

With most of his gang members captured or killed in robberies over the years, especially at the September 1876 Northfield, Minnesota, bank heist—which turned into an all-out war between the town's residents and the James-Younger gang and from which only Jesse and Frank escaped—Jesse often had to recruit new hands to assist him in upcoming jobs. While Jesse was living in Kansas City in 1881, he recruited Charley Ford, a man in his early twenties whom Jesse had met at Ford's house near Richmond, Missouri, a couple of summers earlier through Edward Miller, a mutual friend and member of the James gang. Ford, and his brother Robert, would later move in with the James family, an act that would cause Jesse's demise.

Jesse and his family—his wife, Zee, and their two children—moved by wagon from Kansas City on November 5, arriving three days later at St. Joseph, Missouri, where on November 9 they settled in a house on 21st and Lafayette Streets. Jesse used the alias of Thomas Howard, purporting to be a railroad worker looking for employment. On Christmas Eve, 1881, the so-called Howard family moved into a city councilman's house at 1318 Lafayette Street, which they rented for $14 a month.

Soon they were joined by Charley Ford, who all the while had the intention of cashing in on the tempting $10,000 reward for Jesse James. He was aided by his younger brother, Robert. Robert was a grocery clerk and a habitual liar who would later falsely claim that in July 1881 he had become a detective. On January 13, 1882, Robert Ford had a private meeting with Governor Crittenden at the St. James Hotel in Kansas City about the capture of Jesse James, whom he said he had known for three years.

With Charley's plan of capture a well-kept secret, it was easy for him to bring his brother Robert into Jesse's circle. Charley and Jesse were going to pull a bank robbery and would need more men. Jesse asked Charley if he knew anybody, and Charley of course recommended his brother. Jesse remembered Robert from an earlier meeting and went to meet with him. Twenty-year-old Robert became a member of Jesse's gang, and the three made a stop at Jesse's mother's house before returning to the Howard home at 1318 Lafayette.

Jesse was plotting his next bank robbery. He rode with Charley Ford to Nebraska, where they surveyed banks in several cities. Jesse would typically case a bank by giving the teller a large bill and asking for change, all the while scrutinizing the tellers, security, and layout. But it was the bank at Platte City in northwest Missouri that they settled on robbing. There was going to be a murder trial, and when everybody was at the courthouse listening to the proceedings, they planned to hold up the bank.

While Jesse was concentrating on his next job, the Ford brothers were planning the assassination of their comrade. As Jesse had said he would never surrender to anyone, they realized they would never take him alive; the only recourse was to kill him outright when his gunbelt was off. Jesse rarely disarmed himself, but they would stand ready for the first opportunity to open fire on him. It was about twenty-four hours before the three were to ride to Platte City to rob the bank there that that opportunity presented itself.

It was on the morning of April 3, 1882—exactly a hundred days after the James family had moved into the 1318 Lafayette Street house—that the Fords carried out their plot to do away with Jesse James. After breakfast had been served, Jesse and Charley went out to the stable to curry and feed the horses. Robert, who had moved into the house the week before, stayed inside during the day because Jesse had told him it would look suspicious for three healthy men to live idly under the same roof together.

Between eight and ten o'clock—depending on the account—Jesse and Charley returned to the house, where Zee was in the kitchen and the children were playing in one of the bedrooms. Observing that it was warm, Jesse took off his jacket. Then he decided to either dust off or straighten a picture hanging on the wall.* Wary that the suspicions of any passerby might be aroused by the sight of his gunbelt, which held two pistols, he took it off and placed it on his bed under his coat before mounting a chair.

Charley winked at Robert to signal that this was the opportunity they had been waiting for. Jesse James, the infamous outlaw, was unarmed and standing with his back to them. They drew their guns.

Something caught Jesse's attention at this moment—either the sound of the guns being cocked or the furtive movements of the Ford brothers behind

---

*According to various accounts, it was either a picture of a racehorse or a needlepoint working of the aphorism "God Bless Our Home," which, along with "In God We Trust," was a motto popular in homes at the time. Some historians suggest Jesse was straightening the picture rather than dusting it; having been in the house only a hundred days, they reason, it wouldn't have had time to get very dusty, and while a little dust would probably not bother an outlaw, a crooked picture might.

him—but whatever it was, he started to turn his head toward the boys. The shooting took place so swiftly—Robert fired before Charley could pull his trigger—that before Jesse had finished turning his head, a bullet struck him behind his right ear, felling him instantly.

Zee rushed out of the kitchen to see her husband lying bleeding on the floor. According to her account, she then went to the door and saw Robert and Charley Ford in the yard, Robert climbing over a fence. Charley denied shooting Jesse, blaming his brother. Zee then returned to Jesse, whose head she cradled in her arms. He was still alive but died moments later. He was thirty-four years old.

The Ford brothers immediately repaired to a saloon three blocks away, at Tenth and Lafayette Streets, which had a telephone. They placed a call to the telegraph office and gave instructions for a telegram to be sent to Governor Crittenden notifying him that the outlaw Jesse James had been shot dead. Charley and Robert then went looking for City Marshal Enos Craig, to give themselves up, but the marshal wasn't in his office. With a policeman accompanying them, the Ford brothers continued walking through the streets in search of the marshal.

Marshal Craig couldn't be found. He had already received a telephone call about the shooting and with some other officers had rushed out to the James's house on the hill overlooking St. Joseph. The lawmen found a man lying dead on the floor, and the man's wife at first denied that the shooting victim was Jesse James. She offered descriptions of the gunmen, and the officers arranged to close down all streets from which anyone could leave town. But soon the Fords showed up, and Robert admitted killing the man on the floor, whom he identified as Jesse James. To add credibility to their identification, the Fords told what jewelry and valuables Jesse had in the house, and the authorities found pins and rings with either Jesse James's initials or first name engraved on them.*

For killing the incorrigible Jesse James, the Fords presumed they would not only collect the $10,000 reward but become public heroes. But instead there was a large public outcry against them for shooting James from behind, and Mrs. James charged them with murder in a sworn warrant. The brothers eventually pled guilty to the charge of murder in the first degree and were sentenced to hang, but they were pardoned instead by Governor Crittenden. While they may have collected a small reward, their execution

---

*Jesse James, who seemed to live from hand to mouth—pulling off a job, living off the money until it ran out, then going out to pull off another job—apparently left little in the way of funds for his family. After his death, his wife, in need of money, had the sheriff sell the family possessions. The sale brought in about $113, including $15 for Jesse's dog.

The four-room house in which Jesse James was shot and killed by Robert Ford on April 3, 1882. Shortly after word got out about the killing, a crowd gathered in front of the house.

of the notorious James proved their own undoing: Charles, devastated by shame (and perhaps also suffering with tuberculosis), committed suicide; Robert opened a saloon in Colorado, only to be murdered in 1892 by a patron who sought to avenge James's death.

After the shooting, an inquest was held in which Zerelda Mimms James, Charley and Robert Ford, Zerelda Samuel, and others testified. During this time, as from the moment news got out that Jesse James was dead, people gathered everywhere in St. Joseph to talk about the killing. The death of the infamous outlaw had been falsely reported so many times in the past, that people were at first uncertain whether to believe that Jesse James was in fact gone. While Jesse James was a famous bandit, few people knew what he looked like, and the authorities were unsure if the murder victim was indeed James. But it became clearer over time with personal identifications by those who knew him that the dead man unequivocally was the elusive fugitive.

Concerned that some people might try to avenge the murder of Jesse

James by killing the Fords, the authorities placed the brothers in jail, letting them retain their weapons, and augmented the number of guards. Mobs of people congregated around St. Joseph, and stories and rumors grew about associates of Jesse James planning to exact revenge for the murder of their fallen comrade. Some of the stories may have been true; others were apparently fanciful concoctions. Several people reported seeing packs of heavily armed and rough-looking men, sometimes up to a half dozen in number, riding through different parts of St. Joseph bent on retribution. The newspapers fueled the stories and rumors by printing outrageous reports, including warnings of gang members coming by train to kill the Fords. The governor of Missouri was called on to send soldiers to the city. Public sentiment began mounting against the Fords. People said that even if the victim was Jesse James, the well-known robber and killer, shooting him in the back of the head without affording him due process in a court of law was as heinous as the crimes of which he himself was guilty.

Jesse James's body was taken to a St. Joseph undertaker, Seidenfaden's, where Dick Liddle, an accomplice of Jesse's who had surrendered a couple of months earlier, and Sheriff Timberlake of Clay County identified the body as that of Jesse James, and the coroner performed an autopsy of the outlaw's head. While this was being carried out, a photographer was setting up in a back room to take pictures of the corpse. J. W. Graham had heard of Jesse's death the day before at the St. Joseph picture studio where he worked. He told his manager a lot of money could be made by selling photos of Jesse James in death, and he received from the city marshal the exclusive right to photograph the bandit's remains.

Graham had difficulty making it into Seidenfaden's, with the hordes of curiosity-seekers gathered outside and stretching for blocks. He repaired to a back room and set up some boxes there as a stand for his ponderous studio camera. Soon Jesse's body, stretched out on a board, was carried into the back room. A rope was tied under Jesse's arms and around the back of the board, and the dead outlaw was propped up. Graham took two photos. On his way back to the studio Graham was followed by a crowd of people wanting to purchase an image of Jesse James's corpse. Graham's two pictures sold well, with orders coming in from all across America, and they were both widely published.

So many people were congregating at Seidenfaden's that the coroner finally consented to permit a viewing of Jesse's body for a few hours. Jesse's corpse had been placed in a "cooling box" to preserve it. While rain poured, crowds streamed into the undertaking establishment, but with all those wishing to enter, many people, even prominent local citizens, did not

get the opportunity to see the body of
the infamous bandit who had for so
long eluded the law.

Because Jesse James's criminal past
was heavily associated with Kansas
City, some authorities thought his
body should be remanded to the
authorities there, but after Governor
Crittenden was satisfied that the
remains were in fact those of Jesse
James, St. Joseph officials were successful in having the body conveyed to
the James family. Zerelda Samuel, Jesse
James's mother, took possession of his
body, afraid it might end up displayed
at a carnival or become the object of
derision in a traveling sideshow.

Zerelda Samuel buried her son
beside the coffee-bean tree in the
backyard of her farm near Kearney,
Missouri, to prevent anyone from
invading his grave. Twenty years later,

*Jesse James, shortly after he was mur-
dered, with his stickpin in his cravat.*

in 1902, Mrs. Samuel, too old now to live on her farm, moved (by this time
Jesse's wife was dead) and had Jesse's body reinterred at the Mount Olivet
Cemetery in Kearney. It was raining on the day of reinterment. Supposedly
the skull of the corpse fell off, and Jesse's son, Jesse Edward James, picked
it up to see where the fatal bullet had gone inside his father's head. The
remains were then placed into a different coffin, a painted wooden box
bearing a metallic hue.

For many years after Jesse James's death, numerous people stepped forward claiming to be the real Jesse James. Indeed, between 1882 and the
1930s perhaps some twenty people turned up heralding themselves as the
notorious Wild West outlaw. One of the strongest assertions was registered
in the 1940s by J. Frank Dalton in Lawton, Oklahoma. Dalton, who died
in 1951 at an age he gave as 104, had several bullet wounds on his body,
but they didn't correspond to those of the real Jesse James.

With all the bogus claims that had cropped up over the years, some people in the latter part of the twentieth century wanted to use modern science
to determine once and for all if the alleged remains of Jesse James buried at
the Mount Olivet Cemetery in Kearney were in fact his real remains.

That task was taken up by James E. Starrs, a professor of forensic science at George Washington University in Washington, D.C., who had been involved in a number of other high-profile exhumations, including the remains of Dr. Carl Weiss, the alleged assassin of Senator Huey Long, and the five victims of Alfred Packer, the Colorado cannibal.

Starrs obtained a court order and on July 17, 1995, exhumed the remains in the Jesse James grave.* There was no nameplate on the coffin, and almost all the wood had decayed, although the metallic coffin handles were intact. Jesse James had been buried in the clothes he was wearing when he was killed. After the coroner had released his body, he was redressed in these clothes, which the death photo reveals to be rather dapper—but nothing, not even a fragment of his clothes, was found in the remains or in the grave.

Starrs and his team of scientists visually examined the remains. Someone—knowingly or inadvertently—had put the bones back in the casket the wrong way; the corpse was lying prone, with the head and body facing down.

The 1902 coffin had been crushed by the weight of the soil above it to a height of four to six inches, smashing the skull into numerous fragments. After reconstruction of the skull, a bullet entrance wound was found in the rear of the skull that matched exactly the records of the bullet that struck Jesse James behind the right ear. However, contrary to contemporary newspaper accounts (a newspaper issued after James's murder had reported a hole in a wall of the James house made by the fatal bullet) no exit hole was found anywhere in the reconstructed skull. A bullet was found in the right lung area of the remains, and Jesse was known to have carried a bullet in his chest from the time he had tried to surrender near Lexington, Missouri, in 1865 and was shot; the bullet, a .36-caliber round ball, even matched the type of gun, a Navy Colt, that was allegedly used. (The other bullet Jesse was known to have carried may have been found in the original burial site in 1975. It can't be said with certainty that it came from Jesse James, since his body was removed from that grave in 1902; over a period of seventy-three years, the bullet might have come from anywhere.) There was a lateral cut around the skull that coincided with a saw mark from the skull autopsy; this also disproved the notion that the remains, as was conjectured, could have been those of Jesse's wife, whose body had not been autopsied after she died. (A St. Joseph physician reportedly kept the brain

*Starrs obtained the court order in Clay County, where Jesse was buried, but later learned he had obtained it in the wrong court. It should have been obtained from Buchanan County, where Jesse was killed.

of Jesse James, supposedly removed during the autopsy, on his desk for many years.)

Starrs planned to conduct mitochondrial DNA testing of the remains to determine if they were those of the real Jesse James. Mitochondrial DNA testing requires obtaining adequate and interpretable DNA from the bones, and that was a major deterrent for Starrs's team, since the bones found in Jesse James's grave had decomposed substantially and were in such a serious state of degradation that they were literally falling apart.

The mitochondrial DNA testing initially did not go well. Starrs's team went from one bone to another and were unable to obtain anything that could be used for comparison purposes. Finally, the scientists tried the teeth, which are usually well protected by the enamel outer coating. DNA is found under the enamel, in the dentin. Starrs's team obtained DNA from the molars, which are typically very durable.

It was possible there had been contamination of the remains from microorganisms in the soil and from the hands of the several scientists who had handled them without wearing protective rubber gloves. So before the scientists went to Jesse James's relatives for their DNA, to ensure that the DNA sequence the scientists had obtained from one molar could be replicated (that is, duplicated in another molar), they tested a second tooth. When they came up with the same sequence as they had obtained from the first one, it was virtually certain either would be representative of the DNA of the person in the grave.

The next step was to take the sequence obtained from the teeth of the corpse and match it against a sequence from known relatives in Jesse's maternal line who had the same mitochondrial DNA as Jesse James's sister. Starrs found two living relatives, both, as it turned out, from Oklahoma City. They were two males, one the uncle of the other, and their line of descent was directly back to Jesse James's sister.

Jesse James's sister, Susan Lavenia James (1849–1889), married Allen Parmer on November 24, 1870. They had six children before she died from complications of childbirth. One of the daughters, Feta Parmer, married Bert A. Rose. They had a daughter, Dorothy Ann Rose, who married William Jackson. Dorothy and William Jackson had a son, Bob Jackson, a great-grandnephew of Jesse James. It was Bob Jackson, who became an attorney in Oklahoma City, and Jackson's nephew, Mark Nickol, who donated blood for the DNA tests. Starrs painstakingly verified their lineage with census records, birth and marriage certificates, and other records, and was certain that their mitochondrial DNA would be the same as Jesse James's.

After scrupulous testing, the DNA from Jesse's teeth, as well as from a lock of hair Jesse's family had saved, was found to match that of the two James descendants. As a coup de grace, a piece of archaeological evidence, discovered by X-ray technology, proved clearly that the exhumed remains were indeed those of Jesse James.

Starrs had been trying to determine if there were any bullets or bullet fragments in the grave. There was much debris around the bones in the pit, maybe a thousand different items from the rock and soil, and rather than combing though it inch by inch to find any metallic fragments, Starrs's team laid out the debris on a screen and X-rayed it. Anything that was metallic in nature would show a radiopacity on the X ray. One object in particular, from the chest area, stood out. It was in the shape of a square.

The object was a bit of a mystery to Starrs, but his ten-year-old grandson, whose hobby was rock collecting, identified it as obsidian, a type of volcanic stone. Later testing confirmed the boy's conjecture, revealing it to be obsidian, a cheap stone, not a precious one by any means. Starrs also had found very small fragments of a pin that was obviously connected to the stone. Voilà! This was Jesse James's stickpin. A close inspection of the Jesse James death photographs revealed a stickpin in the cravat he had been buried in.

Starrs likened the discovery of the stickpin stone not just to finding a needle in a haystack but to finding a needle in twenty haystacks. By a stroke of luck, this discovery added nonscientific confirmation to his scientific conclusions. Indeed, the evidence, scientific and archaeological, irrefutably proved that the remains in Jesse James's grave were those of the infamous bandit himself. The findings confirmed as well that all the people over the years who claimed to be Jesse James after the real outlaw's demise were, in fact, imposters.

Under the court order, the exhumed remains had to be reburied within three months at the Kearney cemetery. The bones of Jesse James were returned in a cardboard box which was sealed inside a wooden coffin, and on October 28, 1995, in what was Jesse's third funeral, the remains were reinterred not only with the teeth but with the gold found in them. But the Jesse James Home—the preserved home of the outlaw, now moved to a different site and run as a museum—kept and preserved the soil that had seeped into the pelvis and cranium, because it evidently contained ashes and dust from the remains. This material was stored in sacks with the idea that if a scientific method superior to mitochondrial DNA testing came along in the future, there would be dirt samples from the grave of Jesse James that could be tested so the remains would not have to be dug up again.

After the completion of the DNA tests, Starrs returned the artifacts gathered from the exhumation to the James family. They were placed in the custody of Jesse's great-granddaughter Betty Barr. With the consent of the other five great-grandchildren, Betty Barr turned them over to their current location.

The thieves and murderers of modern history have always run the risk of being callously done in by fellow desperadoes who seek the same thing that brought the infamous criminals notoriety: money. This twist of fate was visited on Jesse James, who in his lifetime robbed, killed, and terrorized the citizenry. In death, the legendary outlaw left a host of macabre memories, as well as his stickpin, astonishingly recovered more than a century after he was killed and one of the few tangible artifacts he left behind—a cheap piece of jewelry that is a memento of the last day of his tawdry life and his violent death.

LOCATION: Jesse James Home, St. Joseph, Missouri.*

---

*The Jesse James Home displays only the stone of the stickpin and its partial mounting, keeping the pieces of the pin, along with all other remnants of the 1995 exhumation, in storage.

${U}$lysses S. Grant's Smoking Stand

DATE: 1885.

WHAT IT IS: A decorative piece of furniture designed to hold cigars that belonged to the Civil War general and eighteenth president of the United States.

WHAT IT LOOKS LIKE: The stand has a three-pronged footed pedestal and a rounded top with indentations on which to put cigars; it is 38¾ inches high. It is made of brass, and in the center at the top is a removable goblet used to hold cigars that bears the initials "USG" on one side and an etching of a horse in mid-leap on the other. The goblet sits on a tray that is 13 inches in diameter; under the tray is a drawer in which reading glasses could be placed.

As its shrewd military leader, Ulysses S. Grant was instrumental in guiding the Union to victory in the American Civil War. He planned and led daring campaigns and forced Confederate strongholds to surrender, surviving it all with such heroic aplomb that he was elected by popular vote to lead the nation he helped reunify. Yet his most perilous battle was against the army of stogies he encountered almost daily during his military and political leadership, a continuing engagement in which the toxins in the dark tobacco cylinders ravaged his body and inflicted torturous pain upon him until he eventually succumbed.

Perhaps it was a combination of the Victorian times he lived in and his own fame that launched the American soldier onto this path of self-destruction, because prior to the 1862 battle at Fort Donelson on the Cumberland in western Tennessee, Ulysses S. Grant was merely an occasional pipe smoker. But with his victory over the Confederates at Fort Donelson—in which he responded to Brigadier General Simon B. Buckner's proposal for an armistice by making his celebrated written stipulation, "No terms except an unconditional and immediate surrender can be accepted"—

his admirers honored him, as was customary, with gifts, in his case cigars and related paraphernalia, as a token of their appreciation. Grant would often take the time to thank his admirers, as he did in this letter of June 5, 1863, to Mrs. Mary Duncan of New York City: "My Dear Madam I have just received your beautiful present of a Cigar Case and will continue to carry and, appreciate it, long after I could have done 'smoked' any number of cigars the Express Company are capable of transmitting. . . ."

Indeed, by the time of the Battle of the Wilderness in Virginia in May 1864, in which Grant was attacked hard by Confederate forces but valiantly held his ground, the general was a heavy smoker—thanks in no small part to those who continued to ply him with cigars. In early October 1864, Grant thanked U.S. Representative John Bidwell in a letter: "I have the pleasure of acknowledging the receipt of two boxes of very superior segars sent by you. Please accept my thanks for this mark of your esteem and recollection of your visit to this Army."

The tobacco continued to roll his way until the general had become thoroughly addicted. Here's Grant himself in 1865, recalling how he had developed a fondness for cheroots:

> I had been a very light smoker previous to the attack on Fort Donelson, and after that battle I acquired a fondness for cigars by reason of a purely accidental circumstance. Admiral Foote, commanding the fleet of gunboats which were cooperating with the army, had been wounded, and at his request I had gone aboard his flag-ship to confer with him. The admiral offered me a cigar, which I smoked on my way back to headquarters. On the road I was met by a staff-officer, who announced that the enemy were making a vigorous attack. I galloped forward at once, and while riding among the troops giving the directions for repulsing the assault I carried the cigar in my hand. It had gone out, but it seems that I continued to hold the stump between my fingers throughout the battle. In the accounts published in the papers I was represented as smoking a cigar in the midst of the conflict; and many persons, thinking, no doubt, that tobacco was my chief solace, sent me boxes of the choicest brands from everywhere in the North. As many as ten thousand were soon received. I gave away all I could get rid of, but having such a quantity on hand, I naturally smoked more than I would have done under ordinary circumstances, and I have continued the habit ever since.

Despite warnings that cigars could adversely affect his health, Ulysses S. Grant, pictured above, was an inveterate cigar smoker.

Horace Porter, an aide to Grant who chronicled some of the general's later military campaigns, reported that after breakfast Grant's servant would bring the general two dozen cigars, one of which he would smoke immediately; the others he would stuff in his pockets to give out to others or puff on later in the day, whether in the heat of battle or while relaxing. Porter noted that "a lighted cigar was in his mouth almost constantly." Indeed, Grant smoked from morning to night. As Porter described one memorable day, "Deducting the number he had given away from the supply he had started out with in the morning showed that he had smoked that day about twenty, all very strong and of formidable size. But it must be remembered that it was a particularly long day. He never afterward equaled that record in the use of tobacco."

In January 1865 Porter wrote, "When the chief had lighted his cigar after the morning meal, and taken his place by the camp-fire, a staff-officer said: 'General, I never saw cigars consumed quite so rapidly as those you smoked last night when you were writing despatches to head off the ironclads.' He smiled, and remarked: 'No; when I come to think of it, those cigars didn't last very long, did they?' "

When the Civil War ended in 1865, Grant was a war hero, and he would soon find that his admirers' desire to honor him was insatiable. Private citizens, soldiers, businesspersons, politicians, and others relentlessly imparted to him all types of gifts, and there seemed to be no limit to the expense to which they would go. In August 1865, Grant was given a hero's welcome in a gala celebration that included a parade and fireworks when he returned to Galena, Illinois, where his family had settled five years earlier, and some citizens of the town bequeathed him a two-story furnished brick house, not the first such gift, which he would only occasionally visit.

After the war Grant determined to moderate his cigar habit. In a newspaper interview that took place in May 1866, during a sitting for noted

Maine sculptor Franklin Simmons, Grant said, "I am breaking off from smoking. When I was in the field I smoked eighteen or twenty cigars a day, but now I smoke only nine or ten."

But aware of his fondness for stogies, soldiers were adamant in lavishing upon Grant, now General of the U.S. Army (the first to hold that rank), a veritable torrent of cigars. Shortly after the USS *Susquehanna* anchored in Havana harbor in mid-November 1866, Lieutenant General William Tecumseh Sherman, famous for leading the "March to the Sea" in which his soldiers destroyed rail lines and supplies from Atlanta to the Atlantic Ocean, remarked in a letter to Grant, "I will be sure to lay in for you five thousand cigars of good quality trusting to bring them to you in due season." Sherman made good on his word, writing Grant just three weeks later from Brazos Santiago, Texas: "When at Havannah I bought you five thousand segars, three thousand at $57, and two thousand at $34." These notes about the cigars were embedded in detailed reports Sherman made about his military mission to Mexico. Grant himself was not too preoccupied to acknowledge Sherman's kind interest, as Bvt. Brigadier General Cyrus B. Comstock shortly wrote to Sherman, "General Grant requests me to enclose the within check for the cigars, for $210 in coin. The cigars have arrived but I don't believe the general who has been under the weather has opened them yet. He sends his thanks."

Grant continued diligently to thank those who bestowed cigars and related paraphernalia on him. Here's Grant in a letter of January 21, 1867, to Miss Mary Jane Safford:

I owe you an apology for not earlyer acknowedeing the beautiful token of remembrance which you were so kind as to send me about one month ago. The box containing it came duly to hand and supposing it to be a box of cigars, a present which I often get, it was sent to the house where I have several dozen boxes just like it, though with different contents. I supposed that a letter would come along through the Mail announcing who had favored me, as is usually the case. But no letter came and the matter was forgotten until last evening I had occasion to open a fresh box of cigars, and accidentally opened the one you sent me, and there found your letter and beautiful present. It was the first I knew of your return from Europe. I was indeed glad to hear from you and shall also prize most highly both your letter and the cigar holder which I shall preserve in remembrance of the donor.

Even in Grant's time, the dangers of tobacco were suspected, and some didn't hold back in letting the general know it. In an open letter to Grant that appeared in the *Chicago Times* in April 1867, George Trask, a Massachusetts gentleman who railed against the health risks of smoking, took him to task for his habit and the example he set:

> Public men we regard as public property; hence their public acts are legitimate subjects of public animadversion. Newspaper reporters . . . identify you with your cigar, and find pleasure in pro-claiming . . . that you are a great smoker as well as a great general. Whether they report you in one battle or another, in the siege of Richmond or the capitulation of Lee, receiving the homage of fair women or the noisy applause of men, they "ring the changes" on "Grant and the inevitable cigar." You conquered, general, in spite of your cigar. . . . We addres you, general, with sincere respect and gratitude; still . . . we make no apologies for assaulting a vice which you persistently obtrude upon public notice. The war we wage is simply defensive. Your habit is contagious, and, associated with your powerful name, is doing irreparable mischief in the great com-munity. . . . Dear general, we ask you to set a better example to our military and naval schools, to our army and nation. You have con-quered a city; the world calls it a great achievement. We ask you to conquer a despotic habit . . . and God's Word will justify us in call-ing it a great achievement.

Evidently, this warning, and others that he undoubtedly received, did not deter Grant. In May 1868, Grant wrote to H. Bernd of Danbury, Connecticut, "Please forward to my address, pr. Adams Ex. One Thousand 'Colfax' segars to collect on delivery."

Grant was elected president in 1868, and when he took office the fol-lowing year for the first of two terms, he continued his cigar smoking in the Executive Mansion (later officially called the White House), spending con-siderable amounts on orders for new cigars. In the early 1870s, for exam-ple, he sent checks to John Wagner, a Philadelphia cigar dealer, in the amounts of $118, $182, and $240, not insubstantial sums at the time, and on several occasions ordered a thousand or two thousand cigars at a time. The fact that he was president did not deter people from continuing to bestow stogies upon Grant. In February 1873, William Gouverneur Morris, the U.S. marshal for California, wrote to Grant's private secretary, Orville Babcock, "I send to your address a couple of boxes of Manillas, commonly

Ulysses S. Grant's smoking stand at his home in Galena, Illinois.

called 'Philopenas' which I imported myself from the Phillipine Islands, and beg to request, you will ask the President if he will honor me by accepting them."

Grant was reelected in 1872, and the Republican Old Guard tried to have him nominated for a third run in 1880, after the intervening term of Rutherford B. Hayes. On June 3, 1880, he was waiting anxiously in an office in Galena when a convention wire arrived reporting that James Garfield had received the Republican nomination for president. Disappointed, Grant strode out of the office and threw to the ground what was left of the stogie he had been puffing, then extracted a new one. Leo LeBron, looking out the window of his jewelry store across the street, attentively observed this scene and sent a boy to retrieve the butt the former president had just dropped. Even as mundane an object as a cigar butt was appreciated by LeBron because of its association with the celebrated Civil

War general and president of the United States, and LeBron determined to save Grant's cigar butt (Galena–Jo Daviess County Historical Society & Museum, Galena, Illinois).

The years of continuous cigar smoking took their toll on Grant's health; by the mid-1880s, when he was retired from public life, he was a dying man. But unfortunately, even in his last years, his health wasn't the only thing in his life in ruins. He was also at this time insolvent after investing with a Wall Street swindler. Out of desperation he pledged all his possessions of value, including medals, swords, proclamations, and commissions as collateral against a loan from the industrialist William Vanderbilt, who was embarrassed about receiving these items and later offered them to Grant's wife, but finally gave them to the Smithsonian Institution.

In the fall of 1884, Grant's physicians did not expect him to live past the following April. Grant was dying from cancer and in great pain—he was being administered cocaine and morphine—but did live to see the following April, and beyond. He was believed to have kept himself alive by sheer will, determined to finish the personal memoirs he was writing to provide some money for his wife and children.

On July 23, 1885, the former Civil War general and U.S. president succumbed to throat cancer at the age of sixty-three at Mount McGregor in upstate New York. Just days before, however, Grant had finished his two-volume *Memoirs,* which became a valuable work of literature and a great historical contribution, not to mention a commercial triumph that provided substantial income for his family.

As a result of his habit of smoking cigars, Ulysses S. Grant was defeated by carcinogenic toxins in his ultimate battle, but we have today a grim reminder of his insidious habit, a brass smoking stand with the Civil War hero's initials inscribed on the goblet that rests on top of it.

LOCATION: U. S. Grant Home State Historic Site, Galena, Illinois.

Jumbo the Elephant

CJCJCJCJCJCJCJCJCJCJCJCJCJCJCJCJCJCJCJCJCJCJ

DATE: 1885.
WHAT IT IS: The remains of the famous nineteenth-century circus elephant.
WHAT IT LOOKS LIKE: The bones are currently disassembled.

Six tons of walking, breathing bulk, he stood a towering eleven and a half feet tall and drew cheering, adoring crowds wherever he stomped his thunderous legs. Trapped in the wilds of Africa, Jumbo was the bush elephant that captured the world's imagination, only to meet a tragic fate when he lumbered into the path of modern technology.

Jumbo was born in freedom in the late 1850s on the continent of Africa. There are different accounts as to when and where he was captured, but most likely it was near a river in Abyssinia, which later became Ethiopia.

The gentle young animal landed in a Paris zoo, then was shipped across the English Channel to the London Zoo. The older he got, the more he ate. By the time he was seven, he was devouring gargantuan supplies of food, supposedly even including whiskey. Jumbo became huge.

As the floppy-eared beast was making a name for himself, he caught the attention of an American showman—Phineas Taylor Barnum. Born in 1810, Barnum achieved fame in the 1830s for displaying an elderly black woman slave he had purchased, whom he claimed was George Washington's nurse. He had continued to make large sums of money exhibiting freaks such as the dwarf General Tom Thumb, or sponsoring talent like opera singer Jenny Lind, known as "the Swedish Nightingale."

The celebrated showman, who fancied himself "the Shakespeare of advertising," knew that the pachyderm would be a popular attraction for his Greatest Show on Earth. In a low-profile deal that created a storm of controversy, Barnum purchased Jumbo from the London Zoo for the then-large sum of $10,000. The people of England were enraged that their beloved giant elephant had been taken from them—although one story has it that Jumbo had grown too violent to keep at the zoo, perhaps because he was suffering from the pain of an impacted wisdom tooth.

From the late nineteenth century to 1975, when his hide burned, Jumbo was displayed at Tufts University's Barnum Museum of Natural History, which later was renamed Barnum Hall and became the location of the school's biology department. A tradition had developed among biology students facing a difficult exam to stick a coin in Jumbo's upturned trunk for good luck.

In America, Jumbo thrilled crowds, whether plodding up Broadway in a festive procession or in the Barnum, Bailey & Hutchinson circus shows that toured the country. Displayed in the early 1880s, when the country was still recovering from the Civil War and the era of cowboys and Indians was drawing to a close, Jumbo was a lively diversion, a genuine wonder.

But in 1885, after only a few years on the new continent, the African bush elephant's destiny became disastrously intertwined with the technology of the civilized world. At 9:30 on a mid-September evening, as a Barnum, Bailey & Hutchinson performance was taking place in St. Thomas, Ontario, Canada, all thirty-one of the circus's elephants save Jumbo and the dwarf elephant Tom Thumb had been loaded into their cars. These two were being led along a track by their caretaker, Mr. Scott, known as Scotty, to their cars. A freight train was heading their way, but only when it drew within five hundred yards were its lights visible to Scotty, and likewise the engineer couldn't see the pachyderms on the track until it was too late. Mr. Scott urged the animals along, and while they did speed up, the train could not stop in time, despite the engineer summoning three times for the brakes. The train first struck Tom Thumb, then smashed into Jumbo from behind. Tom Thumb, hurled into a gully, was badly injured but survived the crash. Jumbo died fifteen minutes later, as workers were trying to free him from underneath the locomotive.

Even Jumbo's death couldn't stop the huckster Barnum from capitalizing on the animal's fame. To keep Jumbo's name in the headlines, Barnum invented stories of how Jumbo had heroically saved Tom Thumb even at the cost of his own life. Barnum had Jumbo stuffed—when Jumbo was cut open the technician found the enormous stomach full of everything from trinkets to coins—and his bones mounted at the famous Rochester, New York–based Professor Henry A. Ward's Natural Science Establishment. He exhibited the mammoth preserved corpse in his traveling circus.

As Barnum's business ventures took a different course, he donated Jumbo's hide to Tufts University in Medford, Massachusetts, and his bones to the American Museum of Natural History. Over the years, Jumbo, in his stuffed reincarnation, lived on as the mascot of Tufts University. But even the beast's effigy met a tragic fate. In 1975, the hide was consumed by a fire. Jumbo's bones survive, however, a reminder of the nineteenth-century beast that captured the world's imagination and whose name entered the English vocabulary as an adjective applied to anything very large.

LOCATION: American Museum of Natural History, New York City.

*F*reud's Couch

DATE: 1890.
WHAT IT IS: The couch, or divan, used by the psychiatric patients of Sigmund Freud's practice.
WHAT IT LOOKS LIKE: The couch has a scroll headrest covered with a loose cushion at one end and is upholstered in heavy cotton, over which is draped an Iranian Qashqa'i rug (dated to the 1920s). The couch measures 5 feet 7.32 inches from one end to the other, 2 feet 3.95 inches high from its base to the top of its pillow at the rear, 1 foot 4.93 inches from its base to its top at the front, and 2 feet 9.46 inches across.

It was the stage upon which patients of the founder of psychoanalysis uttered whatever thoughts came to their minds, leading Sigmund Freud to formulate the theories that revolutionized our understanding of human nature and behavior. Like its Jewish Viennese owner, this famous symbol of psychotherapy—a couch—narrowly escaped being destroyed by the Nazis after Austria was invaded by Germany.

Freud pioneered his psychoanalytic method to treat emotional disorders such as insecurity, confusion, and anxiety by encouraging the patient to speak spontaneously about early childhood, dreams, and personal experiences. Freud believed that the emotional scars of traumatic episodes, disappointments, and embarrassments of people's early years lingered in the subconscious, where they could cause difficulties later in life. The methods of psychoanalysis, he claimed, served to relieve neuroses and other psychological problems.

Freud actually began his work in psychotherapy using hypnosis, during which patients were guided to recall the feelings and events that were causing their present symptoms. But around 1896 he dropped these techniques in favor of a new technique he had developed, which he called free association.

During psychoanalysis, the patient, referred to as the analysand, reclined on Freud's couch. Freud sat in a chair behind and out of view of the analysand, so as not to be a distraction when the person free-associated. Freud would begin treatment by telling analysands they were to talk about themselves, but that rather than trying to impose a logical structure on what they said, they should simply utter whatever came into their minds, no matter how seemingly absurd, trivial, or disconnected.*

Free association, Freud believed, provided the raw material for understanding the unconscious thoughts and fantasies that influenced the patient's conscious ideas and behavior. This raw material offered a window into what was going on beneath the surface—that is, beneath the conscious and logical thinking of the analysand—and from it the forces operating at that level could be understood and interpreted to the patient. When Freud first started using free association, he thought that allowing the analysand to say whatever came to mind was itself therapeutic, but he quickly came to realize that the so-called cathartic effect was short-lived and of little value to the patient. It was connecting the unconscious impulses revealed by free association with the analysand's conscious state that offered the potential for therapeutic integration.

To Freud, the couch was a practical tool for learning about what went on in a patient's psyche, much as a stethoscope is a valuable instrument for discovering what is taking place in a patient's body. The couch provided a way to reduce external stimuli that might be distracting to the patient, who, in a recumbent position and unable to see the psychoanalyst, would not be tempted to guess at the meaning of the psychoanalyst's facial expressions or bodily movements. Rather, the couch made it possible for the analysand to relax and speak freely, inspired solely by the promptings of his or her own internal impulses.

The couch was given to Freud in about 1890 by an appreciative patient, Mme. Benveniste. Freud placed the couch in his office in Berggasse 19, a

---

*The notion that Freudian analysts remain impassively silent throughout a therapeutic session, allowing the patient to babble on endlessly without interruption, is a misconception. The myth may have originated with an American who had gone to Vienna to consult the famous psychiatrist. Freud supposedly said almost nothing during their sessions, and when the American returned and reported his experience, his listeners assumed silence was an important feature of Freud's approach. However, it seems the real story was that the good doctor had found this American patient's free-associative ramblings so excruciatingly boring that he was simply unable to come up with any helpful comments.

Freud's couch, with its pillows and coverings, was comfortable for patients undergoing the psychotherapeutic process.

five-story building in Vienna. The couch was in the style of a divan, with a scrolled headrest at one end. Freud always kept the couch covered with an oriental rug.

Freud wrote scholarly monographs about the psychoanalysis of his patients, whose real names he did not, of course, reveal. Instead, these patients became known by nicknames that summarized their fantasies—such as the "Rat Man," who had obsessive thoughts about being attacked by rats, and the "Wolf Man," who had a pivotal dream in which a tree outside his bedroom was filled with wolves—or were otherwise descriptive, such as "Little Hans" for a young boy.

From 1891 to 1938, Freud lived and practiced psychiatry at Berggasse 19, using the couch in psychotherapy sessions with his patients. But after the Germans invaded Austria on March 11, 1938, life became dangerous for Jews in the country. In Vienna, Nazis poured onto the streets shouting "Death to Judah!" In the climate of terror that permeated the city, Jews were beaten and arrested, and their property was seized.

On March 15, Nazis went to Berggasse 19, where a swastika flag was already hanging above the building doorway. They forced their way into the

Freud family's apartment, confiscated the Freuds' passports, and seized their money.

Freud's friends, including Princess Marie Bonaparte, beseeched the internationally celebrated psychoanalyst and his family to leave Vienna. Having lived in Vienna for nearly half a century and now ill with cancer, the eighty-two-year-old Freud was reluctant. But on March 22, after his daughter, Anna, was taken from the Freud home by the Gestapo and detained and questioned, Freud decided his family should flee to England.

Getting out of Austria was no easy task. Diplomatic intervention by William C. Bullitt, the U.S. ambassador to France, helped, but there was also the matter of paying an exit tax to the Nazis. The Nazis' seizure of Freud's bank account had left him nearly penniless. But Marie Bonaparte came to his rescue and paid the tax. Most refugees left Austria without any money or belongings, and for a time it appeared this would be the case with the Freuds as well. But ultimately, because of Freud's fame and the diplomatic efforts on his behalf, he was granted unusual permission to take his personal possessions out of the country.

There were many items Freud wanted to take with him to England. A passionate collector of antiquities, he had a large collection of statues and objects from ancient Greece, China, Egypt, and other lands. The Viennese firm of Bauml was hired to handle the shipping arrangements for Freud's possessions, including his celebrated couch.

On June 4, 1938, two days after he received his tax clearance, Freud left Vienna with his wife, Martha, daughter, Anna, and two friends. (Four older sisters of Freud stayed behind, ultimately dying at Auschwitz.) The party arrived by train in Paris the next day, where Freud was greeted by Marie Bonaparte and Ambassador Bullitt. Then the Freud party crossed the English Channel.

In England, Freud was greeted with the fanfare accorded a distinguished guest. Freud wrote, "For the first time and late in life I have experienced what it is to be famous."

Freud briefly took up residence at 39 Elsworth Road in London, but on September 27 he moved to 20 Maresfield Gardens in the London suburb of Hampstead. It was to this residence that Freud's possessions, including the analytic couch, were sent. Freud used the couch for his therapy sessions until he closed down his practice on August 1, 1939, when his medical condition became grave. He died seven weeks later, on September 23.

Freud's teachings, including how people's sexual development explained their behavior patterns, have always been controversial. Since the development of antidepressant, antipsychotic, and other types of effective medications,

The "father" of psychoanalysis, Sigmund Freud.

as well as various forms of short-term talk therapy, many modern clinical psychotherapists have discarded Freud's painstaking psychoanalytic approach to treatment, considering it cumbersome and outmoded, although it nevertheless remains a viable treatment method used by some practicing psychotherapists. But Freud's influence on how we think about the dynamics of the human psyche has been profound, permeating all aspects of our culture.

Narrowly escaping the threat of death at the hands of the barbarous Nazis, Freud was reunited in freedom with his personal belongings, including his longtime couch. Today most patients sit in chairs facing the therapist, who interacts freely with them instead of remaining out of sight taking notes. But the couch, in tribute to the man who contributed so much to our understanding of the mysteries of the unconscious, has remained the symbol of the psychotherapeutic process.

LOCATION: Freud Museum, London.

The Hoof of Fire Horse Number Twelve

cⵊⵏⵊ℔ⵊ℔ⵊ℔ⵊ℔ⵊ℔ⵊ℔ⵊ℔ⵊ℔ⵊ℔ⵊ℔ⵊ℔ⵊ℔ⵊ℔ⵊ℔℔

DATE: 1890.
WHAT IT IS: The hoof of a horse that was cut off by the wheels of an engine it was drawing while racing to a fire.
WHAT IT LOOKS LIKE: It is a complete hoof, four inches high, with a diameter of about 6 inches and a shoe about 6 inches.

In the annals of animal-heroism stories, all sorts of four-legged and winged creatures have aided people in times of emergency and distress. Legend has it, for example, that one night in ancient Rome the raucous honking of the sacred geese in the Temple of Juno woke up a patrician named Manlius and caused him to leap out of his bed and run to the edge of the Capitol, where he found a ferocious Gaul army scaling the fortress. The increasingly clamorous geese awakened other Romans, who came to help Manlius successfully repel the invaders. And during the Battle of Verdun on June 4, 1916, Commander Raynal dispatched his last homing pigeon with the desperate message: "We're still holding out but we are under attack by gas and smoke. It is very dangerous and urgent that we get out of here. . . . This is my last pigeon." The pigeon, named Le Valliant, flew over battlefields and arrived, badly poisoned, at its destination, where it died shortly after delivering its crucial message.

Sometimes, animals selflessly—as we humans understand the word—carry out a task that saves human lives even when it ultimately results in their own demise, such as Le Valliant, or the anonymous late–nineteenth-century horse that in early morning darkness pulled a company of firefighters to a blaze, only to suffer a mishap on the way that made it an enduring symbol of bravery.

Fire has always been a menace to humans. Early humans found that flames could be used to cook meat or keep warm, but they were plagued by the consequences of reckless handling of fire. Firefighting was apparently a vital concern of early civilizations, as many societies organized special groups to combat the potential hazards unwanted fires posed.

In ancient Rome, for example, special lookouts on the street would shout out an alarm when they spotted a fire, whereupon large squadrons of men wearing battle gear and carrying hatchets, mallets, hand pumps, and other equipment, as well as fire officials, investigators, and physicians, would come rushing by foot and chariot to the fire scene. In colonial times in America—where dense forests led to the construction of wooden buildings—firefighting was a community effort in which human chains would pass buckets of water to dousers at the front, with another chain passing the empty buckets back for replenishment. The statesman and philosopher Benjamin Franklin recognized the need for organized fire companies, and in 1736 formed America's first volunteer group of firefighters, the Union Fire Department.

In the early nineteenth century, hand pumps with hoses handled by several firefighters simultaneously shot water onto fires, but around 1830 these were replaced by steam engines, which pumped out heavier water flows. As cities grew ever larger in the nineteenth century, organized fire departments sprang up; London, for example, had its first official public fire department in the mid-1860s, and it often fought fires in buildings several stories high. Before the age of power-driven vehicles, the heavy engines had to be drawn to the fire scenes, and to this end, firefighters employed horses to pull the carts on which these were mounted.

Which brings us to this story of four-legged heroism in the late nineteenth century, before the age of the gasoline engine, its protagonist an intrepid horse with no name. The horse is known only by the number assigned to it, perhaps designating its hitching post assignment at the fire station.

Richard Hayne was an elderly resident of 1011 Sixth Street, Southwest, between K and L Streets, in Washington, D.C. After his wife had died just over a year earlier, Hayne, who lived alone, had taken to drinking rum whenever he had the chance, and was so careless in the way he carried around his coal-oil lamp that several times police officers who walked his beat had to come to Hayne's house to make sure he went to bed safely. Indeed, a small fire had once broken out in his house; Patrick Hurley, Hayne's next-door neighbor, lived in constant fear that one day Hayne would start a larger fire that would spread to nearby homes.

Richard Hayne had been out drinking and returned shortly after midnight on the morning of March 28, 1890. Not long after, police officers Cook and Kelly discovered Hayne's house in flames, and sent out an alarm over call box number 415. Minutes later Patrick Hurley's worst fears were realized: his own house caught fire.

The District of Columbia Fire Department's Engine Company Three responded to the alarm. At about 1:30 A.M., as the company's hose carriage and engine were racing to the scene, a collision between the vehicles occurred at the steam railroad crossing at First and C Streets, Southwest. In the accident the wheels of the heavy engine ran over the left foot of horse number twelve, which, with another horse, was drawing the hose carriage. The accident severed the hoof of the horse.

Unaware of the animal's injury, the firefighters continued on feverishly as horse number twelve—along with the other horse—pulled the engines more than half a mile on the stub of its injured leg.

The firefighters employed their hoses at the scene and within minutes of arriving had the fire under control. Hayne's house had been burned to the ground, and in the rubble firefighters found Hayne's charred body. Next to it was a key, a silver dollar, and a pipe; Hayne had probably fallen asleep smoking. Patrick Hurley's house was destroyed, but all the inhabitants escaped safely.

At the scene the firefighters made the gruesome discovery of the horrible injury to the leg of horse number twelve. The firefighters were flabbergasted that the horse had raced for more than half a mile on the cobblestone street on the exposed bone of the stump where the hoof had been torn off. Somebody went back to the scene of the accident and retrieved the sheared hoof.

Had horse number twelve not carried on after the accident, the men of

After Fire Horse Number Twelve's hoof was severed as he was rushing to a fire, it was recovered and became a symbol of bravery to Washington, D.C., firefighters.

Engine Company Three would not have been able to reach the fire scene promptly, the fire may have spread, and more lives could have been lost. The steed had performed its duty nobly, but the injury was irreparable, and it was immediately put out of its misery. District of Columbia Fire Department Chief Parris was quoted by the *Washington Evening Star* as saying, "Never since I have been in the fire department, and I have seen twenty-five years' service, were my sympathies so appealed to as last night when I ordered that horse killed. Truly he had more grit and sagacity than any horse I ever saw."

To honor the horse's courage and devotion to duty, the fire department entered the horse high on its Roll of Honor. The department also had a tangible reminder to firefighters, as well as the public and all posterity, that firefighting is a dangerous enterprise in which both humans and four-legged creatures can be heroes—a sad but honorable souvenir, the severed hoof of fire horse number twelve.

LOCATION: National Museum of American History, Washington, D.C.

Take Me Out to the Ball Game"

⌒⌒⌒⌒⌒⌒⌒⌒⌒⌒⌒⌒⌒⌒⌒⌒⌒⌒⌒⌒⌒⌒⌒

DATE: 1908.

WHAT IT IS: The original handwritten draft of the lyrics to the famous song.

WHAT IT LOOKS LIKE: The lyrics are written in pencil on a sheet of paper that measures 9⅞ inches long by 7¾ inches wide. Two small illustrations, one by the verse, the other by the refrain, adorn the page.

On a summer day in 1908, twenty-nine-year-old Jack Norworth stepped into a New York City subway car and turned an ordinary train ride into a journey to immortality. For on this day he conceived "Take Me Out to the Ball Game," the song that became a paean to baseball, a musical shrine to the game, a timeless ode that captured baseball fans' passion for the sport. Pretty good work, one might say, for a guy who had never before been to a baseball game!

Despite his lack of baseball knowledge, Norworth was no novice when it came to music. A professional vaudeville performer and former blackface comedian, he was also a successful songwriter, and songwriters of his day were always looking for new trends to write about. So when he traversed the elevated tracks on the subway that day, it was not unusual for something that had caught his attention to end up being set to music.

When Norworth spotted a sign among the cluster of advertisements in the subway car that invited people to come see a baseball game at the Polo Grounds—the upper Manhattan stadium that was the home of the New York Giants—Norworth assumed no one had ever before written a song about the national pastime. If he could come up with something, it just might catch on!

By the time his thirty-minute uptown train ride was over, Norworth had batted out the goods—a verse and a refrain. Verses in this era of popular music were typically far less melodious than their refrains and tended to be forgotten over time, but they set up the refrain, the musical and lyrical essence of the song, which was repeated over and over and which normally contained the words in the song's title. Norworth's verse told about a young woman named Katie Casey, an avid baseball fan ("Katie Casey was baseball mad/Had the fever and had it bad"), whose beau calls her on a Saturday to invite her to a show. She declines, then adds, "I'll tell you what you can do"—and the song launches into the rollicking refrain, "Take me out to the ball game."

Norworth took his subway-scribed ditty to his sometime musical collaborator, Albert Von Tilzer, a former shoe salesman who was the manager of the York Music Company, a Tin Pan Alley music publisher. The thirty-year-old Von Tilzer, who had never set foot in a baseball stadium either, came from a musical family. His brother Harry, a composer, had already scored big with such hits as "A Bird in a Gilded Cage" (with Arthur J. Lamb) and "Wait Till the Sun Shines Nellie" (with Andrew B. Sterling). Another brother, Jack, was Albert's partner at York. Albert rose to the challenge of setting music to Norworth's lyrics, composing a melody that was at once catchy, bouncy, singable, infectious, and highly memorable.

A vaudeville singer, Norworth himself tried out the song at Brooklyn's Amphion Theatre, but it met with a cool response. In a discussion with his collaborator, Von Tilzer, he attributed this to his bungled and deadpan delivery of the lyrics. A few weeks later he performed the song again at an engagement at Hammerstein's Victoria Theater in Manhattan. This time it caught on, going over well the first night and growing more popular every night thereafter.

Meanwhile, the song's publisher, York Music, went to work promoting the tune. Publishers in the young but burgeoning music industry typically dispatched song-pluggers to department and music stores to introduce their new tunes and to persuade the singers and band leaders who performed in theaters, clubs, restaurants, and hotels to put the company's songs in their acts. At the time, the piano was a common household item, played for fun and amusement by folks of every social stratum, and people avidly purchased the sheet music of popular new songs.

But in 1908, when "Take Me Out to the Ball Game" was published, an exciting new form of entertainment was capturing the public's fancy, and music publishers were quick to hop on the bandwagon and share in the public's craving for amusement—not to mention grab a piece of their pocketbooks. Songs were, after all, entertainment too! This new form of enter-

Lyricist Jack Norworth conceived "Take Me Out to the Ball Game" on a New York City subway and even adorned his original lyric sheet with a couple of illustrations.

tainment was something called the motion picture, which Thomas Edison had introduced to the public back in 1894. At first the kinetoscopes, as they were called, featured short scenes of people doing amusing things and were considered a novelty, but not long after, story films began to be made, and these grew in popularity with the public each year.

The films were exhibited in nickelodeons—auditoriums or theaters that

If songwriter Jack Norworth, pictured above, had followed his father's wishes and pursued a career in the merchant marine, the world of baseball would never have had its immortal anthem, "Take Me Out to the Ball Game."

were actually converted stores, penny arcades, or the like—so named because the admission price was five cents. By 1908 there were thousands of nickelodeons spread across the United States exhibiting motion pictures, whose production increased each year to fill the public demand. The nickelodeons were open almost all day, and when the films weren't playing, local singers were busy introducing Tin Pan Alley's latest releases. But rather than just passing out sheets of a song and leading the audience in singing it, the song-pluggers also had a gimmicky tool: illuminated glass slides depicting the story of the song lyrics that could be projected onto a screen. Music publishers hired special companies to produce these slides and distribute them around the country.

Following the projection of the illuminated slides, during which a recording of the song would be played or a singer would perform the song, usually to the accompaniment of a piano, the singer would lead the audience in singing the new song. Rounds and rounds of crooning provided entertainment for the audience members and—it was hoped—left them scrambling to purchase the sheet music to that infectious new tune.

Illuminated slides were made of "Take Me Out to the Ball Game," with hired actors playing the characters in the verses. These were no doubt widely distributed and probably helped boost the song's popularity. Soon "Take Me Out to the Ball Game" was sweeping the country. Vaudeville singers everywhere were singing the tune, and one night so many performers on Norworth's bill used it that he had to scratch it when he himself came on. But the song's popularity also had a profound personal affect on its lyricist. One night while he was at Proctor's Fifth Avenue Theatre, a singer on the bill, Nora Bayes, came to his dressing room to say that she liked the song and to ask if she could include it in her act. Norworth consented and not only had another promotional vehicle for "Take Me Out to the Ball Game" but—just one week later—had a wife as well.

Norworth eventually found out he hadn't written baseball's first song. In fact, baseball songs dated back to the mid–nineteenth century, with such pre– and post–Civil War ditties as "The Baseball Polka" and "Home Run Polka." In the wake of the success of "Take Me Out to the Ball Game," a spate of baseball numbers followed—including efforts by such acclaimed musical scribes as George M. Cohan, Irving Berlin, and John Philip Sousa— but none enjoyed the success of Norworth and Von Tilzer's tune, nor endured over the years as it did. Even Von Tilzer's brother Harry, as well as Norworth and his wife, Nora, in a cooperative effort, tried penning new baseball songs, but these too fell far short of "Ball Game." It seemed there was only one song that could swell the hearts and lungs of baseball fans, and that was "Take Me Out to the Ball Game."

Baseball derived great promotional benefits from the jaunty song that everybody seemed to know. But if Norworth's father had had his way, the world might never have known the song that was to become a baseball classic, for he had strenuously objected to the starry-eyed show business aspirations of his son. Norworth's father had successfully urged Jack, who was born in Philadelphia on January 5, 1879, to embark on a naval career. To the world's benefit, however, after six years an illness cut short Jack's marine vocation—he had become a quartermaster—enabling him to make a successful attempt at breaking into vaudeville as a blackface comedian.

Eventually, Norworth would retire from vaudeville as this form of theater itself grew outdated, but his royalties from "Take Me Out to the Ball Game" would continue throughout his lifetime.* Indeed, like many songs of its era, "Ball Game" made more money for its authors—and their heirs— years later than it did at first because of the later development of the recording industry and radio, and because such a classic song is always reincarnated by future artists.

When "Take Me Out to the Ball Game" became a hit in 1908, a musical composition's main source of income was from sales of sheet music. It wouldn't be until the following year, 1909, that a revision of the U.S. copyright law provided a statutory royalty for recordings of two cents per song sold in a "mechanical reproduction"—that is, records, which at this time were chiefly in the form of cylinders. This so-called mechanical royalty was split equally between the publisher and the writer. If there was more than one writer, they would split this share, in equal terms for the composer and the lyricist. (This royalty rate remained in effect until January 1, 1978, when the new Copyright Act of 1976 took full effect.)

---

*Royalties earned by Norworth's songs were bequeathed by the writer and his second wife, Amy, to the ASCAP Foundation, which assists young composers and songwriters in their work.

While songs could easily sell a million or more copies in sheet music form, music publishers and songwriters at the time were being short-changed in another area, that of performing-rights revenue. Although there was a statutory basis for copyright owners to collect royalties for public performances of their songs at the time "Take Me Out to the Ball Game" was first published in 1908, music publishers were unable to collect these monies. An amendment to the U.S. copyright law in 1897 granted copyright owners the exclusive right of public performance, which meant that no one could perform their songs in public without their permission—and payment of a fee. But restaurant, hotel, and other venue operators felt that by having songs performed on their premises, they were promoting and popularizing the songs, and they shouldn't have to pay for providing this service. Thus there was virtually no compliance with the statutory mandate. Music publishers and songwriters were initially afraid to fight the owners of premises where their music was performed for fear of having it boycotted. But eventually, in 1914, the music community banded together to form the American Society of Composers, Authors and Publishers (ASCAP), whose goal it was to test and enforce the performing-rights provision of the copyright law so they could collect revenues for performances of their songs in clubs and hotels and by other types of music users, as well as later from radio and TV stations.

In the early 1940s, more than three decades after he had celebrated the sport in song, Jack Norworth reportedly went to his first baseball game. Even though he hadn't attended a game until this time, he nevertheless had developed into an avid fan of the sport, and of his home team, the Brooklyn Dodgers. In the 1950s, after moving to Laguna Beach, California, the one-time vaudeville performer even helped start a Little League for young ballplayers. A true-blue baseball fan, even residing all the way across the country, he never lost his passion for his home team. In a letter dated October 10, 1953, to Alexander G. Law of Englewood, New Jersey, to whom he had transmitted his original draft of "Take Me Out to the Ball Game" for conveyance to what became its permanent home, Norworth couldn't help but complain about the Brooklyn Dodgers losing to the New York Yankees in the recently completed World Series. "I was rooting for the 'Bums' to win the World Series," he wrote. "Doggone it. Maybe they will turn the trick next year."

The "Bums" were soon moved to Los Angeles, where Norworth himself was acknowledged for his contribution to the game of baseball. On a July day in 1958, fifty years after "Take Me Out to the Ball Game" first inspired the baseball fans of America, Norworth was honored by the Los Angeles

Dodgers on the field at the Los Angeles Coliseum with a lifetime pass signed by the presidents of the American and National baseball leagues.

Jack Norworth died at the age of eighty, three years after his "Ball Game" collaborator, Albert Von Tilzer, passed away. But the two writers left a legacy for baseball fans of all time. In its joyous simplicity, the song captures the affection of the baseball fan for the game, the yearning to be in the ballpark enjoying the game with masses of people, to munch on snacks, and to cheer for one's home team.

By popular accord, "Take Me Out to the Ball Game" is indisputably the most famous song associated with the sport, but it has never been accorded any official title of "theme song" or "anthem" of Major League Baseball. Still, there is no refuting its status, even if unofficial, as the musical ambassador of the baseball world. Over the years Norworth was continually asked how he could pen a baseball hit without ever having attended a game. He never thought this should be an impediment, noting that authors frequently wrote stories about fictional places and that his buddy, Harry Williams of Manhattan, wrote the smash hit, "In the Shade of the Old Apple Tree," probably without ever having seen "a blade of grass." It was the imagination, Norworth insisted, that enabled creation without personal experience.

Who's to argue with such blockbuster success? While some people over the years have maintained that the lyric doesn't postulate the narrator's love for baseball, that does not seem to matter. "Ball Game" is a standard that has transcended the literal meaning of its lyrics. It has become for all time a clarion call of fans' love for the sport. It even spawned in 1949 an MGM motion picture with an eponymous title, which starred Frank Sinatra, Gene Kelly, and Esther Williams, and was directed by Busby Berkeley.

When Jack Norworth wrote his baseball song, he undoubtedly hoped it would be successful, but he couldn't have imagined that for untold decades to come baseball fans would be gleefully singing his words, as second nature to them as the national anthem, during the halcyon days of spring and summer in ballparks across America. Yet in a sentimental sense every rendition by young and old alike is a tribute to Norworth's creativity, which gave birth to a musical gem in a New York City subway car in 1908. Because Jack Norworth took care to preserve his original writing, we have today the actual handwritten draft of the immortal tune.

LOCATION: National Baseball Hall of Fame and Museum, Cooperstown, New York.

*M*ark Twain's Orchestrelle

DATE: 1909.

WHAT IT IS: A musical instrument owned by the American writer that gave him great pleasure in his last years and which figured prominently in one of the most poignant scenes of his life.

WHAT IT LOOKS LIKE: The orchestrelle measures 8 feet 4 inches high; 6 feet 6 inches wide; and 3 feet 3 inches deep. Its exterior is made of dark-stained wood.

The Yuletide season is traditionally a joyful time for people around the world, but on Christmas Eve, 1909, one of the world's most esteemed humorists was confronting disaster of the worst kind. Having over the years lost two children and his wife, and now old and infirm himself, Mark Twain had managed to stay active in his work, continuing to amuse the public with his brilliant wit; indeed, over the past few months he had penned, as he put it, several "bubbling and hilarious articles for magazines." But now tragedy had struck again—deep, piercing tragedy—and his personal world was shattered. Standing at a window on the second floor of his home, Mark Twain looked out at the snowy street scene below, struggling to come to grips with the event while music filled his house from his orchestrelle—which, ironically, he had purchased to help him overcome just such an earlier tragic happening.

Five years previously, in 1904, Mark Twain had taken his beloved wife, Olivia Langdon Clemens, who had been ill, to Florence, Italy. It was while on a European jaunt several decades earlier that Twain had become enamored of Olivia when he saw a miniature portrait of her in her brother's room, and he later met, courted, and married her. But alas, Olivia died in Italy. To help him overcome his grief, Twain's daughter Clara, a trained musician, encouraged him to buy an orchestrelle, a kind of pump organ.

Twain finally agreed that the instrument might be therapeutic, and for the then-hefty sum of $4,600, he ordered a wall-sized Aeolian with a large range of octaves and many instrument pairings.

Twain installed the instrument in his Redding, Connecticut, home (which he called "Stormfield" after his science fiction story, *Captain Stormfield's Visit to Heaven*, about a man who pilots a cometlike conveyance to the holy firmament). By the time Twain built the house in 1907, he was one of the most celebrated writers in the world. His oeuvre was substantial, including articles for newspapers and magazines and numerous books, and he was the author of some of the most popular works of fiction ever published, including *The Adventures of Tom Sawyer*, *Adventures of Huckleberry Finn*, *A Connecticut Yankee in King Arthur's Court*, and *The Prince and the Pauper*. Indeed, Twain, whose real name was Samuel Langhorne Clemens, infused his writings with so much wit and satire that he was renowned as a humorist. His whimsical aphorisms alone could fill a volume or two. Among them are such classics as:

Few things are harder to put up with than the annoyance of a good example.
— *Pudd'nhead Wilson's Calendar*

In the first place God made idiots. This was for practice. Then he made School Boards.
— *Pudd'nhead Wilson's New Calendar*

Always do right. This will gratify some people, and astonish the rest.
— *Mark Twain in Eruption*

Nothing so needs reforming as other people's habits.
— *Pudd'nhead Wilson's Calendar*

Truth is stranger than fiction, but it is because Fiction is obliged to stick to possibilities; Truth isn't.
— *Pudd'nhead Wilson's New Calendar*

Familiarity breeds contempt—and children.
— *Mark Twain's Notebook*

This musical instrument, an Aeolian orchestrelle, brought humorist Mark Twain comfort in some of the most grievous moments of his life.

Stormfield was a large stone house with spacious rooms and a porch, and Twain put the orchestrelle in the first-floor library. The orchestrelle could either be played manually, or a music roll could be inserted that churned out a piece of music mechanically, like a player piano. Twain derived much delight from his orchestrelle, not only from playing it himself—he often entertained guests by playing Negro spirituals he had learned in the Midwest*—but from listening to others play it. Many evenings he would sit back in a chair and listen while his maid, Katie Leary, or secretary, Isabelle Lyon, pumped the orchestrelle for him.

Ever the jester, Twain was not above using the orchestrelle to pull off a prank. There was the time, for example, that a young girl named Dorothy Quick (whom Twain had met and befriended while on a ship returning from England, where he had received a Doctor of Laws honorary degree from Oxford University) was sitting at the orchestrelle, pretending to play a complex piece of music as the roll was turning behind its closed cabinet. Just then, a visitor entered the room and was enraptured at the sight of this brilliant young organ player moving her fingers over the keyboard with such virtuosity. When Mark Twain appeared, the stunned woman exclaimed, "It doesn't seem possible a child could play the organ like that!" Twain admiringly acknowledged the young girl's extraordinary talent, and before the roll end could snap off and reveal the secret of the canned performance, he coaxed the woman out of the room.

Twain was a doting and devoted father and was saddened when his daughter Clara, who had married concert pianist Ossip Gabrilowitsch (later the conductor of the Detroit Symphony), moved to Europe in 1909. But with his daughter Jean by his side, he felt the reassuring comfort of familial warmth. Jean would be his only surviving child to live at home with him.

Twain and his wife, Olivia, had had four children. The first and only

*Twain learned Negro spirituals in Hannibal, Missouri, where he lived until he was seventeen, and at his uncle's farm, which had slaves, in Florida, Missouri.

boy, Langdon Clemens, was born on November 7, 1870. Then came Olivia Susan, commonly called Susy, in 1872. Clara Clemens was born in 1874, and the youngest child, Jane Lampton, called Jean, was born on July 26, 1880.

Twain would survive the first two children. Langdon Clemens died on June 2, 1872, at the age of nineteen months. And when Twain, accompanied by his wife and daughter Clara, arrived in England at the conclusion of his round-the-world lecture tour in 1896, a cablegram was waiting for them stating that Susy had contracted spinal meningitis and was very ill. Mrs. Clemens and Clara immediately left by ship to return to the United States. Mark Twain was alone in England when he received word that Susy, twenty-four, had died.

Mark Twain in 1903.

Jean had epilepsy, but her malady did not prevent her from embracing life with zest and compassion. Indeed, Twain was proud of Jean's endearing qualities and good-hearted nature, and in his autobiography he wrote about how she crusaded for animal rights, donated her allowance to charities, and diligently answered all letters to her famous father, even those he had read and discarded. But tragedy struck on Christmas Eve, 1909, when Jean suffered a seizure while taking a bath. It was a devastating episode; she went into shock and drowned in the bathtub.

Jean's body was removed from her room on Christmas afternoon and placed in the library, clothed in the bridesmaid's dress she had worn at her sister Clara's wedding. "Her face was radiant with happy excitement then," Twain wrote. "It was the same face now, with the dignity of death and the peace of God upon it."

Twain, unfortunately, knew only too well himself the personal pangs of death and was compelled to repeatedly gaze upon his daughter's beloved face as she lay there before being taken away. Here is how he describes that experience in his autobiography:

> I went into Jean's room at intervals and turned back the sheet and looked at the peaceful face and kissed the cold brow and remembered that heart-breaking night in Florence so long ago, in that cavernous and silent vast villa, when I crept downstairs so many times

and turned back a sheet and looked at a face just like this one—Jean's mother's face—and kissed a brow that was just like this one. And last night I saw again what I had seen then—that strange and lovely miracle—the sweet contours of early maidenhood restored by the gracious hand of death! When Jean's mother lay dead, all trace of care and trouble and suffering and the corroding years had vanished out of the face, and I was looking again upon it as I had known and worshipped it in its young bloom and beauty a whole generation before.

It was a sleepless night for Twain, who wrote of "wandering about the house in deep silences, as one does in times like these, when there is a numb sense that something has been lost that will never be found again."

The writer drifted into Jean's study to look at her things. He found a stack of books she had been saving for him to autograph for people unknown to him, and vowed to save them, for "her hand has touched them—it is an accolade—they are noble now." He found hidden in the closet a present for him, something he had frequently expressed a desire to have—a large globe.

At about six P.M. on Christmas Day, a horse-drawn hearse came to take away Jean's body. It was a grim scene as the undertakers carried her casket out of the house. Twain stood at a window on the second floor, knowing it would be the last time he would see her.

As he stood gazing at the removal of his daughter's body on the street below, snow falling from the sky, music from the orchestrelle filled the house. The man to whom he was dictating his autobiography, Albert Bigelow Paine (who later penned his own Twain biography), sat at the pipe organ on the first floor and played Schubert's *Impromptu,* Mascagni's *Intermezzo,* and Handel's *Largo.* Twain had asked Paine to play the pieces in honor of his two deceased daughters and his wife. The music, its reedy tones floating from the pipe organ, provided a mournful but elegant sound track to whatever thoughts were swirling through the humorist's mind on this sad occasion.

Twain was old and in poor health, and Jean's passing no doubt exacted a further toll, for the next year, 1910, the literary legend followed his daughter to the grave. He left behind not only his inimitable legacy of words, but his splendid orchestrelle, an elaborate instrument which for six years had brought him pleasure and joy, and which had provided a measure of comfort on one of the most terrible days of his life.

LOCATION: Mark Twain Museum, Hannibal, Missouri.

The Zimmermann Telegram

DATE: 1917.

WHAT IT IS: The Zimmermann telegram was a secret German World War I telegram whose interception had a profound effect on the course of the war. This is a photostat of the telegram as filed by the German ambassador to the United States for transmission to Mexico City.

WHAT IT LOOKS LIKE: The photostat measures 8 inches high by 6 inches wide and has the State Department file number, 862.20212/82A, in the right-hand margin. The message it contains is encoded in seventeen rows of three-, four-, and five-digit numbers.

Neither the British propaganda campaign, the German sabotage of American munitions factories, nor the invasion of neutral Belgium by German forces was able to wrest America from her self-imposed policy of isolation during the early years of World War I. Not even the sinking of the British passenger liner *Lusitania*, with more than 125 Americans aboard, was sufficient to rouse the country to military action. But a one-page Western Union telegram consisting of a series of numbers was enough to trigger a chain of events that burst America out of its cocoon of neutrality and launched the country into the deadly arena of warfare, resulting in the deployment of millions of soldiers and the expenditure of millions of dollars to fight on the side of the Allies.

Shortly after World War I broke out in 1914, President Woodrow Wilson made it clear that America would not take the side of either the Central Powers of Austria-Hungary, Germany, Bulgaria, and Turkey, or the Allied forces of France, England, and Russia. First came his Proclamation of Neutrality, in which he beseeched citizens of the United States to be "neutral in fact as well as in name," echoed two weeks later by a personal plea for Americans to be neutral in thought as well as in deed. Save for a period of colonialism after the Civil War, America had historically embraced isolationism, a policy that had been urged by its departing first president. In his 1796 Farewell Address, George Washington declared, "It is our true policy to steer clear of permanent alliances, with any portion of the foreign world."

The threat of European powers reconquering for Spain the former Spanish colonies in Latin America, and of Russia's expansion to the northwest coast of the American continent (it had already claimed Alaska), led in 1823 to the Monroe Doctrine. An extension of America's isolation policy, the Monroe Doctrine stated that the American continents "are henceforth not to be considered as subjects for future colonization by any European powers." The doctrine stated that the United States would consider any attempt by European powers "to extend their system to any portion" of the Western Hemisphere as dangerous to its peace and safety, but that it would not interfere with existing European colonies or the internal concerns of any of the European powers.

But with its explosive industrial growth and dwindling frontier after the Civil War, the United States in the late nineteenth century took its own course of imperialism, exercising control over islands in the Pacific and Caribbean and going to war with Spain to force its military presence out of Cuba. With the Roosevelt Corollary to the Monroe Doctrine in the early 1900s, the United States warned that it would exercise international police powers in the Western Hemisphere in flagrant cases of wrongdoing or impotence that "results in a general loosening of the ties of civilized society" in any Latin American countries, a position put into effect over the coming years in such nations as the Dominican Republic and Haiti. With the outbreak of World War I, Americans retreated to their traditional policy of isolationism and determined to focus not on the battles on the other side of the world but on issues that directly affected them at home and in the hemisphere, as in Mexico, whose political instability strained its relations with the United States.

But as the war raged on the oceans and in Europe, events occurred that tugged at the emotions and judgment of Americans—and their elected officials. America's neutral commerce on the seas was shattered by blatant violations on the part of the warring nations. The British navy, which controlled the Atlantic Ocean, put up blockades, directed neutral vessels to their ports, and appropriated cargoes, preventing shipments from reaching Germany. Germany initiated a policy of unrestricted submarine warfare, firing not only on enemy warships but on merchant and passenger vessels

British Naval Intelligence officers deciphered Arthur Zimmermann's
telegram, and it caused an uproar in the United States.

as well, in the belief that the latter vessels could be carrying munitions to
Germany's enemies. President Wilson had warned that firing on neutral
ships carrying civilian passengers would result in retribution, but the
Germans did not heed the president's words. In May 1915 they sunk the
British liner *Lusitania*, taking the lives of some one thousand passengers.

Still, America clung to neutrality and refrained from choosing a side and
entering the war. On U.S. shores, belligerents carried out actions to enlist
American support. In a multitude of forums, from leaflets and cartoons to
public addresses, word of mouth, and much more, the British propaganda
mill carried on a widespread campaign designed to paint the Germans as
barbarians determined to stamp out liberty and freedom. The Germans
likewise fomented a propaganda campaign in the United States, but, conducted at a greater remove from American culture and sentiment than the

British, not to mention under the cloud of bad press the Germans received for many of their acts of warfare, it failed to garner much American sympathy.

Although the United States had business ties to the Allies through exports and loans, England's interference with American shipping caused friction between the countries. The sundry German transgressions against America caused greater enmity. But through it all President Wilson—and the American public—maintained their resolve to steer clear of European embroilment. Wilson endeavored to negotiate a peaceful settlement to the shipping problem (he dispatched an aide, Colonel Edward House, to Europe for the purpose), and even after Germany decided to revive its policy of unselective submarine attacks, Wilson proclaimed that nothing short of overt belligerency, such as destroying passenger vessels without warning, would pull the United States into the war. Then an incident occurred—sensitive enough that the details of its unfolding had to be disguised—that sparked a public reaction of such intense outrage that it spurred President Wilson to take action.

On January 16, 1917, the German foreign minister, Arthur Zimmermann, dispatched a message via a U.S. State Department cable route to the German ambassador to the United States, Count Johann von Bernstorff, requesting him to forward it to the German ambassador to Mexico, Von Eckhardt. Von Eckhardt delivered the message to the Mexican president, but along the way the British intercepted the telegram.

The British had been secretly intercepting and deciphering German diplomatic cables for some time and keeping the information strictly confidential. But in this particular instance the message was so hot that British authorities turned it over to the U.S. government with the understanding that the British did not want it revealed that they had intercepted and deciphered the cable, lest it become known they had the capability to do so. The British also feared raising the suspicion that they had fabricated the telegram as a means to get the United States into the war.

After it was decoded, the text of the telegram was turned over by British authorities to the American Embassy in London. U.S. ambassador Walter Page then forwarded the message to President Wilson and the U.S. secretary of state.

The decoded German message was incorporated in a telegram dated February 24, 1917, which read:

> Balfour has handed me the text of a cipher telegram from Zimmermann, German Secretary of State for Foreign Affairs, to the

German Minister to Mexico, which was sent via Washington and relayed by Bernstorff on January nineteenth. You can probably obtain a copy of the text relayed by Bernstorff from the cable office in Washington. The first group is the number of the telegram, one hundred and thirty, and the second is thirteen thousand and forty-two, indicating the number of the code used. The last group but two is ninety-seven thousand five hundred and fifty-six, which is Zimmermann's signature. I shall send you by mail a copy of the cipher text and of the de-code into German and meanwhile I give you the English translation as follows:

> We intend to begin on the first of February unrestricted submarine warfare. We shall endeavor in spite of this to keep the United States of America neutral. In the event of this not succeeding, we make Mexico a proposal of alliance on the following basis: make war together, make peace together, generous financial support and an understanding on our part that Mexico is to reconquer the lost territory in Texas, New Mexico, and Arizona. The settlement in detail is left to you. You will inform the President of the above most secretly as soon as the outbreak of war with the United States is certain and add the suggestion that he should, on his own initiative invite Japan to immediate adherence and at the same time mediate between Japan and ourselves. Please call the President's attention to the fact that the ruthless employment of our submarines now offers the prospect of compelling England in a few months to make peace. Signed, ZIMMERMANN.

The receipt of this information has so greatly exercised the British government that they have lost no time in communicating it to me to transmit to you, in order that our Government may be able without delay to make such disposition as may be necessary in view of the threatened invasion of our territory.

According to a strictly confidential paragraph in Ambassador Page's telegram, the British were able to break the German codes by gaining access to a secret printed source:

> Early in the war, the British Government obtained possession of a copy of the German cipher code used in the above message and have made it their business to obtain copies of Bernstorff's cipher

telegrams to Mexico, amongst others, which are sent back to London and deciphered here. This accounts for their being able to decipher this telegram from the German Government to their representative in Mexico and also for the delay from January nineteenth until now in their receiving the information. This system has hitherto been a jealously guarded secret and is only divulged now to you by the British Government in view of the extraordinary circumstances and their friendly feeling towards the United States. They earnestly request that you will keep the source of your information and the British Government's method of obtaining it profoundly secret but they put no prohibition on the publication of Zimmermann's telegram itself. . . .

The text of Zimmermann's telegram was released to the American news media and published in newspapers on March 1, 1917, the cover story being that the U.S. government had intercepted the telegram at a Galveston, Texas, telegraph office to which it had been transmitted, and from which it was to be relayed to the German ambassador to Mexico, Von Eckhardt. As a result of the incendiary message that Germany would help Mexico recover its lost territories—three states of the United States of America—there resulted a media storm and public outrage. Aware of the threat to America's safety if the Central Powers defeated the Allies, President Wilson asked Congress to declare war on Germany on April 2, which it did four days later, on April 6, 1917.

Many causes were at the root of America's entry into World War I, significantly Germany's policy of unrestricted submarine warfare. But there is no doubt that an important catalyst to the United States taking up arms against the Central Powers was the provocative telegram sent in January 1917 by the German government's foreign minister, Arthur Zimmermann.

LOCATION: National Archives and Records Administration, College Park, Maryland.

The Fourteen Points

~~~~~~

DATE: 1918.

WHAT IT IS: President Woodrow Wilson's program for world peace, announced in an address to Congress ten months before World War I ended.

WHAT IT LOOKS LIKE: There are several drafts of the Fourteen Points, including a shorthand version and typed drafts with corrections made by Wilson in pencil. One of the typewritten versions has some of its pages cut and pasted together so the pages are of different lengths.

To the casual observer, the marks on the small paper sheets look like nothing more than a bunch of meaningless squiggles and symbols, but they were inscribed in the hope that they would be nothing less than a blueprint for world peace, an antidote to the war that was tearing civilization apart in the second decade of the twentieth century. From 1914 to 1917, nations all over the world declared war on each other, fighting so harshly and brutally that millions of people lost their lives. War continued to rage and an armistice was badly needed, but the opposing forces were ideologically far apart. Was the unreadable blueprint some sort of secret code? An encrypted strategic plan shared among the top leaders of the Allies? No, it was simply Woodrow Wilson's original version of his dream for world peace—written in shorthand.

World War I had its roots in the nationalism of the nineteenth century, which resulted in the unification of provinces and states and the establishment of empires such as the German empire, the unified nation of Italy, and the Austrian empire. Leaders of powerful countries sought wars with other nations so that nearby states would join forces with them against a common enemy, and subsequently merge into a single, unified power.

Such was the case with the Franco-Prussian War of 1870–71, pursued by the Prussian chief minister, Otto von Bismarck, who, by enticing France into war—and invading the country, later gaining the iron-rich provinces of Alsace and Lorraine in a treaty—inspired the south German states to join forces with his country, creating a united Germany of which Bismarck declared the king of Prussia, William I, the emperor. National leaders continued to pursue imperialistic policies, forging political alliances with various countries to strengthen their power but leaving defeated nations embittered over shattered treaties and the forced ceding of their territories. Beginning in the early 1900s, one crisis after another made Europe a hotbed of tension. Germany clashed with France over Morocco. Austria-Hungary annexed Bosnia despite Serbia's protests. Poland, Czechoslovakia, and other countries desired independence. France wanted to reclaim Alsace and Lorraine. The Balkan nations of Bulgaria, Serbia, Greece, and Montenegro, backed by Russia, fought Turkey. A conference was called to address the clash and a new country, Albania, was formed as a result of Austrian demands, the intention being to deny Serbia an approach to the Mediterranean and keep it from growing strong enough to threaten the Austrian empire.

Soon a chain of events occurred that was to ignite World War I. A young Serbian gunman, a member of a secret society supported by the Serbian army, which wanted the Austro-Hungarian empire dismantled, assassinated Archduke Francis Ferdinand, the heir to the Austro-Hungarian throne, and his wife, Sofia, at Sarajevo on June 28, 1914. Subsequently Austria, with the full support of Germany, made various demands on Serbia, to most of which the latter acquiesced. But when Serbia gathered its armed forces, Austria, on July 28, 1914, declared war on the country. Russia then mobilized an army, leading Germany to declare war on Serbia, Russia, and soon afterward, France. World War I was in ugly bloom, and through the end of the year, numerous declarations of war were made, with such countries as England, Montenegro, and Japan jumping into the fray. The Central Powers, beginning with Austria-Hungary and Germany, later joined by Turkey and Bulgaria, fought the Allies—first France, Serbia, England, Japan, and Belgium, subsequently bolstered by Italy, Romania, the United States, Panama, Cuba, Greece, China, Brazil, and other countries.

From the outbreak of World War I, President Wilson determined to stay neutral. On August 18, 1914, he made known his intention of keeping the United States out of the war with his Proclamation of Neutrality. But as the conflict grew, events took place that angered the American people and caused Wilson to change his position. Among these was the sinking of American ships by German submarines (as well as the British vessel *Lusitania,* with many Americans aboard), efforts by Germans to blow up buildings, bridges, and other structures in the United States, the Zimmermann telegram, and the general threat to the country's safety if the Central Powers defeated the Allies. In early April 1917 the president asked Congress to declare war on Germany.

Congress debated the proposal and two days later, on April 6, 1917, approved the declaration. The War Resolution document, already signed by Vice President Thomas R. Marshall and Speaker of the House Champ Clark, was carried by Rudolph Forster, the Senate's sergeant of arms, to the White House to be signed by the president. It was early in the afternoon, and the president was eating lunch with his wife, Edith Bolling Galt Wilson, in the state dining room. Wilson quickly finished his meal and went with his wife and another dining companion to the office of Ike Hoover, the chief White House usher. The president sat down and requested a pen; Edith suggested he sign the proclamation with a gold pen (Woodrow Wilson House, Washington, D.C.) he had given her. The somber-faced president read over the War Resolution, then put his name to the document, bringing the United States of America into World War I. Ike Hoover signaled the Navy Department, and messages were sent out to all U.S. warships that the country was now at war.

The draft would find some 10 million American men registering. It would be some time before troops were dispatched into action, and it was not until almost three months later, on June 26, that the first American soldiers arrived in Europe, landing in France. Troops of the American Expeditionary Force first engaged in combat on October 23, 1917. The brass casing of the first shell fired by American soldiers against the enemy in World War I survives (Woodrow Wilson House, Washington, D.C.). The thirteen-and-a-half-inch-long casing was picked up by soldiers; Major General William L. Sibert, commander of the First Division of the American Expeditionary Force in France, sent it to chief of staff General Tasker H. Bliss, because, as Sibert wrote, "it occurred to me that this would be an acceptable souvenir to the President." The general sent it to Washington along with a letter in which he documented its authenticity and requested that it be given to President Wilson.

In March 1917, the Russian government and tsar were overthrown by liberals who had been fighting on the side of the Allies; but because of fatigue and lack of food, supplies, and arms, the liberal forces withdrew from the conflict. This opened the way for German soldiers to capture many Russian cities and territories. In late 1917, however, the Bolshevik Revolution occurred, in which working-class people and soldiers took control of Moscow and Petrograd, overthrowing the provisional Russian government.

This new government, with Vladimir Ilyich Lenin and Leon Trotsky as its leaders, discontinued fighting with Germany and tried to negotiate a treaty, but the Germans refused to relinquish the territories they had captured. Still, the revolution of the Bolsheviks—who wanted an armistice and foreign evacuation of their land—stopped the Russian war effort.

With the goal of inducing the Central Powers to end their hostilities by promising an equitable world peace, Woodrow Wilson devised what became known as his Fourteen Points program for peace, which he wrote in the White House. Many of the points had already been formulated by the president by the time the United States entered the war, but input came also from Colonel Edward House, who had been Wilson's emissary in Europe over the previous two years, trying to determine what needed to be done to achieve a successful peace. In an address to a joint session of Congress on January 8, 1918, President Wilson delivered his Fourteen Points address.

Wilson summarized the progress of peace talks up to that time. The parley at Brest-Litovsk between representatives of the Central Powers and Russia, held for the purpose of determining whether there could be a peace conference, had resulted in confusion, with the Russians asserting the terms on which they would accept peace, and the Central Powers presenting a basis for settlement which, as Wilson characterized it, "proposed no concessions at all either to the sovereignty of Russia or to the preferences of the populations with whose fortunes it dealt." With the Russians insisting that the conferences be held with open doors for all the world to hear, Wilson asked rhetorically if the world were listening to the liberal parties of Germany who supported peace, or to those who demanded subjugation.

The Central Powers, Wilson noted, had once more declared their war objectives and had challenged their enemies to state what they would deem a fair settlement. "There is no good reason why that challenge should not be responded to," Wilson stated, "and responded to with the utmost candor." The Russian people, shattered and helpless in this debacle against the unrelenting and pitiless might of Germany, Wilson continued, were calling for clarity in objectives and terms. Despite their tenuous position, they would not lower their principles. The Russian people had stated with a straightforward and generous spirit what they thought was "humane and honorable for them to accept," declared Wilson, and had called for others to say what their own desires were. Wilson expressed the hope that America might help the Russian people obtain freedom and peace.

The United States did not demand anything specific for itself, asserted Wilson, only that "the world may be made safe and fit to live in," and that peaceful nations might enjoy justice, self-determination, and freedom from attack by belligerent nations. All countries were partners in this enterprise, Wilson pointed out. Without justice served to other peoples, it would not be served to Americans, and therefore the world's peace was America's peace. "The programme of the world's peace, therefore, is our programme," Wilson declared, "and the programme, the only possible programme," was the Fourteen Points, which were as follows:

1. Open peace agreements with diplomacy in the public view and not with any secret international understandings.
2. Complete freedom to navigate the seas in war and peace except as closed by international agreements.
3. The creation of equal trade conditions among all nations that agree to peace, with all economic barriers removed.
4. The reduction of national armaments to the lowest level guaranteeing domestic safety.
5. The adjustment of colonial claims on an impartial and open-minded basis, with strict observance of the principle that questions of sovereignty are determined with the interests of the concerned populations having equal weight with the claims of the foreign governments.
6. The evacuation of foreign forces from Russia and the settlement of issues enabling Russia to independently determine its own political development and national policy.
7. The evacuation of foreign forces from Belgium and restoring it to its former position without limiting the sovereignty it has in common with other free countries.
8. The liberation of all French territory and rectifying the wrong done to France by Prussia in 1871 by returning to France the provinces of Alsace and Lorraine.
9. The reestablishment of Italy's borders in accordance with recognized lines of nationality.
10. Autonomous development for Austria-Hungary.
11. The evacuation of foreign forces from Romania, Serbia, and Montenegro, and international guarantees made for the political and economic independence of the Balkan states.
12. The assurance of a secure sovereignty for the Turkish territories of the Ottoman Empire, and the assurance of a secure life and autonomous development for other nationalities under Turkish rule.
13. The creation of a free Polish state.
14. The establishment of an association of nations whose purpose is

to guarantee political independence and territorial integrity to large and small countries alike.

Wilson believed the terms he outlined were just and worthy of insisting on. "For such arrangements and covenants we are willing to fight until they are achieved," he declared, "but only because we . . . desire a just and stable peace such as can be secured only by removing the chief provocations to war." He also said that the United States was not envious of German achievement and did not wish to hurt Germany if it was willing to join other countries in implementing justice and fair dealing. "We wish her only to accept a place of equality among the peoples of the world,—the new world in which we live now,—instead of a place of master," Wilson proclaimed.

Wilson wound up his address by noting that running through his whole program was the thread of "justice to all peoples and nationalities, and their right to live on equal terms of liberty and safety with one another, whether they be strong or weak." This was the principle upon which the people of the United States acted and to which they devoted their lives, honor, and property. "The moral climax of this culminating and final war for human liberty has come," Wilson concluded, "and they are ready to put their own strength, their own highest purpose, their own integrity and devotion to the test."

President Wilson typed out the final draft of his Fourteen Points speech at the White House and made handwritten corrections in pen. It was basically a clean copy, with some misspelled words corrected such as "parleys" for "parlies," some extraneous words or phrases deleted, and some words substituted for others, such as "settlement" for "arrangement" and "definitive" for "actual."

After President Wilson had delivered the speech and returned to the White House, he gave the pages of his address that he typed on his own typewriter to his daughter, Jessie. This copy contained pages that were cut and pasted together.

Wilson originally wrote his Fourteen Points address in shorthand as a matter of habit. He had learned shorthand in college so he could take copious notes, and as president he customarily wrote his speeches first in shorthand for his own convenience. Wilson developed a bastardized form of shorthand that he taught to a man named Charles Swem, who became his transcriber. He and Swem were the only two persons who could read the squiggles. Wilson trusted few around him other than Swem, and his personal shorthand may have been a way of keeping others from knowing exactly what Wilson was formulating. Wilson's shorthand version of the Fourteen Points, his first draft, was close to the final draft.

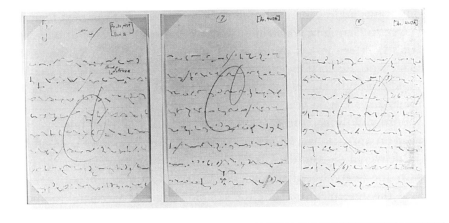

Some of the pages of Woodrow Wilson's shorthand draft of the Fourteen Points.

The Fourteen Points received worldwide attention and became an invaluable political tool for the Allies. Heavily publicized, the proposal made its way behind enemy lines and weakened the morale of the Germans; citizens of the Central Powers nations looked upon Wilson's plan as an assurance that the Allies would establish peace rather than defeat and subjugate their countries.

An armistice was signed on November 11, 1918, which brought an end to the fighting, but the terms of peace still needed to be ironed out. To this end, the Paris Peace Conference was held, beginning on January 18, 1919, with some thirty nations attending. President Woodrow Wilson led an American delegation at the conference but made a political blunder in not choosing a Republican leader from the Senate to be a member.

President Wilson hoped to push through his Fourteen Points as the basis of a treaty, but his American war aims were not shared by other Allied countries. One of the problems was that some Allied nations had already entered into secret treaties providing for them to split up territories of the Central Powers. Wilson's biggest challenge was to win acceptance of his proposal for a League of Nations, but he was ultimately able to convince other delegates to support it. The conference was dominated by the "Big Four" leaders, who were, in addition to President Wilson, Premier Georges Clemenceau of France, Prime Minister David Lloyd George of England, and Premier Vittorio Orlando of Italy. Each had particular goals he wanted to achieve as a result of the conference. Finally, after four months of wrangling, in April 1919 a treaty was finalized that contained compromises and modifications addressing the different countries' aims. (The next month it was given to Germany, which approved it in late June.) Many of Woodrow Wilson's Fourteen Points were not included in the Treaty of Versailles, but it did incorporate his principles of territorial readjustment based on nationality and a world political association, the League of Nations, which he felt necessary for a lasting peace.

Woodrow Wilson returned to the United States and on July 8, 1919, received an uproarious welcome in New York City. Two days later, on July 10, he delivered the Versailles Treaty himself to the Senate, urging the body to ratify the treaty. But after much debate, the Republican-majority Senate rejected the agreement, judging the sanctions against Germany too harsh and believing that the League of Nations would force the United States out of its longtime isolation from European imbroglios. The repudiation of the Versailles Treaty by the United States, which would emerge from World War I a major world power, as well as the denial of membership to certain countries, kept the League of Nations from being a strong and effective world organization that could resolve disputes between nations and promote peace in the world.

Following the Paris conference, the Allies made a treaty with Austria (the Treaty of St. Germain), and the next year, 1920, treaties were made with Hungary (the Treaty of Trianon), Turkey (the Treaty of Sèvres), and Bulgaria (the Treaty of Neuilly, revised in 1923, pursuant to a new Turkish government, in the Treaty of Lausanne).

Although many of its provisions were specific, the Fourteen Points might well be considered a covenant for world peace for all time. Its general principles in their essence champion freedom of the seas, equity in commerce, open peace covenants, reduction of national armaments, self-determination, autonomous development, and political independence and territorial integrity for all nations. Such provisions, if observed, would be timeless in their ability to ensure that powerful nations do not conquer and subjugate weaker ones. The Fourteen Points were composed during the darkest hours of the early twentieth century, but they give voice to the eternal hopes and dreams of all freedom-loving men and women.

LOCATIONS:

Shorthand version: Library of Congress, Washington, D.C.

Typewritten version: Library of Congress, Washington, D.C.

Typeset reading copy for Wilson's congressional address: Library of Congress, Washington, D.C.

The Truce Flag That Ended World War I

DATE: 1918.

WHAT IT IS: A fragment of the cloth that was carried as a truce flag by German soldiers to the armistice ending World War I.

WHAT IT LOOKS LIKE: The rectangular fragment is white and measures 5 inches long and 4½ inches wide; its edges are tattered. The cloth, which has printed on it the military unit and name of the soldier who received it, as well as the date on which it was received, is pinned to a letter.

It was the first monumental conflict of modern warfare. Armies swept into combat carrying new types of sophisticated weapons. Agile submarines navigated the ocean depths, destroying in their unrestricted warfare battleships and passenger ships alike. Airplanes for the first time in war unleashed terror and death from the sky. Some 60 million soldiers from all over the globe were deployed; approximately 10 million lost their lives, with another 29 million injured, taken prisoner, or reported missing.* Warring nations wreaked havoc on one another on an unprecedented scale, and civilian populations were further devastated by rampant disease and hunger. More than four years after the commencement of World War I, the most massive international conflict in the history of humankind up to that time, its hostilities came mercifully to an end, symbolically brought to a halt by a beat-up old tablecloth.

Armistice Day was the day armies ceased their advances, the cannons stopped thundering, the bloodshed ended. It transpired on the 11th of November, 1918, pursuant to French Marshal Ferdinand Foch's announcement to the Allied commanders that hostilities would cease on that date at eleven o'clock in the morning, and that there would be no movement of

*Estimates of fatal casualties range from a few million less to a few million more.

Allied troops beyond their positions on that date until further orders. For people in every corner of the globe, the long-hoped-for Armistice Day, which just a few weeks earlier had seemed impossibly far away, came into reality.

Indeed, by the end of October 1918 the Central Powers' alliance had crumbled. Turkey and Bulgaria had already had enough of the war and wanted to negotiate a treaty with the Allies. Austria-Hungary had accepted Woodrow Wilson's proposal to negotiate peace and in early November was given treaty terms from the Allies. The surrender of its partners was a severe blow to Germany, as the Allies could now launch attacks from inside the borders of the fallen countries.

In its weakened position, Germany's descent to defeat came quickly. Soon the Kaiser, informed that German soldiers would no longer carry out his orders, abdicated, and the crown prince announced that he would not succeed him (both would flee to Holland). Groups of working-class people and soldiers commenced a movement that flourished across Germany and took over Berlin. The war was still being waged on the Western Front, but the Allies fought aggressively, forcing the German armies to retreat.

The German government corresponded with the Allies on a peace negotiation. The Allies informed the Germans that Wilson's Fourteen Points would be the foundation of peace, and that Marshal Ferdinand Foch of France would provide their representatives with the armistice terms. The world awaited the outcome of the armistice.

Four German envoys carrying a "surrender flag," an old, stained tablecloth improvised to appear as a white flag of capitulation, were received by a French Army unit shortly after 8 P.M. on November 7 and were taken to La Capelle, where they were put on a train that took them to Rethondes. Soon after their arrival, the Germans were greeted by Allied commander in chief Marshal Foch and other high-ranking Allied commanders. The armistice terms were presented to the German delegates, who, because of the terms' harshness—among other conditions the terms required evacuation of all occupied territories and the surrender of submarines and war supplies—requested permission to transmit them to their provisional government in Berlin, whose members convened and approved the terms on November 10. The German government informed their delegates, and at 5 o'clock the next morning, on November 11, 1918, they signed the armistice. As of that day, per Marshal Foch's instructions to the Allied armies, hostilities ended.

The Paris Peace Conference would follow in January 1919, attended by Woodrow Wilson for the purpose of incorporating as much of his Fourteen

A patch of the World War I truce flag pinned to the letter to Georges Clemenceau that accompanied it.

Points as possible into the Treaty of Versailles that would be drafted at the conference. Wilson arrived in France on December 13, 1918, meeting with the premier of France and then traveling to England and Rome before the conference began the following month.

Shortly after his arrival in Paris in December, President Wilson made an official call on Georges Clemenceau at the War Office. Jubilant at the Allied victory, which the United States had greatly facilitated with its entrance into the war, the premier greeted Wilson with outstretched arms, saying, "I'm so glad to see you, Mr. President. It is so good of you to come to see me. I want to say to you right here that I am going to swear eternal friendship to you."

During the meeting Clemenceau presumably presented the German truce flag fragment to Wilson as a token of friendship. Pinned to the flag was a letter detailing the provenance of the cloth, which had accompanied the truce fragment when it was originally given to Clemenceau. On the first page of this letter, the French premier wrote an inscription: "Presented to M. Wilson by Clemenceau." The letter, written in French in a formal military style, reads in translation:

November 11th, 1918
La Fortelle (Belgium) Sector 210

Monsieur G. Clemenceau,
President of the Council
Minister of War, in Paris

Captain Chuillier, Infantry Officer
"Chevalier de la Legion d'Honneur,"*
Commander of the 171st Infantry Regiment

Mr. President,

This is a French "Poilu"† who is offering you a piece of the white flag waved by the German negotiators sent to the French front lines and received by himself on November 7th at 8:20 pm, east of "la Capelle," hill 234.

This was already a precursory symbol of victory.

This is where arrogant Germany begged for peace.

This is where the "Krauts" surrendered to the immortal French "Poilu."

Mr. President, would you please accept this gesture of gratitude from the last remaining "Poilu" and last souvenir of war.

The happiest officer in France,
M. Chuillier

It was with no small measure of pride that the Wilsons received the World War I truce flag. In a letter to her family from Paris, dated Tuesday, December 17, 1918, Edith Wilson wrote of receiving the fragment. After mentioning her husband's busy schedule and that he had rid himself of his cold, she then noted, "Yesterday he called on M. Clemenceau & when he left M. C. gave him a piece of the German flag of truce—to give to me. It looks like an old piece of table cloth, but it is such an interesting thing to have. I must stop now & write him a note to thank him."

Edith Wilson again called attention to the World War I armistice artifact in her 1938 autobiography, *My Memoir*. Reminiscing about her 1918 visit to Paris, she wrote:

---

*Cavalier of the Legion of Honor, a military award reserved for exceptional service in the armed forces, as well as for dignitaries and political figures.
†"Poilu" literally means "hairy man"; it was a term for French soldiers of World War I.

That same morning M. Clemenceau brought me a small piece of the flag of truce which the Germans had carried when they came to sign the Armistice terms. It is a square about two and one half inches large of what looks like an old piece of damask tablecloth. The French premier wrote a few lines on a sheet of paper and pinned the bit of cloth to it: a very gracious thought on the part of this old man. . . .*

While the armistice ended the hostilities of World War I, peace treaties still needed to be carved out. This would be effected through the Treaty of Versailles and other subsequent treaties, but the fealty pledged to Wilson by Clemenceau seemed to dissolve as the French premier (along with other Allied leaders) declined to support Wilson's Fourteen Points as a foundation for peace. But Armistice Day in effect was the end of the war, and the truce flag is a symbol of the surrender of Germany, the last nation to hold out against the Allies, and the paving of the way for peace.

The truce flag returned to the White House with the Wilsons. Woodrow Wilson collapsed in 1919 after giving a speech in Pueblo, Colorado, to rally public support for his proposed League of Nations. His health in decline, he stepped down after his second term as president ended in 1921. Soon thereafter the Wilsons moved into a home at 2340 S Street, N.W., in Washington, D.C., taking with them the truce flag fragment. Woodrow Wilson died in February 1924, and his wife continued to keep the truce cloth at her home until she died in 1961, when it became a part of the National Trust for Historic Preservation.

Artifacts of momentous chapters of history are often simple, seemingly innocuous, everyday sorts of things. But of course it is the actions behind them that turn them into the special objects they are, extraordinary emblems of past events. In this sense, the countless human dramas, the remarkable heroism and untold suffering of a global catastrophe the likes of which had never been seen before, are invisibly woven into the extant piece of the truce flag that ended World War I.

LOCATION: The Woodrow Wilson House, Washington, D.C.

---

*Edith Wilson miscalculated the actual size of the small piece of cloth. She also wrote that "the French premier wrote a few lines on a sheet of paper," when Clemenceau, in fact, wrote a brief inscription on the first page of the letter written by Chuillier.

$\mathcal{W}$yatt Earp's Drawing of the O.K. Corral Gunfight

DATE: 1926.

WHAT IT IS: A sketch made by the legendary marshal of one of the most famous shoot-outs of the Old West.

WHAT IT LOOKS LIKE: The drawing is made in pencil on thin typing paper; on the reverse side is another drawing showing the location in Sulphur Springs Valley of the ranch owned by the McLaurys, who fought in the O.K. Corral gunfight. The paper measures 8½ inches wide by 11 inches long.

In the twilight of his years, Wyatt Earp determined to preserve for posterity the story of his adventurous days as a lawman on the American frontier. At this time, 1926, with automobiles, airplanes, motion pictures, and radio common fixtures in the tapestry of everyday life, the world was a vastly different place from the Old West he had known. An old-time frontier officer about whom there was increasing nostalgic curiosity, Earp undertook this task not to exalt himself and his exploits, but from a sense of responsibility: he thought he should record for history an eyewitness account of the heroics of a colorful bygone era.

To help any potential biographer—and he was courted by many—Wyatt Earp sometimes drew illustrations of gunfights to explain how they had played themselves out. On a September day at his Los Angeles home, the elderly law officer collaborated with his secretary, J. H. Flood, Jr., in casually sketching out a diagram of his most famous fight, the shoot-out at the O.K. Corral. As Earp sifted through his memory to bring into focus that crucial day forty-five years earlier, he undoubtedly conjured up vivid images of bitter adversaries tensely arrayed against each other, ready for a showdown—in which, in the space of a few seconds, a blaze of gunshots would give birth to one of the most provocative and stirring legends of the Old West.

Through the popular media of books, film, and television, the story of the gunfight at the O.K. Corral is well known. It took place in Tombstone, Arizona, in 1881. Trouble between the Earps and Clantons had been brewing for about a year, ever since the Earp brothers had arrived in Tombstone, a mining boomtown that was attracting gamblers and thieves in addition to common folk eager to hit paydirt with the area's resources. The Earp family was an itinerant clan, the father, Nicholas Earp, having moved back and forth between the Midwest and California in the 1860s and 1870s, and some of the children having settled and worked in various locations in between.

Wyatt Earp had four brothers—James, Virgil, Morgan, and Warren; a sister, Adelia; and a half brother, Newton. Through the end of the 1860s and 1870s, Wyatt, born in 1848, was a gambler and horse thief who had taken assorted legitimate jobs such as railroad construction before becoming a policeman in Wichita in 1875 and thereafter continuing work as a peace officer. His brothers also worked as lawmen, as well as in other jobs. Settling in Tombstone around 1880, Wyatt, Virgil, Morgan, and Warren tried to establish themselves politically, Virgil becoming city marshal and Wyatt running, albeit unsuccessfully, for sheriff of the newly formed Cochise County.

Ever since Virgil's predecessor, Marshal Fred White, had been killed in October 1880 by a friend of the Clantons (a family of local ranchers), whom he was trying to arrest, the Earps and the Clantons had loathed each other. But in March 1881 an incident happened that would really set Ike Clanton off.

There had been a stagecoach robbery in which two men were killed, and Wyatt Earp, as a Wells Fargo detective, investigated the crime. Wyatt deduced that three men—Harry Head, James Crane, and Billy Leonard—had committed the robbery and murder, but a diligent search for them was unsuccessful. One day when Ike Clanton and Frank McLaury were in Tombstone, Wyatt, knowing the wanted men were associates of Clanton and McLaury, tried to entice them with the reward money, $3,600, for the apprehension of the outlaws, if they would tell him where to find them. Earp's aim was purely political—if he could capture the wanted men he would be a hero, and the people of Cochise County would elect him to the coveted office of sheriff.

Wyatt and Clanton secretly devised a plan whereby Joe Hill, an associate of Clanton's, would draw the outlaws out of hiding by enlisting their help in robbing a (fictitious) miners' paymaster purportedly traveling from Tombstone to Bisbee. Earp would have a posse waiting to apprehend the wanted men at the McLaurys' ranch near Soldier's Holes. But the plan fell through when Hill discovered that Head and Leonard had been murdered before he could meet them, supposedly by horse thieves (Earp would later learn that Clanton-McLaury gang members, unaware of Clanton's collusion with Earp, had murdered the wanted men).

Then Wyatt's close friend, Doc Holliday, an erstwhile dentist turned gambler and drifter, was arrested for playing a role in the fatal March 1881 stagecoach robbery, and Tombstone residents began publicly to question the integrity of the Earps and their associates. The Earp faction responded by drawing attention to the criminal activities of the Clanton-McLaury gang.

The imbroglio was gathering momentum like a tornado, and as each side was making nasty claims about the other, an Earp acquaintance told Ike Clanton that he knew Ike had agreed to give up Harry Head, James Crane, and Billy Leonard for the reward money. Feeling betrayed, Ike Clanton and Frank McLaury accused Earp of having divulged their secret plan to Doc Holliday and to Marshall Williams, the Tombstone agent for Wells Fargo, which had put up the reward money. Ike Clanton and his gang members began to make threats against the Earp brothers, who stayed on their guard, knowing their adversaries were cold-blooded killers.

On October 26, on the streets of Tombstone, Ike Clanton had an altercation with Wyatt, Virgil, and Morgan Earp. Clanton swung his rifle at Virgil, but the marshal seized it and smacked Clanton with the side of his revolver. The Earps escorted Clanton to the Grand Hotel for a search, then Wyatt and Morgan took their prisoner to the courtroom of Justice Walker. There Clanton and the Earps exchanged more threats. Later Wyatt ran into Tom McLaury outside the courtroom, where they had an exchange of words and Wyatt slapped McLaury in the face, challenging him to draw his gun. McLaury didn't respond, and Wyatt, who didn't appreciate the threats made on his life by McLaury, whacked him on the head with his gun, then ambled off to go buy a cigar.

Soon Ike Clanton was released from custody and went to join his brother, Billy, and friends Tom and Frank McLaury at a gunsmith shop on Fourth Street, where a watchful Wyatt observed them inserting cartridges into their belts. Then they left the shop and strolled along Fourth Street to the corner of Allen. Wyatt stopped following them as they continued down Allen toward Dunbar's Corral. The men would have to be disarmed given their openly murderous intentions, but Virgil, whose job as city marshal it was to do so, would need assistance.

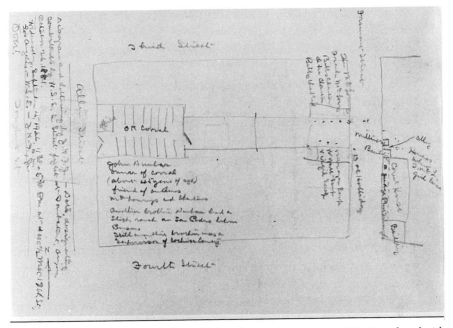

On September 15, 1926, Wyatt Earp recalled his famous gunfight at the O.K. Corral, and with the help of his secretary, J. H. Flood, Jr., recorded on paper the positions of the gunmen.

Ten minutes later, Wyatt Earp joined his brothers Morgan and Virgil and their friend Doc Holliday on the corner of Fourth and Allen. Aware of the building tension between the Earps and the Clantons, a small crowd had gathered. One man warned, "There's going to be trouble with those fellows." Another announced that the Clantons and McLaurys had "just gone from Dunbar's Corral to the O.K. Corral, all armed," adding, "I think you had better go and disarm them."

City marshal Virgil Earp adjusted his gunbelt and told his comrades to follow him.

The three Earp brothers and Doc Holliday cautiously made their way down Fourth to Fremont. At the corner they glimpsed Billy Clanton, the McLaurys, and Sheriff Beehan—who was known to consort with the Clantons—standing in the space between Fly's photograph gallery and the adjacent building to the west. The Earps and Holliday headed toward them, walking on the left side of Fremont.

When they were about fifty yards from their adversaries, a short distance from the O.K. Corral, Wyatt could see that the group included Ike Clanton,

Billy Claiborne, and another man Earp didn't recognize. As Wyatt's group took a few steps farther, Sheriff Beehan stepped away from the Clanton group and approached Earp's men, nervously glancing back over his shoulder.

"For God's sake," Beehan begged Virgil Earp, "don't go down there. You'll get murdered!"

"I'm going to disarm them," the Tombstone marshal responded, unperturbed. Beehan—whose lady friend, Josephine Marcus, was the object of romantic affection by Wyatt Earp—stared at Earp for a moment, then moved off apprehensively down the street. The Earps and Doc Holliday continued their guarded advance.

When the groups were in close range Virgil Earp called out, "Throw up your hands. I have come to disarm you."

Billy Clanton and Frank McLaury placed their hands over their pistols.

Virgil shouted to his partners to hold their fire, but suddenly shots were exploding from both sides. Wyatt Earp saw Billy Clanton and Frank McLaury both aiming at him, but knowing McLaury was the better shot, Wyatt fired at McLaury. Billy Clanton's shot missed its mark, and McLaury went down with a bullet in the stomach, having failed to hit Earp with his own shot. Tom McLaury scrambled behind a horse but was hit and also fell to the ground. Billy Clanton took a bullet in the chest. At this point Ike Clanton turned and ran down an alleyway, out of sight; Billy Claiborne and the sixth man also took off, disappearing in different directions.

There was a heavy silence as the Earps and Doc Holliday surveyed the field. Before them were sprawled the casualties of their gunfight, three lifeless bodies.

If the shoot-out at the O.K. Corral wasn't enough by itself to give rise to Wild West folklore, in its aftermath the confrontation acquired a vastly expanded mystique. The gunfight became the focal point of intense controversy: Sheriff Beehan tried to arrest the Earps, and many people claimed that the Earp brothers and Doc Holliday had shot at unwilling combatants, although it never was determined which side had fired first. An inquest followed on November 16, 1881, and the defendants were cleared, but acts of vengeance followed: Virgil was shot (but survived); Morgan was shot to death in a saloon, and Wyatt took off after their attackers, killing several people, including Frank Stilwell, a law officer Earp believed had participated in Morgan's murder.

Wyatt hid out for a time, then became a drifter and gambler. His partners in the gunfight likewise led itinerant lives involving gambling and even murder. Wyatt finally settled in Los Angeles, where at the age of seventy-eight on September 15, 1926, he assisted his secretary, J. H. Flood, Jr., in making a drawing of the shoot-out at the O.K. Corral.

Soon Wyatt's tale would begin to ignite the public imagination, thanks in part to Walter Noble Burns's 1927 book, *Tombstone* (Wyatt's legend would be launched to greater heights with Stuart Lake's posthumous biography of him, *Frontier Marshal*). But for now, in this era not too far removed from nineteenth-century cowboy days, he was a celebrated relic of the Old West whom Western movie actors such as Tom Mix and William Hart, who got a kick out of hanging around real veterans, would portray on the screen.

But several authors, including Lake, had communicated with Wyatt about collaborating on his autobiography, and he did dictate portions of his autobiography to Flood. The infamous O.K. Corral shoot-out was of prime fascination, and Wyatt probably made the drawing of it to set the record straight rather than to exonerate himself, his brothers, and Doc Holliday. As John D. Gilchriese, a noted Earp authority and collector involved in an Earp museum in Tombstone, later wrote:

> During the time Wyatt & John Flood were jointly writing a book [which was never finished or published] explaining Wyatt's lively career, they met frequently in order that Wyatt could read Flood's weekly efforts. Wyatt suggested to Flood that he would draw several sketches & diagrams that would explain his various gunfights, and locate the ranches of those killed during the gunfight of October 26, 1881. . . . Often in an animated way he would remember some detail, once taking his ten gauge shotgun & demonstrating to Flood how he shot Frank Stilwell, in the Tucson trainyard. Naturally, Wyatt discussed how the adversaries stood, placing dots to show their location. . . . Often latent bitterness crept into his voice when he described how they shot Morgan in the back. . . . The historical value of these diagrams is obvious, for it clearly illustrates what Wyatt Earp remembered & also what he wished to reveal. These two diagrams handed to me by Flood are to the best of my knowledge exactly what he said they were.

The O.K. Corral gunfight possessed the ingredients of a timeless fable: bold outlaws, fearless protagonists of dubious rectitude, a bitter feud, and, of course, the romantic Old West setting. But with scholarly interpretation over the years, the Earps would be perceived by some as antiheroes, scurrilous and malevolent, as corrupt as the criminals they had gunned down. After Wyatt Earp died in 1929, books appeared that celebrated his career, followed later by television shows and movies that permanently inscribed the Earp brothers into the folklore of the Old West. The magnitude of that fame was elusive to the Earps in their own lifetimes, as legends are frequently born after death, but Wyatt Earp in his simple drawing of the O.K. Corral gunfight left a legacy that endures for posterity as the firsthand account of an unforgettable day in the annals of the Wild West.

LOCATION: Autry Museum of Western Heritage, Los Angeles, California.

The Maltese Falcon

DATE: 1941.
WHAT IT IS: A prop from the eponymous motion picture.
WHAT IT LOOKS LIKE: The prop (which exists in two versions) is a statuette of a falcon. One is made of lead and bronze, weighs 50 pounds, is nearly 12 inches high, and has slash marks on the head. The other statuette is also made of lead and has a bent tail feather.

Few pieces of movie memorabilia have captured the public imagination like the Maltese falcon, the prop from the film *The Maltese Falcon*. And real life has mirrored movie fiction. As in the movie, the prop has been both shrouded in intrigue and the object of relentless desire.

In the 1920s, Dashiell Hammett's tale of the search for a bejeweled statue of a bird of prey ran in serial form in a magazine. Hammett's story was inspired by a falcon legend derived from real-life history, which records that the Holy Roman Emperor Charles V, who was also the king of Spain, granted the island of Malta in 1530 to the Knights of St. John, who had been driven from the Aegean island of Rhodes by the Turks. There were two conditions: should the knights ever abandon Malta, the Mediterranean island would become imperial property again; and as recognition that the island was still under Spanish dominion, once a year on All Saints' Day, the knights would send a falcon to Charles.

The legend picks up some years later with one of the annual falcon levies. Sometimes, instead of providing a live falcon, the knights sent falcon statues bedecked with precious gems. In the late 1530s, a bejeweled falcon statue was shipped to King Charles but during its voyage was snatched by marauders. It was discovered hundreds of years later, in the early 1900s, in a Parisian antique shop, from which it was again stolen, thus setting in motion the drama of a suspenseful hunt.

The Maltese falcon movie prop that has a bent tail feather.

Hammett's fictional story of the hunt for the fabulous historical artifact was so popular that it was published in book form in 1930. The following year, *The Maltese Falcon,* the first of three film adaptations, was released, starring Ricardo Cortez and Bebe Daniels.

Five years later, the next film adaptation was playing in movie theaters. Called *Satan Met a Lady* and starring Bette Davis, Warren William, and Arthur Treacher, the priceless object of pursuit in this movie was a ram's horn.

In 1941 the third adaptation, also titled *The Maltese Falcon,* was released, with Humphrey Bogart, Peter Lorre, Mary Astor, and Sydney Greenstreet. The movie was not expected to be successful for several reasons: the story had been done twice before; John Huston had never directed a movie before; and the actors were not then stars. But Huston, who felt that the earlier films had not captured Dashiell Hammett's wonderful dialogue, wrote a script that was faithful to Hammett's fast-paced, suspenseful prose and gave the film a dark and edgy feel. Huston's *Maltese Falcon,* costing less than $400,000, was a low-budget production that became a huge success, launching Humphrey Bogart, who played Detective Sam Spade, and director John Huston into instant stardom.

In the Huston production, the statue of the Maltese falcon has a long history of intrigue as shady people take huge risks to find the figurine. Sydney Greenstreet's con-artist character, Kasper Gutman, finally acquires it, but it turns out to be a worthless carving of lead.

Two lead statues were made to represent the Maltese falcon in the movie. The future value and importance of these props probably wasn't recognized during the filming, as one of the prop men reported they used the fifty-pound statues as weights on the movie set.

Over the years, as the film itself has acquired legendary status, the Maltese falcon prop has been widely counterfeited. In 1993 Christie's, the auction house, put up for sale a five-pound resin Maltese falcon statue allegedly used in the Humphrey Bogart movie. The authenticity of the Christie's figurine was disputed, and the auction was canceled. It has never been proved that this statue matches any image of the Maltese falcon seen in the movie.

One of the two real props made for the classic Bogart film was auctioned by Christie's the following year, this one coming from the estate of actor and director William Conrad, who used the prop as a bookend after supposedly receiving it as a gift from Jack Warner, the head of Warner Brothers.

As in the movie, the statue in real life turned out to be an object of consuming desire, even if it had no inherent value. In December 1994, jeweler Ronald Winston purchased the statue for a hefty $398,000. In the film the raving character played by Sydney Greenstreet uses a penknife to slash the Maltese falcon and discovers it is not made of gold but lead. The statue purchased by Winston is believed by some to have been a practice prop as its slash marks are too deep and abundant, and does not have a bent tail feather as seen in the film.*

After acquiring the prop, Winston, son of the famed jeweler Harry Winston, who donated the Hope Diamond to the Smithsonian Institution, decided to fulfill the dreams of the characters. He created the Winston falcon, a ten-pound, 11¼-inch-high solid-gold statue with two Burmese cabochon ruby eyes and a 42.98 carat pear shaped diamond on a platinum chain hanging from the beak, all mounted on a four-inch-square malachite base. It was initially valued at $8 million. Winston, however, reportedly sold the movie-prop Maltese falcon for one million dollars within a few years after acquiring it.

The other Maltese falcon prop from the Humphrey Bogart movie was purchased in 1987 by Dr. Gary Milan, a Beverly Hills dentist and artifact collector. Milan's falcon, like the one usually seen in the film, has a bent tail feather, unlike the other Maltese falcon prop from the movie, as well as some slash marks.

Humphrey Bogart's Sam Spade detective character poignantly observed that the Maltese falcon was "the stuff dreams are made of." Indeed so in big-screen make-believe, but the statuettes would have little actual value if they hadn't been the centerpiece of one of the most popular motion pictures of all time. Plucked from the set of a fictional movie where they represented an unobtainable object of desire for a cast of colorful, unforgettable characters, the Maltese falcon statuettes—by virtue of their metamorphosis from cheap props into fabulously expensive collectors' items—may now be said to have become dreams made into stuff.

LOCATIONS: Warner Bros. Museum, Burbank, California (on temporary loan from Dr. Gary Milan); the Winston falcon is owned by a person who wishes to remain anonymous.

---

*The bent tail feather may have resulted from an accident on the set in which the falcon was dropped, just missing actress Lee Patrick's foot and slightly injuring Bogart's toes.

*M*onty's Battle Caravans

ᘓᘓᘓᘓᘓᘓᘓᘓᘓᘓᘓᘓᘓᘓᘓᘓᘓᘓᘓᘓᘓᘓ

DATE: 1942–1945.

WHAT THEY ARE: The three trailers used by the revered British commander of the Eighth Army, Bernard Law Montgomery, during his North African and Northwest European military campaigns in World War II.

WHAT THEY LOOK LIKE: Two of the caravans were made in Italy. The first one used by Montgomery, remounted on a British Leyland chassis, is 24 feet long, 8 feet wide, and 10 feet, 6 inches high. The next caravan acquired by the British commander was remounted on an American Mack chassis and measures 27 feet long, 8 feet wide, and 12 feet high. The map lorry (motortruck) measures 31 feet long, 7 feet, 6 inches wide, and 11 feet high.

The subtle ironies of war are sometimes best appreciated after the smoke has cleared and historians have been able to sift through the ashes of events and weigh in with their assessments. Not so with Bernard Law Montgomery, who at the time of his greatest military challenge zestfully embraced the ironies of war and rode their crest to victory—roaming the desert sands of North Africa in the mobile home of an Italian enemy general, its walls adorned with pictures of his nemesis, Erwin Rommel, and other top German commanders.

By the summer of 1942, Adolf Hitler's master plan for global domination hung darkly over the free nations of the world. Poland, Norway, Denmark, France, Greece, Belgium, Yugoslavia, the Netherlands, and other countries had one after another been swallowed up by Germany, which had by now invaded Russia and was penetrating ever deeper into its heart. German submarines and mines were destroying American and British merchant vessels on the seas. Japanese forces dominated the western Pacific and Southeast

Asia. There were Allied victories, to be sure, but the future looked grim and doubtful, promising more warfare and death and hinting at the unthinkable: an Axis victory.

In February 1941, about four months before Germany launched its invasion of Russia, German major general Erwin Rommel arrived in Africa to help Mussolini, who had promised Hitler to bring Africa under Axis control. Germany was now eager to conquer North Africa, with Egypt, including the Suez Canal, the prized target, and move on to the Middle East oil fields. The Italian army in Libya needed help, and that would come with great vigor from Rommel leading the German Afrika Korps.

Rommel penetrated Egypt without much resistance. The British Eighth Army was repelled by Rommel's relentless drive, and it appeared Egypt was about to fall to the Germans. But Rommel's offensive, begun in January 1942, would eventually falter, thanks in part to the decision to bring in Bernard Montgomery to command the British troops.

On July 1, an advance by Rommel's Afrika Korps, bolstered by Italian forces, reached El Alamein in Egypt, the final Allied barrier to fend off an Axis drive to Alexandria and the Suez Canal, Cairo, Iraq, Iran, and ultimately India. But the British held off the German-Italian army, and in mid-August Montgomery, selected by Winston Churchill, replaced Sir Claude Auchinleck as commander in chief of the British Eighth Army in North Africa.

Montgomery's task was formidable indeed, but his mission was crucial. When Monty, as his soldiers called him, came to the desert to take command of the Eighth Army, he was assigned for his quarters the mobile home of the Eighth Army commander—a caravan captured from the Italian general Berganzoli, known to his troops since the Spanish Civil War as "Barba Electrica" (Electric Beard, probably derived from his bushy and spiky beard and mustache), and dubbed "Old Electric Whiskers" by the British. The caravan not only had been made in Italy, an enemy country, but bore pictures of enemy leaders: a signed pastel of Rommel and two photographs each of two esteemed German field marshals, Albrecht Kesselring and Gerd von Rundstedt.

Monty's battlefield caravan was more than just a bed on wheels. In the confines of this trailer he spent much time strategizing, reflecting, and letting his imagination spark his insight into human nature.

But why didn't the British commander take down the photographs of the German leaders?

As Monty would later say, "I used to look at the photograph of the general I was up against at the moment and try and decide what sort of person

Field Marshal Montgomery outside his caravans on November 5, 1946, greeting the man he defeated, Field Marshal Ernst Busch, the commander in chief of the German armies in northwest Europe, accompanied by General Gareis, the senior German liaison officer, at Luneburg Heath, a previous training site for the Wehrmacht.

he was and how he was likely to react to any moves I might make against him. In some curious way this helped me in the battle."

Monty painstakingly prepared attack plans against the enemy, which had superior armor, and in the late night and early morning darkness of October 23–24, 1942, the British Eighth Army began an all-out assault on the combined German-Italian force at El Alamein. The battle would prove to be one of the most important of World War II, a decisive strategic gain and morale boost for the victor.

When the battle erupted, Monty was in his first caravan (mounted on the Leyland chassis), which had served as his "home" at the Battle of Alam Halfa on August 31, 1942. The military leader was resting comfortably when the firing began at 9:40 P.M. on October 23. As Monty would later write in his *Memoirs*: "The barrage of over one thousand guns opened, and the Eighth Army which included some 1200 tanks went into the attack. At that moment I was asleep in my caravan."

The Allied attack at El Alamein was ferocious. Against a wide swath of German land mines, tanks, and infantry, Allied artillery units bore down with determination. Royal Air Force raids destroyed Axis planes waiting on airfields to be deployed in bombing missions. Dummy armor, equipment, pipelines, and other displays were used to confuse the Germans about where the attacks would be launched. On November 4, less than two weeks after the drive began, the badly battered Axis forces retreated. The Allied victory was a major success for Monty, whose brilliant leadership launched him into legend.

As the war blazed on, Monty's Eighth Army captured another caravan in the desert in Tunisia. Like Monty's mobile home, this had also been used by an Italian commander, Marshal Giovanni Messe, and been manufactured in Italy. Messe had succeded Rommel, who was ill and had returned to

Germany. At Monty's headquarters, where Messe was taken after his capture following the surrender of Italian forces in May 1943, the Italian commander told Monty that Rommel had used the caravan himself.

Monty adopted this prize as his living quarters, adapting his previous home to serve as his office. His new dwelling was a major step up from the previous one: it had a bath. Visitors to his new quarters were frequent, but the British commander would not displace himself except for the most esteemed guests. As he would later say, "I would turn out of this new caravan only for two people: the King, George VI, and Winston Churchill. Other and less important VIPs were given a tent."

Montgomery's caravans went with him to the Mediterranean island of Sicily and to Italy when he waged a campaign there before the invasion of Normandy, where Monty was in charge of the Allied ground forces.

Monty's third caravan was the only one not captured from an enemy; it had been tailor-made for its military purpose by a British manufacturer. The caravan served as a map center, in which were hung maps that Monty and his staff assessed daily in planning their strategies; it was also used as a communications center.

Of the three caravans, Monty deemed this last one the most important. As he later recalled:

> The third caravan, with the maps, is in my view the most interesting and historic of the three. During the campaign in the desert, in Sicily, and in Italy, I had always felt the need of a map lorry from which I could conduct the war and have telephone conversations with my subordinate generals. I decided this lack must be made good for the battle for Normandy and the campaign in North West Europe. So when I arrived back in Italy in January 1944 my staff approached the British Trailer Company Limited of Trafford Park, Manchester, and asked if they would make me an articulated caravan to our design. They willingly agreed.

In this map lorry, Monty regularly received the reports of his staff from which he made strategic decisions. Much of Monty's later war effort was conducted in this caravan. As he also noted, "It was in this map lorry that my team of liaison officers gave me every night the latest situation on the various parts of the fronts visited by them. Winston Churchill always liked to listen to these reports whenever he stayed with me and so did King George VI."

In early January 1944, Montgomery returned to England to begin

French fighting forces guard Montgomery's caravan (the Eighth Army Advanced Head-quarters) in Tripolitania.

planning with General Dwight D. Eisenhower the Allied invasion of Europe; Monty would lead the ground units, while Eisenhower would act as supreme commander. Monty relinquished his ground command to Eisenhower in September and took over leadership of the British 21st Army Group, with responsibility for over a million soldiers. During this command, which continued until the conclusion of World War II, Monty used all three caravans as a mobile headquarters in the field.

After the war Monty claimed the three battle caravans for himself, in the face of opposition from the British War Office. Finally the War Office relented and decided to allow the commander to keep them during his lifetime. Monty in turn pledged that they would after his death be turned over to their current home.

From African deserts to the beaches of Normandy to the streets of Berlin, Montgomery's caravans served a vital purpose. They were like faithful old companions, which is why he insisted on keeping them after the war despite the objections of the British War Office. Indeed, Montgomery, who rose in rank to field marshal, considered his battle caravans important historical artifacts. "In years to come," he wrote, "historians and scholars will learn with interest how the commander in chief of the British Army in the field lived during the war against Hitler's Germany, and will be able to see the map lorry from which he conducted operations of great armies of over one million men."

Today the caravans testify not just to the fortitude, brilliance, and resourcefulness with which Monty commanded the Allied armies during World War II, but to the heroism of a gallant commander and the million soldiers he led to victory over the Axis powers in the most destructive war in history.

LOCATION: Imperial War Museum, London.

The World War II Japanese Surrender Table

⊂⊃⊂⊃⊂⊃⊂⊃⊂⊃⊂⊃⊂⊃⊂⊃⊂⊃⊂⊃⊂⊃⊂⊃⊂⊃⊂⊃⊂⊃⊂⊃⊂⊃⊂⊃

DATE: 1945.

WHAT IT IS: The table on which Japanese dignitaries and Allied representatives signed the document providing for Japan's surrender in World War II.

WHAT IT LOOKS LIKE: It is a silvery metal folding table that measures 96 inches long by 27 inches wide by 30 inches high when standing. The table has many scratches, and its underside is stamped in two places with the name of its manufacturer, "Metal Office Furn. Co., Grand Rapids, Mich."

With the proceedings about to commence, peace would officially be restored to a world ravaged by a war unprecedented in violence. On sea, on land, and in the air, combatants had wreaked havoc on foe and civilian alike on a scale never seen before. With concentration camps, human ovens, mass executions, prisoner-of-war camps, and atomic bombs, humans inflicted unspeakable atrocities upon one another. But Japan's surrender would ensure that the last battles would be brought to a halt, that imprisoned soldiers would no longer suffer barbarities at the hands of their captors, and that civilian populations would be relieved of the anguish of war. Japan's official capitulation was a monumental event long dreamed of by most of the world, one that would allow armies to disperse and restore human liberty and dignity to millions of noncombatants—and, it was hoped, would launch the world into a new era of peace and tranquility.

Present for the signing of the surrender instrument would be the most distinguished commanders of the Allied powers, as well as political and military dignitaries of the vanquished nation of Japan. With the elaborate preparations made for this historic encounter, how is it that a simple mess table, a plain piece of furniture on which sailors ate their humble meals, became the stage on which World War II was brought to an end?

•   •   •

With Germany and Italy defeated, Japan was the last major Axis power still fighting at the end of World War II. Several Allied declarations preceded the catastrophic events that would compel the Japanese government to yield, notifications that warned of the Allies' determination to fight Japan and that the country's ultimate surrender might come at a great cost.

In the Cairo Declaration, released on December 1, 1943, the U.S. president, Franklin D. Roosevelt, the Chinese general, Chiang Kai-shek, and the British prime minister, Winston Churchill, resolved that:

> The several military missions have agreed upon future military operations against Japan. The three Great Allies expressed their resolve to bring unrelenting pressure against their brutal enemy by sea, land, and air. This pressure is already rising. The three Great Allies are fighting this war to restrain and punish the aggression of Japan. They covet no gain for themselves and have no thought of territorial expansion. It is their purpose that Japan shall be stripped of all the islands in the Pacific which she has seized or occupied since the beginning of the first World War in 1914, and that all the territories Japan has stolen from the Chinese, such as Manchuria, Formosa, and the Pescadores, shall be restored to the Republic of China. Japan will also be expelled from all other territories which she has taken by violence and greed. The aforesaid three great powers, mindful of the enslavement of the people of Korea, are determined that in due course Korea shall become free and independent.
>
> With these objects on view the three Allies, in harmony with those of the United Nations at war with Japan, will continue to persevere in the serious and prolonged operations necessary to procure the unconditional surrender of Japan.

Fourteen months later, on February 11, 1945, an agreement was signed at Yalta stating: "The leaders of the three Great Powers—the Soviet Union, the United States of America and Great Britain—have agreed that in two or three months after Germany has surrendered and the war in Europe has terminated the Soviet Union shall enter into the war against Japan on the side of the Allies. . . ."

On July 26, 1945, the leaders of the United States, the Republic of China, and Great Britain issued the Potsdam Proclamation, in which they demanded that the terms of the Cairo Declaration be carried out, that those Japanese authorities who had deceived the Japanese people into embarking on world conquest be ousted, that Japan's war-making power be destroyed, that the Japanese military forces be disarmed—that there be an immediate and unconditional surrender. If these terms were not carried out, the Allied powers promised Japan's "prompt and utter destruction."

The Japanese cabinet debated a surrender to the Allies, and while many members favored surrendering, not all did, and in an official statement issued on July 28 Prime Minister Kantaro Suzuki nonchalantly dismissed the Potsdam Proclamation, asserting it offered little improvement over the Cairo Declaration. American newspapers responded by reporting that Japan ignored the demand for surrender.

By this time the United States had readied an atomic bomb—if it had been ready months earlier it might well have been dropped on Germany— and the Soviet Union, conducting its own military offensive, had swept across Eastern Europe. Russia seemed ready to invade Japan, and on July 24 Harry Truman, who succeeded Roosevelt as president of the United States, had mentioned to Stalin that the U.S. military had a potent new weapon. Through Russian spies, Stalin knew exactly what Truman was referring to, but he did not seem to appreciate the destructive potential of the new American bomb.

On July 16, 1945, an implosion-type atomic bomb with a force greater than 18,000 tons of TNT was tested successfully in an isolated area of New Mexico. President Truman thought the Japanese would surrender before the Soviets launched an invasion, but a surrender was not forthcoming. Perhaps this influenced the U.S. president, who may not have wanted to compete with Russia over Japan, to take a harsh step.

Truman interpreted Japan's recalcitrance to accept the Potsdam Proclamation as a rejection of the demand to capitulate. Finally, in an effort that was intended to spare Allied lives and hasten the end of the war, Truman ordered the dropping of the atomic bombs on Japan. Truman did not specify which cities to bomb; rather that would be a military decision based on the importance of Japanese cities militarily and favorable weather conditions for bombing.

As it turned out, two cities were chosen to be bombed. Hiroshima was decimated on August 6, Nagasaki three days later, and on August 10, Emperor Hirohito relayed through the Swiss Political Department Japan's acceptance of the terms of the Potsdam Conference with the stipulation that the emperor be allowed to continue as the sovereign ruler. The next day, August 11, James F. Byrnes, U.S. secretary of state, on behalf of the governments of the United States, the United Kingdom, the Soviet Union, and China, replied that the emperor and Japanese government would be allowed to rule Japan subject to the terms of the Allied supreme commander, "who will take such steps as he deems proper to effectuate the surrender terms." On August 14 Japan acceded to the provisions of the Allied joint declaration. A date in late August was set for the formal surrender of Japan, but it was moved back because of a typhoon. Another date, Sunday, September 2, was set; the ceremony was to take place on the 45,000-ton battleship USS *Missouri*.*

In what was to be the first foreign occupation in its history, Japan became subjugated when Allied forces began arriving on August 28. The next day, August 29, the *Missouri* entered Tokyo Bay. The flagship of Admiral William F. Halsey's Third Fleet, the *Missouri* anchored about a half-dozen miles off Yokohama, with other battleships of the Allied fleet. One day later, Douglas MacArthur, the Supreme Commander for the Allied Powers, landed at Atsugi Airfield outside of Tokyo.

Thousands of soldiers, sailors, dignitaries, and others converged on Tokyo, and all seemed to be in order for the historic ceremony, except for a simple snafu that occurred before the signing on September 2. There were to be two copies of the Instrument of Surrender that the representatives of Japan and the Allied nations would sign. The surrender documents were to be laid out on a stately mahogany table that had been brought on board a day earlier from HMS *Duke of York*, the flagship of Admiral Sir Bruce Fraser, commander of the British Pacific Fleet. On the morning of the historic signing it was discovered that the table was too small to hold both sets of surrender documents, and orders were given for an appropriate table to be procured from the officers' living quarters. But the wardroom tables were screwed tightly into the floor, so crew members scrambled to the sailors' mess room as it was being cleaned up after breakfast and picked out a table just as it was being put away. Although its pedigree was inadequate for the momentous event shortly to come, the humble folding mess table would have to do. The table was whisked to the veranda deck of the *Missouri*, where it was set up and a woolen green tablecloth from the officers' wardroom (which sported a coffee stain in the center) was placed over

---

*The practice of naming capital ships after states began in 1815 by a decision of the Board of Navy Commissioners, with the approval of the U.S. secretary of the navy. Lots were drawn to begin the ship-naming practice, which waned after the 1830s but returned to fashion in the 1890s, with the naming of such ships as the USS *New York* and the USS *Maine*. Later, it became the practice to use the names of states for strategic missile submarines, as well as for some guided missile cruisers in the U.S. fleet.

it.* Two considerably more grand mahogany chairs with black leather seats from HMS *Duke of York* were placed on either side of the table. Spread out over the tablecloth were the two copies of the Instrument of Surrender (National Archives and Records Administration, College Park, Maryland, and the Diplomatic Record Office of the Ministry of Foreign Affairs of Japan, Tokyo) and other documents.†

With the frantic search for a surrender table successfully completed, the ceremony was ready to commence. Having arrived on an American destroyer about an hour earlier, the Supreme Commander for the Allied Powers, General Douglas MacArthur, strode up the gangway of the *Missouri* with Col. Bernard Thielen, an army officer who had arrived by plane from Washington, D.C.; Thielen carried the surrender instruments, which had been prepared by the U.S. War Department. The Japanese delegation—two signers plus nine representatives of the Navy and War Departments, and the Foreign Office—traveled to the *Missouri* on the *Lansdowne,* an American destroyer.

Many witnesses were present for the formal Japanese surrender on the starboard side of the *Missouri,* and the mess table was the center of attention. Behind the table stood the Allied powers' representatives; in front of it stood the Japanese delegation. Around the sides of the table, on other decks, and just about everywhere on the ship scores of top commanders, officers, crew members, journalists, photographers, and other visitors were packed together to watch the proceedings. These witnesses included American sailors, soldiers, and marines, high-ranking officers who had directed U.S. war efforts in the Pacific theater, and Americans released from Japanese prisoner-of-war camps.

The ceremony opened with an invocation by the *Missouri* chaplain,

---

*An Associated Press dispatch that appeared in *The New York Times* a few days before the signing reported that the *Missouri*'s ventilator head was going to serve as the Japanese surrender table.
†There were two identical sets of papers on the table, one in a green buckram-leather volume (kept by the Japanese), the other in a black buckram-leather volume (kept by the Americans). The papers consisted of the two-page Instrument of Surrender (the first page contained the surrender terms in eight paragraphs written in English; the second page was for the representatives' signatures); an imperial rescript issued and signed by Emperor Hirohito and countersigned by the Japanese prime minister that proclaimed that the signers accepted the terms of the Potsdam Declaration, had ordered the Japanese imperial government and military to sign the Allied Instrument of Surrender on their behalf, and had commanded "all Our people forthwith to cease hostilities, to lay down their arms and faithfully to carry out all the provisions of Instrument of Surrender . . ." (the two-page rescript was written in Japanese and followed by an English translation); the credentials of General Yoshijiro Umezu in Japanese and English; the credentials of Foreign Minister Mamoru Shigemitsu in Japanese and English.

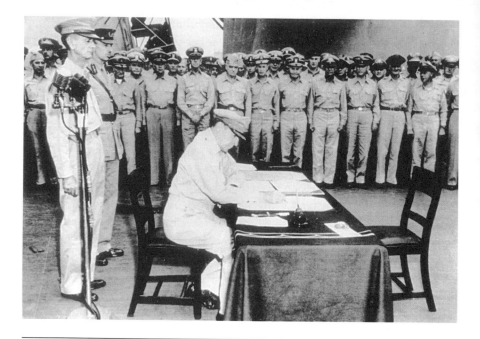

General Douglas MacArthur accepts Japan's surrender in World War II on board the USS Missouri on September 2, 1945. A stately mahogany table had been chosen for the Japanese surrender instruments, but because it was too small to hold all the documents, a simple sailors' mess table was used.

followed by the playing of a recording of America's national anthem, "The Star-Spangled Banner." Then General MacArthur, clad in his military uniform and hat, emerged from a cabin and walked over to a microphone stand to lead the ceremonies. Shortly after nine o'clock, the five-star general began with some introductory remarks about the meaning of the surrender and his vision for its aftermath, his hands trembling as he held his speech:

> We are gathered here . . . to conclude a solemn agreement whereby peace may be restored. The issues . . . have been determined on the battlefields of the world and hence are not for our discussion or debate. Nor is it for us here to meet, representing as we do a majority of the peoples of the earth, in a spirit of distrust, malice or hatred. But rather it is for us, both victors and vanquished, to rise to that higher dignity which alone benefits the sacred purposes we are about to serve. . . .
>
> It is my earnest hope and indeed the hope of all mankind that

from this solemn occasion a better world shall emerge out of the blood and carnage of the past—a world founded upon faith and understanding—a world dedicated to the dignity of man and the fulfillment of his most cherished wish—for freedom, tolerance and justice. . . .

As Supreme Commander for the Allied Powers, I announce it my firm purpose . . . to proceed in the discharge of my responsibilities with justice and tolerance, while taking all necessary dispositions to insure that the terms of surrender are fully, promptly and faithfully complied with.

After making his remarks, MacArthur invited the Japanese delegation to come forward to sign the surrender instrument. The eight-paragraph instrument stipulated that the emperor of Japan, the Japanese government, and the Japanese Imperial General Headquarters accept the provisions of the Potsdam Declaration; proclaim the unconditional surrender of the Japanese Imperial General Headquarters and of all Japanese armed forces; command all Japanese forces to cease hostilities; command the Japanese Imperial Headquarters to order commanders of all Japanese forces to surrender unconditionally; command all civil and military officials to obey and enforce all proclamations and orders of the Allied Powers Supreme Commander to effectuate surrender; carry out the provisions of the Potsdam Declaration in good faith; and liberate all Allied prisoners of war and civilian internees under Japanese control. To fulfill the surrender terms, the emperor and Japanese government were to rule Japan subject to the Allied forces' supreme commander.

Japan's foreign minister, Mamoru Shigemitsu, who years before had lost his left leg to a bomb and wore a wooden limb, hobbled with a cane to the table on which the instruments were laid out and sat down on a chair at the table. As the people on deck watched solemnly, he signed the two documents, officially bringing World War II to an end. He signed on behalf of the emperor of Japan and the Japanese government, and after writing his name in Japanese he wrote the time, 0904.* The chief of the general staff of the Imperial Japanese Army, Yoshijiro Umezu, next signed the surrender documents on behalf of the Japanese Imperial General Headquarters.

Then at 9:08 A.M., General MacArthur, who had invited Lieutenant General Jonathan M. Wainwright and Lieutenant General Arthur E. Percival of the British Army to stand next to him, signed his acceptance of

*That is, 9:04 A.M. Tokyo time.

The Japanese delegation stands before the table on which rested the documents providing for Japan's surrender in World War II.

the Japanese surrender on behalf of the Allied nations. Appreciating the momentousness of the occasion, MacArthur used six fountain pens to sign the two surrender instruments, intending to distribute the pens for posterity. Four of the fountain pens were obtained from the headquarters supply in Manila by Major Courtney Whitney, one was the personal property of Whitney, and one belonged to MacArthur's wife, Jean. The general broke up the writing of his name to use the six pens.

With the first pen he used, the five-star general wrote "Doug," and then handed the pen over to Wainwright, commander of the Philippine units who had been captured and imprisoned by the Japanese after Bataan fell (the pen is now at the United States Military Academy, West Point, New York). With another pen he wrote the second syllable of his first name, then gave the pen to Percival (Cheshire Regimental Museum, Chester, England). MacArthur continued signing with the other pens and distributed them as well (two are at the MacArthur Memorial, Norfolk, Virginia; General Whitney's pen was given to his son Richard; Mrs. MacArthur's pen was stolen years later from her apartment in the Waldorf-Astoria hotel in New York City).

When he was finished, MacArthur called for representatives of the different Allied countries present to sign the instrument: for the United States of America, Fleet Admiral Chester W. Nimitz; for the Republic of China, General Hsu Yung-Ch'ang; for the United Kingdom, Admiral Sir Bruce A. Fraser; for the Union of Soviet Socialist Republics, Lieutenant General Kuzma Derevyanko; for the Commonwealth of Australia, General Sir Thomas A. Blamey; for the Dominion of Canada, Colonel L. Moore Cosgrave; for France, General Jacques Le Clerc; for the kingdom of the Netherlands, Admiral Conrad E. L. Helfrich; for the Dominion of New Zealand, Air Vice Marshal Leonard M. Isitt.

After the twelve men had affixed their signatures to the documents,* MacArthur ended the ceremony by saying, "Let us pray that peace be now restored to the world, and that God will preserve it always. These proceedings are closed."

After the ceremony MacArthur walked to a microphone set up at another area and delivered a concluding speech:

> Today the guns are silent. A great tragedy has ended. A great victory has been won. The skies no longer rain death—the seas bear only commerce—men everywhere walk upright in the sunlight. The entire world is quietly at peace. . . . I speak for the thousands of silent lips, forever stilled among the jungles and the beaches and in the deep waters of the Pacific which marked the way. I speak for the unnamed brave millions homeward bound to take up the challenge of that future which they did so much to salvage from the brink of disaster. . . .
>
> We have known the bitterness of defeat and the exultation of triumph, and from both we have learned there can be no turning back. We must go forward to preserve in peace what we won in war.
>
> A new era is upon us. Even the lesson of victory brings with it profound concern. . . . The destructiveness of the war potential, through progressive advances in scientific discovery, has in fact now reached a point which revises the traditional concept of war. . . .
>
> We have had our last chance. If we do not now devise some greater and more equitable system Armageddon will be at our door.

*Colonel Cosgrave of Canada, who walked unsteadily and by some accounts may have been drunk, nervous, or consumed with a headache, signed the Japanese document in the wrong place and MacArthur's chief of staff, Lieutenant General R. K. Sutherland, had to cross out the names of all the countries that followed Canada and rewrite them in ink to correspond with the signatures written by the representatives of France, the Netherlands, and New Zealand.

The problem . . . involves a spiritual recrudescence and improvement of human character. . . . It must be of the spirit if we are to
save the flesh. . . .

To the Pacific basin has come the vista of a new emancipated
world. Today, freedom is on the offensive, democracy is on the
march. Today, in Asia as well as in Europe, unshackled peoples are
tasting the full sweetness of liberty, the relief from fear. . . .

And so, my fellow-countrymen, today I report to you that your
sons and daughters have served you well and faithfully with the
calm, deliberate, determined fighting spirit of the American soldier
and sailor . . . their spiritual strength and power has brought us
through to victory. They are homeward bound—take care of them.

The ceremony was recorded but not broadcast live. After the ceremony
the recordings were immediately taken to another ship, from which they
were broadcast to the four corners of the earth.

The signing was followed by a spectacular aerial display of about a thousand airplanes roaring over Tokyo Bay and the more than 250 Allied warships anchored there. Other fanfare marked the ceremony. The steel
quarterdeck of the *Missouri* was gaily decorated with ribbons. And displayed on the surrender vessel during the ceremony was the first American
flag officially carried into and flown in Japan, the thirty-one-star pennant
that Commodore Matthew Perry and his crew had brought into the country in the mid–nineteenth century when the United States tried to open trade
and diplomatic relations with Japan.

The genesis of the historic return of the Perry flag for this occasion was
when the U.S. Naval Academy superintendent, Rear Admiral J. R. Beardall,
wrote in a letter dated October 27, 1944, to the secretary of the navy, "It is
not generally known that the first U.S. flag hoisted over Japanese territory
is the one hoisted by Commodore Matthew Calbraith Perry, U.S. Navy, on
July 14, 1853, when first landing at Uraga . . . its possible use at some
future date is obvious." In August 1945 the Naval Academy Museum curator sent a copy of this letter to the U.S. Navy's director of public information, along with a note in which he mentioned radio announcements about
MacArthur receiving the Japanese surrender and wrote, "I have no idea
whether it has occurred to anyone the implication set forth therein." On
August 29, the flag, packed in a wooden box, was delivered to Admiral
Halsey.

With the formal surrender ceremony concluded at 9:25 A.M., the Japanese delegation departed the *Missouri*. One of the surrender instruments had been given to Foreign Minister Shigemitsu.

In the elation of the aftermath of the proceedings, the Japanese surrender table of World War II would likely have been lost had someone not had the foresight to retrieve this now-historic piece of furniture. After the ceremony, during a coffee break in the cabin of Captain Stuart Murray, it was suggested that the furniture and paraphernalia just used in the proceedings might be appropriate artifacts for the Smithsonian Institution. The table, found in the galley area, and tablecloth, found on the deck, were secured (someone had already obtained the two chairs, but one has been lost over the years). The Japanese surrender items never made it to the Smithsonian. They were instead assigned to a different, permanent home in January 1946 by Fleet Admiral Chester W. Nimitz.

With Japan having capitulated, American troops continued entering the country for the occupation, and Japanese forces in the Philippine Islands, Korea, Singapore, Wake, the Marianas, and other areas surrendered. Pursuant to the imperial rescript issued by Emperor Hirohito, instruments of surrender were signed by Japanese commanders for the surrender of Japanese-occupied Southeast Asian battlefields.

World War II was the deadliest conflict in the history of humankind— some 40 million people were killed, 25 million were wounded in action, and millions of soldiers imprisoned or missing in action. Its conclusion came only after incalculable suffering. But with the signing of the surrender documents on September 2, 1945, soldiers laid down their weapons, subjugated people were liberated, the terror that had gripped the world faded into oblivion, hope for a new era of peace blossomed in the hearts of people around the world, and an anonymous table from the mess hall of the *Missouri*,* pressed into service to support the instrument that officially brought an end to the horror that had engulfed the globe, became an immortal artifact.

LOCATION: United States Naval Academy, Annapolis, Maryland.

*In 1998 the *Missouri*, which had an original displacement of 45,000 tons and a draft of 28 feet 11 inches, and whose overhaul in 1988 gave it a displacement of 57,500 tons and a draft of 37 feet 9 inches, was towed to Pearl Harbor, Hawaii. Plans are for the *Missouri* to be open to public visitation and for it to be permanently berthed on the seaward end of Battleship Row, within sight of the battleship USS *Arizona*, which was bombed and sunk by the Japanese in the attack on December 7, 1941.

NIAC

~~~~~~

DATE: 1946.

WHAT IT IS: The first large-scale general-purpose electronic computer.

WHAT IT LOOKS LIKE: Only portions of ENIAC survive, including panels (units that performed various mathematical operations such as addition and multiplication) and function tables (devices which stored numeric constants that were used by ENIAC's program). The panels are 10 feet tall and 3 feet wide, and are painted black. Prominent features include round knobs and cables with plugs on the ends (the cables are of the patch-cord kind, and the plugs are large).

Deftly pushing contemporary technology to its limits and working without any kind of manual to guide them with regard to design, components, circuitry, assembly, or any other detail, the inventors of the electronic computer built what is arguably the first modern "thinking machine" by creating an electronic version of the mechanical adding machines of the day. They produced a device that by later standards was immensely heavy and huge; it weighed thirty tons and was shaped like a giant U with the two parallel sides each running sixty feet long, the bottom measuring thirty feet, and the whole contraption rising ten feet off the ground. It was large and cumbersome, indeed, and with its flashing lights and immense tangled forest of vacuum tubes, knobs, lights, and wires it resembled a contraption worthy of an old science fiction novel. But the machine was a landmark invention. After centuries of dreaming about an automatic calculating device, humans created ENIAC, the first general-purpose electronic digital computer, and with it ushered in the information age.

The first computing device, simply enough, was the human hand. A primitive digital computing device, fingers could be counted to solve basic arithmetical problems. The Romans and the Chinese each developed an abacus, a wire frame containing rows of movable beads that made possible more complex mathematical operations.

In the mid-1830s, Charles Babbage, an English mathematician who had built mechanical calculation machines, began designing an analytical engine in which tabulating cards were used for the performance of operations. Babbage, who through the years lost government support for his inventions, never finished building this forerunner of the modern automatic computer.

In 1944, Harvard professor Howard Aiken demonstrated a general-purpose electromechanical machine. Called the Automatic Sequence Controlled Calculator, it had moving parts—principally, electromagnetic relays—that were powered by electricity, but it was still essentially a mechanical device. ASCC contained some three-quarters of a million parts in total and was a huge punch card machine. An electronic computer had yet to be built.

Thanks to the U.S. Army, one was actually on its way. During World War II the army employed "computers" (people, typically women) to prepare firing tables for its guns. Using calculators, the workers—many of whom were Women's Auxiliary Corps mathematicians—took between ten and forty hours to compute just one trajectory. But the tables contained up to four thousand trajectories each, and there simply weren't enough people available to grind out the calculations. Some kind of device that could do the math much more quickly was needed.

John Mauchly, a physics professor at Ursinus College in Collegeville, Pennsylvania, who was interested in using mathematics to predict weather, had proposed in a memo an electronic computer for making faster calculations. His idea caught the attention of Herman H. Goldstine of the Ballistic Research Lab in Aberdeen, Maryland. Goldstine, who was seeking an efficient way to calculate artillery trajectories, requested that Mauchly develop a proposal. Mauchly was practical about funding and understood that, at least at the time, ballistics took priority over weather. He undertook to write the proposal with a gifted electronic engineering graduate student named J. Presper Eckert. They submitted a proposal on April 2, 1943, for a machine called ENIAC, the Electronic Numerical Integrator and Calculator, and two months later they were awarded a contract.

A team of engineers headed by Eckert, with Mauchly the principal consultant, secretly built ENIAC in the Moore building at the University of Pennsylvania in Philadelphia; because it was wartime, and the output of ENIAC was needed to operate large guns, the project was kept under wraps. The machine, in which over 17,000 vacuum tubes, 6,000 switches,

ENIAC, the first modern general-purpose electronic digital computer. Could the inventors of this large-scale thinking machine ever have envisioned the laptop?

10,000 capacitors, and 70,000 resistors were encased in black steel, occupied 1,800 square feet.

Unlike Howard Aiken's Automatic Sequence Controlled Calculator, ENIAC was an electronic device in that it was based not on mobile metal parts but moving electrons; it did not have moving mechanical parts but electrons moving in a vacuum. ENIAC's main components were the panels, which numbered forty in total. Numerous cables plugged into each panel. The other ends of the cables plugged into digit trays, which connected the panels. The panels had numerous rotary switches, or knobs, that indicated a particular number or function.

ENIAC worked in base ten, as opposed to modern computers, which work in base two. The foundation of the entire ENIAC was the accumulator, which was essentially an electronic version of an adding machine. The accumulator added ten-digit decimal numbers, and kept them in base ten. A panel would have the capability to display one decimal number ten digits long by using an array of lights, going from top to bottom, so it would have ten columns of ten lights each. These lights would signify numbers. The accumulators would be connected together to perform mathematical calculations. Essentially, Eckert, Mauchly, and their team of engineers strung together decimal adding machines, or mechanical accumulating calculators, of their day and made them electronic.

Unveiled in a ceremony on February 14, 1946, ENIAC, which punched results onto cards, performed high-speed calculations not feasible on other computing devices.

But its operation was delicate. Vacuum tubes were not always reliable, and with more than seventeen thousand of them emitting a hundred thousand pulses per second, there were almost two billion chances every second that ENIAC could fail. Furthermore, the complexity and interdependence of ENIAC's circuits meant that a failure of just one of the thousands of solder joints could render the whole electronic brain unusable.

But the marvel was that ENIAC worked, and it was unquestionably a major improvement over the computing devices of the day—indeed, the inventors of ENIAC successfully harnessed the power of the vacuum tube to create a machine that worked more than a thousand times faster than these devices. Although the war was by this time over, ENIAC could compute a firing trajectory in just half a minute.

Despite its immense size and cost (over $486,000), ENIAC convinced an array of professionals of the potential of electronic computing, launching the modern computing era. The rest, as they say, is history: the FORTRAN language, magnetic disks for storage, transistors replacing vacuum tubes, keyboards and monitors replacing punched cards, minicomputers, microprocessors, silicon chips, personal computers, graphical user interfaces, Windows 95, laptops, the World Wide Web.

The programming capability of ENIAC can be approximated today with a small calculator that costs under $40. ENIAC's clock speed was 100,000 pulses per second or 0.1 megahertz. This compares with modern computers that run at about 600 megahertz or more.

Today, the PC is the offspring of the computer revolution. A common household and office item, a PC can be purchased for under $1,000. But anyone who has ever clicked a mouse owes a debt to that monstrous hunk of metal and wires, ENIAC, which quietly sparked the revolution and forever changed the way we live.

LOCATION: National Museum of American History, Washington, D.C. This is the main repository of ENIAC's panels. Of the sixteen panels the museum owns, some are on loan to other institutions, including the School of Engineering and Applied Science at the University of Pennsylvania in Philadelphia, the Computer Museum in Boston, and the Heinz-Nixdorf Museumsforum in Patterborn, Germany. Other panels and parts of ENIAC are located at other institutions.

$\mathcal{M}$arilyn Monroe's Billowing Dress from *The Seven Year Itch*

DATE: 1955.

WHAT IT IS: A dress the actress wore in a famous movie scene in which she stands over a subway grating and a rush of air lifts up her dress to expose her upper thighs and panties.

WHAT IT LOOKS LIKE: The bodice is a sleeveless halter top, and the skirt is full-flowing and pleated. The dress is white.

Thomas O'Malley sniffed circumspectly around the storage-bin area, searching for clues. A gumshoe right out of Philip Marlowe, the Tenth Squad NYPD detective surveyed the crime scene, making mental notes as he went along.

Just minutes before, O'Malley had been sitting in the squad room at the Tenth Precinct on West Twentieth Street. It was late afternoon on the 13th of September, 1993. He was banging out a "Five"—a detective report—in the typewriter when the call came in. A 10-21, a past burglary. A storage bin at Chelsea Mini-Storage on West Twenty-eighth Street had been broken into. Property had been stolen. A mere garden-variety crime, except that the stolen goods included priceless, original personal property of perhaps the most famous movie actress of all time: Marilyn Monroe.

By mere serendipity, Detective Thomas O'Malley, a burly six-foot-two Irishman with over twenty years on the job, was up on the squad rotation order, so he would be the "catching," or head, detective on the case. O'Malley and his partner, rookie Detective Richie O'Brien, left the stationhouse and piled into their unmarked Chevy Caprice.

The report of the burglary had been made by Anna Strasberg, widow of the renowned acting teacher Lee Strasberg. Marilyn Monroe, who died of an overdose of sleeping pills at the age of thirty-six in 1962, had bequeathed her former acting coach 75 percent of her estate, which had been valued at over $1.5 million.

Strasberg kept a large amount of Marilyn Monroe memorabilia in a seventh-floor bin at Chelsea Mini-Storage: the actress's white dress and pumps from *The Seven Year Itch,* the sequined dress in which she had sung "Happy Birthday, Mr. President" to John F. Kennedy at Madison Square Garden in 1962, garments, letters, vanity kits, a clock given her by Clark Gable, personal mementos, commemorative merchandise, and sundry other objects. When one of Strasberg's employees went to bin number 744 to catalog the contents in preparation for a planned exhibit to benefit a child-welfare organization, the employee discovered that the lock on the bin had been clipped and replaced by a different lock, and boxes inside had been stolen. The employee dialed 911, and the call filtered down to Tom O'Malley.

Experienced cops have gut instincts, hunches they play out like Vegas poker games. A veteran of thousands of homicide, assault, robbery, and burglary cases, O'Malley had razor-sharp instincts when it came to crime scenes. A few observations lit up O'Malley's intuition. He felt that the chances were excellent that at least some of the stolen Monroe goods were still somewhere in the building, probably in a bin rented by the thief himself. And if O'Malley could find even one of the items in someone else's bin, he'd have his perp.

Such thieves don't always feel a need to remove their booty immediately, O'Malley knew. Sometimes people store their belongings for long periods, six months to a year, before returning to inspect their possessions or take them out. And skillful purloiners know that if security sees a lock broken, an investigation will immediately be launched, so they're careful to replace the broken lock with one identical or very similar to the original. This gives the perp time to smuggle items out of the facility in small packages at leisurely intervals without arousing suspicion.

But obviously O'Malley couldn't just search through all the bins in the huge storage facility. He had to figure out, somehow, who had rented a bin for the purpose of storing stolen goods, before the perp sold all the pilfered merchandise.

There were video cameras in the storage facility, but none on the upper floors, where the burglary had occurred. The precinct print man dusted for fingerprints, and these would have to be run and sorted.

O'Malley had his work cut out for him.

Working in a busy house, or precinct, O'Malley investigated the case of the stolen Marilyn Monroe artifacts while juggling dozens of other cases. While to the public eye, detectives employed ingenious techniques to find

Marilyn Monroe's pleated white skirt cascading in the famous movie scene.

their prey, O'Malley knew he would solve this case the same way he solved all his others: with hard work.

Over the next six and a half months, O'Malley pursued his leads on the Marilyn Monroe theft and tried to develop new ones. While the local press had a field day with the case—the *Daily News* ran a story about it under the banner, "Sticky Fingers in Pinch of Marilyn's 'Itch' Dress"; *Newsday's* headline blared, "Burglars Got Dress, But Will It Fit?"; and the *New York Post* trumpeted on its front page, "Marilyn's Dresses Ripped Off"— O'Malley canvassed for witnesses, fingerprinted the storage facility's employees and compared them with the crime-scene prints, asked around on the street, ran names through the police department's central computer, checked the storage facility's customer list, debriefed prisoners. One jailbird said he had heard that someone who had a "house" (bin) in the storage facility had done the crime, but he couldn't give a name. O'Malley thought the guy was on to something, but he also knew that crooks would give up their mothers to extricate themselves from the crib.

Names surfaced over the months, which O'Malley and O'Brien considered as cops do, eliminating some and keeping others in mind, until O'Malley, who likened criminal investigations to beauty contests, told his partner that they were down to three finalists. After further checking he found out that one of the suspects, a man named Davila, had a prior arrest in Manhattan for a storage-bin burglary. "I like him," O'Malley said to O'Brien of his pick for a "winner."

At 3:10 P.M. on March 28, 1994, O'Malley and O'Brien returned to the scene of the crime to ask if anyone by the name of Davila had ever conducted business at the storage facility. A review of the establishment's records revealed that a Jesus Davila had rented storage bin number 13-734, which was located on the same floor as Anna Strasberg's and was only a few aisles away.

"Let's go have a look," O'Malley said.

At about 4:00 P.M., O'Malley, O'Brien, and two storage-facility managers repaired to the suspect's bin. Some of the metal bins at the storage facility had had their tops removed so their areas could be extended; wire screens ran from the top of the metal lockers to the ceilings. Jesus Davila's bin had such a wire mesh, and O'Malley asked security to fetch a long ladder so he could take a gander. O'Malley climbed the ladder and looked down. After a few moments he guffawed. "Hey, Richie," he said to his partner, "do me a favor. Sometimes I don't know if I see something because I want to see something. You go up and take a look."

When O'Malley cracked a case, a sense of euphoria sometimes overwhelmed him. He liked to share the feeling with his partner.

O'Brien climbed the ladder and saw below a box that had a mailing label with Anna Strasberg's name printed on it. He waved O'Malley a high five. One of the facility managers also climbed the ladder and confirmed the detectives' discovery.

Back in the squad room, O'Malley called Anna Strasberg, who was in California at the time, asking her to send a representative to make a positive identification of the alleged stolen property. Soon a man in his late twenties by the name of Michael Martin Theuringer reported to the Tenth Precinct detective unit. O'Malley and O'Brien drove Theuringer to the Chelsea facility and shepherded him to Davila's bin, where he climbed the ladder, looked through the screen, and declared, "That is her box, taken from Ms. Strasberg's bin."

O'Malley contacted the New York County District Attorney's Office, and after conferring with an ADA (assistant district attorney), found himself standing before a judge. The Hon. William Mogulescu granted his request for a search warrant.

Armed with the vital document, O'Malley returned to the Chelsea building to execute the search. He clipped the lock on Jesus Davila's bin and removed Anna Strasberg's property, which her representative, up close and without a barrier now, once again confirmed as belonging to Ms. Strasberg.

O'Malley hoped the recovered boxes would yield the *Seven Year Itch* dress. He badly wanted to recover the dress, not just for Anna Strasberg's sake, not just to do his job as a detective, but for Marilyn Monroe. The dress was a piece of movie history, a symbol of its sexiest star. He had heard there were other copies of Monroe's dress from *The Seven Year Itch*—leading actors and actresses often had multiple sets of the same outfits for important scenes in case the primary costume was damaged or lost—but he was convinced that if anyone had retained the actual dress filmed in the immortal subway-grating scene, it was Marilyn Monroe herself, and this was the dress she had bequeathed to Lee Strasberg.

Indeed, of all the Marilyn Monroe items stolen from the Strasberg bin, the most famous was the dress Monroe wore in *The Seven Year Itch*. Monroe made this Billy Wilder–directed comedy (released in 1955) after she was divorced from baseball great Joe DiMaggio. It was a difficult time for her personally, but she enjoyed great success in this movie, playing a dumb-blonde role with such panache, charm, and sexiness that she became one of the most popular movie actresses of the day. In one scene, she stood over a New York City subway grating, and a rush of air swirled the pleated skirt of her white dress around her waist. This would be her signature film scene, one that would be forever imitated.

The boxes were opened, but alas, the *Seven Year Itch* dress was not among the recovered contents. There was still a perp to be arrested, however.

At 1:30 P.M. the next day, March 29, O'Malley and O'Brien left the Tenth Precinct and headed uptown to St. Luke's–Roosevelt Hospital on Ninth Avenue. Two hospital security officers escorted the detectives to Jesus Davila, who worked at the hospital. Confronted with the fact of the detectives' discovery, the thirty-five-year-old man quickly confessed his crime; he was placed under arrest and advised of his Miranda rights. Davila also admitted that he had given some of the Marilyn Monroe pieces to his co-workers and a neighbor who lived upstairs in his apartment building. The detectives found the co-workers and told them they had until eight o'clock that night to return the stolen goods, otherwise they would be arrested. Three Marilyn Monroe commemorative dishes were promptly returned.

Back in the squad room O'Malley interviewed Davila, who gave further details. He said that in August 1993 he had clipped the lock on the Chelsea storage bin that contained the Marilyn Monroe objects and removed the boxes within, but he was unaware their contents had belonged to Marilyn Monroe until he saw the media reports.

Davila had placed the stolen boxes in his bin, intending to recover them at a later date, but had removed some of the items and taken them home. O'Malley asked Davila to sign a letter granting permission to search his home, and Davila consented. Davila and O'Malley initialed the note, which was witnessed by O'Brien, who initialed it also. Davila said the neighbor to whom he had given some of the stolen goods lived in the apartment above his.

Shortly before 4:30 P.M. on March 29, O'Malley and three other detectives took Jesus Davila to his home on East 106th Street. They went to a sixth-floor apartment, where Davila requested his friend to bring him the black plastic bag he had given him to hold. The resident retrieved the bag and turned it over to Davila, who in turn gave it to the detectives. The bag contained only a few hats, a fur piece, and some plates. The detectives then went to Davila's apartment one floor below, which he shared with his sister and brother, and searched it, but they found no items stolen from Anna Strasberg's bin. Davila was brought back to the Tenth Precinct for the arrest process to be completed.

The arrest caught the attention of the media. The *New York Post* reported that Davila had "reportedly emptied a storage bin at a West Side storehouse of $10 million in movie star memorabilia," including property that had not only belonged to Marilyn Monroe, but other stars and former Lee Strasberg students as well, including Marlon Brando, James Dean, Montgomery Clift, and Al Pacino. The *Post* noted that while most of the stolen items had been recovered, Marilyn Monroe's dress from *The Seven Year Itch* was still missing.

But it wasn't long before O'Malley was told by his superiors to stop looking for the *Seven Year Itch* dress. It seems it hadn't been stolen after all. The perp had been arrested, but the official word now was that during the course of the investigation, the dress had been found in the Strasberg bin.

The dress hadn't been stolen after all? O'Malley registered a sudden jolt on his shock meter, but the arrow quickly returned to zero. After all his years of experience working with the legal system, he understood how these things worked.

If a stamp collection with one world-famous stamp were stolen and most of it recovered except for the premier stamp, the owner would of course do anything to get it back; and if the perp had a half-decent lawyer, he would know that that stamp was his bargaining chip. The lawyer could offer to return the stamp provided his client didn't get any jail time. Probation, maybe, but no jail time.

O'Malley pictured the *Seven Year Itch* dress in his mind. "Here's a guy who got himself a get-out-of-jail-free card," he mused.

O'Malley had seen this sort of thing over and over again in his career, although he wasn't always privy to the fine details. Lawyers make deals with the district attorney's office, they don't make deals with the police department. The DA has the last lick. So if the cop is looking for a world-famous stamp and the DA tells him to stop poking around, what's he to do but stop looking?

But how do you explain the stamp all of a sudden showing up? Of course, the media would ask the police if they had recovered the stamp. The detective would respond, "I never recovered that stamp." So the media would say, "Wait a minute, what's going on here? If the police didn't recover it, how was it found?" To save face, the DA might say, "The stamp was reported stolen in error. It was in the back of the safe, and we didn't see it. But it was always there."

O'Malley knew that that sort of response eliminates the whole issue of impropriety. Nobody is going to question anybody, and the deal is done. The owner's got his stamp back. The perp does soft time, the district attorney is happy because the case is closed with probation, and the police department is happy because before the case was taken out of their hands an arrest was made, and it was a good arrest.

Using the NYPD nomenclature, O'Malley closed out the case on paper with an A, which is a good clearance, as opposed to any of the C designations, which are negative clearances.

He sighed with satisfaction. Thanks to good old-fashioned detective work, Marilyn Monroe's billowing white dress from the immortal *Seven Year Itch* subway scene was back where it belonged and would endure as a memento of one of the most famous scenes in movie history and popular culture.

LOCATIONS: New York City (for the Strasberg dress); another dress is in the collection of actress Debbie Reynolds. (As mentioned, stars in major motion pictures often have multiple identical costumes for particular scenes. Hence the reason for at least two dresses identified as having been worn by Marilyn Monroe in the subway-grating scene from *The Seven Year Itch*.)

*E*lvis Presley's Purple Cadillac

CLOCLOCLOCLOCLOCLOCLOCLOCLOCLOCLOCLOCLOCLOCLOCLO

DATE: 1956.

WHAT IT IS: An automobile purchased by Elvis Presley that, according to legend, was repainted purple after he had made his color preference known in a manner that was quintessentially Elvis.

WHAT IT LOOKS LIKE: The car is purple and has white upholstery, whitewall tires, tail fins, and massive chrome detail.

The car languished in a backyard shed for many years, then was left out in an open field, where, exposed to the elements, it began to crumble away. The 1956 convertible Cadillac Eldorado Baritz had been a precious possession of Elvis Presley's when he was a hot young rock 'n' roll star, but just as he faded from public view for a time in his later years only to reemerge in a new blaze of glory, so his car was forgotten until it was rescued at an auction and restored by a used car dealer and his wife, both Elvis fans.

Elvis Presley had a passion for cars. Once his new fame had accorded him sufficient income, he purchased a pink Cadillac in December 1954. Some months later this car caught on fire and was destroyed, and in the summer of 1955 Elvis acquired another Cadillac, a pink Fleetwood. The next year he bought a pink Cadillac limousine. When it became widely known that Elvis was driving pink Cadillacs, he was forced to give them up, as his car would be mobbed. He gave his 1955 Fleetwood to his parents, but it wasn't long before Vernon and Gladys couldn't drive it either. Thinking Elvis must be driving the car, fans beseiged his mother and father.

The Presleys had been relatively poor, and with Elvis's escalation to stardom, Cadillacs were seen as a suitable reflection of the family's newfound wealth and rise in social status. Whatever the psychological reasons that drew Elvis to Cadillacs, 1956, the year he bought his Eldorado Baritz, was a watershed year for him; the cost of the sumptuous vehicle was not an issue. (Elvis's taste in cars eventually broadened, and his later purchases included a Rolls-Royce, a Ferrari, an MG, and a Stutz Blackhawk.)

The well-known story of Elvis's transformation from impoverished country boy to the "king of rock 'n' roll" is classically American. Born in Tupelo, Mississippi, on January 8, 1935, with a stillborn twin brother, Elvis was his parents' only child. The family had little money but found inspiration at church, where Elvis was exposed to gospel music. Recognition of his musical talent came early, as he won fourth place in the Tupelo State Fair talent contest in which he was entered by his fifth-grade teacher at East Tupelo Consolidated School (later renamed Lawhon Elementary School). Elvis attended Humes High School in Memphis, where his family moved in 1948, and after graduating he worked for a tool company, then drove a truck.

One summer day in 1953, shortly after he graduated, during a lunch break from his job Elvis went into a recording studio and paid four dollars to record a couple of songs so he could present the acetate demo to his mother as a gift. The following January he returned to the studio, owned by Sun Records' head Sam Phillips, to record some more songs, and met Philips there for the first time. Phillips was looking for a white male who could sing soulfully and invited Elvis to record some songs with top-notch musicians he hired for the occasion. One of the songs in this session in early July 1954, "That's All Right," became a regional smash, and Presley began appearing on local television shows and having additional local hits. He had two different managers before Colonel Tom Parker took over the reins of the young singer's career. In late 1955, RCA bought out Presley's Sun Records contract for a then-exorbitant sum, and with the proceeds, Elvis purchased the Cadillac that he later gave to his parents. RCA and Elvis wasted no time in readying the new product for the market, and the following January Elvis went into a Nashville recording studio and recorded a package of new songs that would make him a star.

Indeed, 1956 was a banner year for the young singer. Elvis topped the national pop charts with "Heartbreak Hotel," "I Want You, I Need You, I Love You," "Don't Be Cruel," "Hound Dog," and "Love Me Tender," and he appeared on the national television shows of Jimmy and Tommy Dorsey, Milton Berle, and Steve Allen, in addition to making two of his three famous appearances on *The Ed Sullivan Show* (his third *Ed Sullivan* appearance was in January 1957). Sullivan had initially refused to book Presley, but changed his mind after the singer had performed on the other shows, paying $50,000 for Presley's three appearances. In March 1957, the now-celebrated twenty-two-year-old icon of the young generation purchased an estate in Memphis called Graceland for $102,500.

With his suave looks, shiny black pompadour, and unique singing style, not to mention a selection of up-tempo songs that showcased his electric rhythm—his nickname "Elvis the Pelvis" referred to his whirling gyrations—the southerner had by now captured the public's imagination and was in the process of transforming the relatively new genre of rock 'n' roll into the cultural idiom of the younger generation. Indeed, Elvis Presley was on his way to becoming not only rock's most famous and enduring individual star, but the most imitated, recognizable, and celebrated singer of the twentieth century. In 1956 he even commenced what became a flourishing movie career, debuting in the Civil War drama *Love Me Tender*, the first of thirty-three feature films he would star in.

With his outstanding success, Elvis had the financial freedom to indulge himself. And so after having picked out and paid for a brand-new white 1956 Cadillac Eldorado Baritz while in Houston on one of his concert tours—Elvis frequently performed in Texas, Arkansas, and Louisiana—on June 12 Elvis flew with his eighteen-year-old girlfriend June Juanico (who purchased her airline ticket under the name June Pritchard) to Houston to pick up his new Eldorado. Elvis wasted no time trying out his new set of wheels, and the next day drove it back to Memphis with June.

Elvis adored the car, but after only about a year and a half he decided he needed a new one. In December 1957 he traded in his Eldorado Baritz. Having "inside" information on the crooner's swap, Lena Moskovitz, an acquaintance of Elvis's mother and fan of the singer, rushed to the dealer and purchased it for $4,000 in cash and a trade-in on her 1954 Cadillac. Moskovitz drove the car until around 1964, then parked it in a shed at her Phoenix City, Alabama, home. Here the car remained hidden away. When Lena Moskovitz Smith died in 1974, her husband, Herbert O'Dell Smith, a stuntman whose specialty was being buried alive, moved to College Park, Georgia, leaving the Eldorado in an open field, probably in Phoenix City, Alabama. Here the car was exposed to the elements and to vandals who scribbled graffiti on it.

Although Elvis never regained his '50s stature, he wasn't long out of the public mind in later years. His biggest career slump occurred from 1966 through early 1968. His so-called comeback concert in 1968 at a Hollywood studio (his first concert since 1961) was number one in the ratings, and this reception showed that the indifferent box-office success of his movies had not been his fault. Elvis, who had 105 charted hits, was the number two artist of the '60s, number eleven in the '70s, and the number one concert

After rotting for years in an open field, Elvis Presley's 1956 purple Cadillac was recovered and restored to its original splendor.

box-office draw in both 1973 and 1977—the year he died, in August. During his last few years, Elvis, who was damaging his health by abusing prescribed drugs, was no longer so drawn to the limelight, but he wasn't a recluse. He undertook concert tours, as well as regularly attending movies in Memphis, driving around town, and signing autographs for eager fans at the gate of Graceland.

In 1976, the car was purchased for $975 at an auction by James Cantrell, a used car dealer, and his wife, Jean, from Columbus, Georgia. The Cantrells spent $30,000 of their own money to restore the car and repaint it purple. The couple intended to show the restored car to Elvis as a surprise. Unfortunately, just before the restoration of his 1956 purple Cadillac was completed, Elvis Presley died at the age of forty-two.

Elvis is dead (sightings notwithstanding), but his Eldorado is a reminder not only of the star's lavish tastes as a young man, but of his flamboyant nature.

On July 27, 1957, just over a year after he bought it, Elvis drove his Cadillac Eldorado Baritz into the Jimmy Saunders Custom Auto Shop in Memphis to have it painted. He also had mechanics add taillight bullets, convert the interior to purple and white, and inscribe the floor mats with his EP monogram, but painting the exterior of the car weighed heavily on his mind. In fact, shortly before he took the car over to Jimmy Saunders's, Elvis demonstrated to his maternal aunt, Lorraine Smith, exactly what shade of purple he had in mind.

Young Elvis, conversing with his Aunt Lorraine at Graceland, mentioned his intention to have the car painted. A simple announcement of a common task to be sure, but there was to be no mistake about the color. Picking up a bunch of purple grapes, he asked his aunt to follow him outside. In the driveway, Elvis lifted his arm and smashed the grapes down heavily on the car's gleaming white surface. Then he turned to her and declared, "That's the color I want it to be!"

LOCATION: Graceland, Memphis, Tennessee.

$\mathcal{A}$ble the Space Monkey

~~~~~~

DATE: 1959.

WHAT IT IS: The stuffed remains of a rhesus monkey that was one of the first two primates to be launched into space and return alive.

WHAT IT LOOKS LIKE: The monkey is preserved in an upright position and is held in a harness.

The goal: To determine if human beings could travel safely aboard rockets into space.

The experiment: To send living animals into space and bring them back without any adverse effects.

Experiment coordinator: National Aeronautics and Space Administration (NASA).

Jupiter C missile supplier: U.S. Army Ballistic Missile Agency.

The date: May 28, 1959.

The political situation: The Soviet Union and the United States are at the height of the Cold War, and the Russians are leading the space race. . . .

The cosmos, with its array of twinkling lights, diverse celestial bodies, and vast expanse apparent as one looks up into the black night, no doubt intrigued the earliest human beings. Over time, humans charted the heavens, first with the naked eye and later with the telescope, but actually traveling into those infinite reaches of space seemed a wildly fantastic dream. By the mid–twentieth century, however, technology and science had progressed to the point where humans were on the verge of soaring into space for firsthand exploration. The crusade to the stars was the result of brilliant scientific achievements—hastened, in part, by the political struggle between two superpowers.

As the Cold War between the Soviet Union and the United States was smoldering in the 1950s, technology had made it possible to send rockets outside the earth's atmosphere, and a space race between the nations was heating up. On October 4, 1957, the Russians launched Sputnik I, which became the first artificial satellite to orbit the earth and collect and transmit data on space conditions. With this celebrated leap and their subsequent highly publicized achievements in space, the Russians appeared to have taken a threatening lead in the space race. The ultimate goal, of course, was to put a human being in space, and both sides labored assiduously toward this goal.

As a precursor to manned space flight, numerous tests were conducted to help scientists make the spacecraft safe to carry humans, including launching animals into space so they could predict how humans would react to the conditions of flight. Animal reactions to flight conditions such as acceleration, deceleration, rotation, noise, and other phenomena would aid in the design of equipment and the training of astronauts.

As the year 1959 marched in, attempts to send animals up and return them had been mostly unsuccessful. As long as a decade before, the United States had launched monkeys and mice in rockets, and in most of these tests the animals died. In November 1957 the Russians sent up Laika, a Siberian husky, aboard the satellite Sputnik 2, but the dog, fed liquids in a specially constructed capsule, died after a few days in orbit when the life support system stopped, its batteries worn out. In December 1958 the Americans launched a squirrel monkey, Gordo (nicknamed "Old Reliable"), but the nose cone the animal was in was not recovered, and Gordo perished. But the Americans had other animals in the wings, tested and trained for space flight, waiting to be selected for an experimental launch.

While the U.S. Army was conducting tests with its Jupiter intermediate-range ballistic missiles—a primary goal of the Jupiter program was to develop a way for the nose cones to reenter the earth's atmosphere without burning up—a biomedical project was undertaken in which primates would be launched into space to determine what effect the missile firing and reentry would have on them.

Rigorous testing was conducted before the final selection of the project's primates. A program at the Walter Reed Army Institute of Research had conducted studies with rhesus monkeys, all less than two years old. Flight conditions were simulated with respect to g-forces, weightlessness, restraint, and other physical phenomena; the researchers maintained copious records of the monkeys' responses. Three days before the launch, physicians selected from a group of eight rhesus monkeys a seven-pound specimen named Able. At the U.S. Navy School of Aviation Medicine in Pensacola, Florida, a one-pound squirrel monkey named Baker was trained for the same mission.

Because army missiles fell under its domain, the U.S. Army Ordnance Missile Command supervised the biomedical testing. The army's Ballistic Missile Agency, which supervised the Jupiter program, developed and built the biomedical capsule in which Able was placed. The U.S. Navy School of Aviation Medicine, with ABMA's assistance, likewise designed and built the capsule for Baker. Input for the biomedical experiment and the design of the capsules came from other armed forces units as well as civilian research institutions. The capsules would be specially equipped not only to maintain the life support of the passengers but to gather and transmit data.

The heating of the nose cone presented a major problem. After a craft is launched straight up, it plummets back into the atmosphere at high speed. The craft experiences tremendous friction as it reaches the upper edges of the atmosphere, and as it reenters the atmosphere it generates intense heat.

American scientists worked to solve the problem of the heating of the nose cone at reentry, making the cones with ablative material that absorbed heat. There were several layers of this ablative material. As the first layer absorbed heat and reached a certain temperature, the layer would fall off, leaving a cool surface underneath. Then that layer would heat up, and after it reached a certain temperature would fall off in its turn, exposing another cool surface, and so on. An August 1957 flight demonstrated that the solution was successful, and with this accomplishment, the next step for the Americans was to conduct medical research on an animal launched aboard a missile in the unused space of the nose cone.

On May 28, 1959, the Americans prepared to send the two primates, Able and Baker, into space in the nose cone of a Jupiter intermediate-range ballistic missile. The monkeys were restrained in separate compartments of the nose cone. Able was set in a fiberglass seat with restraints that held her in place, with foam-rubber padding to help prevent injury from being tossed around in her seat. Baker, the smaller monkey, was kept in place in her seat by a perforated metal piece that fit over her body from her chin down (both restraints are at the U.S. Space and Rocket Center, Huntsville, Alabama). A climate-control mechanism utilizing liquid nitrogen kept the temperature inside the cone that carried the monkeys at a comfortable level.

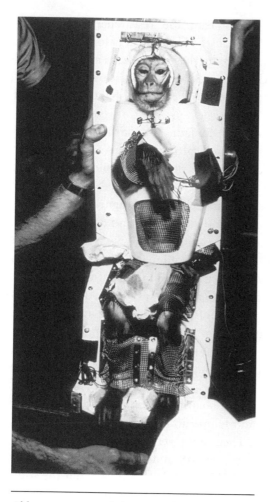

Able, a seven-pound rhesus monkey, is secured in her fiberglass seat prior to her historic space flight.

At 2:35 A.M. in Cape Canaveral, Florida, the missile was launched. Able, wearing a "space helmet" containing headphones that sent sixteen channels of data on her physical reactions to ground scientists, lay facedown. Baker, wearing a plastic helmet, lay on her back on her silicone-rubber bed in a fetal position.

The missile, launched on a ballistic trajectory, reached a maximum speed of 10,000 miles per hour and an altitude of 300 miles. At its maximum altitude the missile traveled in the thermosphere, almost into the exosphere. (Space starts about 50 miles above the earth's surface; the thermosphere is the area 50 to 310 miles above the earth; and the exosphere is the region from 310 miles above earth to deep space.) On the missile's reentry into the earth's atmosphere, the temperature of the ablative nose cone (with its two primate passengers) soared to a searing 5,000 degrees Fahrenheit. The capsule splashed down in the Atlantic Ocean, at a downrange distance from its launch site of 1,500 miles.

To recover the nose cone of the Jupiter missile, several navy ships, including destroyers, cruised the splashdown area in the Atlantic Ocean, while navy planes circled overhead. The nose cone had been fitted with paraphernalia to assist searchers in locating it; retrieval apparatus included a brightly colored inflatable balloon with a signal light and a radio communications device. At 3:20 A.M. a navy flier spotted the nose cone and guided several ships to the area where it had splashed down. Several frogmen secured ropes to the nose cone (U.S. Space and Rocket Center, on loan from the Smithsonian Institution), hoisted it aboard, and recovered the space travelers Able and Baker, both alive and apparently unharmed.

The successful flight, from launch to touchdown, lasted approximately fifteen minutes, but its short duration belies its remarkable accomplishment. It marked the first time that primates were launched into space aboard a missile, survived the rough conditions of the journey, and returned alive to earth.

Indeed, Able and Baker endured the high-velocity stresses of the launch, reentry, descent, and splashdown. The weightlessness and g-force, or pull of gravity, that Able and Baker were subjected to was of prime interest to scientists, as it showed that primates could tolerate these physical changes. During acceleration into space, the animals experienced a maximum g-force of fifteen, then were weightless for nine minutes, and during reentry experienced thirty-eight times the normal force of gravity. Thus on reentry, the seven-pound Able felt as though she weighed 266 pounds. (A 180-pound human subjected to the same g-forces would temporarily experience a weight of over three tons!)

Able and Baker were not only alive but in good health. Researchers compiled the data on their physiological reactions to the journey, as well as on environmental conditions in their space capsules. This information was used by scientists to prepare for human space flight.

Able and Baker were first taken to Puerto Rico, then to Washington, D.C. The monkeys were space heroes, but Able's days on earth were numbered. On June 1, three days after the flight, a sensor that had been planted under Able's skin was being removed when she suffered an adverse reaction to the anesthesia she had been given and died. She was subsequently stuffed.

In what may be a reflection of the adaptability of animals, including humans, to extreme changes in conditions, Baker went on to live a healthy life. She was placed in a specially designed habitat at the U.S. Space and Rocket Center in Huntsville, Alabama. The cylindrically shaped environment was approximately eight feet in diameter and four feet high with clear Plexiglas walls and a floor comprising stainless steel bars covering a drainage system that washed away waste products; the temperature was maintained between 72 and 75 degrees. "Miss Baker," as she was called, had several mates but never reproduced. She died on November 29, 1984, at the age of twenty-seven—about three times the life expectancy of a squirrel monkey in captivity—and was buried on the grounds of the U.S. Space and Rocket Center in Huntsville, adjacent to the front entrance, with a five-

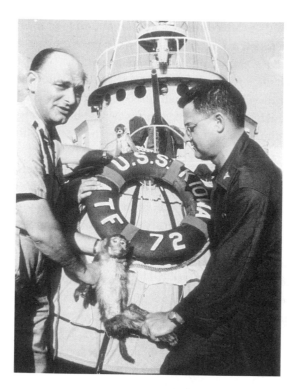

Two sailors aboard the USS Kiowa hold Able after she splashed down with Baker in the Atlantic Ocean.

foot granite memorial marking her grave and an epitaph citing her birth date, death date, and role in history.

After their May 1959 flight, Able and Baker received substantial attention in the media, but then they were quickly forgotten, probably because advances in space exploration at the time were so rapid that new accomplishments were constantly making headlines. Less than two years later, on April 12, 1961, the Soviets launched the first human being into space, and a little over ten years after Able and Baker were carried aloft, the Americans landed two men on the moon.

In the tense Cold War era, the Russians and Americans were competing fiercely to be the first to accomplish some great mission or other to prove which of their socioeconomic systems was best and to gain military advantage. Early on the Russians seemed always to be one step ahead of the Americans; they sent up the first satellite (Sputnik I), the first dog (Laika), the first cosmonaut (Yuri Gagarin), and the first unmanned spacecraft to land on the moon (Lunik 2), all historic achievements. But while the Soviets were first, their missions were not always completed. The Sputnik I satellite was essentially a transmitter that could be tracked, as opposed to

Explorer I, the first U.S. satellite, which was a complete scientific package (it discovered the Van Allen radiation belt). The Soviets put the first dog in space but could not recover it alive. The first Soviet cosmonaut had no control over his capsule, as opposed to the early American astronauts, who had at least a degree of maneuverability. Unlike Able, Baker, and Yuri Gagarin, the astronauts were part of the system instead of just being along for the ride.

The Jupiter-C missile in which Able and Baker were launched, like other U.S. missiles at the time, was a modified military weapon. To mitigate the military implications of the space race, the National Aeronautics and Space Administration was formed as a civilian space agency. With NASA, advances in space-exploration technology made by the military were used for peacetime purposes.

With all the fantastic accomplishments of space exploration, and all the monumental missions on the horizon, the space monkeys Able and Baker were pioneers in space exploration and an indelible part of early space history. Indeed, before the human pioneers—astronauts such as Neil Armstrong, Alan Shepard, John Glenn, Edward White, John Young, Frank Borman, and James Lovell, as well as cosmonauts like Yuri Gagarin, Gherman Titov, Andrian Nikolayev, and Valentina Tereshkova—there were Able and Baker, the primate space voyagers, who in their own way helped advance the U.S. space program. These were the first animals to soar beyond the earth's atmosphere and return to earth alive, a remarkable feat that carved their niche in history. In addition, they also have the distinction of being the first successful female space travelers.

Indeed, the potential for manned space flight received a major boost in the predawn hours of a spring day in 1959 when Able and Baker soared into space and returned safely to earth, suggesting that their more advanced primate cousins could likewise survive the perilous trip. Today, the space monkey Able, frozen in eternal sleep, reminds us of one of the most significant first steps in humankind's inevitable journey into the cosmos.

LOCATION: National Air and Space Museum, Washington, D.C.

Odyssey

DATE: 1970.

WHAT IT IS: The Apollo 13 command module.

WHAT IT LOOKS LIKE: It is nearly 11 feet high and weighs approximately 13,000 pounds. From its violent reentry into the earth's atmosphere, *Odyssey*'s exterior has been burned a rusty orange.

"Okay, Houston, we've had a problem here."
—*Apollo 13 command module pilot*
Jack Swigert

"Failure is not an option."
—*Mission Control Flight Director*
Gene Kranz to the ground crew

Two hundred thousand miles away from earth, a manned spacecraft is soaring through the vast darkness of space when suddenly an explosion reverberates harshly through the vessel. The main supply of oxygen, power, and water is lost, the mission is aborted, and the three-man crew is faced with a life-and-death predicament. How can they get themselves back home to earth when the backup battery in their command module offers only a fraction of the energy needed to return safely?

What follows is one of the most remarkable tales in the annals of space travel, a testament to the ability of humans to triumph over their machinery when it goes awry in the most perilous of circumstances. And with the vessel that served as a main stage for this dramatic event having survived, we have today a remnant of that tale—a mute, scarred witness to one of the most daring, daunting, and miraculous voyages of all time.

After the Russians had unmistakably moved ahead in the space race by making Yuri Gagarin the first human in space on April 12, 1961, the pride of the United States was deeply tarnished. Three weeks after Gagarin orbited the earth, astronaut Alan B. Shepard, Jr., became the first American to be launched into space, but Shepard made only a fifteen-minute suborbital flight in which he spent five minutes flying outside the earth's atmosphere. Although it was an important accomplishment, America's manned space-flight debut was not as impressive as the Russian mission. The next year, in an address at Rice University in Houston, Texas, on September 12, 1962, President John F. Kennedy affirmed that America would put a man on the moon and return him safely to earth "before the end of this decade."

With only limited success in its space program, the idea of the United States being able to send a crew into space to reach the moon in under eight years was not just an ambitious goal, but an incomprehensibly huge task, certainly the vision of a dreamer. But the National Aeronautics and Space Administration (NASA) relished arduous challenges, and it established the Apollo space program to accomplish the impossible: in a relatively short time, to put a human being on a different world.

The Apollo program began tragically, however; Apollo 1 never made it into space. During routine ground exercises, a fire erupted on the vessel, killing the three astronauts scheduled to make the first manned flight of the program. Unmanned Apollo flights followed, and eventually the first manned mission, Apollo 7, in which the spacecraft, comprising both command and service modules, orbited the earth. Apollo 8 was the first manned mission to go to the moon, but it only orbited the moon without setting any crew members on the surface. The manned Apollo 9 flight tested a lunar module in earth's orbit, and Apollo 10 was the final dress rehearsal for the first manned lunar landing: the astronauts took their craft's lunar module into lunar orbit, flying within several miles of the lunar surface but not setting it down. Apollo 11, in which the first lunar landing was made, was truly a historic voyage, and Neil A. Armstrong became the first human being to set foot on another celestial body. Apollo 12 was a subsequent manned mission to the moon to collect soil and rock samples.

Apollo 13 was to be America's third lunar mission. While the landing crew of Apollo 11 had explored the moon's Sea of Tranquillity and Apollo 12 the Ocean of Storms, the lunar landing crew of Apollo 13 was to explore the Fra Mauro Formation, particularly a hilly upland area north of the Fra Mauro

Apollo 13 is launched from Pad A, Launch Complex 39, at the Kennedy Space Center at 1:13 P.M. (CST) on April 11, 1970. Little did the space vehicle's astronauts—James A. Lovell, commander; John Swigert, command module pilot; and Fred Haise, lunar pilot—know what was in store for them, but soon the whole world would be following their dramatic flight.

crater, deploying equipment for scientific experiments, conducting geological surveys, and photographing future potential exploration sites. The equipment they would set down to measure such events and phenomena as meteoroid crashes, variations in lunar atmosphere temperature, and heat flow from underground to the moon's surface constituted ALSEP, the Apollo Lunar Surface Experiment Package.

Three astronauts made up the Apollo 13 crew: James A. Lovell, Jr., the commander; John L. Swigert, Jr., the command module pilot; and Fred W. Haise, Jr., the lunar module pilot. Swigert was actually a backup member chosen to replace Thomas K. Mattingly III after backup lunar module pilot Charlie Duke accidentally exposed the crew to the German measles, and it was found that Mattingly did not have antibodies for immunity to the contagious disease.

There were three major components of the Apollo 13 spacecraft: the command module, named *Odyssey*; the service module; and the lunar module, named *Aquarius*. The command-service module (the two components were connected through the flight until reentry) was the main ship—the astronauts would sleep and work in the command module, the vessel's life-support and propulsion systems being located in the service module—and was the vessel in which the astronauts would return to earth. The two-man lunar module was an ancillary craft that would separate from the command-service module in its orbit of the moon, take the landing party to the moon's surface, and then, after the lunar mission was complete, ascend to reunite with the command-service module orbiting the moon. The lunar module would be jettisoned back to the moon to test the seismological equipment left on it.

At 1:13 P.M. CST on Saturday, April 11, 1970, Apollo 13 was launched from the Kennedy Space Center at Cape Canaveral, Florida. The lunar module was scheduled to set down on the moon four days later, on April 15. The landing crew would venture out twice to conduct their explorations and investigations—at 1:13 A.M. and 8:58 P.M. CST, both on April 16. The next day, April 17, the landing crew would depart from the moon to link up with the orbiting command module. Early in the afternoon of April 18, the spacecraft would propel itself out of its moon orbit and splash down in the Pacific after 2:17 P.M. CST on the 21st of April.

For the first forty-six hours the journey to the moon proceeded according to schedule—so well, in fact, that the Mission Control capsule communicator (CapCom), astronaut Joe Kerwin, remarked, "The spacecraft is in real good shape as far as we are concerned. We're bored to tears down here."

But then forty minutes later, when the fans for oxygen tank number two were routinely turned on, the tank's oxygen quantity reading zoomed from normal to "off-scale high." Within the next few hours the crew turned on the fans twice more, still obtaining "off-scale high" readings, then rested. In the meantime, the ground crew at the Manned Spacecraft Center in Houston had observed a malfunction in hydrogen tank number one, and, almost fifty-six hours after Apollo 13's launch, asked the astronauts to activate the fans and heaters of the cryogenic systems. At this time Apollo 13 was about 200,000 miles from earth.

The fans for oxygen tank number two were turned on, and the tank's pressure began to rise as the stabilization-control system signaled a power transient. The tank's pressure reached its maximum, then jumped to "off-scale high" again. Then it started to decrease, and seconds later its temperature plunged to "off-scale low." The master caution and warning alarm sounded, signaling an electrical problem. Oxygen flow to fuel cells one and three began decreasing, then ceased. Then there was a rise in temperature of the service propulsion-system helium tank. At 9:07 P.M. CST on Monday, April 13, there was a loud bang on board Apollo 13.

James Lovell, in the lower equipment bay, and Jack Swigert, in the left seat of the command module, thought the bang they heard was just a joke played by Fred Haise, who had previously moved a valve that had triggered a similar rumble. But Haise was innocent of any horseplay, and he quickly assured Lovell and Swigert that the explosion they had heard and felt was no joke.

The crew observed that the voltage on DC main bus B was low and realized they were in trouble. "Okay, Houston," Jack Swigert announced to ground control. "We've had a problem here." "Say again?" responded CapCom Jack Lousma, and this time Lovell reported, "Houston, we've had a problem here. We've had a main B bus undervolt."

The explosion had emanated from liquid-oxygen tank number two. As would later be determined in more detail, combustion had caused the tank, which supplied oxygen to the fuel cells that powered the command and service modules, to fail. But for now, the spacecraft, the mission—and indeed the astronauts—were in a state of crisis. Oxygen tank number one was out. The command module had no power, the service module was dead, and only the lunar module was operational. The spacecraft was more than eighty-five hours from earth, and the backup battery in the command module offered a maximum life of only ten hours—and that had to be preserved for reentry to earth to supply power to the command module's reentry computers.

With the mission aborted, a decision had to be made about how Apollo 13 would return home. One option was simply to turn the spacecraft right around and head back, but that would have consumed too much fuel. The method finally chosen was fraught with danger; if not carried out correctly, it could have meant the demise of the spacecraft's passengers.

An hour after the explosion, Mission Control announced to the Apollo 13 crew, "We are starting to think about the LM lifeboat." The use of a lunar module in an emergency had for years been considered, but implementing it in such dire circumstances required the examination of previous studies. With the command module running out of power, a plan had to be settled on soon.

It was decided that the Apollo 13 crew would try to come home using the lunar module as a lifeboat. The astronauts would leave the command module for the lunar module, where they would navigate the spacecraft around the moon, then use the moon's gravitational pull to increase their speed and hurtle them back toward earth. At some point the earth's gravity would grab them and pull them back in, and the command module would be used for the final approach to earth. In theory it was plausible, but would it actually work?

According to the laws of physics, it could. With Apollo 13 continuing toward the moon, at some point the gravitational pull of the moon would start to take over, sending the spacecraft around the back of the moon. The spacecraft would be caught in a kind of whirlpool, but at a proper point in its lunar orbit, the lunar module would fire its rockets to escape the moon's gravitational pull and slingshot the craft toward earth. From this point, the vessel would pretty much be on cruise control, building up speed as it headed home. It was important that Apollo 13 hit the earth's atmosphere at exactly the right angle; if it came in too shallow it would skip off the earth's atmosphere and go into an eternal orbit around the earth, and if it came in too steep it would burn up as soon as it entered the atmosphere.

As Odyssey is kept afloat in the South Pacific Ocean after it splashed down at 12:07 P.M. (CST) on April 17, 1970, astronaut John L. Swigert is lifted in a Billy Pugh net to a helicopter, where Fred W. Haise has already been taken. James Lovell waits in a life raft with a U.S. Navy underwater demolition swimmer, while other navy team swimmers involved in the recovery operation are in the water.

With such a small margin for error, the flight had to be planned precisely. There were several obstacles. With *Aquarius,* whose mass and center of gravity differed from the command module, driving the entire spacecraft, corrections in the course had to be calculated and effected. The velocity of the craft had to be increased using *Aquarius*'s descent engine, an operation it was not designed to handle. And simply trying to stay alive inside the spacecraft was becoming a greater challenge as the consumables (chiefly oxygen and water) were being depleted and the temperature inside the cabin was dropping by the minute.

Indeed, *Aquarius,* with its limited power and air, wasn't made for such an excursion. Its engines were designed for the ascent and descent of the lunar module. It was like taking a car designed to drive on city streets and trying to drive it over rocky mountains. But the principles were there. If a truck could be driven through mountainous terrain, a car ought to be able to as well, even though that had not been its intended use, and even if it had never been tried before. But the bottom line was that there really wasn't much of a choice. It was either that or lose the crew.

Many of the potential problems of such a lunar-module excursion were addressed by members of the Mission Control team, who called in specialists from the companies that had participated in the manufacture of the various systems aboard Apollo 13. They used computers and simulators to conduct tests and maneuvers, and the results of these were used to guide the space-traveling astronauts. The ground crew investigated numerous trouble areas, and astronauts at Kennedy Space Center in Florida and Houston's Manned Spacecraft Center ran emergency tests in lunar-module simulators.

The lunar module was the "lifeboat" for most of the trip back to earth. It supplied oxygen and power, and the astronauts worked in there and even rested there. Because of the conservation of power, the men found it too cold to sleep in the command module, but though *Aquarius* was warmer, at 38 degrees Fahrenheit it was still cold, and Mission Control was concerned that this would prevent the astronauts from getting the rest they needed to handle the tricky navigation of the craft. But the astronauts held up, and so did *Aquarius*.

As the three astronauts worked their way out of their cosmic dilemma, the world beneath them watched closely, following every scrap of news broadcast about the crew. A dozen countries offered to help in recovering the landed spacecraft. People all over the globe prayed for the successful return of the astronauts, then glued themselves to their television sets to watch coverage of the flight.

Meanwhile Apollo 13, having been whipped out of lunar orbit, was hurtling back toward earth. All the systems on board the command module had been shut down save those for life support and communication, and its power consumption was lowered to enable it to sustain its occupants. Because the lunar module had no heat shield, the landing would have to take place in the command module. More than four hours before the spacecraft would reenter the earth's atmosphere, with Lovell and Haise in the lunar module, Swigert jettisoned the damaged service module. As the service module drifted away the crew got their first look at the damage it incurred in the explosion. Due to the extent of the damage questions were raised as to whether the explosion had caused structural damage to the heat shield; if it had been damaged the ship could burn up during reentry into the earth's atmosphere. The answer would not be known until reentry.

About ninety minutes before reentry the astronauts got back into the command module, and the lunar module, the astronauts' deliverer and savior, was ejected. Mission Control bade farewell to *Aquarius,* as did the astronauts. It was up to *Odyssey* now to deliver the Apollo 13 crew safely back to earth.

Shortly after noon CST on Friday, April 17, nearly eighty-seven harrowing hours after the accident and after more than five days and twenty-two hours in space in total, the three parachutes of Odyssey opened, permitting the craft with the three astronauts aboard to gracefully drop into the Pacific Ocean. Instead of being doomed to endless orbit in outer space, Odyssey—with its precious human cargo—was home again.

Odyssey, the Apollo 13 command module, is set down by a cable on the USS Iwo Jima in the South Pacific.

And so Odyssey lives on,* a shrine to the valor of the men and women who participated, in space and on the ground, in Apollo 13's mission, and a grand testament to the fact that while the journey to the cosmos may be fraught with danger, the unbridled spirit and boundless ingenuity of human beings can overcome even the most formidable of obstacles.

LOCATION: Kansas Cosmosphere and Space Center, Hutchinson, Kansas.†

*In the 1960s and early 1970s, after command modules returned to earth, they would routinely, for budgetary reasons, be gutted so that their parts could be installed in other spacecraft to reduce costs. Odyssey was likewise stripped of its parts, and when it arrived at its current home in Kansas, staff members devoted much time to locating its lost hardware. Many interesting tales attend the recovery of the parts, including the long search for one of Odyssey's major control panels, which ended only when it was found and identified by its serial number in one of the holding institution's own exhibit crafts.
†Odyssey is on permanent loan to the Kansas Cosmosphere and Space Center from the Smithsonian Institution's National Air and Space Museum, which has in its collection from the Apollo 13 flight the astronauts' space suits, a parachute, photographic equipment and accessories, a slide rule, the astronauts' chronographs, and a microform Bible that one of the astronauts brought on board.

The Gun That Killed John Lennon

DATE: 1980.

WHAT IT IS: A .38-caliber special Charter Arms Undercover revolver used in pop music's most famous assassination.

WHAT IT LOOKS LIKE: The Lennon murder weapon has a 2-inch barrel and a 5-chambered cylinder. It is a "blued" gun—bluing is a process in which a preservative coating is put over the metal to keep it from rusting—that appears to have a black finish. The serial number inscribed on the gun is 577570.

The 8th of December 1980 was a mild winter day in New York City, the temperature dropping into the fifties as darkness descended. Midtown Manhattan was alive and vibrant, as it typically is on a weekday night, with traffic navigating the crowded thoroughfares and pedestrians briskly negotiating the sidewalks. Neon lights flickered over Broadway, skyscapers stretched to the heavens along the Avenue of the Americas, stately apartment buildings presided over Park Avenue, and trendy restaurants and boutiques graced the fashionable West Side. Below ground, long subway trains clattered through the dark serpentine tunnels, their passengers perhaps a little wary of the dangers of night travel in the city's subterranean trenches.

On West Forty-fourth Street, in the heart of the theater district, a couple left the Record Plant recording studio and climbed into a limousine. A glut of long black cars routinely clogged the streets in Gotham, ferrying the wealthy, the famous, and those who wanted to impart these images, but this particular limo harbored two world-renowned passengers. He was a rock star, one of the most idolized persons in the world, the erstwhile co-creative force of what many considered the greatest rock 'n' roll band of all time. A towering figure, the man was a widely acclaimed musical genius, an artist with sublime musical and lyrical gifts, a poet, a peace activist, and a thinking person's renegade—not to mention the world's most famous former full-time househusband. Although personal and professional rifts were given as the underlying reasons, his wife had been vilified as the dragon lady who had catalyzed the sundering of the iconographic Sixties music group, which had bestowed on the world a catalog of tunes that not only changed the face of the popular music scene, but which ushered in a whole cultural shift. The Beatles were not only the most inventive, most celebrated, and most successful pop musical group in the history of the music industry, but they spawned a revolution that reverberated for decades, perhaps permanently changing the sociological and cultural tapestry of civilized society.

Together the two limo passengers, husband and wife John Lennon and Yoko Ono, were a pop-music duo in their own right, having released several recordings since their controversial 1968 album *Two Virgins,* whose front and back covers were graced by photographs of their fully naked bodies.

The husband-and-wife music team had been working at the Record Plant on a song for a planned new album. This project was part of Lennon's musical rebirth since the birth of his and Ono's son, Sean, in 1975, after which the ex-Beatle Lennon decided to take the radical step of becoming a full-time father and nurturer to his newborn child. With his substantial earnings from his days as a Beatle, as well as the vast self-perpetuating royalties earned daily for radio airplay of the songs he wrote and of repackaged Beatles records, money would not be a problem for the wealthy Lennons in their New York City digs.

An English expatriate, John Lennon had had to fight to make America his home, after initially being denied permanent residence because of an earlier drug conviction in England, but finally he became a legal resident of New York City.

From the late 1950s, Lennon, Paul McCartney, and George Harrison had been members of a musical group, eventually known as the Beatles. The band built up local followings in Hamburg, Germany, where they played on several visits, and in their hometown of Liverpool, England. In 1961, a record-store proprietor named Brian Epstein heard the band play and got them a contract with the Parlophone label of EMI. There were a couple of early personnel changes, and the band soon became famous as the foursome of Lennon, McCartney, Harrison, and Ringo Starr (born Richard Starkey, Jr.).

In October 1962 the Beatles hit the English charts with "Love Me Do," followed a few months later by "Please Please Me." But the Beatles hadn't caught on yet in the United States, the world's largest record market, because EMI's American subsidiary, Capitol Records, had no faith in the combo's commercial potential in America.

Despite Capitol's refusal to release the Beatles' records, Epstein himself traveled to America to play for an East Coast Capitol chief a dub of the Beatles' "I Want to Hold Your Hand," which generated a lot of excitement. On February 1, 1964, "I Want to Hold Your Hand" reached the top position on the U.S. singles chart, followed in the next few months by "She Loves You," "Can't Buy Me Love," "Love Me Do," and "A Hard Day's Night." (Not only were all these songs written by Lennon and McCartney, but the pair even had another number-one tune as writers during this time with Peter and Gordon's "A World Without Love.") By now, Beatlemania had grabbed the world and was changing the face of the music scene.

Lennon and McCartney wrote the Beatles tunes and sang the lead vocals on most of them as well. They created infectious melodies and married lyrics to them that could be fun, ponderous, silly, provocative, romantic, cryptic, optimistic, pessimistic.

As the Sixties wound through their critical social upheavals with the assassinations of John and Robert Kennedy and Martin Luther King, Jr., and the Vietnam War, the Beatles not only supplied the musical sound track, but led the revolution with their faddish hairstyles and attire and their maverick attitudes on everything from religion and philosophy to sex and politics. The Sixties were a time of psychedelic drugs, sexual liberation, mysticism, antiwar demonstrations, and rabid environmentalism. John Lennon was perhaps the most progressive Beatle, the experimenter, the articulate spokesperson, the elder statesman of the Fab Four. Even though they had stopped touring in 1966 and produced music only on vinyl from that point on, millions of Beatles fans worldwide received the news of their breakup, announced by Paul McCartney in April 1970, with immense disappointment, and the Japanese artist Yoko Ono was fingered by some as the culprit. But Lennon had found his soulmate in Ono, his second wife.

As Lennon and Ono cruised uptown in their limo, a deranged fan waited at their destination. The limousine pulled up to the Dakota at Central Park West and Seventy-second Street, the home of its passengers. The massive yellowish stone building with castlelike turrets was surrounded by a wrought-iron fence topped with a long row of truculent sculpted male heads. At the entrance was an imposing arched stone gate that opened into the building's large interior courtyard. A small guardhouse stood in front of the gate on the right-hand side, from which security personnel could keep watch over the driveway into the courtyard and the twin walkways that bordered it.

John Lennon and Yoko Ono got out of their limousine and were about to step onto the right-hand walkway when the armed intruder emerged from the shadows of the arched entrance. Earlier in the day the stocky, bespectacled man had asked John Lennon for his autograph, which the rock star had willingly scribbled on the cover of his recently released album, *Double Fantasy.* Now the interloper called out.

"Mr. Lennon!"

Famous the world over, Lennon was recognized everywhere he went, and people were constantly beseeching him for autographs. It was well known that New York City was his adopted domicile and that he had taken up residence at the Dakota, a building known for its famous show-biz inhabitants. Lennon was probably not surprised to hear the voice of a stranger call to him, but this time he was met not with gushing admiration but with lethal action.

At about 10:50 P.M., the sound of a flurry of shots echoed from the face of the massive stone building across the intersection and into the park across the avenue, followed by a woman's scream. Four bullets struck John Lennon—two in the back, two in the left shoulder. As Yoko Ono, who was not hit, cried out for help, the wounded Beatle staggered up the walkway past the guardhouse, collapsing as he emerged into the Dakota's courtyard.

The gunman did not bother to run or toss away his gun, but rather just paced about under the archway holding his weapon, getting into a verbal altercation with the frantic doorman, then quietly waiting for the police.

By the time police arrived minutes later, scores of people had gathered around the entrance to the Dakota. Word of Lennon's shooting spread with amazing rapidity. Tears streamed down the shocked faces of many of the onlookers. Television crews pulled up shortly afterward. Soon the world would receive the news that John Lennon had been shot and possibly killed.

New York City police officers lifted the mortally wounded victim and placed him into the back of a police car, where he sprawled across the seat. An officer asked him if he was John Lennon, and the dying man, barely conscious, muttered, "Yeah." During the ride to the emergency room Lennon moaned. The police sped to nearby Roosevelt Hospital, but by the time they arrived the life had already trickled from the once-vibrant musician. In the emergency room doctors pronounced John Lennon, forty years old, dead at 11:15 P.M.

Yoko Ono, driven to the hospital in a police car, became hysterical, begging, "Tell me it isn't true." A crowd was building outside the hospital now, and by one in the morning about a thousand people stood outside the Dakota, some mute and numb, others softly chanting one of Lennon's musical mantras about giving peace a chance.

The gunman was identified as twenty-five-year-old Mark David Chapman. He had traveled to New York City from his home in Hawaii, making a stop in Georgia where he had lived as a teenager. He brought with him a gun that he had purchased for a reported $169 in Hawaii to carry out the execution. Chapman did not have a criminal record, but he had tried to commit suicide twice—once in 1977, the second time a couple weeks earlier while he was in New York City stalking Lennon.

Until recently Chapman, who had previously done social work for the YMCA, had worked as a security guard at a condominium in Hawaii. After the first of his suicide attempts, he had been temporarily confined to an institution. A high school rock-band guitarist who was obsessed with the Beatles, Chapman, like Lennon, was married to a Japanese woman. Although a fan of the former Beatle, some dark impulse in Chapman had driven him to destroy his idol.

The news of the death of John Lennon stunned the world. Society had become inured to the premature death of its cultural icons; many popular entertainers had died prematurely due to fatal accidents, drug overdoses, or other calamities. Buddy Holly, Elvis Presley, Mama Cass, Jimi Hendrix, Janis Joplin, and Jim Morrison had all succumbed at relatively young ages. But the killing of John Lennon was different, a new phenomenon: the murderer committed the deed merely to have his name linked with a famous person.

In the last months of his life, John Lennon had become musically active once again. The preceding summer he had begun recording with Yoko Ono the album *Double Fantasy*. Shortly before he was fatally shot, a single, "(Just Like) Starting Over," was released and became a hit. With the song an overture to his musical resurrection, it was one of life's cruel jokes that Lennon was cut down just as he was returning to music after a period of quiet domesticity.

One man, one gun, one psychotic impulse, and the world was deprived of one of its great musical geniuses. With the voice silenced, people everywhere mourned the man who had brought pleasure to their lives and in his songs pled for peace.

Meanwhile, on December 9, the day after the murder, the New York City Police Department's Ballistics Squad received from the morgue three bullets in association with complaint number 14854, the designation given to the John Lennon murder case, which was caught by (that is, assigned to) the

20th Precinct Detective Unit. One piece of lead bullet found at the crime scene was so deformed that ballistics examiners could not match it with the gun. The other two bullets delivered to the squad were taken from John Lennon's body by the medical examiner. Both were .38-caliber lead hollow-point bullets. Of these two, one bullet was in good condition, the other in fair condition. The alleged murder weapon, a .38-caliber Charter Arms Undercover revolver that was vouchered by the arresting officer, was received by the Ballistics Squad around the same time the spent bullets came in.

On the eighth floor of the NYPD Police Academy on East Twentieth Street in Manhattan, a ballistics test was performed to determine if the weapon seized from Chapman had fired the two bullets found in Lennon's body. After a ballistics examiner made an identification study of the gun and recorded its serial number, caliber, barrel size, number of chambers, and manufacturer, he fired it to make sure that it was in fact an operable firearm. Then he placed a couple of .38-caliber cartridges into chambers of the Charter Arms revolver and shot into a large water tank. The water absorbed the kinetic energy of the bullets, slowing them down so that they wouldn't cause damage. But now the bullets bore the unique markings of the imperfections in the barrel of the gun.

The two test bullets retrieved from the water tank were placed in small envelopes and forwarded to the squad's Microscopic Section. Here a microscopic comparison was performed in which the markings of the test bullets were compared to the markings of the two bullets recovered from John Lennon's body. As a result of the test, the Ballistics Squad matched the two bullets from the body with the Charter Arms firearm, the weapon recovered from Mark David Chapman at the Dakota on the night John Lennon was shot.

On December 10, two days after the fatal shooting, John Lennon's remains were reportedly cremated at a Hartsdale, New York, crematorium. The body that once was a familiar sight on millions of album covers was now a pile of ashes. But although his life was terminated, his songs endure as a testament to the

A New York City Police Department Crime Scene Unit photograph of the gun used to kill John Lennon.

indomitable spirit and creative genius of one of the twentieth century's great musical talents. The gun that discharged the fatal bullets survives as well and will continue to be a grim reminder of the day John Lennon became a martyred icon for the ages.

LOCATION: New York City Police Museum, Manhattan, New York.

ACKNOWLEDGMENTS

The Tooth of the Buddha

Kurunegoda Piyatissa of the New York Buddhist Vihara invited me into his sanctuary and with extraordinary patience spent many hours explaining the subject material of this chapter to me. Over the course of time Reverend Piyatissa continued to assist me; he was always a kind and generous purveyor of information, and I am most grateful to him.

The Gold Larnax of King Philip II

Andreas G. Vlachopoulos, Hellenic Ministry of Culture; Dr. Angeliki Kottardi, Archaeological Museum of Vergina.

The Magna Carta

Dr. Christopher Fletcher, Curator, Literary Manuscripts, The British Library; Dr. Andrew Prescott, The British Library; A. C. Dawson, Salisbury Cathedral; Darlene McClurkin, Exhibits Staff, National Archives.

The Stone of Scone

I am most indebted to Christine Reynolds, Assistant Keeper, Muniment Room and Library, Westminster Abbey, for answering my questions and providing additional details. Ms. Reynolds's correspondence was invaluable to me in writing this chapter. Christopher J. Tabraham, Principal Inspector of Ancient Monuments, Historic Scotland.

The Essex Ring

Christine Reynolds, Westminster Abbey; John J. Doherty, Reference Librarian, Montana State University Library; John Ulatowski graciously conducted valuable research for me.

Galileo's Middle Finger

Mara Miniati, Institute of the History of Science, Florence, Italy. Permission to reproduce the Tommaso Perelli quote was kindly provided by the Institute of the History of Science.

George Washington's Schoolboy Copybooks

I am indebted to Dr. Gerard W. Gawalt, a historian at the Library of Congress, who extended to me a rare privilege by granting me permission to personally examine two of the three extant George Washington copybooks (one of the volumes was on display during my visit). This was a most thrilling and exhilarating experience for me. I was able to spend a day touching and combing through the very pages George Washington wrote on as a youth in the 1740s. As one who is passionate about historical artifacts, I am grateful to Dr. Gawalt for the opportunity to examine firsthand a fabulous national treasure.

John Harrison's Fourth Marine Timekeeper

Jonathan Betts, National Maritime Museum, London.

The Virginia Declaration of Rights

I am grateful to Dr. John Sellers of the Library of Congress not only for the information he provided but for setting me on the trail to pursue the thesis of this chapter; Dr. Gerard W. Gawalt, Library of Congress; Zanne Macdonald, Research Librarian, Thomas Jefferson Memorial Foundation; Rebecca Bowman, Research Historian, Thomas Jefferson Memorial Foundation; John Butler, Old Military and Civil Branch, Textual Services Division, National Archives; Tom Albro, Head of the Book and Paper Treatment Section of the Conservation Division of the Library of Congress.

The Rising Sun Chair

Robert L. Giannini, Ann Marie Dube, and Karen Diethorn of Independence National Historic Park.

The Louisiana Purchase Treaty

John Butler, National Archives; Michael E. Pilgrim, Archives Reference Branch, Textual Reference Division, National Archives; Rebecca Bowman, Research Historian, Thomas Jefferson Memorial Foundation; Aloha P. South, National Archives.

The Lewis and Clark Journals

Generous assistance for this chapter came from Carolyn Gilman, Special Projects Historian, Missouri Historical Society. Ms. Gilman read the chapter and suggested many valuable changes. Scott DeHaven, Assistant Manuscripts Librarian, American Philosophical Society; David F. Moore, Mauscript Specialist, Western Historical Manuscript Library; Jane Ehrenhart, Supervisor, Reference and Technical Services, Illinois State Historical Library; Carol M. Spawn, Archivist, The Academy of Natural Sciences; Rebecca Bowman, Research Historian, Thomas Jefferson Memorial Foundation; Maureen D. Heher, Public Services Assistant, The Beinecke Rare Book and Manuscript Library.

Beethoven's Ear Trumpets

Dr. M. Ladenburger, Beethoven House; S. Brandenburg and Nicole Kämpken, Beethoven Archive; Marla Sivak Rachlin, Lexington School for the Deaf.

Harrison's Peace Pipes

Lisa Ann Shockley, Registraral Assistant, The Kansas City Museum (Ms. Shockley provided the information on the history of the Dyer collection); Jim Crocker, National Museum of Natural History; Kristen Froehlich, The Historical Society of Pennsylvania.

John Adams's Pigtail

Barbara Tomlinson, Curator, Antiquities, National Maritime Museum, London.

The Doubleday Ball

I enthusiastically give credit for this chapter to Thomas R. Heitz, a consummate baseball historian. Mr. Heitz laid out the whole story of the Doubleday myth for me, and provided a comprehensive explanation of the history of baseball, including its roots, evolution, and development as a professional sport in America. Mr. Heitz's historical baseball knowledge is encyclopedic and he is a passionate and articulate spokesman of the game. He also generously faxed me many pages of rare baseball documents, and was always available to answer questions and provide additional information, anecdotes, and colorful stories.

For a physical description of the Doubleday Ball I would like to thank Tim Wiles and Peter Clark, and for research documents, Frank Vito, all of the National Baseball Hall of Fame and Museum.

Vondovi's Head

Dr. David Hunt, National Museum of Natural History; Gary E. Cantrell and the Special Collections section at Swirbul Library, Adelphi University.

The Battle Sword of Colonel Najera

Generous assistance was provided by James Nottage, Vice President and Chief Curator of the Autry Museum of Western Heritage. Mr. Nottage brought this artifact to my attention and provided information on it, including a physical description of the sword.

Charles Dickens's Prompt-Copy of A Christmas Carol

Kenneth Benson; Rodney Philips, Curator of the Berg Collection, New York Public Library; Lou Ellen Davis. The opening scene of the chapter is reconstructed from various sources including newspaper reviews of Dickens's "final" reading.

The First American Flag Raised in Japan

James W. Cheevers, Associate Director and Senior Curator, U.S. Naval Academy.

The Emancipation Proclamation

Much gratitude is due to Dr. John Sellers of the Library of Congress for providing information and documents and answering questions. James Corsaro, The New York State Library; Judith Giuriceo, The Brooklyn Historical Society; Michael E. Pilgrim, National Archives.

Slices of Tom Thumb's Wedding Cake

I am especially grateful to Chris Coenen, one of the best authorities around on Tom Thumb. Mr. Coenen not only graciously shared with me his knowledge of Tom Thumb, but also provided many rare documents. I also wish to thank Dr. Marvin Kranz of the Library of Congress and Barbara Celitans of the San Antonio Public Library.

Thomas Edison's Original Tinfoil Phonograph

Douglas Tarr, Edison National Historic Site.

Jesse James's Stickpin

Gary Chilcote of the Patee House Museum and the Director and National President of the James-Younger Gang generously provided information and rare documents on Jesse James; James Starrs; Sarah Elder and Marilyn Taylor, St. Joseph Museum.

Ulysses S. Grant's Smoking Stand

For this chapter I was most fortunate to have the generous assistance of one of the foremost Grant scholars, John Y. Simon, U. S. Grant Association, Morris Library, Southern Illinois University. I also wish to thank Terry Miller, Sheila Cottral, and Peggy Ruthenberg, U. S. Grant Home State Historic Site; Nancy Wolfe, The Galena–Jo Daviess County Historical Society and Museum.

Jumbo the Elephant

Chris Coenen.

Freud's Couch

I am very grateful to Dr. Henry Mallard of the Psychoanalytic Society and Institute for kindly giving me a mini-course on Freud and providing colorful anecdotes; Erica Davies, Director, Freud Museum. (The Freud Museum, located at 20 Maresfield Garden, London, is open Wednesday to Friday from 12:00 noon to 5:00 P.M.)

The Hoof of Fire Horse Number Twelve

Jane Rogers, National Museum of American History; Herbert Collins; Marilyn Higgins.

"Take Me Out to the Ball Game"

Timothy J. Wiles, Director of Research, National Baseball Hall of Fame and Museum; Thomas R. Heitz; Barbara Alejandro and Michael Kerker, American Society of Composers, Authors and Publishers.

Mark Twain's Orchestrelle

Henry H. Sweets III, Director, Mark Twain Museum, kindly provided information and research documents. Astute readers may notice in the text of this chapter the titles *The Adventures of Tom Sawyer* and *Adventures of Huckleberry Finn* and wonder why the word "The" does not precede the latter title. It may have been a printer's error, but the word "The" does not precede the title in the original publication of the book.

The Zimmermann Telegram

Milton O. Gustafson, National Archives.

The Fourteen Points

Frank J. Aucella, Woodrow Wilson House; John Haynes, Mauscript Historian, Twentieth Century Political History, Manuscript Division, Library of Congress, kindly granted me permission to personally examine the papers of Woodrow Wilson, including his Fourteen Points address.

The Truce Flag That Ended World War I

Frank J. Aucella, Woodrow Wilson House.

Wyatt Earp's Drawing of the O.K. Corral Gunfight

James Nottage, Vice President and Chief Curator, Autry Museum of Western Heritage.

The Maltese Falcon

Dr. Gary Milan.

Monty's Battle Caravans

Dr. Neil Young, Imperial War Museum; Peter Simkins.

The World War II Japanese Surrender Table

James Cheevers, U.S. Naval Academy; James W. Zobel, MacArthur Memorial; Kenneth D. Schlessinger, National Archives.

ENIAC

I am grateful to Paul Shaffer, ENIAC curator, University of Pennsylvania, who critiqued the various drafts of my chapter and made corrections and suggestions for revision; Dr. David Allison, National Museum of American History.

Marilyn Monroe's Billowing Dress from The Seven Year Itch
Detective Thomas O'Malley, Tenth Precinct Detective Squad, New York City Police Department; Detective William Oldham, Major Case Squad, NYPD; Alfred J. Marini and John J. Healy, Detectives Endowment Association of the NYPD.

Elvis Presley's Purple Cadillac
Greg Howell, Graceland. Mr. Howell stated that the source for the grape-smashing incident is Lorraine Smith, the deceased sister-in-law of Gladys Presley, Elvis's mother. Lorraine Smith related she was present when Elvis smashed the grapes into his Cadillac.

Able the Space Monkey
My utmost appreciation goes to Tom Giles of the U.S. Space and Rocket Center. Mr. Giles kindly provided information and research materials, answered my questions, and read the chapter and suggested revisions. He was always cheerful, enthusiastic, and a pleasure to work with. Shelly Helmer, U.S. Space and Rocket Center; Allan Needell, Curator, National Air and Space Museum; Klaus Martel, U.S. Army Ordnance Missile Command.

Odyssey
Jeff Ollenburger, Kansas Cosmophere and Space Center; Allan Needell, Curator, National Air and Space Museum.

The Gun That Killed John Lennon
Detective Steven Fiorica, Detective Desi Stokes, and Police Officer Edward Accardi of the Firearms Analysis Section, NYPD. Detective Fiorica kindly gave me a crash course in ballistics.

David Sobel is the editor of this book, as he was of its predecessor, *Lucy's Bones, Sacred Stones, and Einstein's Brain,* and my debt to him is enormous. He is a caring, gentle, perceptive editor, and I shall always be grateful to him for giving literary life to my concept for these books—using artifacts as springboards for relating fascinating events and stories of history.

Anne Geiger, David Sobel's capable assistant, made numerous editorial suggestions to improve the manuscript. I am most grateful for her historical insights and editorial thoroughness.

I would like to thank Glen Hartley and Lynn Chu for their efforts in making this book become a reality.

My dear friend Judith Stein perused the manuscript and offered many acute and honest suggestions. I owe much to Judy for her great judgment and meticulousness.

Many other people were helpful in one way or another and at the risk of omitting anybody's name, I would like to extend my appreciation to Gretchen Worden, Nancy Constantine, Albert Quartaroli, Marisa Nadel, Sally Schiller, Agnes Dubin, Jeff Burke, William Hayden, Bonnie Barchichat, Emile Barchichat, Cliff Share, Paul Share, Manny Bekier, Paul C. Maloney, and William H. Davis at the Center for Legislative Archives at the National Archives.

My parents, Philip and Mazie Rachlin, were, as always, pillars of support.

My wife, Marla, and son, Glenn, put up with my taking over too many corners of our house with file folders, reference books, and other unwieldly research materials, as well as my long and irregular work hours. They are to be commended for their unwavering patience, love, and support. I would to thank Elyssa and Lauren Goldwert for their enthusiasm and support as well.

Virtually every author dreams of his or her work being adapted for presentation on the small or big screen, if their work is suitable for such adaptation. My own dream came true when Charlie Maday of the History Channel saw the potential for television adaptation of *Lucy's Bones, Sacred Stones, and Einstein's Brain,* and patiently shepherded the book through the labyrinthine legal and creative process that translates print to moving images. So I am eternally grateful to Mr. Maday, who, like my editor, David Sobel, is, as I would call it, a "dream maker." I would also like to thank all the other wonderful people at the History Channel, including Susan Werbe (the network's terrific executive producer of the series), Abbe Raven, Dan Davids, Harriet Georgiopoulos, LaDebra Moore Fletcher, and Barbara Shornick. For making *History's Lost and Found* a success, they're all "dream makers" too!

The actual creators of *History's Lost and Found* are the people who make up the fabulous team of Atlas Media Corporation. These people—the producers—really know how to take an idea and run with it! And so my great appreciation is extended to Bruce David Klein, Maria Lane, Pam Wolfe, Scott Tiffany, Christine Shuler, Michael Husain, Bill McClane, Ruby Lopez, Ted Schillinger, Alissa Krimski, Debbie Katz, Matthew Goldfine, Alexis Robie, Catherine Scheinman, Faye Moore, and the rest of the staff. Producer Charles Grinker and television executive Rand Stoll, who are intimately involved with the series, also helped bring the concept to the air and have been invaluable creative resources for the series.

SOURCES AND BIBLIOGRAPHY

Numerous reference works consulted in the research for this book were used so frequently that they merit being listed here as general sources for the entire book. These reference works are: *Encyclopaedia Britannica* (Chicago: Encyclopaedia Britannica, 1963); *The New Encyclopaedia Britannica* (Chicago: The New Encyclopaedia Britannica, 1997); *Collier's Encyclopedia* (New York: Collier's, 1997); *Academic American Encyclopedia* (Danbury, Conn.: Grolier, 1996); *World Book Encyclopedia* (Chicago: Field Enterprises Educational Corporation, 1958; Chicago: World Book, 1995); *The Book of Knowledge* (New York: Grolier Society, 1928); *The Concise Dictionary of National Biography: From the Beginnings to 1930* (London: Oxford University Press, 1939); *Encyclopedia Americana International Edition* (Danbury, Conn.: Grolier, 1988).

Introduction

Men's Journal, July 1995, with source attribution to *Molecular Medicine,* vol. 1, 1995: pp. 1–12, for the one-in-300-million-sperm statistic.

The Tooth of the Buddha

Kavsalyayan, Bhadant Anand. *An Intelligent Man's Guide to Buddhism.* Nagpur, India: Kashinath Meshram, 1992.

Payutto, Bhikkhu P. A. (Translated from the Thai by Bhikkhu Puriso.) *Good, Evil and Beyond . . . Kamma in the Buddha's Teaching.* Bangkok: Buddhadhamma Foundation Publications, 1993.

Piyatissa, Pidiville. *An Exposition of Buddhism.* Taipei, Taiwan: The Corporate Body of the Buddha Educational Foundation, 1994.

Santina, Peter D. *Fundamentals of Buddhism.* Taipei, Taiwan: The Corporate Body of the Buddha Educational Foundation, n.d.

Thera, Narada. *Buddha and His Teaching.* Kuala Lumpur, Malaysia: Missionary Society, 1973.

Thera, Narada. *Buddhism in a Nutshell.* Taipei, Taiwan: The Corporate Body of the Buddha Educational Foundation, 1982.

The Gold Larnax of King Philip II

Andronicos, Manolis. *Vergina: The Royal Tombs and the Ancient City.* Athens: Ekdotike Athenon S.A., 1992. (This is Andronicos's first-person account of his discovery of the tomb of King Philip II. It is the premier record of the finding of the tomb and its contents and my source for the description of the gold larnax and the tomb contents, as well as the cremation and burial of King Philip.)

The Magna Carta

British Library exhibition labels and reference cards from its permanent exhibition of the Magna Carta.

Davis, G. R. C. *Magna Carta.* London: The British Library, n.d.

Kelliner, Hilton, and Sally Brown. *English Literary Manuscripts.* N.p., 1985.

McKechnie, William S. *Magna Carta: A Commentary on the Great Charter of King John, with Historical Introduction.* New York: B. Franklin, 1914.

Prescott, Andrew. *English Historical Manuscripts.* N.p., 1989.

The Stone of Scone

Breeze, David, and Graeme Munro. *The Stone of Destiny.* Scotland: Historic Scotland, 1997.

"The Coronation Chair and the Stone of Scone" (information sheets). London: Westminster Abbey, n.d. (Source of the Latin inscription.)

The Essex Ring

Boyce, Charles. *Shakespeare A to Z.* New York: Facts on File/Roundtable Press, 1990.

"The Essex Ring, a Gift to Westminster Abbey." *The Times* (London), July 15, 1927.

Hibbert, Christopher. *The Virgin Queen: Elizabeth I, Genius of the Golden Age.* Reading, Mass.: Addison-Wesley, 1991.

Ogburn, Charlton. *The Man Who Was Shakespeare: A Summary of the Case Unfolded in the Mysterious William Shakespeare.* McLean, Va.: EPM, 1995.

Rowse, A. L. *The Annotated William Shakespeare* (Vol. II). New York: Potter, 1978.

Strachey, Lytton. *Elizabeth and Essex.* New York: Harcourt, Brace, 1928. (Source of the Shakespeare quote.)

Universal Standard Encyclopedia. Unicorn Publications, n.d.

Untitled information sheet on the Essex Ring. London: Westminster Abbey, n.d.

Untitled Westminster Abbey Library chart (for the female lineage of the Essex Ring).

Galileo's Middle Finger

Miniati, Mara (ed.). *Museo di Storia della Scienza Catalogo.* Florence: Giunti, 1991.

Web site pages of the Institute and Museum of the History of Science, Florence, including "Condemnation of Galileo" and "Abjuration of Galileo."

George Washington's Schoolboy Copybooks

DeWan, George. "Birth of a Nation," *Newsday,* May 24, 1987. (Source of the Charles Biddle quote about George Washington.)

Rauscher, Ann M. (annotator). *George Washington's Rules of Civility & Decent Behavior in Company and Conversation.* Mount Vernon, Va.: The Mount Vernon Ladies' Association, 1989.

Washington, George. *George Washington Papers* (Series 1, Sub-Series A; Forms of Writing and School Copy Books). In the collection of the Library of Congress.

Washington, George. *George Washington's School Copy-Book, 1745.* In the collection of the Library of Congress.

Washington, George. *1744–1748: School Exercises.* In the collection of the Library of Congress.

John Harrison's Fourth Marine Timekeeper

Betts, Jonathan. *John Harrison.* London: National Maritime Museum Publications, 1997. (A short but invaluable book about Harrison's endeavors to build a workable marine timekeeper.)

Greenhill, Basil (ed.). *The National Maritime Museum.* London: Scala Books, 1982.

Longitude Symposium. *The Quest for Longitude.* Cambridge, Mass.: Harvard University, 1996.

Sobel, Dava. *Longitude.* New York: Walker, 1995.

Web site of the Institute and Museum of the History of Science, Florence.

The Virginia Declaration of Rights

Becker, Carl. *The Declaration of Independence: A Study in the History of Political Ideas.* New York: Harcourt, Brace, 1922.

Bell, Whitfield J., Jr. *The Declaration of Independence, Four 1776 Versions: Jefferson's Manuscript Copy, The First Official Printing by John Dunlop, The First Newspaper Printing, A Unique Printing on Parchment by John Dunlop.* Philadelphia: American Philosophical Society, 1986. (Source of the John Hancock quote.)

Ellis, Joseph J. "Editing the Declaration." *Civilization,* July/August 1995.

Gustafson, Milton O. "The Empty Shrine: Transfer of the Declaration of Independence and the Constitution to the National Archives." *The American Archivist,* vol. 39, no. 3, July 1976.

Locke, John. *Two Treatises of Civil Government.* London: J. M. Dent & Sons, 1955.

Maier, Pauline. *American Scripture: Making the Declaration of Independence.* New York: Knopf, 1997.

Malone, Dumas. *The Story of the Declaration of Independence.* New York: Oxford University Press, 1975.

Mason, George (Robert A. Rutland, ed.). *The Papers of George Mason* (Volume 1). Chapel Hill, N.C.: Institute of Early American History & Culture Ser., 1970.

Padover, Saul. *Thomas Jefferson on Democracy.* New York: Appleton-Century, 1939.

Peterson, Merrill (ed.). *Thomas Jefferson: Writings.* New York: Library of America, 1984. (Source of the Thomas Jefferson letter of May 8, 1825, to Henry Lee.)

Printed Journals of the Continental Congress (Vol. 4). Washington, D.C.: Library of Congress, 1906.

Rutland, Robert Allen. *George Mason, Reluctant Statesman.* New York: Holt, Rinehart, and Winston, 1961.

Shuffleton, Frank. *Thomas Jefferson: A Comprehensive, Annotated Bibliography of Writings About Him (1826–1980).* New York: Garland Publishing, 1983.

Shuffleton, Frank. *Thomas Jefferson, 1981–1990: An Annotated Bibliography.* New York: Garland Publishing, 1992.

The Rising Sun Chair

Bruns, Roger A. (introduction). *A More Perfect Union: The Creation of the United States Constitution.* Washington, D.C.: National Archives and Records Administration, 1978 (reprint 1986).

Dube, Ann Marie. *A Multitude of Amendments, Alteration and Addition: The Constitution of the United States.* (The Web site that lists the locations of the different drafts of the U.S. Constitution is www.nps.gov.)

Farrand, Max. *The Framing of the Constitution of the United States.* New Haven, Conn.: Yale University Press, 1913.

Independence National Historical Park museum catalog records and information sheets, Philadelphia, Pa.

Jackson, John W. *With the British Army in Philadelphia, 1777–1781.* San Rafael, Calif.: Presidio Press, 1930.

Jameson, John Franklin. "Studies in the History of the Federal Convention of 1787," *Annual Report of the American,* n.d.

Jensen, Merrill (ed.). *The Documentary History of the Ratification of the Constitution.* Madison: State Historical Society of Wisconsin, 1976.

Journal of the House of Representatives of Pennsylvania, 1776–1781.

Milley, John C. (ed.). *Treasures of Independence National Historical Park and Its Collections.* New York: Main Street Press/Mayflower Books, 1980.

Pryor, Hubert C. "Summer of Destiny," *Modern Maturity,* February/March 1982. (Source of the Madison quote.)

Rapport, Leonard. "September 1786," National Archives pamphlet, National Archives Trust Fund Board, Washington, D.C., September 1986.

Smith, Page. *The Constitution: A Documentary and Narrative History.* New York: Morrow, 1978.

The Louisiana Purchase Treaty

"American Originals, December 8, 1995 Through December 1998," pamphlet, National Archives and Records Administration, Washington, D.C.

Ford, Paul Leicester (ed.). *The Works of Thomas Jefferson* (Vol. 9). New York:

Putnam (Knickerbocker Press), 1905. (Source of the Thomas Jefferson quote of April 18, 1802, to Robert R. Livingston.)

Greer, Curtis Manning. *The Louisiana Purchase and the Westward Movement.* Philadelphia: G. Barrie & Sons, 1904.

Hosmer, James K. *The History of the Louisiana Purchase.* New York: Appleton, 1902.

Lamar, Howard B. (ed.). *The Reader's Encyclopedia of the American West.* New York: Thomas Y. Crowell, 1977.

Miller, Hunter (ed.). *Treaties and Other International Acts of the United States of America* (Vol. 2). Washington, D.C.: U.S. Government Printing Office, 1931. (This was my source for the treaty quotes in this chapter.)

The Written Word Endures. National Archives and Records Administration, Washington, D.C.

The Lewis and Clark Journals

Academy of Natural Sciences, Philadelphia, interoffice memorandums and Lewis and Clark inventory holdings sheets, n.d.

Allen, John Logan. *Passage Through the Garden: Lewis and Clark and the Image of the American Northwest.* Urbana: University of Illinois, 1975.

Ambrose, Stephen E. *Undaunted Courage: Meriwether Lewis, Thomas Jefferson, and the Opening of the American West.* New York: Simon & Schuster, 1996.

Bakeless, John. *Lewis & Clark: Partners in Discovery.* New York: William Morrow, 1947.

Catlett, Stephen. *From St. Louis to Philadelphia: Tracking the Lewis and Clark Journals—an Exhibition of the Journals and Documents.* Philadelphia: American Philosophical Society, August 10, 1982.

Catlett, Stephen (ed.). *A New Guide to the Collections in the Library of the American Philosophical Society.* Philadelphia: American Philosophical Society, August 10, 1987.

Conrad, Howard L. (ed.). *Encyclopedia of the History of Missouri* (Vol. 2). New York: Southern History Company, 1901.

Coues, Elliott. *History of the Expedition Under the Command of Lewis and Clark, To the Sources of the Missouri River, thence across the Rocky Mountains and down the Columbia River to the Pacific Ocean, performed during the Years, 1804–5–6, by Order of the United States Government. A New Edition.* New York: Francis P. Harper, 1893.

Crawford, Anthony R. (ed.). *The Lewis and Clark Expedition: A Guide to the Holdings in the Division of Library and Archives of the Missouri Historical Society.* St. Louis: Missouri Historical Society, 1981.

Cutright, Paul Russell. *Lewis and Clark: Pioneering Naturalists.* Urbana: University of Illinois Press, 1969.

Halsey, Ashley, Jr. "The Air Gun of Lewis & Clark," *American Rifleman,* vol. 132, no. 8, August 1984.

Lamar, Howard B. (ed.). *The Reader's Encyclopedia of the American West.* New York: Thomas Y. Crowell, 1977.

Mayer, Robert W. "Wood River, 1803–1804," *Journal of the Illinois State Historical Society,* vol. 61, no. 2, 1958.

Moulton, Gary E. (ed.). *The Journals of the Lewis & Clark Expedition, August 30, 1803–August 24, 1804* (Vol. 2). Lincoln: University of Nebraska Press, 1986. (The first of an eleven-volume set that reproduces the journals and is an invaluable reference source on the expedition, with details on the writing of the journals, reprinted by permission of the University of Nebraska Press, copyright 1986 by the University of Nebraska Press.)

"The Mystery of Meriwether Lewis" (Associated Press), *Newsday,* June 4, 1996.

Norton, W. T. (ed.). *Centennial History of Madison County, Illinois and Its People, 1812 to 1912* (Vol. 1). Chicago: Lewis Publishing, 1912.

Peterson, Merrill (ed.). *Thomas Jefferson: Writings.* New York: Library of America, 1984. (Source of the Thomas Jefferson letter of June 20, 1803.)

Quaife, Milo M. *The Journals of Captain Meriwether Lewis and Sergeant Ordway.* Madison: State Historical Society of Wisconsin, 1965.

Western Historical Manuscript Collection microfilm, University of Missouri–Columbia, Columbia, Missouri.

Yale University Library catalog cards, n.d.

Beethoven's Ear Trumpets

Cross, Milton, and David Ewen. *Milton Cross' Encyclopedia of the Great Composers and Their Music* (Vol. 1). Garden City, N.Y.: Doubleday, 1953. (Source of the quote, "For me there can be no recreation in the society of my fellows . . .")

Komroff, Manuel. *Beethoven and the World of Music.* New York: Dodd, Mead, 1961. (Source of the quotes, "To give you an idea of this curious condition . . ." and "whistle and buzz.")

Orga, Ates. *Beethoven: His Life and Times.* New York: State Mutual, 1981.

Solomon, Maynard. *Beethoven.* New York: Associated Music Publishers, 1977.

Swift, Frederic Kay, and Willard I. Musser. *All About Music.* Rockville Centre, N.Y.: Belwin, 1960.

Harrison's Peace Pipes

Belden, Bauman L. *Indian Peace Medals Issued in the United States.* New York: American Numismatic Society, 1927. (Source of the Wayne quote, which itself is quoted from the American State Papers, Indian Affairs, Vol. 1.)

Eighteenth Annual Report of the Bureau of American Ethnology, no. 14, part 2. Washington, D.C., 1896.

Josephy, Alvin M., Jr. *The Indian Heritage of America.* New York: Bantam, 1969.

Kansas City Museum catalog cards on the Shawnee peace pipe and the Washington medal.

Lamar, Howard B. (ed.). *The Reader's Encyclopedia of the American West.* New York: Thomas Y. Crowell, 1977.

Lindsay, G. Carroll. "The Treaty Pipe of the Delawares," *Antiques Magazine,* July 1958.

McClinton, Kim. *Collecting American 19th Century.* New York: Scribners, 1968.

Powell, J. W. *Fourteenth Annual Report of the Bureau of Ethnology to the Secretary of the Smithsonian Institution, 1892–93.* Washington, D.C.: U.S. Government Printing Office, 1896.

Prucha, Francis Paul. *Indian Peace Medals in American History.* Madison: State Historical Society of Wisconsin, 1971.

John Adams's Pigtail

Bligh, William. *Mutiny Aboard H.M. Armed Transport "Bounty" in 1789.* N.p.: Bowker and Bertram, 1978. (The source for the "wanted description of Alex: Smith.")

Danielsson, Bengt. *What Happened in the Bounty.* London: Allen & Unwin, 1962.

Hough, Richard. *Captain Bligh and Mr. Christian: The Men and the Mutiny.* New York: Dutton, 1973.

Kemp, Peter (ed.). *The Oxford Companion to Ships and the Sea.* London: Oxford University Press, 1976.

Kennedy, Gavin. *The Mutiny of the Bounty.* Boston: David R. Godine, 1980. (This book contains an abridged version of Sir John Barrow's *The Eventful History of the Mutiny and Piratical Seizure of H.M.S. Bounty: Its Causes and Consequences,* London: John Murray, 1831. Barrow's book, written anonymously, is probably the definitive account of the whole *Bounty* mutiny and is the source of my quotes in this chapter as reproduced in Gavin Kennedy's book.)

McKee, Alexander. *HMS Bounty.* New York: Morrow, 1962.

National Maritime Museum, London, accession records related to John Adams's artifacts.

Paine, Lincoln. *Ships of the World: An Historical Encyclopedia.* Boston: Houghton Mifflin, 1997.

Scott, Brian W. "Pitcairn: What Happened," in *Mutiny on the Bounty, 1789–1989: An International Exhibition to Mark the 200th Anniversary, 28 April 1989–1 October 1989.* (An excellent article that tells why John Adams used the name Alexander Smith and reveals that when Adams as a young man left England on the *Bounty* he left behind a child he had sired.)

The Doubleday Ball

Chadwick, Henry, letter of March 20, 1908, to A. G. Mills. National Baseball Hall of Fame and Museum Library, Cooperstown, N.Y.

"A Challenge," *Delhi Gazette,* Hamden, New York, July 12, 1825.

Franco, Barbara. *The Cardiff Giant: A Hundred Year Old Hoax.* Cooperstown, N.Y.: New York State Historical Society, 1990.

Gould, Stephen Jay. "The Creation Myth of Cooperstown," *Natural History,* November 1989.

Guilfoile, Bill (ed.). *National Baseball Hall of Fame & Museum 1990 Yearbook.* Cooperstown, N.Y.: National Baseball Hall of Fame and Museum, 1990.

Heitz, Thomas R., and John Thorn. "Leatherstocking Base Ball Club—Early Baseball Chronology" (sheets), n.d.

Heitz, Thomas R., and John Thorn. "Leatherstocking Base Ball Club—The 1845 New York Game Rules" (sheets), n.d., Knickerbocker Rule Book, 1845.

"Home of Baseball," *The Freeman's Journal,* March 26, 1908.

Lewin, Jonathan, and Jay Maeder. "The Crown and Flower of 19th-Century Magic," *New York Daily News,* March 2, 1998.

Mills, A. G., letter of December 30, 1907, to James Sullivan, Secretary, Special Base Ball Commission. National Baseball Hall of Fame and Museum Library, Cooperstown, N.Y.

Rader, Benjamin G. *Baseball: A History of America's Game.* Urbana: University of Illinois Press, 1992.

Spalding, Albert G. (Revised and reedited by Sam Coombs and Bob West.) *America's National Game.* San Francisco: Halo Books, 1991.

Spalding, Albert G. (With an introduction by Benjamin G. Rader.) *America's National Game.* Lincoln: University of Nebraska Press, 1992. (Originally published in 1911. Source of the Spalding quotes.)

Thorn, John, and Pete Palmer, with Michael Gershman. *Total Baseball* (3rd ed.). New York: Harper Perennial, 1993.

Ward, Geoffrey, and Ken Burns. *Baseball: An Illustrated History.* New York: Knopf, 1994.

Woodward, William E. *The Way Our People Lived.* New York: Washington Square Press, 1965.

Wright, Marshall D. *Nineteenth Century Baseball, Year-by-Year Statistics for the Major League Teams, 1871 Through 1900.* Jefferson, N.C.: McFarland, 1996.

Vendovi's Head

Herman, J. K. "Vendovi: Cannibal and Curio," *U.S. Navy Medicine,* vol. 77, no. 2, March/April 1986.

Stewart, T. D. "The Skull of Vendovi: A Contribution of the Wilkes Expedition to the Physical Anthropology of Fiji," *Arch. & Phys. Anthrop. in Oceania,* vol. 13, nos. 2 and 3, July and October 1978.

Wilkes, Charles. *Narrative of the United States Exploring Expedition During the Years 1838, 1839, 1840, 1841, 1842.* Philadelphia: C. Sherman, 1849. (A fascinating work of five volumes that was the source of the quotes that appear in this chapter.)

The Battle Sword of Colonel Najera

Greer, James Kimmins. *Colonel Jack Hays: Texas Frontier Leader and California Builder* (rev. ed.). College Station: Texas A&M University, 1987. (Probably the best biography of Hays. The source for my description of the duel between Hays and Lt. Col. Najera.)

Lamar, Howard B. (ed.). *The Reader's Encyclopedia of the American West.* New York: Thomas Y. Crowell, 1977.

Charles Dickens's Prompt-Copy of A Christmas Carol

Ackroyd, Peter. *Dickens.* New York: HarperCollins, 1990.

Collins, Philip (ed.). *Charles Dickens: The Public Readings.* Oxford: Clarendon Press, 1975. (An excellent book and the source for the review from the *Portland Transcript,* February 4, 1868.)

Collins, Philip (ed.). *Dickens: Interviews and Recollections.* London: Macmillan, 1981.

Dickens, Charles. (With introduction and notes by Philip Collins.) *A Christmas Carol, the Public Reading Version, a Facsimile of the Author's Prompt-Copy.* New York: New York Public Library, 1971. (The term "prompt-copy" insofar as it relates to Dickens's stage readings appears to have been coined by Philip Collins.)

Gordan, John D. *Reading for Profit: The Other Career of Charles Dickens: An Exhibition from the Berg Collection.* New York: New York Public Library, 1958. (Another excellent source on Dickens's reading career.)

"Mr. Chas. Dickens's Farewell Reading," *Illustrated London News,* March 19, 1870. (The source for Dickens's farewell speech.)

Szladits, Lola L. (compiler). *Charles Dickens, 1812–1870: An Anthology from the Berg Collection.* New York: New York Public Library, 1990.

The First American Flag Raised in Japan

Barrows, Edward M. *The Great Commodore: The Exploits of Matthew Calbraith Perry.* Indianapolis: Bobbs-Merrill, 1935.

"Fillmore's Authorization of 'Five Full Powers in Blank' to Commodore Matthew C. Perry" (sheet), United States Naval Academy, n.d.

Hawks, Francis L. (ed.). *Narrative of the Expedition of an American Squadron to the China Seas and Japan, Performed in the Years 1852, 1853, and 1854, Under the Command of Commodore M. C. Perry, United States Navy, By Order of the Government of the United States Compiled From the Original Notes and Journals of Commodore Perry and His Officers at His Request and Under His Supervision* (Vols. 1–3). Washington, D.C.: Published by Order of the Congress of the United States, Beverly Tucker, Senate Printer,

1856. (My account of Perry's mission to Japan is chiefly based on material in Volume 1 of this three-volume set.)

Morison, Samuel Eliot. *"Old Bruin": Commodore Matthew C. Perry, 1794–1858.* Boston: Atlantic Monthly Press/Little, Brown, 1967.

"USNA *55.1 Flag: U.S. Ensign: 31 Stars: Japan Expedition: Commodore Matthew C. Perry (1853)" (sheets), United States Naval Academy, n.d.

The Emancipation Proclamation

Basler, Roy P. (ed.). *The Collected Works of Abraham Lincoln.* New Brunswick, N.J.: Rutgers University Press, 1953. (Source of the letter to Horace Greeley of August 22, 1862.)

"The Emancipation Proclamation" (pamphlet), Albany, New York StateLibrary.

The Emancipation Proclamation: Milestone Documents in the National Archives. (Foreword by John Hope Franklin.) Washington, D.C.: National Archives and Records Administration, 1993.

Franklin, John Hope. *The Emancipation Proclamation.* Wheeling, Ill.: Harlan Davidson, 1995.

Heffner, Richard D. *A Documentary History of the United States.* New York: Mentor/New American Library, 1965.

Hill, Walter B., Jr. "Military Service and the Emancipation Proclamation," *National Archives Bulletin,* January 1998.

Johnson, Sally. "Dust Blown Off, Paper Reveals Lincoln's Hand," *New York Times,* May 14, 1989.

"Library of Congress Opens Special Exhibition for Centenary of Emancipation Proclamation," Press Release No. 63-5, Advance—for Publication on Friday, September 21, 1962, Washington, D.C.: Library of Congress.

Nevin, Allan, and Henry Steele Commager. *A Pocket History of the United States.* New York: Washington Square Press/Pocket Books, 1981.

"The Property of Mr. William Hotine . . . The Pen of Liberty," in "Printed Books and Manuscripts Including Americana," Christie's, New York.

Rawley, James A. *Abraham Lincoln and a Nation Worth Fighting For.* Wheeling, Ill.: Harlan Davidson, 1996.

Slices of Tom Thumb's Wedding Cake

Barnum, Phineas T. *Struggles and Triumphs.* New York: American News Company, 1871.

The Lives of Tom Thumb and Wife (pamphlet), New York: Popular Publishing, n.d. (c. 1881).

Malone, Dumas (ed.). *The Dictionary of American Biography.* New York: Scribner's, 1964.

"The Tom Thumb Wedding," *The New York Herald,* February 11, 1863.

"The Loving Lilliputians," *The New York Times,* February 11, 1863.

Romaine, Mertie. *General Tom Thumb and His Lady.* Taunton, Mass.: William S. Sullwold Publishing, 1976.

Thomas Edison's Original Tinfoil Phonograph

Bergerac, Cyrano de. (Translated by Richard Adlington.) *Voyages to the Moon and the Sun.* New York: Orion Press, 1962.

"Build the Edison Tin-Foil Phonograph" (sheets), West Orange, N.J.: Edison National Historic Site, n.d.

Gelatt, Roland. *The Fabulous Phonograph: From Tin Foil to High Fidelity.* Philadelphia: J. B. Lippincott, 1955.

Koenigsberg, Allen. *Edison Cylinder Records, 1889–1912, with an Illustrated History of the Phonograph.* Brooklyn: APM Press, 1987.

"One Hundred Years of Sound Recording" (press release), New York: Recording Industry Association of America, 1977.

Rachlin, Harvey. "The Sound Recording Industry," *Songwriter's Review,* vol. 33, no. 3, June/July 1978.

Rosenberg, Robert A., et al. (vol. eds.). *The Papers of Thomas A. Edison, Menlo Park: The Early Years, April 1876–December 1877* (Vol. 3). Baltimore: Johns Hopkins University Press. (Source of the quotations that appear in this chapter.)

Tarr, Douglas. "Sound Recording" (sheet), West Orange, N.J.: Edison National Historic Site, May 15, 1998.

Jesse James's Stickpin

"The Dead Outlaw," *Daily Gazette,* St. Joseph, Mo., Wednesday, April 5, 1882.

"Jesse by Jehovah," *Daily Gazette,* St. Joseph, Mo., Wednesday, April 5, 1882.

"Jesse James" (sheets), Jesse James Home, St. Joseph, Mo., n.d.

"Jesse James Is Very Definitely Dead, Says a Man Who Photographed His Body," *Kansas City Times,* November 12, 1948.

Lamar, Howard B. (ed.). *The Reader's Encyclopedia of the American West.* New York: Thomas Y. Crowell, 1977.

Settle, William A. *Jesse James Was His Name, Or Fact & Fiction Concerning the Careers of the Notorious James Brothers of Missouri.* Lincoln: University of Nebraska Press, 1977.

Ulysses S. Grant's Smoking Stand

Bowman, John S. (exec. ed.). *The Civil War Almanac.* New York: World Almanac Publications, 1983.

DeGregorio, William A. *The Complete Book of U.S. Presidents.* New York: Dembner, 1989.

Galena Historical Society Accession Record on U. S. Grant's cigar butt.

Goldhurst, Richard. *Many Are the Hearts: The Agony and the Triumph of Ulysses S. Grant.* New York: Reader's Digest, 1975.

Grant, Ulysses S. (E. B. Long, ed.) *The Personal Memoirs of U. S. Grant.* Cleveland: World Publishing, 1952.

"Grant's Old Cigar Butt," newspaper unknown, December 30, 1890. (Source of the Ulysses S. Grant–Leo T. LeBron cigar-butt story.)

Pitkin, Thomas M. *The Captain Departs: Ulysses S. Grant's Last Campaign.* Carbondale, Ill.: Southern Illinois University Press, 1973.

Porter, General Horace. *Campaigning with Grant.* New York: Da Capo Press, 1986. (Source of Porter's quote.)

Simon, John Y. *The Papers of Ulysses S. Grant.* Carbondale, Ill.: Southern Illinois University Press. (© by the Board of Trustees, Southern Illinois University; Volume 8 © 1979, source of the Mary Duncan letter quote; Volume 16 © 1988, source of the U. S. Grant quote in the interview during the Franklin Simmons "sitting," the William Tecumseh Sherman telegram aboard the USS *Susquehanna,* the William Tecumseh Sherman telegram to Ulysses S. Grant, the Comstock letter to William Tecumseh Sherman, the Ulysses S. Grant letter to U.S. Representative John Bidwell; Volume 17 © 1991, source of the Ulysses S. Grant letter to Mary Jane Safford, the George Trask letter that appeared in the April 9, 1867, edition of the *Chicago Times;* Volume 18 © 1991, source of the letter to H. Bernd of Danbury, Conn.; Volume 19 © 1995, source of the William Gouverneur Morris letter to Orville Babcock; Volume 21 © 1998, source of the costs and amounts of cigars ordered by Ulysses S. Grant.)

"U. S. Grant Home State Historic Site" (pamphlet), Illinois Historic Preservation Agency, 1994.

Jumbo the Elephant

"The Great Jumbo Killed," newspaper article, publication unknown, n.d.

Reingold, Adam. "The Greatest Show on Earth," *New York,* January 25, 1993.

Saxon, Arthur. *P. T. Barnum: The Legend and the Man.* New York: Columbia University Press, 1989.

Freud's Couch

Dudar, Helen. "The Unexpected Private Passion of Sigmund Freud," *Smithsonian,* August 1990.

Freud, Sigmund (Marie Bonaparte, ed.). *The Origins of Psycho-Analysis: Letters to Wilhelm Fliess, Drafts and Notes, 1887–1902.* New York: Basic Books, 1954.

Gay, Peter. *Freud: A Life for Our Time.* New York: Norton, 1988.

Jones, Ernest. *The Life & Work of Sigmund Freud.* New York: Basic Books, 1957.

Kelman, Harold (ed.). *New Perspectives in Psychoanalysis.* New York: Norton, 1965.

Molnar, Michael (ed.). *The Diary of Sigmund Freud, 1929–1939: A Record of the Final Decade.* New York: Scribner's, 1992.

The Hoof of Fire Horse Number Twelve

National Museum of American History catalog cards.
"An Old Man Burned to Death in His Lonely Home," *Washington Evening Star,* no date but circa March 30, 1890.
"A Pipe Found Beside Him," *Washington Post,* March 30, 1890.

"Take Me Out to the Ball Game"

Anderson, Bruce. "The National Pastime's Anthem." Publication unknown, n.d.
ASCAP biographical sheet on Jack Norworth, n.d.
Bauman, Richard. "An All-American Hit Since 1908," *American Songwriter,* November/December 1996.
Debus, Allen G. "Celebrity Corner: The Records of Jack Norworth," *Hobbies—The Magazine for Collectors,* September 1957.
"Dodgers' Dots & Dashes," *Los Angeles Dodgers Line Drives,* vol. 1, no. 3, July 1958.
Feist, Leonard. *An Introduction to Popular Music Publishing in America.* New York: National Music Publishers' Association, 1980.
Friedman, Ralph. "Best-Loved Baseball Song Born During Subway Ride" (newspaper article), Central Press Association, c. 1959.
Fusselle, Warner. "Take Me Out to the Ball Game," in *Total Baseball* (4th ed., edited by John Thorn and Pete Palmer). New York: Viking, 1995.
Law, Alexander G., letter of October 29, 1953, Englewood, N.J., to Sid C. Keener, Director, Baseball Hall of Fame.
Lynn Farnol Group (compilers). *The ASCAP Biographical Dictionary of Composers, Authors and Publishers.* New York: American Society of Composers, Authors, and Publishers, 1966.
Mote, James. *Everything Baseball.* New York: Prentice-Hall, 1989.
New York Herald Tribune, November 24, 1940.
Rachlin, Harvey. *The Encyclopedia of the Music Business.* New York: Harper & Row, 1981.
Ripley, John W. "Baseball's Forgotten Casey," *Ford Times,* June 1974.
Rosenthal, Harold. "Take Me Out to the Ball Game" (publication unknown), March 19, 1958.
Walsh, Jim. " 'Take Me Out to the Ball Game' Still Champion," *Variety,* n.d.

Mark Twain's Orchestrelle

Harnsberger, Caroline. *Mark Twain, Family Man.* New York: Citadel Press, 1960.
Harnsberger, Caroline Thomas (compiler). *Everyone's Mark Twain.* South Brunswick, N.J.: A. S. Barnes, 1972.
"Mark Twain's Orchestrelle," *The Fence Painter* (Bulletin of The Mark Twain Boyhood Home Associates, Hannibal, Mo.), vol. 4, no. 1, Spring 1984.
Quick, Dorothy. *Enchantment: A Little Girl's Friendship with Mark Twain.* Norman: University of Oklahoma Press, 1961. (The source of the woman's quote on seeing the little girl playing the instrument.)

The Zimmermann Telegram
Bredhoff, Stacey. "Zimmermann Telegram" (sheet), National Archives, n.d.
Friedman, William F. *The Zimmermann Telegram of January 16, 1917 and Its Cryptographic Background.* Washington, D.C.: U.S. Government Printing Office, 1938.
O'Toole, G. J. A. *Honorable Treachery: A History of U.S. Intelligence, Espionage, and Covert Action from the American Revolution to the CIA.* New York: Atlantic Monthly Press, 1991.

The Fourteen Points
Address of the United States President Delivered at a Joint Session of the Two Houses of Congress, January 8, 1918 (pamphlet), Washington, D.C., 1918.
Sibert, General William L., letter of November 5, 1917, to General Tasker H. Bliss.
Woodrow Wilson House accession and catalog cards.
Woodrow Wilson Papers (series 7B, box 2) and the Sayre Papers (box 7) at the Library of Congress, including Wilson's shorthand and typewritten versions of his Fourteen Points address.

The Truce Flag That Ended World War I
Allen, George H., et al. *The Great War: The Triumph of Democracy* (vol. 5). Philadelphia: George Barrie's Sons, n.d.
Link, Arthur (ed.). *The Papers of Woodrow Wilson, Volume 53, 1918–1919.* Princeton, N.J.: Princeton University Press, 1966. (Source of the Edith Wilson letter.)
Wilson, Edith. *My Memoir.* New York: Arno Press, 1980. (Source of the quote.)
Woodrow Wilson House accession and catalog cards.

Wyatt Earp's Drawing of the O.K. Corral Gunfight
Boyer, Glenn G. (collector and ed.). *I Married Wyatt Earp: The Recollections of Josephine Sarah Marcus Earp.* Tucson: University of Arizona Press, 1976.
Clum, John P. *It All Happened in Tombstone.* Flagstaff, Ariz.: Northland Press, 1965.
Greer, James Kimmins. *Texas Ranger Jack Hays in the Frontier Southwest.* College Station: Texas A&M University Press, 1993.
Jahns, Pat. *The Frontier World of Doc Holliday: Faro Dealer from Dallas to Deadwood.* Lincoln: University of Nebraska Press, 1979.
Lake, Stuart N. *Wyatt Earp: Frontier Marshal.* Boston: Houghton Mifflin, 1931.
Lamar, Howard B. (ed.). *The Reader's Encyclopedia of the American West.* New York: Thomas Y. Crowell, 1977.
Marks, Paula Mitchell. *And Die in the West: The Story of the O.K. Corral Gunfight.* New York: William Morrow, 1989.

Turner, Alford E. *The Earps Talk*. College Station, Tex.: Creative Publishing Company, 1980.

Turner, Alford E. *The O.K. Corral Inquest*. College Station, Tex.: Creative Publishing Company, 1981. (Source of the quotes from the O.K. Corral participants.)

Waters, Frank. *The Earp Brothers of Tombstone: The Story of Mrs. Virgil Earp*. Lincoln: University of Nebraska Press, 1976.

The Maltese Falcon

"Maltese Falcon Is Exec's New 398G Gem," *New York Daily News* (News Wire Service), December 7, 1994.

Saltonstall, Dave. " 'The Stuff That Dreams Are Made Of,'" *New York Daily News*, September 18, 1994.

" 'The Stuff Dreams Are Made Of': Harry Winston Falcon Completed" (press release), New York: Harry Winston Jewelers, n.d.

Monty's Battle Caravans

Dupuy, Trevor Nevitt. *European Land Battles, 1939–1943. The Military History of World War II* (vol. 1). New York: Franklin Watts, 1962.

Imperial War Museum, Department of Sound Records (Accession No. 000657/01): "Field Marshal The Viscount Montgomery of Alamein, Field Marshal Bernard Law Montgomery Talks About the Three Caravans He Used in the Field During the Second World War." (The source of some of the Montgomery quotes.)

Miller, Francis Trevelyan (with a board of historical and military authorities). *War in Korea and the Complete History of World War II* (Armed Services Memorial Edition). N.p., 1952.

"The Montgomery Caravans," Imperial War Museum Exhibit Leaflet, No. 1.

Polmar, Norman, and Thomas B. Allen. *World War II: The Encyclopedia of the War Years, 1941–1945*. New York: Random House, 1996.

Young, Brigadier Peter (ed.). *The World Almanac Book of World War II*. New York: World Almanac Publications (A Bison Book), 1981.

The World War II Japanese Surrender Table

"Address by General of the Army Douglas MacArthur Aboard the Battleship USS Missouri, September 2, 1945" (War Department press release). (Source of MacArthur's pre-signing remarks and concluding address made on the USS *Missouri*.)

Adler, Julius Ochs. "Horrors in Japanese Prisons Like Those of Nazi Camps," *New York Times*, August 31, 1945.

"Allies Rush Final Preparations for Signing of Surrender Terms" (Associated Press), *New York Times*, September 1, 1945.

"Atsugi 'Parade' On . . . Commander Lands" (Associated Press), *New York Times*, August 31, 1945.

"Battleship's Ventilator to Be Surrender Table" (Associated Press), *New York Times*, August 29, 1945.

Brooks, Lester. *Behind Japan's Surrender: The Secret Struggle That Ended an Empire.* New York: McGraw-Hill, 1968.

Butow, Robert J. C. *Japan's Decision to Surrender.* Stanford, Calif.: Stanford University Press, 1954.

Clayton, James D. *The Years of MacArthur, Volume II, 1941–1945.* Boston: Houghton Mifflin, 1975.

Egeberg, Roger O. *The General: MacArthur As Seen by His Aide & Physician.* New York: Hippocrene Books, 1983.

Hunt, Frazier. *The Untold Story of Douglas MacArthur.* New York: Devin-Adair, 1954.

Japan Surrenders. Washington, D.C.: National Archives and Records Administration, 1989.

Kase, Toshikazu. *Journey to the Missouri.* New Haven: Yale University Press, 1950 (reprinted by Archon Books, 1969).

Kluckhorn, Frank. "Japan's Surrender Ordered over Military Opposition," *New York Times*, September 2, 1945.

Marshall, Maj. Gen. R. J. His personal diary.

Perret, Geoffrey. *Old Soldiers Never Die: The Life of Douglas MacArthur.* New York: Random House, 1996.

Polmar, Norman, and Thomas B. Allen. *World War II: The Encyclopedia of the War Years, 1941–1945.* New York: Random House, 1996.

"Surrender Ceremony Marking Japan's First Defeat in Her 2,600-Year-Old History," *New York Times*, September 3, 1945.

"Tokyo Aides Weep as General Signs" (Associated Press), *New York Times*, September 2, 1945.

USNA 46.45.1: Furniture: Mess Table: USS Missouri (BB 63) (1945). U.S. Naval Academy Museum, n.d.

USNA 46.45.2: Furniture: Chair: HMS Duke of York/USS Missouri (BB 63) (September 2, 1945). U.S. Naval Academy, n.d.

USNA 46.45.3: Textile: Tablecloth: Officers' Wardroom: USS Missouri (BB 63) (1945). U.S. Naval Academy, n.d.

USNA *55.1: Flag: U.S. Ensign: 31 Stars: Japan Expedition: Commodore Matthew C. Perry (1853). U.S. Naval Academy, n.d.

"War Comes to an End" (Associated Press), *New York Times*, September 2, 1945.

Whitney, Maj. Gen. Courtney, letter of September 2, 1945, to his wife.

ENIAC

Eckstein, Peter. "J. Presper Eckert," *IEEE Annals of the History of Computing*, vol. 18, no. 1, Spring 1996.

Goldstine, H. H., and A. Goldstine. "The Electronic Numerical Integrator and Computer (ENIAC)," *IEEE Annals of the History of Computing*, vol. 18, no. 1, Spring 1996.

Marcus, Mitchell, and Atsushi Akera. "Exploring the Architecture of an Early Machine: The Historical Significance of the ENIAC Machine Architecture," *IEEE Annals of the History of Computing*, vol. 18, no. 1, Spring 1996.

Shaffer, Paul. "ENIAC Fast Facts" (fact sheet), University of Pennsylvania, 1996.

Strauss, Robert. "Birth of a Machine, Dawn of a New Era," *Newsday*, February 13, 1996.

Winegrad, Dilys, and Atsushi Akera. *ENIAC 50: The Birth of an Information Age: An Overview of the History of the First Large-Scale, General-Purpose Electronic Digital Computer.* Philadelphia: University of Pennsylvania, 1996.

Marilyn Monroe's Billowing Dress from The Seven Year Itch

Marzulli, John. "Sticky Fingers in Pinch of Marilyn's 'Itch' Dress," *New York Daily News*, September 16, 1993.

New York Police Department paperwork: case reports and complaint follow-up reports of the burglary in the Strasberg locker.

Rashbaum, William K. "Burglars Got Dress, But Will It Fit?" *Newsday*, September 16, 1993.

Travis, Neal, and Philip Messing. "Dress Dragnet," *New York Post*, n.d.

Elvis Presley's Purple Cadillac

Bronson, Fred. *The Billboard Book of Number One Hits.* New York: Billboard Publications, 1985.

Cotten, Lee. *All Shook Up: Elvis Day by Day.* Ann Arbor: Popular Culture, 1998.

Pareles, Jon, and Patricia Romanowski (eds.). *The Rolling Stone Encyclopedia of Rock & Roll.* New York: Rolling Stone Press/Summit Books, 1983.

UPI dispatch (Phoenix City, Ala.), August 3, 1976. (Source of the information on Herbert O'Dell Smith and the car auction.)

Able the Space Monkey

Curtis, Anthony R. "Russian Dogs Lost in Space," on "Space Today Online" Web site (www.tui.edu/STO/sto.html).

Needell, Allan A. "Able Bio-Capsule" (fact sheet), March 2, 1998.

U.S. Army Ordnance Missile Command. "Fact Sheet, Able-Baker Experiment," n.d.

U.S. Army Ordnance Missile Command. Untitled press release on the presentation of a space capsule to the Smithsonian Institution, n.d.

Odyssey

"Apollo 13: A Successful Failure" (MR 7), *NASA Mission Report*, May 20, 1970.

Compton, David W. *Where No Man Has Gone Before: A History of Apollo Lunar Exploration Missions.* Washington, D.C.: NASA SP-4214, 1989.

Cook, Robert, and Earl Lane. "A Space Hero Dies, Alan Shepard Jr., 74, Pioneer U.S. Astronaut," *Newsday,* July 23, 1998.

Jones, Eric M. (ed.). "The Frustrations of Fra Mauro: Part 1" from the *Apollo Lunar Surface Journal,* 1995 (from the Internet).

Lovell, Jim, and Jeffrey Kluger. *Apollo 13.* New York: Pocket Books, 1995.

NASA Logo. "Detailed Chronology of Events Surrounding the Apollo 13 Accident" (from the Internet).

NASA News Release No. 70:50: "Apollo 13 Third Lunar Landing Mission," National Aeronautics and Space Administration, Washington, D.C., April 2, 1970.

"Summary Analysis of the Apollo 1 Accident" (loose sheets), n.d.

The Gun That Killed John Lennon

Bronson, Fred. *The Billboard Book of Number One Hits.* New York: Billboard Publications, 1985.

Clendinen, Dudley. "Lennon Murder Suspect 'Different Person' to Father," *New York Times,* December 11, 1980.

Ledbetter, Les. "John Lennon of Beatles Is Killed; Suspect Held in Shooting at Dakota," *New York Times,* December 9, 1980.

Montgomery, Paul L. "Police Trace Tangled Path Leading to Lennon's Slaying at the Dakota," *New York Times,* December 10, 1980.

Montgomery, Paul L. "Suspect in Lennon's Slaying Is Put Under Suicide Watch," *New York Times,* December 11, 1980.

Palmer, Robert. "Lennon Known Both as Author and Composer," *New York Times,* December 9, 1980.

Pareles, Jon, and Patricia Romanowski (eds.). *The Rolling Stone Encyclopedia of Rock & Roll.* New York: Rolling Stone Press/Summit Books, 1983.

Rockwell, John. "Leader of a Rock Group That Helped Define a Generation," *New York Times,* December 9, 1980.

INDEX

ILLUSTRATION CREDITS

Temple of the Tooth Relic, sacred relic casket containing the tooth of the Buddha:
New York Buddhist Vihara; *Princess Hemamala and Prince Danta:* Ven. Dr.
Kollupitiye Mahinde Nayaha Maha Thero of Kelani Raja Maha Vihara; *Gold
Larnax of King Philip II:* Hellenic Republic Ministry of Culture, Archaeological
Receipts Fund, Athens; *Magna Carta:* Lincolnshire County Council at Lincoln
Castle, Lincoln, England; *coronation chair with the Stone of Scone, Stone of Scone:*
the Dean and Chapter of Westminster; *Essex Ring:* the Dean and Chapter of
Westminster; *Galileo's middle finger in its casket:* Institute and Museum of the
History of Science, Florence; *Galileo in prison, Galileo reading a book:* New York
Public Library; *"Rules of Civility" page from one of Washington's schoolboy copy-
books:* Library of Congress, Washington, D.C.; *illustration of George Washington as
a youth:* from *Child's History of the United States* by John Dawson Gilmary Shea,
McMenamy, New York: 1872/New York Public Library; *John Harrison's fourth
marine timekeeper:* National Maritime Museum, London; *page from the Virginia
Declaration of Rights:* Library of Congress, Washington, D.C.; *George Mason portrait: Magazine of American History,* published by A. S. Barnes & Co., New York,
1877–1893, continued by *Magazine of American History,* published in Mount
Vernon, New York/New York Public Library; *Thomas Jefferson portrait:* New York
Public Library, *Rising Sun Chair full shot of the chair, Rising Sun Chair—detailed
shot of the "rising sun" crest, "Signing of the Constitution" by Thomas P. Rossiter:*
Independence National Historical Park, Philadelphia; *Louisiana Purchase Treaty—
cover of French exchange copy, signature page:* National Archives and Records
Administration, Washington, D.C.; *page from a Lewis and Clark journal:* American
Philosophical Society, Philadelphia; *Beethoven's ear trumpets:* Beethoven House,
Bonn, Germany; *Beethoven playing piano:* from *History of the Nineteenth Century,
Year by Year* by Edwin Emerson, Jr., P. F. Collier, 1902/New York Public Library;
Harrison's Peace Pipes—the Shawnee peace pipe: Kansas City Museum, Kansas City,
Missouri; *William Henry Harrison portrait:* U.S. Bureau of Engraving and
Painting/New York Public Library; *John Adams's pigtail, countryside of Pitcairn
Island:* National Maritime Museum, London; *Doubleday Ball:* National Baseball
Hall of Fame and Museum, Cooperstown, N.Y.; *nineteenth-century baseball field:*
Library of Congress, Washington, D.C./New York Public Library; *Abner Doubleday:*
New York Public Library; *Vendovi face illustration:* Smithsonian Institution,
Washington, D.C.; *Najera's sword:* Autry Museum of Western Heritage, Los Angeles;

page from Dickens's prompt-copy of A Christmas Carol: New York Public Library, New York, N. Y.; *Dickens's final farewell reading:* Illustrated London News and Sketch, Ltd.; *delivery of the president's letter, document conveying the "Five Full Powers in Blank" to Matthew C. Perry granted by President Millard Fillmore, photo of the first American flag raised in Japan:* U.S. Naval Academy Museum, Annapolis; *first page of the Emancipation Proclamation:* National Archives and Records Administration, Washington, D.C.; *"Emancipation" scene:* from the collection of Connie and James Malone/photo by Jim Strong; *Tom Thumb's wedding cake:* Frank Leslie's Illustrated Newspaper, New York, February 28, 1863; *Tom Thumb, Lavinia, Commodore Nutt, and Minnie Warren greeting guests at the wedding while standing on a piano:* Chris Coenen; *Thomas Edison's illustration of the original phonograph that he instructed one of his technicians to build, original tinfoil phonograph:* U.S. Department of the Interior, National Park Service, Edison National Historic Site; *house in which Jesse James was killed, Jesse James in death with his stickpin in his cravat:* Jesse James Home, St. Joseph, Missouri; *Ulysses S. Grant's face:* Ulysses S. Grant Association, Southern Illinois University, Carbondale; *Ulysses S. Grant's smoking stand:* U. S. Grant Home State Historic Site, Galena, Illinois; *Jumbo— nineteenth century:* Barnum, Bailey, and Hutchinson; *Jumbo at Tufts University:* Tufts University Archives; *Freud's couch:* Freud Museum, London; *Sigmund Freud— face:* Library of Congress, Washington, D.C.; *Hoof of Fire Horse Number Twelve:* Smithsonian Institution, Washington, D.C.; *original lyric sheet of "Take Me Out to the Ball Game":* National Baseball Hall of Fame Library and Archive, Cooperstown, N.Y.; *Jack Norworth:* American Society of Composers, Authors and Publishers, New York, New York; *Mark Twain's orchestrelle, Mark Twain—face:* Mark Twain Museum, Hannibal, Missouri; *Zimmermann telegram:* National Archives and Records Administration, Washington, D.C.; *Fourteen Points—shorthand page:* Library of Congress, Washington, D.C.; *truce flag that ended World War I pinned to its accompanying letter to Clemenceau:* Woodrow Wilson House, Washington, D.C.; *Wyatt Earp's Drawing of the O.K. Corral Gunfight:* Autry Museum of Western Heritage, Los Angeles; *Maltese Falcon:* Maltese Falcon © 1996 Warner Bros. All Rights Reserved. The Maltese Falcon statue is from the collection of Dr. Gary Milan; *Field Marshal Montgomery outside his caravan greeting other officers:* The Trustees of the Imperial War Museum, London/photo by Sgt. Morris; *caravan camouflaged and guarded by French troops:* The Trustees of the Imperial War Museum, London/photo by Sgt. Palmer; *Japanese delegation before the table on board the USS* Missouri *on September 2, 1945, General MacArthur signing the surrender instrument:* U.S. Army Signal Corps; *ENIAC:* University of Pennsylvania Archives; *Marilyn Monroe's Billowing Dress from* The Seven Year Itch: Archive Photos, New York, N. Y.; *Elvis image—purple Cadillac:* used by permission, Elvis Presley Enterprises, Inc.; *Able the Space Monkey—preflight, Able the Space Monkey—postflight:* U.S. Army photos; *Odyssey— liftoff of Apollo 13, recovery of* Odyssey, *command module (Odyssey) being set down on the USS* Iwo Jima: NASA/Johnson Space Center, Houston; *gun that killed John Lennon:* New York City Police Department.